Sheffield Hallam University
Learning and IT Services
Adsetts Centre City Campus
Sheffield S1 1WS

D1589159

101 914 973 6

KEY TEXT
REFERENCE

This ambitious and provocative study provides a new narrative
of nineteenth-century English political history. Based on extensive research the book draws on recent 'postmodern' critical
theory to read a vast range of hitherto neglected oral, visual and
printed sources, in an attempt to expand our conception of the
politics of the period. Read in this way, nineteenth-century
English politics resolved itself into a story about the struggle to
define the nation's constitution, past, present and future. It
suggests the existence of a popular strain of English libertarian
politics, albeit one that was used in many different ways.
However, the book is also about the erosion of the radical and
democratic potential of both this libertarian tradition and the
constitution. Ironically, the invention of England's liberal
democratic constitution depended upon the demise of the
democratic forms of popular politics which accompanied the
ascendancy of print, and organised mass party politics. Thus,
despite the inclusion of many men within the constitution,
politics became less (not more) democratic: a phenomenon
which the author sees as pertinent for many struggling to live in,
or to establish, liberal democratic constitutions in our own times.

SHEFFIELD HALLAM UNIVERSITY
LEARNING CENTRE
WITHDRAWN FROM STOCK

POLITICS AND THE PEOPLE

POLITICS AND THE PEOPLE

A study in English political culture, c. 1815–1867

JAMES VERNON

British Academy Postdoctoral Fellow, University of Manchester

CAMBRIDGE UNIVERSITY PRESS
Cambridge, New York, Melbourne, Madrid, Cape Town, Singapore, São Paulo, Delhi

Cambridge University Press
The Edinburgh Building, Cambridge CB2 8RU, UK

Published in the United States of America by Cambridge University Press, New York

www.cambridge.org
Information on this title: www.cambridge.org/9780521115087

© Cambridge University Press 1993

This publication is in copyright. Subject to statutory exception
and to the provisions of relevant collective licensing agreements,
no reproduction of any part may take place without the written
permission of Cambridge University Press.

First published 1993
This digitally printed version 2009

A catalogue record for this publication is available from the British Library

Library of Congress Cataloguing in Publication data
Vernon, James.
Politics and the people: a study in English political culture,
c. 1815–1867 / James Vernon.
p.　cm.
Includes bibliographical references.
ISBN 0 521 42090 3
1. Great Britain – Politics and government – 19th century.
2. Political culture – Great Britain – History – 19th century.
I.　Title
JN16.V47　1993
306.2′0941 – dc20　92-34917CIP

ISBN 978-0-521-42090-7 hardback
ISBN 978-0-521-11508-7 paperback

To Ros

... the political, ethical, social, philosophical problem of our days is not to try and liberate the individual from the state, and from the state's institutions, but to liberate us both from the state and from the type of individualization which is linked to the state. We have to promote new forms of subjectivity through refusal of this kind of individuality which has been imposed upon us for several centuries.

Michel Foucault, 'The Subject and Power' in H. Dreyfus and P. Rabinow (eds.), *Michel Foucault: Beyond Structuralism and Hermeneutics* (Chicago, 1982)

Life obliges people over and over again to give birth to themselves.

Gabriel Garcia Marquez, *Love in the Time of Cholera* (London, 1988)

Contents

Plates

Tables

Acknowledgements

In an academic monograph like this the acknowledgement is a privileged site. It stands apart from the narrative logic of the text, hinting at the argument's fragility and the artificiality of its seemingly seamless progress towards closure, with its beginning (introduction), middle (progressively numbered chapters) and end (conclusion). It is a logic which seems ingeniously designed to refuse any signs of the author's doubts, the endless rethinking and rewriting, the elaborations, the cuts, the responses to preliminary readings by friends and colleagues. Only in the acknowledgements can the author reveal such frailties by thanking those who have encouraged or quelled their anxieties. Certainly, what follows is not intended as a display of 'knowingness' (of whom I know and which network I lay claim to), nor as a way of implicating others in the inadequacies of my own work for which I alone am responsible.

None the less over the years I have received so much help that it is impossible to acknowledge it all, and to those I have forgotten or overlooked my apologies and thanks. Firstly, I owe much both to those who taught me that there were alternative histories to those taught at a minor English private school, and to those who kept those instincts fresh. Yet invariably it was my fellow postgraduate at Manchester, Tony Taylor, whose company and conversation kept me nourished and enthused during the long bleak periods. The presence of his endless supply of references and his incisive comments on earlier drafts will, I trust, be evident in the text itself. I would like to thank others who have read, heard, and commented on my work, especially the examiners of my Ph.D. thesis Iorwerth Prothero and John Belchem, and also John Breuilly, J. C. D. Clark, James Epstein, Jonathan Fulcher, John Garrard, Rohan McWilliam, Nicola Richards, Sally Taylor and David Vincent. Their help and encouragement helped me survive an early savaging by E. P. Thompson.

To my postgraduate supervisors, Patrick Joyce and Frank O'Gorman, my debt is legion. At a time of ever increasing workloads they often gave themselves selflessly. Without their friendship, continued support, trenchant criticism, and when all else failed their unfailing sense of humour and humanity, this book would have been half what it is. I hope it does them justice. Yet I fear it is impossible to fully acknowledge Patrick Joyce's contribution to this book. In recent years our work has converged so much that it has often been difficult to trace the genealogies of ideas, sentences, and even phrases. His has been a profound influence, one which I suspect (and hope) will be keenly felt not only in this book, but in others to come.

My thanks also to the librarians, archivists, and curators at the following institutions who, with scant reward I am afraid, made my work so much easier. Oldham Art Gallery, Museum and Local Studies Library, Boston Public Library, Boston Borough Municipal Archives, Boston's Guildhall Museum, British Library Reading and Map Rooms, Lincoln Archives Office, Lincoln Central Library, East Sussex Record Office, Sussex Archaeological Society, Devon Record Office, Plymouth Museum and Art Gallery, Hackney Archives Department, Shoreditch Local History Library, Bishopsgate Institute, Manchester Central Reference Library, John Rylands University Library at Manchester, National Museum of Labour History, Co-Operative Union Archives Office at Manchester, and, finally, the British Library's newspaper collection at Colindale. Needless to say I would have been unable to visit these places or to finish this book without the financial support of a British Academy's postgraduate studentship and postdoctoral fellowship.

Thanks, too, to those at Cambridge University Press: to the anonymous readers for their stringent readings; to Gillian Maude for her patience and good humour in making my turgid prose less unreadable; and to William Davies for his faith.

Lastly, my friends and family have in their own ways, at times unwittingly and at times not, helped me on the way with ideas, money, and shoulders to cry on. They have always reminded me that there is life beyond dusty libraries and word processors. But my biggest debt of all is to Ros. She alone knows how much we have both suffered because of this book, and yet without her it would have been impossible. It is a small gesture and little reward, but this book is dedicated to her with much love and thanks.

Introduction: a new political history?

In these historic times politics are back in fashion. The apparent about turn of the forward march of labour, the Right's electoral successes on both sides of the Atlantic during the 1980s and 1990s, and the collapse of the Berlin Wall in 1989, have led many to reassess their understanding of politics. For some there is a distinct millennial feel to this postmodern world, one in which all the narratives we need to explain and understand politics have disintegrated before our very eyes; while for others these events represent not so much a defeat as a triumph, a triumph of just one narrative, liberalism.[1] Critical to this rethinking of politics has been our understanding of the ways in which political identities, subjectivities, and constituencies of support are created. Just as commentators have chronicled the increasing power of the media in shaping our perceptions of politics, so postmodernist critical theory has turned our attention to the decentred subject and the discursive techniques by which the narrative forms of language construct political subjectivities as stable and coherent.[2] As ever somewhat belatedly, and certainly in Britain somewhat begrudgingly, a new 'cultural history' which critically engages with such postmodernist insights has begun to emerge, one which offers us the possibility of expanding our concept of politics and political history.[3] Although, like a bad smell they wished would go away, most political historians have tried to ignore these new developments, they do have far-reaching implications for the study of nineteenth-century English politics. This book hopes to unravel some of these implications and, in so doing, to advocate a new cultural history of politics.

One of the attractions of such a cultural approach is as a remedy for the deficiencies of the current narratives of nineteenth-century political history, with their triumphalist accounts of the development of England's democratic and libertarian constitution. Following

Lewis Namier, for instance, Tory narratives have concentrated on the aristocratic institutions and actors of high politics, interpreting the constitutional reforms of 1832 and 1867 as the consequences of high political manœuvring, not pressure from outside Westminster.[4] In these accounts it is the political forces of Conservative reaction, not the triumphs of Liberal public opinion, which are brought to the fore. Thus, for D. C. Moore the first Reform Act represented an attempt to reinforce aristocratic electoral control over rural areas, just as for Maurice Cowling the second Reform Act was the result of Disraeli's ambition to dish the whigs, both readings denying extra-parliamentary politics a role in either reform.[5] In such narratives power is seen to emanate from the centre to the periphery, a centre which for some tory historians seems to have become ever more narrow, impervious, and overwhelmingly aristocratic.[6] The central concern, then, of these tory narratives has been to reject the liberal fiction that nineteenth-century politics was about the seemingly ceaseless progression to a liberal democratic constitution. Instead, for tories England's libertarian tradition lies not in the struggle for democracy, but in the struggle for a prosperous, entrepreneurial Protestant nation.

It is a narrative that has recently found forceful, not to say at times vitriolic, support from J. C. D. Clark's portrayal of the persistent presence of England's resilient Anglican, aristocratic, and monarchical *ancien regime* during the nineteenth century.[7] Gradually, the contours of this *ancien regime* are being stretched out to 1914, and for Clark it is this hierarchical regime, not a bourgeois liberal individualist one, which provides the most fruitful setting both for the growth of the market and for liberty. Although the style and content of Clark's work is far from unproblematic, it does represent one of the few serious attempts to rethink the politics of the period.[8] As we shall see, his emphasis upon the continued importance of religion, monarchy, and aristocracy, and his new found (albeit idealist) interest in the language of politics, has much in common with other 'revisionist' accounts written within seemingly competing historiographical traditions. And yet, despite Clark's attempt to liberate politics from the reductionist teleologies of liberal and marxist narratives, he ultimately falls back upon an equally reductionist high political definition of politics and the public sphere. Having opened Pandora's Box he promptly closes it again.

None the less, as I have already indicated, Clark has challenged

those heroic liberal narratives which portray the emerging bour-
geoisie as the guardians of English liberty and democracy, for it was
they who enabled the rise of party and public opinion to defeat
aristocratic hegemony with the electoral reforms of 1832, 1867, and
1872.[9] It was a teleological story of the eclipse of the traditional
politics of interest, influence, and the market by the progressive
politics of individual opinion. And yet, by concentrating on the
growth of those political institutions, organisations, and representative systems which most facilitated the development of such
'progressive' and 'modern' political forms, these liberal narratives
tended to exclude those other forms of popular politics which did not
fit this model. Inevitably this meant that the poor, the disenfranchised, and others dispossessed, were excluded from their accounts of
the triumph of England's libertarian constitution.

Recent revisionist narratives, written from what may be termed
here a broadly social democratic position, have also done much to
question the often complacent teleologies of these liberal narratives.[10]
Thus, while the 1832 Reform Act and the mid-Victorian invention of
party were always privileged within liberal narratives as the engines
which propelled English politics into the 'modern' democratic era,
revisionist narratives have turned our attentions backwards. It is in
the once much neglected world of eighteenth-century politics that
historians now find the genesis of popular party and electoral politics,
politics which were in no way the exclusive domain of the middle
classes. Indeed, the strength of these accounts lies in their treatment
of politics from the bottom up, their recovery of a popular political
culture which had previously been lost to view. And yet, however
long the eighteenth century has now become, there remains an
implicit assumption in much of this body of work that nineteenth-
century politics was qualitatively different, that the emphasis shifted
from the local to the national, from the moral to the commercial, and
from a popular politics to one informed by class. In this sense these
revisionist narratives can be read as merely extending the teleology of
whig interpretations, either liberal or marxist, back into the
eighteenth century.

This is less surprising in light of the shadow E. P. Thompson's
The Making of the English Working Class cast upon many of these
revisionists, a text which romantically and imaginatively redefined
marxist narratives of England's libertarian political past.[11] Thompson's project (perhaps crusade would be a better word) was to rescue

those excluded from liberal and tory narratives by showing that it
was they, 'the people', whose *experience* of their struggle for liberty,
against both a coercive state and the developing market, not only
made them as a class but forced the state to redefine the constitution
in 1832. Thompson's definition of the 'people' as the dispossessed in
political struggle may ultimately have been reduced to the making of
the male working class, but it did provide a counterpoint to the
equally romantic, but restrictive, definitions of 'the people' and
liberty evident in tory and liberal narratives. Despite, or because of,
the teleology and triumphalism of Thompson's narrative, especially
its insistence on the ability of the people to make their own history (so
long as they did so as working-class men), it still dominates much
broadly marxist political history.

Recently, however, historians have begun to question Thompson's
account of the politics and experience of class formation, pointing not
only to the reactionary nature of much plebeian politics, but also to
current interpretations of the industrial revolution as being not so
much a big bang as a long and uneven whimper.[12] Such criticisms
have also been fuelled by the theoretical reservations of those taking
the linguistic turn who have increasingly criticised Thompson's
reflective concept of language, in which the language of politics is
seen as reflecting, rather than actively constituting, social experience.[13] Thus for Stedman Jones the language of Chartism was not a
language of class because it reflected some anterior working-class
experience of industrialisation, but because, in the political context of
mid nineteenth-century England, Chartist language spoke to the
politically excluded people as a class. Although Stedman Jones has
rightly been criticised for replicating that peculiarly Cambridge
tradition of the history of the political ideas – where primacy is
afforded to printed, rather than oral or visual, texts, and the
questions of agency, the instability of meaning, and the play of
differences within texts are simply ignored – his work has proved an
important catalyst to the rethinking of nineteenth-century English
politics.[14] Taking up where Stedman Jones left off, Patrick Joyce has
argued that class was just one of many identities articulated by the
languages of radical politics, all of which, as Joan Scott has
demonstrated, were highly gendered, just as they also spoke to a
dominant *ethnos*, of Englishness against all its Others.[15]

Much of the impetus for this linguistic turn came from the feminist
movement, born of disenchantment with the Left and its social

structural models of subjugation. Of course it is both difficult and dangerous to place feminist narratives so precisely in such a brief survey of the historiography of English politics, for they have always been diverse and heterogeneous, sitting uneasily aside, and yet always apart from, other historiographical traditions, united only by their concern to write women into history.[16] It is clearly significant that it is feminist historians like Joan Scott and Denise Riley who have found the post-structuralist emphasis on the decentred subject, the instability of language and the ordering of factors of difference within it, most useful (or have used them most) to understand knowledge as power so as to subvert and deconstruct the authoritative and repressive languages and categories to which 'women' have been subjected.[17] However, such techniques and concerns have also been evident in those feminist critiques of modern liberal democracy, whose uses of the Enlightenment ideal of the rational, virtuous, individual citizen at its founding moment during the Age of Revolution, was based upon the exclusion of women.[18] In these feminist narratives then, the whole Enlightenment belief in the progress of reason, liberty, and democracy is revealed as a sham, an attempt to fix the political subjects' relations of sexual difference in such a way as to privilege reasonable public men at the expense of natural irrational women. Certainly such a narrative challenges the triumphant teleologies of its whiggish rivals, be they tory, liberal, social democratic or marxist.

And yet the linguistic turn under the influence of post-structuralism, offers so many other possibilities for a new political history than those suggested by feminist histories. By acknowledging that it is language and not some prior social structure that creates the diverse, unstable, and often contradictory identities of the decentred subject, figures such as Patrick Joyce and Geoff Eley have begun to open up new and exciting approaches to the histories of nineteenth-century politics and class.[19] Reading politics as an attempt to put the decentred Humpty Dumpty back together again by making identity fixed, stable, and coherent (however provisionally) through the narrative forms of its languages, they have enabled us to see politics as a discursive struggle to empower people by imagining them as legitimately acting subjects around specific fixed identities. Of course, as feminist narratives remind us, such an attempt to create fixed, centred subjectivities inevitably rely upon an ordering of the factors of difference, so that each secured, stable identity was based upon exclusions of 'Others' and therefore equally liable to disable, as enable, the subject. This consideration of politics as power, as a discursive attempt to create or prevent a sense of agency, represents a significant step forward. It is worth emphasising that, although individual and collective actors are constrained by the finite subjectivities of political languages, they are none the less always able to play at the margins of those languages, extending their possibilities, appropriating and subverting them in unanticipated ways.

So much then is the state of the art. Hopefully, it is now clear how far those of us who have fellow-travelled on the tide of post-structuralism have moved away from the old political histories of 'interests' with their institutions and ideologies. What I am offering here is a new cultural history of the meanings of politics – a history of its subjectivities and identities, the ways in which politics defined and imagined people – which in turn provides, at least in my reading, a new narrative of nineteenth-century English political history. There is, then, little of the stuff of orthodox political history in this book. There is no discussion of the organisations, personnel or policies of the national institutions of politics, nor any detailed analyses of social and economic structures. Those traditional sources of political history which have tended to privilege the most literate and articulate members of the political nation have also been dispensed with, in favour of much neglected traces like ballads, banners, cartoons, handbills, statues, architecture, the uses of time and space, and the rich vein of ceremonial and iconographic forms. Even the standard texts of political history, like newspapers and poll books, have been re-read in innovative ways.

Chronologically, however, the book is rather conventional. It spans perhaps the most well-picked bone on the carcass of British political history, that half-century between the end of the Napoleonic Wars in 1815 and the passing of the second Reform Act in 1867. Of course, such periodisation is inevitably essentially arbitrary, and it is certainly not intended to imply some qualitative change in the nature of politics in the periods preceding or following these dates – indeed often the reader may be aware of passages in the text discussing events before and after them. However, it does serve a rhetorical purpose, as we have been led to believe that this was the period which established English political liberty and democracy. The chronology is a familiar one. The rise of the radical mass platform between 1815 and 1819 paved the way for the successful reform agitation of

1829–32, and yet it was the disappointments of the 1832 Reform Act which fuelled a decade of Chartist activity ending with the collapse of the mass platform in 1848. In the following mid-Victorian decades the working class were either forced, or convinced, to work within the political system which excluded them, seeking inclusion through the nascent Liberal and Conservative parties and the Reform Acts of 1867 and 1884, a process completed with the arrival of independent labour politics and the Representation of the Peoples Act of 1918. It is a teleological chronology which caricatures itself. Even its more recent revisionist versions, where the emphasis is on continuities and the slow and uneven nature of political change, have evoked either a world where nothing ever really happens, or one in which paradise was indefinitely postponed due to lack of interest.[20] In these readings English liberty and democracy, with their engine's party and class, may have taken much longer to arrive than we previously thought, but they were still delivered and proved enabling and progressive. Instead this book will argue that such developments often constituted a disabling retreat. By examining the creation of political sub-jectivities as they were played out in the debate over the meaning of the constitution and the nature of citizenship, I will argue that definitions of the constitution became increasingly exclusive during this period. In short, at the founding moment of English liberty and democracy, it was the closure of democratic political forms, the stifling of a radical libertarian tradition, that was most evident.

Central to such an account is the recognition that politics is about far more than orthodox political institutions and their representative systems. Instead it turns upon the idea of English political culture as an arena of struggle in which competing groups contested each others' definitions of the public political sphere according to their interpretation of the constitution.[21] It was, however, an uneven struggle, a fact recognised in the very organisation of this book. Those who controlled the offices of state – the local and national political institutions with their associated powers over the military, police, and media – those who propagated official definitions of the public political sphere, always had the upper hand. For their definitions and subjectivities were always backed by the force of the law, or sometimes even just plain, brutal force. Yet it would be misleading to overemphasise this coercive aspect, for official definitions of the constitution could not always be imposed by force alone. The illegality of certain types of politics and the risk of imprisonment (or

fates still worse) rarely served as a guarantee that people would not
continue to practise them. Consequently, in Part 1 I analyse the ways
in which popular support was generated for exclusive official
definitions of the public political sphere with their restrictive
subjectivities. Thus the first two chapters reveal the remarkable
degree of popular participation within all levels of official politics,
from the parish meeting to civic ceremony and the parliamentary
election. Clearly, however, this participation was carefully structured, organised, and disciplined around subjectivities which were
unlikely to challenge the legitimacy of the political and social *status
quo*. Conversely, in Parts 2 and 3 I examine the attempts of popular
political groups to contest such exclusive official definitions with their
own expanded and inclusive definitions of the constitution. Chapters
5, 6 and 8 are all concerned with the ways in which radicals and
reformers endeavoured to empower those groups officially excluded
from the constitution by creating subjectivities which spoke to them
as citizens, including them within their cultures and organisations
and providing them a platform within the public political sphere.

Of course this division of the book into 'official' and 'popular'
parts is in many ways artificial and ahistorical, implying fixed,
discrete, and unitary categories which cry out for deconstruction. It
is therefore worth emphasising that I do not intend to imply that
these categories can be referred back to specific social groups, or that
they boasted intrinsic cultural forms, beliefs and practices. Instead in
what follows I am at pains to point to the relationship between these
categories and the differences and tensions within them. It is certainly
possible to read such a formulation as in part a corrective to the
recent trend to afford primacy to the state's attempt to define the
political agenda and its subjectivities, which at times sails perilously
close to reviving a history of high politics.[22] If we are to have a history
of the reception of political languages as well as the history of their
production it is the dynamic relationships between the worlds of
'official' and 'popular', 'high' and 'low', politics that we must strive
to reveal – in any case they make no sense as discrete categories.
Their only utility is that they enable us to imagine and portray
something of the complex process through which political subjectivities and the public political sphere were continually redefined
and contested.

As I have already suggested, the central theme of the book is that,
despite laying the legislative foundations of liberal democracy in 1832

and 1867, English politics became progressively less democratic during this period as political subjectivities and the public political sphere were defined in increasingly restrictive and exclusive fashions. Much of this was due to the changing dynamics of political communication which gradually afforded individuals less and less power in the creation of their own political languages and identities. As we shall see in chapter 3, a mass of legislation sought to discipline popular modes of political communication: partly by regulating the occurrence of meetings, the contents of speeches, handbills, news-papers, and the uses of banners, flags and favours; and partly by privileging the uses of print in political communication, as opposed to customary oral and visual forms. Taken together this body of legislation – often ingeniously labelled anti-corruption laws – encouraged the private, individual, and masculine uses of politics at the expense of more threatening, subversive, and popular public and collective uses. Although this gradual and uneven closure of the public political sphere was by no means complete in 1867, it found little resistance from radicals and reformers. They, too, increasingly sought to discipline popular politics, tempting it out from its customary venue of the pub to purpose-built halls in which audiences could be better regulated, shunning the customary techniques of popular political protest as irrational, and providing women with well-defined roles and identities which would not challenge the ascendancy of the patriarchal discourse of their politics. As we shall see in chapters 4 and 6, read in this way even the mid-Victorian invention of party can be seen as part of this closure of the public political sphere, a means of disciplining popular politics by securing it within certain limited and restrictive subjectivities and practices. And yet, as chapter 7 reminds us, the relationship between political leaders, languages, and their popular constituencies was a complex one, the meaning of the leader lying as much in the mind of the beholder as with the leader himself. Despite the best efforts of leaders to project their own images of themselves, they remained the icon and creation of their followers.

Many of these themes come together in Part 3 in an analysis of the narrative forms of the language of politics. Here I argue that the debate over the meaning of the constitution's past, present, and future, that is the discourse of popular constitutionalism, represented the master narrative of nineteenth-century English politics. It was through their different appropriations and interpretations of this constitutional narrative that political groups articulated their own definitions of the public political sphere, seeking to construct constituencies of support by empowering the decentred subject with a stable and coherent identity. And yet this did not mean that the range or variety of identities available to individual or collective actors was in any sense limited or static, like the narrative of the constitution they were multi-vocal, amenable to a myriad uses and meanings, both empowering and disabling. Indeed, one of the advantages of such a reading is that it enables us to escape from the historiographical preoccupation with class, to conceptualise how subjects were imagined as members of a sex, religion, a nation, or as a people, as well, and as often, as members of a particular class.[23] It enables us to acknowledge that the languages, categories, and identities of nineteenth-century politics were both shared – in that they all drew their authority from the same constitutional master narrative – and different – in that each individual or collective subject appropriated those languages, categories, and identities in different ways. Thus, just as we cannot imagine difference without the unity of a shared code, neither can we imagine that unity without an awareness of its different uses.

This is also apparent in the typology of the book. At the outset this study was intended as a comparative account of five parliamentary constituencies with very different geographic, demographic, political, social, and economic contexts, differences which I assumed would be reflected in their political cultures. Geographically the constituencies stretched from Oldham in the north-west to Tower Hamlets and Lewes in the south-east, from Boston in the east Midlands to Devon in the West Country. The two urban and industrialising constituencies of Oldham and Tower Hamlets were deliberately offset by the small market-towns of Boston and Lewes, and the predominantly rural county of Devon as such places have tended to be neglected by historians intent on finding models for social and political development.[24] Of course these images are themselves caricatures. Tower Hamlets was notoriously by-passed by the sort of intensive industrial production of cotton, coal, and engineering evident in Oldham. If the industrial proletariat was to be found anywhere in nineteenth-century England it was in Oldham, not Tower Hamlets which remained dominated by small-scale domestic artisan production, despite its large fluid population and commercial docks.[25] And yet both constituencies came to represent, in the imagination of the legislators at least, great urban industrial centres which had to be included within the political nation as boroughs in the 1832 Reform Act. In contrast, Boston, Lewes, and the county of Devon had long been part of the unreformed electoral system – Lewes as an important Sussex market town, which also boasted its own paper, grain, and malt trades, and Boston as a thriving provincial port responsible for the export of the grain and wool produced in the surrounding agricultural hinterland and the import of timber from the Baltic. Before its division into two constituencies in 1832 (of which I concentrate on south Devon) Devon was second only to Yorkshire in size, representing predominantly a rural England of large aristocratic landowners, yeoman tenant farmers, and agricultural workers.

Despite the substantial contrasts and differences between these constituencies, it soon became apparent that it was their similarities that were most striking and interesting, suggesting, as they did, the existence of a national political culture, albeit with strong local and regional mediations. I therefore largely abandoned a strict comparative analysis of the five constituencies in order to avoid having to manufacture political differences to which I would then have to attach undue structural significance. In emphasising the similarities between the five constituencies I have tried not to reduce their politics to one text with a stable, unified set of meanings. I hope I have been as alive to their differences as to their similarities. Inevitably I am afraid, in a study of this size, such a technique favours the most well-documented groups and constituencies, particularly those involved in electoral politics whether at parish, municipal, county or parliamentary level.

PART I

Politics, community, and power

CHAPTER I

Power legislated: the structure of official politics

INTRODUCTION

This chapter will examine the official structure of nineteenth-century English politics as defined by law. Officially the political arena was defined by the legal framework upon which it rested, that is the institutions, offices, and representative structures of local and national government. It was through these legal structures that official definitions of the public political sphere were created. Here one is aware of the discursive role of the law. This chapter represents an analysis of official uses of the discourse of the law to formalise and close down the public political sphere by providing ever more restrictive definitions of property as the legitimate basis of political participation and authority. Theoretically the connection between politics, property, and power had been implicit since 1688 and all that, but it was during this period, with the political reforms of parliament, parish, and municipality, that it took a practical, legal root in English constitutional history. If such a connection proved restrictive for poor, property-less men, it quickly became calamitous for women, properties or not, as by the mid-1830s property had become an exclusively male category. Henceforward, the official political subject was propertied and male.[1]

As we shall see, it is difficult to talk of one, singular, exclusive official definition of a male propertied political arena. The official political structure was a curious mixture of the old and the new, the local and the national, combining the remnants of a medieval political system with that created by nineteenth-century reforms. The five constituencies studied here reflect this heterogeneity, although in no sense do they represent all types of official political structures found at parish, civic, county, and national levels.[2] It is striking not only how structurally diverse official politics were in the five constituencies, but how vibrant popular participation was within the official political arena. Significantly, this was true of all levels, including the parish, town, and county, even though political historians have tended in the past to concentrate exclusively upon parliamentary politics.[3] If the scale and intensity of official politics was greater than previously thought, then it becomes doubly important to examine the ways in which popular participation was shaped, regulated, and disciplined by officially defined political structures.

PAROCHIAL POLITICS

To the historian of England between the Revolution and the Municipal Corporations Act, if he is not to leave out of the account the lives of five-sixths of the population, the constitutional development of the parish and the manifold activities of its officers will loom at least as large as dynastic intrigues, the alternations [sic] of Parliamentary factions, or the complications of foreign politics.[4]

As the Webbs recognised, most people's experience of the official political process began with their own parish, at the public parish vestry. As we shall see, vestries existed in all five constituencies and, contrary to the Webbs' opinion, continued to be centrally important in many areas well after the Municipal Corporations Act of 1835. Broadly, there were three types of vestry in use – the public parish vestry, the Sturges Bourne select vestry, and the closed select vestry – and this section will examine their respective uses in the five constituencies.[5]

Officially the public parish vestry did not exist in law before 1818; that is, it was regulated by common law and custom, not by official statute. Consequently, the rights of attendance at these vestries were ambiguous, fluctuating between either householders or ratepayers in different parishes, although most vestries tried to prevent those who had received parish relief over the preceding twelve months from attending their meetings. However, it would be hard to describe the public parish vestry as an exclusive body. The turnout for meetings varied from a handful of ratepayers to several thousand inhabitants.[6] Invariably the press reported that vestry meetings had been adjourned from the church or its yard to much larger open-air venues like a market-place or some derelict open space. In such meetings the distinctions between householders, ratepayers and inhabitants were notoriously difficult to maintain, and whichever side felt itself to be losing the argument or the vote always questioned the legitimacy of the meeting and its participants.[7]

Moreover, as Keith-Lucas has noted, it has often been overlooked that women householders and ratepayers often played a full part in the politics of the parish vestry, not only attending and voting at vestry meetings, but even holding parochial offices.[8] The legal test-case of Olive v. Ingram in 1739 had upheld the right of women to vote at vestries and to be elected as sextons, if only because it was 'an office that did not concern the public, or the care and inspection of the morals of the parishioners, there was no reason to exclude women'.[9] This ruling was immensely significant, for, although women were clearly not regarded as men's equals, it established the legal precedent with which propertied women could legitimately claim their right to participate in official politics. In effect it provided an official definition of property which accepted women's legitimate political interests. The lingering influence of this ruling was still evident in the Sturges Bourne Acts of 1818 and 1819, both of which failed to specifically exclude propertied women from the vestry franchise, preferring, it seems, to leave the decision to local custom.[10] While Hobhouse's more radical Vestries Act of 1831 was bolder still, using this established legal precedent to officially recognise by statute the right of women ratepayers to the parochial suffrage.

The pre-1818 parish vestry was therefore, at least potentially, a genuinely popular body, although the extent of popular participation varied enormously from parish to parish and from meeting to meeting. Of the five constituencies, Oldham's (pre-1818) public parish vestry generated the greatest degree of popular participation, no doubt partly due to its wide administrative brief: its functions included raising poor and church rates, distributing poor relief, appointing parish constables and surveyors of highways, as well as passing their annual accounts. Before 1818 neither the vestries of Boston or Lewes could claim to be as popular or as powerful, for they were both overshadowed by Boston's unreformed corporation and the Lewes court-leet respectively. The spectre of these popular, even quasi-democratic, bodies wielding increasing powers in new industrialising towns like Oldham, frightened many, both within and outside parliament, who envisaged popular fronts of shopkeepers and working men and women disproportionately levying rates on the burgeoning ranks of urban industrialists.

Consequently, in 1818 and 1819 the whole system of local

government by public parish vestry was reformed and formalised by statute. The Sturges Bourne Vestry Act of 1818 endeavoured, if not to provide a tighter and more exclusive official definition of property, then, at least, to privilege certain definitions of property over others, by introducing a scale of voting whereby ratepayers would have between one and six votes depending on the size of their property. Those inhabitants whose property was assessed at more than £160 received the maximum six votes, while the sliding scale ensured that those assessed at up to £50 only had the minimum one vote. Moreover, those who did not pay rates were excluded not only from voting, but even from attending vestry meetings, while joint stock companies and non-resident ratepayers were enfranchised for the first time. The Act clearly represented an attempt to 'redress' the balance of power at vestry level between the propertied and the poor, indeed it was the first official attempt to limit the public political sphere to the propertied alone. As such it marked a significant formalisation and consolidation of the official political structure by statute, a trend which was to dominate and transform both the structure of local government and the entire province of legislation over the following 40 years.[11]

Unsurprisingly the act was hugely unpopular. Even *The Times*, then as now a paper not renowned for its radicalism, attacked it as too 'sudden an alteration of the constitution of this realm... The laws of the realm, the laws of nature and the laws of God acknowledge no such classification or gradations in man'.[12] Neither did opposition to the Act wane with the passage of time. Indeed, thanks largely to the campaigns of the reforming barrister and historian Joshua Toulmin Smith, the Act remained infamous because 'its object is to give to those who have and to take away from those who have not even that which they have. It gives a number of votes not according to the number of minds, but the amount of property... in the true spirit of Centralization it treats materialism as the sole foundation and criterion of human good... There is no greater blot upon our Statute book than Sturges Bourne's Act.'[13] As we shall see in chapter 5, there can be little doubt that Toulmin Smith's uncompromising language struck a chord with those who felt that the Act, and many of the subsequent 'reforms' which used its provisions, were the pernicious product of Benthamite centralisation which robbed them of their rights as freeborn Englishmen to a voice in local affairs. Partly as a result of its unpopularity the Act was far from successful. Non-ratepayers continued to attend, and even in some cases still to vote, as the system of plural voting proved far too complex and laborious to be used for all vestry decisions. Many parishes seem to have used the plural voting system only for those decisions and elections that went to the poll, while the vast majority of decisions still continued to be taken by a show of hands.[14]

The following year, undeterred by the unpopularity and practical difficulties of his Vestries Act, Sturges Bourne guided through parliament the equally contentious Poor Relief Act. This Act restructured the administration of poor relief and, in doing so, established select vestries of 'substantial householders', which were elected by the public parish vestry specifically to oversee the administration of poor relief. A full-time official with a salary, the assistant overseer, replaced the amateur part-time overseer who had invariably done the job voluntarily, at his own leisure and expense. This Act, therefore, like the earlier one, attempted to transform the structure and processes of vestry politics by linking them to an exclusive definition of property which allowed only the rich to administer and take part in parish affairs.

The clearest indication of Sturges Bourne's attempt to restrict popular participation was the exemption of the old closed select vestries from the clauses of his Vestries Act of 1818. These closed select vestries which had evolved through common law during the seventeenth and eighteenth centuries were found predominantly in the metropolis, especially in the parishes of what became, in 1832, the constituency of Tower Hamlets. Despite having total control of local taxation and expenditure, they were self-elected bodies and, therefore, utterly unaccountable to either the county magistrates or the general ratepayers and inhabitants. The infamy of the 'Parish Tyrants' of London's select vestries, like Joseph Merceron at Bethnal Green, was nation-wide and fuelled a radical campaign that culminated in 1831 with the passing of Hobhouse's Vestries Act.[15]

Hobhouse's Act abolished London's closed select vestries and replaced them with genuinely open, accountable vestries which retained the same wide administrative duties. This Act completely by-passed the structural framework of the earlier Sturges Bourne's Acts and therefore signified a major shift in parliament's conception of the people's role within local government. All those who paid rates (men and women alike) were given a vote of equal worth, which could be cast by secret ballot if demanded by five or more parishioners. Each year a third of the elected vestry members had to stand for re-election, while all the accounts and minutes of the vestry had to be available for inspection by any ratepayer, in order to ensure full accountability: both popular innovations that were adopted 4 years later in the Municipal Reform Act. The introduction of the secret ballot and the formal recognition of women ratepayers' right to vote were major steps forward by the legislature, it represented the first official recognition of these principles in law.[16] Indeed, because of the radical implications of Hobhouse's Act it is hard to resist the feeling that it was passed almost by default by a parliament preoccupied with the parliamentary reform bill.[17] While the champions of the Act argued they were enabling the property-less to become virtuous parochial citizens by educating them in the affairs, issues, and meetings of the vestry, there were those who felt that the Act had set a dangerous precedent by providing an official definition of the propertied and virtuous parochial citizen which was far too inclusive. Some, like Wellington, believed that the Act threatened the very fabric of property itself, as it left 'the property of every man at the disposition of the rabble of his parish, particularly in the towns'.[18] No doubt such fears were soothed by the prohibitive property qualifications for Hobhouse's vestry members. For in the metropolis, and parishes elsewhere with over 3,000 householders, candidates had to be householders assessed at £40 or more, compared to the £10 qualification for resident householders in the smaller parishes.

However, the ambiguity surrounding both the implementation of the Sturges Bourne Acts and the metropolitan parliamentary electorates makes it difficult to decipher the number of voters involved at vestry polls, or for that matter to make any meaningful comparisons between the electorates of Sturges Bourne's and Hobhouse's Acts or either of these with their municipal and parliamentary counterparts. None the less, from the few publicised poll results available, it is possible to make some exploratory suggestions. For instance, polls in the parishes of Oldham, Chadderton, Royton, and Crompton (approximately that area covered by the parliamentary constituency) produced 2,392 votes in favour and 1,804 votes against the reconstruction of Oldham's Anglican church in 1828. Similarly, in 1844 at the Oldham parish vestry's election for an assistant overseer, a relieving overseer and a collector, 2,917, 2,819, and 1,190 votes were cast for the candidates of each office. At Boston's vestry two polls over the church rates in 1834 and 1840 produced a total number of votes of 734 and 689 respectively. While at an election of an assistant overseer at Lewes' St John's parish in 1863 276 votes were cast by 239 voters. All these figures would seem to suggest that even Sturges Bourne's vestry electorates were often substantially larger than their parliamentary or municipal counterparts. For instance at the poll in St John's, Lewes, the only one where the actual number of voters were specified, it is very unlikely that all 239 parochial electors were also members of Lewes' parliamentary electorate of 720, as that electorate was drawn from no less than 8 parishes. Likewise, even if we assume that all those who voted in the 1828 poll on the reconstruction of Oldham's church cast 6 votes on Sturges Bourne's sliding scale, which was less likely than them all casting a single vote, then the poll still represents an electorate of 700 voters, which corresponds favourably with the 1,131 parliamentary electors enfranchised in 1832. We encounter similar difficulties when comparing the vestry polls of the metropolitan parishes operating under the provisions of the Hobhouse Act with their parliamentary counterparts. None the less these figures, which, for instance, range from 3,122 votes polled over the setting of the church rate at St Dunstan, Stepney in 1846, to 4,236 votes polled for no less than 16 candidates at Ratcliff's vestry election in 1859, suggest that there too parochial electorates were greater than the parliamentary electorate in these areas. However, in light of the little evidence available such statements must remain largely impressionistic and provisional.

Despite these quantitative difficulties, it should already be clear that, whatever its form, the vestry was a central component of official politics. As the problems of urbanisation and industrialisation increasingly manifested themselves in England's towns and cities, it was invariably to the vestries that central government turned when dispensing new administrative responsibilities. As Prest has recently shown, a series of permissive legislation enabled the localities to deal with specific problems by establishing committees elected from vestry members by Sturges Bourne's system of plural voting.[19] Despite several attempts, inspired by Chadwick and sponsored by the Whig government, to rationalise the structure of local government by replacing the parish with the new administrative unit of the union through the 1834 Poor Law Amendment Act, the power and influence of the vestry arguably increased. Of course, as we shall see in chapter 5, this varied from parish to parish and locality to locality depending upon what other official representative administrative bodies existed and how much permissive legislation local vestries adopted. Thus although Lewes' vestries were seemingly always dominated by the town's court-leet and town commissioners, Boston's vestry remained influential even after the town's incorporation in 1835 because it remained responsible both for raising the church rate to maintain the huge Anglican church of St Botolph's and electing the Board of Guardians. Similarly, despite attempts by central government to restrict its power in 1820 and 1826 through the Salford court-leet and then by creating the town's police commissioners (an unelected body which assumed the administrative duties of the vestry), Oldham's vestry remained a critical arena of local politics and administration until 1849 when the town was finally incorporated.

Even at the height of Chadwick's rationalising public health legislation, central government remained aware of the importance of the parish vestry.[20] Encouraged by Toulmin Smith's campaigns, the parish experienced a distinct revival as the definitive unit of local administration in the official political mind. A year after Chadwick's centralised union-based General Board of Health had been disbanded in 1854, the Metropolis Management Act was passed. This Act created a two-tier system of local government in London by establishing the Metropolitan Board of Works which appropriated all the functions of the numerous commissioners and boards of London's parishes. However, the Metropolitan Board of Works remained accountable to the parish vestries because it was dependent on them for the election of its members and, crucially, the raising of taxation through the setting of rates. Significantly, the Act also established a uniform electoral procedure and franchise throughout the metropolis based upon the inclusive terms of Hobhouse's Vestries Act of 1831. In part this simply recognised that some of the larger metropolitan vestries used Hobhouse's system since 1831, and it would clearly have been politically awkward for a professedly liberal-minded government to disenfranchise any of London's parish voters. Yet it also represented an important vote of official confidence in the parish vestry and the expansive definition of a propertied, virtuous parochial (even proto-) citizenry pioneered by Hobhouse's Act in 1831. It was not until the London Local Government Act of 1899 created twenty-eight metropolitan borough councils that London's parish vestries with their inclusive franchises were finally made redundant.

CIVIC POLITICS

The term 'civic politics' is used here to describe the politics of those towns legally recognised, and governed, as boroughs. The legal structure of politics in these boroughs took two forms: the manorial borough like Lewes, and the municipal borough like Boston and Oldham. Although the vestry remained central to the official political structure, its functions were increasingly eclipsed by the reformed municipal system of local government. This section will examine the official structures of civic politics, and their development, in the three towns of Lewes, Boston, and Oldham.

The feudal origins of Lewes' status as an ancient borough, entitled to return two members to parliament, is unclear. However, by the advent of the nineteenth century the town was the manor of the most unlikely trio, namely the Duke of Norfolk, the Earl of Abergavenny and the Earl de la Warr. These 3 people, as tenants in common, served in rotation through their respective stewards (whom they appointed) as lords of the borough. Every year, on Affearing Day, these stewards held a court-leet during which the officers of the borough for the ensuing year were chosen. Originally all the inhabitants of the manor over 12 years of age were obliged to attend the court-leet, but this no longer seems to have occurred during this period. The local press conveys the impression that few people even attended the meeting of the court-leet in the town hall, let alone the dinner afterwards, other than the active participants. These participants were the local inhabitants selected by the steward as the jury of the court-leet. The jury usually consisted of about 23 people, although it fluctuated between 16 and 26, and they were invariably tradesmen and merchants.[21]

Although in theory the stewards also appointed the town's officers, in practice they always chose the first 2 names on a list of 4 nominated by the jury. The town's offices included such useful posts as the 'Searcher of Leather' and an 'Ale Conner' but consisted chiefly of the two constables, the two headboroughs, and the town-crier. The constables were the chief officers of the borough responsible for the custody of the borough's muniments, the management of its property, including setting a rate, while also serving as returning officers at parliamentary elections. The headboroughs were assistants to the constables and they, in turn, became constables. At the meeting of the court-leet the jury examined and audited the retiring constable's accounts. However, it was not until the following Whit Monday that the constables called a public meeting of the inhabitants to approve the annual rate they wished to have set. Usually the rate was set at 6 pence in the pound, but an attempt in the 1830s to increase it to 1 shilling in the pound provoked a legal investigation which finally ruled that the constables had no power to enforce a rate. The town then apparently reverted to the old 6 pence rate 'which [was] *voluntarily* paid by the inhabitants with very few exceptions'.[22] The rate was then seemingly based upon the consent of all the inhabitants, regardless of the rateable value of their property. Ironically then, Lewes' essentially feudal administrative system was the most representative, for popular accountability was not limited by exclusive property qualifications.

No doubt mindful of the radical implications of such a political structure the town's propertied elite established a town commission, independent of the county magistrates and the court-leet, by adopting a permissive Act passed in 1806 'for paving lighting cleansing watching repairing and improving the roads streets lanes and other public passages and places within the borough of Lewes for removing and preventing nuisance and encroachments therein' (*sic.*).[23] Membership of the commission was limited to those inhabitants (paying scot and lot) who owned or occupied property rated at a yearly value of £20 within the boundaries of the town. Clearly such a prohibitive property qualification ensured the exclusivity of the commission, although few details are available about the size or composition of this body, perhaps unsurprisingly the local press barely acknowledged its existence. I have found only one reference to the commission which, like the court-leet, met at the White Hart Inn. The report notes that the meeting 'was very thinly attended, there not being half a dozen commissioners present until the rate for the ensuing year was passed. Subsequently, however, the number was increased to fifteen or sixteen.'[24] Over and above the general administration of the borough and the setting of the rate, the commission had also appropriated the power of policing the borough for the 'Constables and Headboroughs are generally persons whose station in life and engagements are incompatible with the duties of the police'.[25] The town commission had then been created to ensure that the town's official political structure was cemented to an exclusive definition of property which effectively made the strangely democratic system of the court-leet redundant.

Boston was also an ancient borough although, unlike Lewes, it had received a Charter of Incorporation in 1545. Before its reform in 1835 Boston's municipal corporation was typical of many unreformed corporations. It consisted of a mayor, a town recorder, and 11 aldermen, all of whom were self-elected, together with 18 councillors appointed by the aldermen. All these offices were held for life. The corporation was responsible for appointing the local magistracy (usually from the aldermen) and managing the borough's estates, although it could not levy the town rate, instead its income came from town tolls and harbour charges. With its reform in 1835, the Boston Corporation inherited these and other responsibilities, such as policing the borough, and, crucially, was empowered to raise and set the town rate. The reformed municipal electorate of 740 ratepayers or burgesses, divided between the 2 wards of Boston and Skirbeck, returned a mayor, 6 Aldermen, and 18 councillors to the council chamber.[26] To qualify as a municipal elector one had to be a male occupier of rateable property and to have fully paid the rates over the preceding two and a half years. Significantly, the 1835 Municipal Reform Act followed the example set by the parliamentary Reform Act of 1832 by explicitly specifiying that the franchise was for 'male persons' only. This represented an important retreat from the inclusion of women in official politics by Hobhouse's Vestries Act and for the rest of this period the official political subject was always a deliberately male one. However, in other ways the 1835 Municipal Reform Act was less exclusive. Boston's municipal electorate accounted for a mere 5.8 per cent of the borough's total population, or 22.6 per cent of adult males. However, with the passing of the Small Tenements Act in 1850, the size of this electorate increased to 1,720 (9.8 per cent of the population, 38.5 per cent of adult males) with a further 1,194 burgesses (6.8% of the population, 26.7% of adult males) excluded by the system of compounding.[27] It is hard to make meaningful comparisons between Boston's municipal and parliamentary electorates as the electoral boundaries were different (see Plate 1) by 1865, however, 719 of Boston's 1,093 parliamentary electors (or 65.8 per cent) were also municipal voters. No less than a thousand of Boston's propertied male ratepayers were then granted citizenship of their town while they were still denied citizenship of the nation. Indeed, Keith Lucas has estimated that the omission of the £10 limit on rateable property in the Municipal Reform Act enfranchised an additional 20 or 25 per cent of the urban popu-

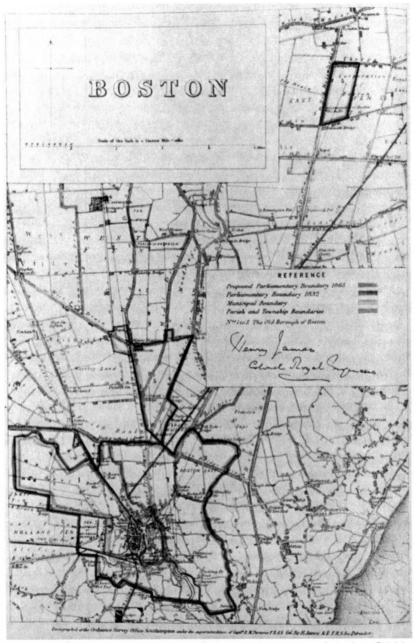

1   Map of Boston's municipal and parliamentary boundaries after 1835 (British
Library)

lation.[28] At both municipal and vestry level a far larger (and possibly different) constituency than the parliamentary electorate was actively participating in the official politic arena.

Nowhere was this extra-parliamentary official political arena more evident or vibrant than in Oldham. So fearful were the local and national authorities of the town's popularly controlled vestry that they sought to subsume its powers, first under the aegis of the Salford court-leet in 1820 and then through the Oldham Police Act in 1826. This Act, which endowed an unelected body of police commissioners with many of the vestry's administrative responsibilities, sought to reduce popular accountability and participation in the town's affairs by once again making local political administration the exclusive preserve of rich propertied men. To qualify as a commissioner one had to own property of a rateable value of at least £60 – a prohibitive clause which severely restricted the possible number of commissioners, thus by 1849 the commission was only some 360 strong.[29] None the less, radical, or at least reforming, shopkeepers, tradesmen, and mill-owners were well represented on the commission, and by the early 1830s they appear to have won effective control of it. The exclusivity of the commission was also checked by its ultimate accountability to the town's vestry where all its accounts had to be approved. As we shall see in chapter 5, this division of powers would prove a source of much political conflict during the 1830s and 1840s, particularly over the contentious issue of the police accounts. It was the increasing use of the rural county police, who were accountable to the county magistrates not the police commission or the vestry, together with the financial and administrative limitations of the commission, which convinced many in Oldham of the need to incorporate the town.

In 1849, therefore, 15 years after the Municipal Reform Act, Oldham received its Charter of Incorporation. The new incorporated borough was twice the size of the borough of Boston, boasting no less than 8 wards across some 4,666 acres. The council consisted of a mayor, 8 aldermen, and 24 councillors, who were returned at the first municipal election in 1849 by an electorate of 2,910 (4 per cent of the total population, 15.7 per cent of adult males) which had risen to 5,067 (4.7 per cent of the population, 18.4 per cent of adult males) by 1866. Unlike Boston, Oldham's municipal electorate was always larger than its parliamentary electorate, despite the municipal

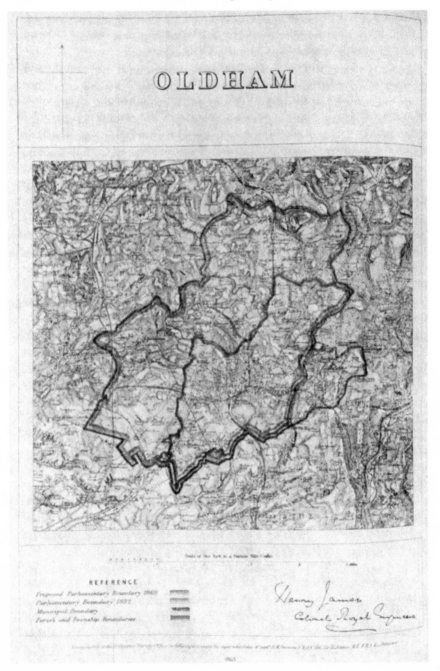

2   Map of Oldham's municipal and parliamentary boundaries (British Library)

boundary being considerably smaller than that of the parliamentary constituency (see Plate 2).[30]

We should not be seduced by these figures into believing that the municipal franchise always expanded the official political arena. We have already seen how the 1835 Act created an exclusive official definition of the propertied, male political subject. Yet, women and the poor non-ratepayers were not the only ones excluded from such official definitions, many ratepayers were disqualified as well. For instance, while some, particularly members of the migrant work-force, were excluded by the two and a half years residency clause, anyone who had hit hard times in the preceding 30 months and received poor relief or some other sort of alms were also disqualified. As, too, were all compounded householders, at least before the Small Tenements Act of 1850. Increasingly used from the 1840s, com-pounding was an administrative device to levy the rates of a rented property (particularly those with a small rateable value) from the owner, rather than the occupier. The owner was then responsible for reclaiming the cost of the rates directly from the tenants. Conse-quently, compounded householders were not on the burgess roll as they were not officially registered ratepayers. The Small Tenements Act was therefore designed to enfranchise those compounders who occupied houses not exceeding a rateable value of £6. However, as a permissive Act it was only adopted in Boston and Lewes out of the five constituencies. It was most effective in Boston where it doubled the number of registered burgesses from 818 to 1,720 overnight.[31] Such dramatic figures exemplify just how exclusive the qualifications for the municipal franchise could be, even amongst those it sought to include. The official structure of municipal politics after 1835 was then something of a half-way house between the often inclusive traditional representative structures of the public parish vestry and court-leet, and the often more exclusive 'reformed' structures of the Sturges Bourne vestry, town or police commissioners or post-1832 parliamentary constituency.

COUNTY POLITICS

The official structure of politics in Devon county was significantly different from that of the other four constituencies. However, like the organisation of both vestry and municipal politics, the administration of the English counties was based on formulas that had existed for centuries, hence their basic uniformity.[32] Despite these feudal origins, or even because of them, there was an emphasis on landed property, as distinct from the urban property of industrial or commercial wealth, as the legitimate source of authority and disinterested, independent county government.

At the apex of the county's political structure stood the Lord-lieutenant and the sheriff, both of whom were nominees of central government. The authority of the sheriff was, however, derived from the ancient institution of the county or sheriff's court, and by the nineteenth century this office was largely ceremonial, responsible for holding county meetings and elections. Conversely, the Lord-lieutenant's office had become increasingly powerful by appropriating the judicial functions of the sheriff's court and thus, critically, the power of appointing the county magistracy. For, by the beginning of the nineteenth century and until 1888, magistrates possessed almost all administrative power within the county – raising the county rate, policing the county, licensing pubs, and regulating the construction and management of roads, bridges, prisons, and lunatic asylums. Although an Act of 1732 had meant that theoretically one could qualify as a magistrate by owning a landed estate of £100, in practice the Lord-lieutenant often set far more exclusive criteria, defining property in terms of land and social prestige rather than wealth and income.[33] Clearly such definitions ensured that the structure of official county politics remained largely the preserve of the landed aristocracy and clergy.

Paradoxically, immediately underneath this governing county elite stood the generally representative parish vestries. None the less, while the vestries enabled county's householders to advise the magistrates on the relief of the poor, the maintenance of roads, and the appointment of constables and overseers, they were ultimately subject to the control of the magistracy at the Quarter Sessions in Exeter Castle. The county meeting was then the only real forum for the inhabitants to voice their complaints to the magistrates and the knights of the shire. Officially, they were meetings of the county court at Exeter Castle and were therefore restricted to the county's propertied freeholders alone. However, the reality was quite different as the German tourist Baron A de Stael Holsten recognised in 1822 'of all public assemblages of persons in England, perhaps none are so striking to a stranger as county meetings ... though the freeholders of the county are the only persons who have a right to vote at them almost anyone that chooses to be present is admitted without distinction. The business is not to decide as legislators or judges on positive rights or interests, but to consult or to guide the opinions of the many.'[34] The county meeting was then an indispensable occasion for the upwards and downwards communication of information and sentiment. It provided the only effective official arena in which those who were not propertied 40s freeholders could question the use and abuse of the offices of county government, although by the 1830s it was increasingly eclipsed by the use of partisan meetings and consequently experienced a steady, if gradual, decline. Despite growing agitation for greater popular control over the levying and administration of the county rate during the 1860s, this largely elitist official structure of county politics remained unchanged until the creation of county councils in 1888.

PARLIAMENTARY POLITICS

This section will analyse the official structure of parliamentary politics in the five constituencies, a structure which was of course famously reformed in 1832 by the 'Great' Reform Act. Of the five constituencies only Boston, Lewes, and Devon were represented in parliament before 1832, each in different ways. The 1832 Reform Act then not only standardised the archaic qualifications of the un-reformed electoral system, but also included the hitherto unrepresented localities of Oldham and Tower Hamlets within the political nation. However, as recent work has suggested, the effect of the 'Great' Reform Act was less than great and considerably less dramatic than has previously been supposed.[35]

Boston's resident freemen had returned two MPs since 1547. As the name suggests, the category and rights of freemen were an exclusively male preserve, handed down from father to son or occasionally purchased from the corporation. Although this gave the corporation considerable power to manage the creation of freemen, and hence the electorate, they were never entirely able, as R. G. Thorne has shown, to control the town's representation, if only because no corporation could ever guarantee that newly created freemen would vote as they were supposed to.[36] Perhaps, as a consequence, Boston's electorate of freemen grew at an unprecedented rate in the 50 years before 1832. Namier and Brooke have estimated that in 1780 Boston's electorate consisted of approximately 200 freemen, a figure which had risen to 378 by 1802 before doubling to 695 by 1832.[37] This steady increase in Boston's electorate before 1832 was replicated in the other un-reformed constituencies of Lewes and Devon. John Phillips reports that in Lewes, where the franchise was vested in the usually male inhabitants paying scot and lot, there was an electorate of some 243 voters in 1790.[38] By 1812, that figure had risen to 378, and by 1830 increased further to 750. Clearly, as Table 1 demonstrates, the unreformed electorates of Boston and Lewes grew rapidly between 1790 and 1832, albeit in proportion with their respective populations. Certainly such evidence of dynamic growth, coupled with the high proportion of adult males that were enfranchised, contradicts the historiographical cliché of a moribund and unrepresentative un-reformed electoral system.

Unfortunately, we can be less sure about the size and growth of Devon's unreformed electorate, as the sheer size of the constituency made registers and poll books impossible to compile. Before 1832 the constituency of Devon was spread across no less than 1,600,000 acres in 398 parishes, 25 market-towns, 10 boroughs, and 1 city. In this massive constituency the franchise was officially held only by those with freehold property rated to a land tax assessment of 40s. per annum. Yet, such a prohibitive property qualification may not have been as exclusive as it seems. Although there is no evidence of women being included within this definition of property, Frank O'Gorman has argued that 'customarily... "freehold" received a generously broad interpretation and included leases, mortgages, offices and annuities as well as freehold land. County voters, therefore, were almost as likely to be office holders, small holders, artisans and even tradesmen, as farmers.'[39] Despite the enormity and the ambiguity surrounding Devon's unreformed franchise it is still possible to estimate the size of the electorate. Namier and Brooke have estimated that the electorate consisted of roughly 3,000 voters between 1754 and 1790, a figure which seems to have more than doubled by the vigorously contested election of 1818 when 7,601 voters were polled.[40] Such figures again reaffirm the impression of rapid and substantial growth within the unreformed electorate in the half-century before 1832. It is important, therefore, to recognise that any increase in the electorate following 1832 did not occur within the context of a static unreformed electoral system. As we shall see, the 1832 Reform Act had very little effect upon either Boston or Lewes' electorate (see

Table 1. *The size of the unreformed electorate as a percentage of the population and as a percentage of adult males in Boston and Lewes*

	Boston			Lewes		
Date	No. of voters	% total population	% adult males	No. of voters	% total population	% adult males
1790	200			239	11.2	43.9
1802	378	6.4	25.1	334	7.6	29.6
1818	503	4.8	18.8	503	11.3	44.3
1830	695	6.2	24.3	750	11.8	46.3

Sources: Boston figures from Namier and Brooke (eds.), *The House of Commons 1754–1790*, I, pp. 324–5; *A True and Correct State of the Poll* (Boston, 1802); *History of the Boston Election* (Boston, 1818); *A Sketch of the Boston Election* (Boston, 1830). Lewes figures from Phillips', *Electoral Behaviour in Unreformed England* with the exception of the figures for the population in 1802 and the electorate in 1830 which were taken respectively from Thorne (ed.), *The House of Commons 1790–1820*, I, p. 395; and *Borough of Lewes. A Poll* (Lewes, 1830).

Table 2. *Social composition of the unreformed electorate in Boston and Lewes* (%)

	Boston		Lewes	
	1818	1830	1812	1830
Category:				
Gentleman/professional	6.5	7.7	13.1	14.9
Merchant/manufacturer	5.2	3.6	5.3	3.7
Retailers	21.9	22	22.8	17.3
Skilled craftsmen	51.4	56	40.7	38.4
Unskilled labour	11.3	9.7	17.5	24.5
Agriculture	3.7	1	0.6	1.2

Sources: *History of the Boston Election* (Boston, 1818); *A Sketch of the Boston Election* (Boston, 1830); *Borough of Lewes – to Wit. A Poll* (Lewes, 1812); *Borough of Lewes. A Poll* (Lewes, 1830).

Tables 3 and 4). The real effect of the Reform Act was that of a brake, or at least a restraining force, upon the already expanding and dynamic unreformed electorate.

If this conclusion owes much to the pioneering work of Phillips and O'Gorman, so too does the recognition of the socially diverse nature

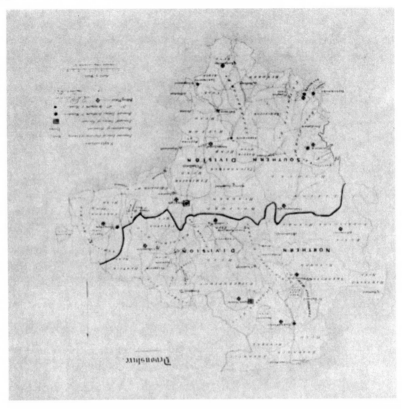

3 Map of Devon constituency with 1832 boundary changes (British Library)

of the unreformed electorate.[41] Table 2 convincingly shows that the weight of electoral power lay not with the upper classes of historiographical mythology, but further down the social scale, with retailers, craftsmen, and even unskilled labourers. In Boston and Lewes at least, these groups accounted for 80 per cent or more of the unreformed electorate. The main occupational group amongst these voters in Boston was not gentlemen or merchants, but cordwainers, who accounted for over a quarter (26.3 per cent) of the voters in 1818, and 17.7 per cent in 1830. While, in Lewes, at the last election before the Reform Act of 1832, over 10 per cent of the electorate were labourers (see Appendix 1).

Of course, such occupational classifications of voters raises considerable methodological problems.[42] Despite these difficulties, these

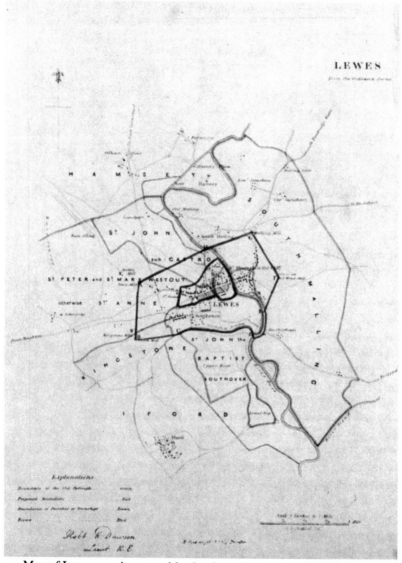

4   Map of Lewes constituency with 1832 boundary changes (British Library)

categories have informed the current work of historians analysing poll books because it allows comparisons to be made between, not only constituencies, but, more importantly, the unreformed and reformed electorates. Such forms of occupational analyses are

Table 3. *Number of registered electors in the five constituencies, 1832–1866*

	1832	1852	1866
Boston	1,257	955	1,093
Lewes	872	713	720
South Devon	7,453	9,569	9,592
Tower Hamlets	9,906	23,534	34,115
Oldham	1,131	1,890	2,316

Sources: J. Vincent and M. Stenton, *McCalman's Parliamentary Poll Book 1832–1914* (Brighton, 1971); C. R. Dod, *Electoral Facts from 1832–1852. Impartially Stated* (Brighton, 1972); *The Poll Book, Together with the Names of the Persons … that did not Vote* (Boston, 1852); *The Oldham Poll Book* (Oldham, 1852); 'Counties, Cities and Boroughs: Registered Voters', *Parliamentary Papers* 1866, (3626) LVII, 215.

inescapable if we are to provide any sort of insight into the social composition of electoral systems. For, despite the historiographical hype that has surrounded the 1832 Reform Act, we shall see that it hardly changed the social composition of the electorate, and certainly did not transform the supposedly aristocratic unreformed electorate into a new improved bourgeois model.[43]

Of the three unreformed constituencies, Devon was perhaps the least effected by the 1832 Reform Act. The enfranchisement of £10 copy-holders, leaseholders, and tenants-at-will paying no less than £50 per annum did little more than officially formalise the notoriously generous interpretation of the 'freehold' qualification that had long existed within the unreformed counties.[44] However, Devon's parliamentary representation was transformed by the revision of the county boundaries in 1832 which divided the county into two separate constituencies, North and South Devon, with each still returning two MPs. (see Plate 3), while in 1867 the second Reform Act created a third constituency of East Devon. Therefore, for practical reasons, after 1832 I concentrate on the constituency of South Devon, whose electorate grew by 77 per cent between 1832 and 1852, from 7,453 to 9,569, before levelling off to 9,592 in 1865.

Conversely, the 1832 Reform Act increased the size of Lewes' constituency boundaries from a comparatively miniature 0.2 to 1.3 square miles (see Plate 4). Yet, despite this increase in the constituency's size, the 1830 unreformed electorate of 750 rose to only 872, before falling back to 713 in 1852, at which level it remained

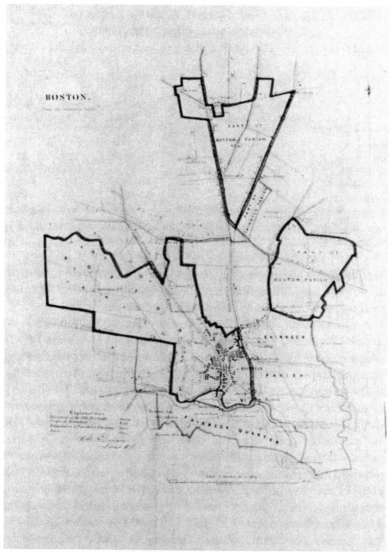

5   Map of Boston constituency with 1832 boundary changes (British Library)

barring a marginal rise to 720 in 1865–6. Despite the seemingly
negligible impact of the 1832 Reform Act, Lewes continued to boast
the highest proportion of electors in its population (see Table 4).
Boston had the next smallest electorate with only 1,257 electors in

Table 4. *The size of the reformed electorate as a percentage of the population and as a percentage of adult males*

	1832		1852		1866	
	% total population	% adult males	% total population	% adult males	% total population	% adult males
Boston	9.8	38.5	5.5	21.4	6	23.7
Lewes	9.7	37.9	7.5	29.3	7.3	28.8
South Devon	2.3	9.1	2.4	9.8	2.3	9.1
Tower Hamlets	2.8	10.8	4.4	17.1	4.8	18.4
Oldham	2.2	13.7	2.6	10.2	2.1	8.4

Sources: See Table 3. South Devon's figures for 1866 calculated from registered electorate of 1864–5 and the population figures of the 1861 census.

1832, which, despite decreasing to 955 in 1852, rose again to 1,093 by 1866 (see Plate 5). None the less, like Lewes, Boston also had a high percentage of voters among its population (see Table 4).

A comparison of Tables 1 and 4 immediately suggests that the reformed electorate was actually less representative than its unreformed counterpart. For instance, if we compare the electorates of Boston and Lewes either side of the 1832 Reform Act it is apparent that the proportion of voters per head of population fell from an average 8.6 to 7.6 per cent and, similarly, that the average proportion of voters as a percentage of adult males fell from 33.8 to 29.9 per cent. Thus, far from being the first step along the road to a model parliamentary democracy, the Great Reform Act actually restricted popular representation, at least in some constituencies. Indeed, the immediate increase in both Boston and Lewes' electorates following 1832 were due, not to the creation of new voters, but to the residual element of unreformed electors, that is those who did not qualify for a vote under the terms of the Reform Act and yet were not disenfranchised by it. Thus, at the 1832 election at Boston, of the 1,257 electors that could be accounted for a remarkable 374 (29.8 per cent) still qualified as freemen. By 1866 that number had decreased significantly to 148, 13.5 per cent of the electorate.[45] Similarly, of Lewes' reformed electorate of 872 voters in 1832, a staggering 79.1 per cent still qualified as scot and lot voters, although by 1866 that figure had also fallen dramatically to 7.7 per cent of Lewes' electorate.

Without these sections of the unreformed electorate still qualifying as voters after 1832, it is probable that the reformed electorates of Boston and Lewes would have been almost identical in size to their old unreformed counterparts. However, even with this residual element included, the increase in the electorate initiated by the 1832 Reform Act was modest by any calculation. By 1852 the reformed electorate of Boston and Lewes had settled down to levels very similar to that of the unreformed electorate of 1831. Certainly, had the unreformed electorate continued to grow at the same pace it had between 1790 and 1832, there can be little doubt that it would have far outstripped its reformed counterpart by the middle of the century. •It is, then, possible to read the Great Reform Act of 1832 not as a great expansive step forward, but as a restrictive step backwards, an attempt to limit popular representation by establishing uniformly exclusive electoral qualifications. Clearly this was the case for women.• For the very first time in English constitutional history the 1832 Reform Act explicitly excluded women property owners from the official political nation by stipulating that the Act concerned male persons only. The significance of this can not be over played. Henceforward, official definitions of property and the public political arena were highly gendered. As Catharine Hall has shown, the creation of this official male political subject allowed the distinction between the rational public world of men and the passionate private realm of women to be brought into sharp relief.[46] It was a distinction which was to dominate politics for the rest of the century. Thus, for women, but also for many men, the 1832 Reform Act represented a retreat, one which had given them less of a chance to be included within the official political nation than the old unreformed electoral system.

Clearly, this was less the case for those constituencies enfranchised in 1832, like Oldham and Tower Hamlets which represented those previously excluded. However, as Table 4 shows, even these constituencies, like the new constituency of South Devon, could only claim to represent less than 3 per cent of their population – a derisory figure. Once again one is struck not only by the modest impact of the 1832 Reform Act, but how inadequate studies of official electoral politics are, for they neglect the politics of 95 per cent or more of the population. Nowhere is this more apparent than in an analysis of the new and essentially artificial constituencies of Oldham and Tower Hamlets. The constituency of Oldham cut across existing parochial

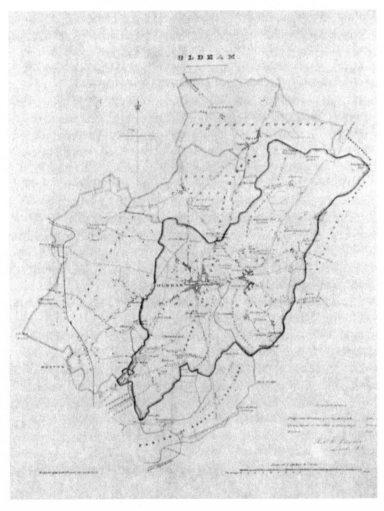

6   Map of Oldham constituency (British Library)

boundaries to include (besides the town of Oldham), the townships of
Chadderton, Crompton, and Royton, together with the surrounding
rural hinterland of 18.8 square miles (see Plate 6). The curious mix of
this constituency, half rural country and half industrialising town,
was reflected in the social composition of its electorate which included
farmers in equal measure to shopkeepers and cotton spinners.
Moreover, the rapid growth of the constituency's population during

this period, from 50,513 in 1831 to 107,729 in 1866, meant that the electorate struggled to maintain its representative proportion. Thus, while the number of registered voters rose from the 1,131 in 1832 to 2,285 in 1866, this actually represented a proportionate decline; from 2.2 to 2.1 per cent of the total population, or from 13.7 to 8.4 per cent of adult males.

Yet, of all the five constituencies examined here, the constituency of Tower Hamlets was the most artificial and most unrepresentative of all. It covered an area of 12 square miles in the impoverished East End of London, including the parishes of Bethnal Green, St Botolph-without-Aldgate, Bow, Bromley, St Katharine, St George, Hackney, Limehouse, Norton Folgate, Poplar, Shadwell, Shoreditch, Spital-fields, Stepney, Tower of London, Wapping, and Whitechapel (see Plates 7a and 7b). In terms of both inhabitants and electors the constituency was huge.[47] Its *registered* population alone increased from 359,864 in 1832 to 710,179 in 1866, while the number of *registered* electors also rose from 9,906 in 1832 to 34,115 in 1866, which represented 2.8 and 4.8 per cent of the population or 10.8 and 18.4 per cent of adult males. The widespread use of compounding meant that the electorate eligible for the franchise was over twice the size of the registered electorate of 23,187 in 1832 and 41,921 by 1852.[48] By 1849, according to Sir William Clay, over 16,000 of his constituents in Tower Hamlets were disenfranchised by the use of compounding in 1849.[49] Consequently, 2 years later, Clay introduced a Compounding Bill to the Commons which aimed to reduce the expensive and lengthy procedure of registration for compounders, from four times a year to once a year. However, its success in parliament was not reflected by its practical success in Tower Hamlets. In the St Leonards parish of Shoreditch for instance, some 15 years after Clay's bill had become law, only 50 of the 4,157 compounded houses had registered as electors. Similarly, in Poplar only 23 of the 4,052 compounders had registered in 1866.[50] Thus, despite Clay's attempt to minimise the bureaucracy associated with compounding, potential electors still failed to register.

The franchise in Tower Hamlets was, like its population generally, complex, volatile, and unpredictable, and consequently produced an electorate of surprising social consistency. The electoral returns of 1866 estimated that 8,107 (23.8 per cent) of the voters in the Tower Hamlets were 'working class'. According to the same electoral

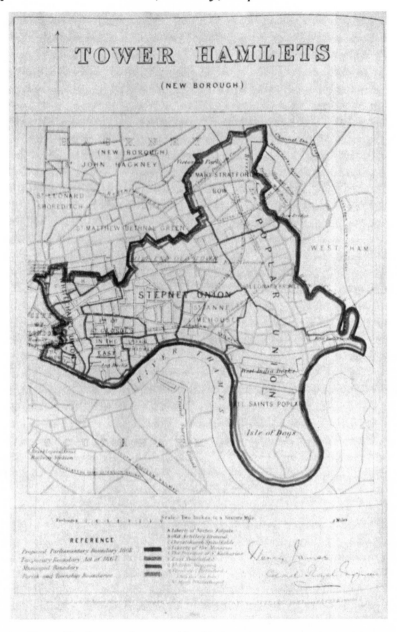

7a   Tower Hamlets constituency with 1867 boundary changes (British Library)

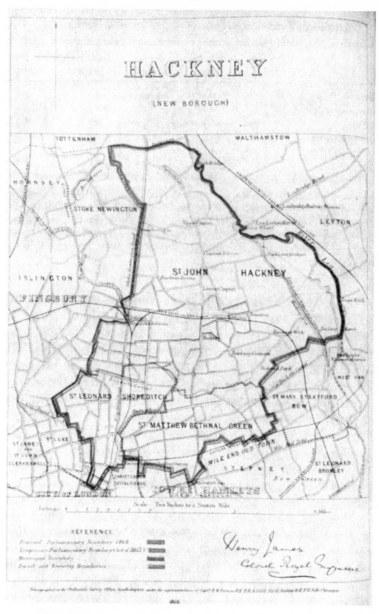

7b   Hackney constituency as created by the 1867 Reform Act.
The Second Reform Act of 1867 divided the original constituency of Tower Hamlets
into these two separate constituencies. No map of the original constituency exists.

Table 5. *Social composition of the reformed electorate (%)*

	Oldham 1832	Lewes 1835	Boston 1852	Oldham 1865
Gentlemen/professional	5.4	15.4	11.6	8.5
Manufacturer/merchant	5.1	5.1	8.5	6.3
Retailers	27.2	23.9	27.3	28.3
Skilled craftsmen	31.3	37.2	25.7	23.8
Unskilled labour	3.7	16.6	12.9	1.4
Agriculture	19.8	1.8	12.4	8.6

Sources: A List of the Voters (Manchester, 1832); *A Poll taken by Mr. George Bailey* (Lewes, 1835); *The Poll Book of the Boston Parliamentary Election* (Boston, 1852); *Election, 1865. The Oldham Poll Book* (Oldham, 1865). These are not exact figures, as voters' occupations were not always listed. For example, in Oldham's poll books for 1832 and 1865 there was no occupation recorded for 7.8% and 23.1% of voters respectively.

returns, of the 5 constituencies, Tower Hamlets was overshadowed only by Lewes, where no less than 26.3 per cent of the electorate were working class, almost double Oldham's 13.6 per cent, and appreciably greater than Boston's 18.2 per cent.[51] The reliability of this electoral return is hard to assess. The definition of 'working-class' employed was not only extremely vague – including artisans, mechanics, and other manual workers – but, like my earlier occupational analysis of the poll books, rests on a materialist, work-based definition of status and class which precludes cultural definitions of these categories. Given these short-comings, the figures seem plausible when compared to my own occupational analysis of the only four poll books in which the voters occupation was listed (see Table 5).

Table 5 shows that Oldham, the most industrialised constituency of the five, had not only the electorate with the lowest proportion of unskilled labourers, gentlemen/professionals and manufacturers/merchants, but also contained the greatest proportion of voters involved in agriculture – in 1832 19.6 per cent of the electorate were farmers (see Appendix 1). Neither does Table 5 endorse the interpretation of the 1832 Reform Act as having wedded the industrial manufacturers and entrepreneurs to the aristocratic state through their joint control of the electoral system. Rather, as Table 6 demonstrates, the social composition of the reformed electorate was remarkably similar to that of its unreformed counterpart. Although

Table 6. *Comparison of the social composition of the unreformed and
reformed electorate in Boston and Lewes (%)*

	Boston		Lewes	
	Pre-1832	Post-1832	Pre-1832	Post-1832
Gentlemen/professional	7.1	11.6	14.0	15.4
Manufacturer/merchants	4.4	8.5	4.5	5.1
Retailers	22	27.3	20.1	23.9
Skilled craftsmen	53.7	25.7	39.6	37.2
Unskilled labour	10.5	12.9	21.0	16.6
Agriculture	2.4	12.4	0.9	1.8

Sources: See Tables 2 and 5.

this was less the case in Boston, where the reformed electorate was
spread more consistently over all 6 categories, largely at the expense
of the craftsmen and skilled workers. However, we should not read
any sign of change as necessarily significant. For, while the proportion
of gentlemen, professionals, manufacturers, merchants, and retailers
all increased in Boston's reformed electorate, so too did the proportion
of labourers and those involved with agriculture. In effect 1832 seems
to have had very little effect, amounting to little more than a cosmetic
redistribution of voters among different occupational categories.
Certainly this reading is affirmed by an analysis of the social effects of
1832 on Lewes' electorate. It would be hard to imagine a constituency
less effected by the 1832 Reform Act, than Lewes. Clearly, in the
constituencies already enfranchised before 1832, the structure of
official parliamentary politics was not fundamentally transformed by
the Reform Act. Despite the creation of the new industrialising
constituencies, the Reform Act served to restrict, rather than to
expand, the official political arena.

CONCLUSION

This chapter has endeavoured to examine the official structure of
politics in the 5 constituencies. Although that structure has varied
considerably from constituency to constituency, certain common
themes have emerged. It has, for instance, been argued that the legal
bases upon which politics were organised defined the official arena of
politics, as well as its hierarchical shape from the parish, to the town,

to the county, and, last but not least, to the nation. However, within this hierarchical structure there was a great deal of interaction between institutions and their electorates which enhanced the sense of mutual dependence between the communities of parish, town, county, and nation. With very few exceptions, political historians have concentrated almost entirely upon parliamentary politics and ignored the crucial areas of vestry, municipal, and county politics.

The structural diversity of official politics was as evident within, as between, the different levels of parish, town, county, and nation. This diversity reflected not only the often ancient and gradual historical development of the representative structures, but also, more significantly, their essentially decentralised and local character. However, within parliament there was a growing degree of uncertainty as to whether such a localised political process could cope with the ever increasing responsibilities heaped upon it by the twin pressures of urbanisation and industrialisation. Following the end of the Napoleonic Wars, such official unease manifested itself in the growing body of legislation designed to reform and rationalise the official structure of local government; from Sturges Bourne's reforms in 1818 and 1819, to Hobhouse's 1831 Vestries Act, to the parliamentary reform of 1832, and the Municipal Reform Act of 1835, not to mention numerous local improvement and public health legislation or the Metropolis Management Act of 1855. Despite the many different shifts of emphasis between the centre and the periphery in this legislation, there has rarely been a more concerted attempt to impose an official and nationally uniform definition of the public political sphere as the preserve of propertied men. By 1835, the franchise, at all levels of the official political process, was dependent on the rateable value of property. Officially political rights were now wedded to property rights and, with the exception of parish politics, property was an exclusively male category.

No doubt such an official definition of the public political sphere was designed to prevent the popular control of the state and its political institutions or, at the very least, to buy some time before this popular control was unavoidable. If this was not the intention, it was certainly the effect. However, despite this narrowing of the official political arena, we should not underestimate the often considerable degree of popular participation in official politics, which was much greater than has previously been allowed by many political historians, especially before the series of so-called 'great' political reforms at vestry, municipal, and parliamentary levels in 1818, 1832, and 1835. As these reforms placed ever more exclusive legal definitions upon official politics, there was renewed urgency to establish extra-legal ways to involve, and win the support of, the very popular constituency now officially excluded from the political nation. In the following chapter, therefore, I shall examine some of the cultural techniques by which the official political arena encouraged popular participation in ways which (it was hoped) reaffirmed its legitimacy.

CHAPTER 2

Power imagined: the culture of official politics

The exercise of power always requires symbolic practices. There is no government without rituals and without symbols, however demystified or unmagical government may seem. Governing cannot take place without stories, signs, and symbols that convey and reaffirm the legitimacy of governing in thousands of unspoken ways.[1]

INTRODUCTION

In this chapter I want to suggest that the culture of official politics reconstituted the increasingly restrictive legal definitions of the political arena examined in chapter 1. Ironically, while people found it increasingly difficult to become citizens of the official political nation, they seemed to be afforded greater opportunities to participate in the ceremonies and symbolic practices that punctuated official political life. This chapter will examine the social dramas enacted through the symbolic practices of official politics, and the way in which they were used to 'convey and reaffirm the legitimacy of governing in thousands of unspoken ways'. It would be wrong to imagine that these symbolic practices were confined to the national celebrations staged in London during this period, rather it was the provincial town, not the metropolis, that was the centre of the official political culture. Each locality had its own official ceremonial calendar, which included parish, town, and county meetings, civic ceremonies such as Mayor's Day, the celebration of royal and national occasions, and last, but by no means least, the sequence of 'events' which structured election campaigns.[2]

It will be seen by this list that I use the term ceremony here in its broadest sense to describe a symbolic practice, usually complete with a full complement of iconography, which was regularly performed.

However inclusive such a definition may be, it does allow us, unlike much of the existing anthropological, sociological, and historical work on ritual, to consider how people used and interpreted ceremonial events in different ways.[3] No longer do we need to read symbolic practices as reflecting pre-existing social realities of conflict or consensus, instead it will become apparent that official political ceremonies were used to transform and reconstitute political 'reality'. Neither do we need to search for a grand explanatory model to tell us why ceremonies occur, rather we need to discover the ways in which they were used and given meaning by contemporaries. This chapter will therefore analyse the ways in which the symbolic practices of official politics were used; both 'from above' to legitimate exclusive official definitions of the political arena, and 'from below' to contest these definitions. Thus, although these attempts to legitimate exclusive official definitions of the political sphere failed as often as they succeeded, they were significantly performed for, and addressed to, all the inhabitants of the locality, voters and non-voters alike, men as well as women. After all it was the disenfranchised, those legally excluded from the official political nation, whose support most had to be won.

THE URBAN CONTEXTS OF PERFORMANCE:
THE TOWN AS TEXT

Every official symbolic practice in the five constituencies was performed upon a civic landscape. These civic landscapes were not just urban backdrops for such performances, rather they were increasingly politicised themselves as rapid urbanisation placed a cumulative pressure on the organisation and use of space in towns and cities.[4] For the historian therefore, civic landscapes can be read as cultural texts in themselves, texts of equal significance to the ceremonies and other symbolic practices that were staged upon them. Then as now, the civic landscape represented the town to itself through public buildings and amenities, street names, statues, and memorials – it articulated not only the competing narratives of the community's historical purpose and destiny, but also the roles of different individuals and groups within those narratives. However, this section is concerned chiefly with the narrative of the official civic landscape as produced by local political elites. Although responses to this are discussed, the reader will have to wait until chapter 6 for

8   Lewes County Hall (Sussex Archaeological Society)

more substantive discussions of the popular reception of the largely elitist narratives articulated by official civic landscapes.

The civic landscapes of all five constituencies were dominated by their central official parochial, civic or county institutions. Thus Boston's unreformed corporation commissioned the construction of the New Assembly Rooms in 1822 to replace the cramped and decaying medieval Guildhall, while (not to be out done) its reformed counterpart built a Sessions House (1841–3) and an Athenaeum and Exchange (1854). Similarly, Lewes' town or county hall (see Plate 8) was built in 1809 on the orders of the recently established town commission, just as Oldham's town hall was commissioned and built by the town's police commissioners in 1841–2 (see Plate 9). Tower Hamlets had no central civic institution, but from the 1850s several parishes built vestry halls, like Mile End Old Town's vestry hall which was finished in 1860 (see Plate 10).[5] Devon was the exception as the county's central administrative building, the session-house at Exeter Castle, had long been completed in 1774.

These buildings were invariably the largest within their respective civic landscapes, and their size did not reflect their function as homes to, albeit ever-expanding, parochial, municipal, or county bureau-

9   Oldham Town Hall (Oldham Local Studies Library)

cracies. As with Oldham's town hall, imposing façades often hid
small and cramped offices. As one of the country's leading architects
and competition judge for many civic commissions, Sir Charles Barry
recognised a town hall should be 'the most dominant and important
of the municipal buildings of the city in which it is placed. It should
be the means of giving due expression to public feeling upon all
national and municipal events of importance. [It should be]...the
life and soul of the city'.[6] Deliberately spectacular then, these
buildings were always sited at the very heart of the civic landscape,
no doubt so that their full splendour could be frequently savoured by
local inhabitants. Boston's assembly room still stands watchfully over
the market-place, obliquely facing the huge St Botolph's church;
Lewes' county hall sits below the castle at the top of the hill; while
Oldham's town hall stood proudly at the town's central junction,
opposite the church and market-place. As Barry advocated, the size
and site of these buildings were supposed to dominate the town's
skyscape and hence its consciousness, just as they also defined the
community's symbolic centre, its sacred ceremonial space.

However, it was the architectural and iconographic styles of the

10   Mile End Vestry Hall

buildings which did most to define the locality's image of itself, or at
least an official interpretation of it. These were produced not simply
by the architect, but also by the local ruling elite who commissioned
the building as well as, to a lesser extent, those masons, builders,
carpenters, and so on who built it. While each building rested on a
different configuration of these influences, a general pattern emerges
from the accounts we have.[7] Usually, the local administrative body
appointed a committee to supervise the construction of the buildings.
This committee then selected a local architect who produced a design

which was acceptable to them both stylistically and financially. The builders, stone masons, carpenters, iron-mongers, stained-glass window makers, and the like were then left with the task of constructing the final design, sometimes making their own modifications for financial, temporal or practical reasons. For the most part, then, local inhabitants were excluded from influencing the choice of architectural style and decoration, especially as Oldham and Lewes' town halls and Boston's assembly rooms were all built by self-appointed, unaccountable, local authorities. However, as Colin Cunningham has argued, to serve their purpose successfully these buildings had to have some popular resonance, 'their symbolic language needed to be readily understood' and, consequently, 'they tended to use an established architectural vocabulary'.[8] None the less, if these buildings can be said to represent the views of one group over and above any other, it was those of the local official political establishment.

The earlier town halls, built before 1850, were neo-classical in style and tended to resemble oversized grand town houses, like Lewes' almost understated town hall, or the regency mansion of Boston's assembly rooms. Oldham's town hall, with its far more imposing classical façade, aspires more to Roman magnificence than modest regency mansion, it is cast more in the role of a Roman temple than a *palazzo* (see Plate 9). Despite the increasing popularity of the Gothic style from the 1860s, the vestry halls of Tower Hamlets continued in the classical vein. The ground floor of Mile End Old Town's vestry hall aspired to the 'Tuscan style', while the upper floor imitated the 'Corinthian style', and 'a portico 19 ft. by 10 ft. 6 in., consisting of eight columns in *antis* and a flight of Portland stone steps' dominated the approach to the building (see Plate 10). All in all, as with Oldham and Lewes' town halls and Boston's assembly rooms, the building had more the air of an Italian city state than a nineteenth-century parochial building in the East End of London. These uses of classical architectural styles then lent an immediate sense of *gravitas* and antiquity to the buildings, as though they had always been there. The invention of tradition was as evident at the parochial and civic levels as it was at the national level.

Further analysis of the iconography of Oldham's town hall, the only one on which we have any sort of detailed sources, reveals the particular type of civic tradition being invented. The large stained-glass window above the principal staircase portrays allegorical figures which supposedly represent the town's qualities and characteristics – art, science, industry, commerce, and the spinning mechanism. Representations of prominent men in the town's official history support these figures, they include: Hugh Oldham, Bishop of Exeter; Sir Ralph Langley, who rebuilt the parish church in 1475; Dr Lawrence Chadderton, the first Master of Emmanuel College, Cambridge; James Assheton, founder of Oldham Grammar School in 1611; John Cudworth, Lord of the Manor during the reign of King John; and Sir Watts Horton, the High Sheriff in 1774. Besides the obvious celebration of the town's masculine, aristocratic, and Anglican pedigree, not to mention the cultural achievements of its select few, the lineage of local self-government is traced back to King John and the Magna Carta. These men are, in turn, surmounted by shields bearing the coat of arms of neighbouring Lancashire towns, thereby fixing Oldham firmly into its regional context – no small matter for a Lancashire town perilously near the Yorkshire boundary. Amongst them all, and above the main entrance, sits the Oldham family's coat of arms. There is no sense of irony that figures of ancient authority from the town's Anglican and aristocratic past sat alongside images of the town's supposedly equally ancient tradition of education and local self-government. All were appropriated by the self-appointed police commissioners to lend themselves an air of historical legitimacy at a time when they were increasingly under pressure to relinquish their authority and incorporate the town.

At the same time as being used to articulate a highly selective version of the town's official identity, the building could also embody the local pride of the inhabitants. Typical of the rest of the buildings considered here, there was no ceremonial opening of Oldham Town Hall at which the town's different social and political groups could assert their right to be included within the town's official political community. However, popular pride in the construction of Oldham Town Hall could manifest itself in other forms, such as the use of local stone, worked upon, and given shape, by local masons who, in turn, worked alongside local bricklayers, slaters, carpenters, plasterers and painters, ironmongers and plumbers.[9] To the inhabitants this use of local materials and labour may have represented a celebration of local crafts, skills, and even local human and material resources, which contradicted the more exclusive definition of the town's identity evident in the building's iconography. Therefore, it is quite possible that the building encapsulated some sense of popular civic pride, albeit for different reasons. Certainly, there was no protest about the expense of the building, as there had been about the rebuilding of the parish church during the late 1820s.[10] There seems to have been a general sense of civic shame that the police commissioners, the very people responsible for the town's sanitation, highway repair, street lighting, and general municipal image, had previously met in a pub.

The ability of people to engraft their own readings and meanings on these buildings was also apparent by the multiplicity of names and uses they were subjected to. Lewes' town hall was, for instance, sometimes known as 'County Hall', the 'Shire Hall', and even the 'Manor Rooms', all of which evoked different conceptions of the town's identity. The 'Manor Rooms' suggested a loyalty to the town's Lord of the Manor and his court-leet, just as the names 'Shire' and 'County Hall' alluded to the town's identity as the capital of Sussex county, while 'Town Hall' implies a recognition that the hall was commissioned by the newly created town commissioners and belonged to the town itself. By using these different names, Lewes' inhabitants were able to ascribe the building with the identity of their choosing. This was by no means unusual. Many parochial, civic, or county buildings had a myriad of uses, and hence identities – as debating chamber, meeting-room/concert-hall, court-rooms, gaol, and offices for police constables, gas, water, and school boards – which were deployed at different times. Indeed, the very range of these uses allowed for a common identification with the building which bound together different elements of the local community. Thus, the meeting-room in Oldham Town Hall was made available for public use by the town's inhabitants for political meetings, private parties, and social and cultural events. Between 1843 and 1868 it regularly housed, among others, meetings by Radicals, Chartists, Liberals and Conservatives, the Oldham Lyceum, the Orange Society, the Licensed Victuallers Association, and the Temperance Society. By meeting in the town hall all these groups asserted their right to be included within the town's official political community. Therefore, if these public buildings were used by local political elites to create an exclusive official civic identity, it was not a tidy consensual identity with which all necessarily shared, for people were able to engraft their own meanings upon the buildings, and this invariably entailed a recognition of diversity and difference within the locality.

The second half of the nineteenth century witnessed the construction of other projects within the official civic landscape besides
these parish, town, and county halls. These civic projects seem to
have reflected a growing recognition of the role of local inhabitants in
the making of the town. Significantly, the opening of Alexandra Park
in 1865 constituted the first ceremonial celebration of a civic project
in Oldham (see Plate 11). For the first time the town's inhabitants
were afforded a chance to assert their contribution to the civic
landscape and hence their right to inclusion within the town's official
identity. Council officials deliberately courted popular involvement,
staging the ceremony on Wakes Monday and inviting voluntary
groups and local notables to take part in the grand procession around
the town. However, heavy rain delayed the start from 10 am to 12
noon, shortened the processional route, and reduced the number of
participants. Even so, as the town's chief constable struggled to
marshal the procession into the marching order, accompanied by
four bands playing different tunes in the pouring rain, a 'considerable
crowd' had gathered outside the town hall. At a quarter-past-twelve
the rain-soaked spectators 'became impatient, so that the Mayor
gave the order to proceed'. The *Oldham Chronicle* was certainly
anxious to stress the popular character of the ceremony. 'There can
be no doubt' it reported, 'that, if the day had been fine, the finest and
most numerous display that Oldham ever witnessed in a procession
would have been made, and with all the drawbacks there were 1,300
people in it, including the bands, which were eight in number'.[11]
Despite these claims the procession was carefully organised by the
council's park committee to display the local elite first, with the usual
mass of voluntary and friendly societies bringing up the rear.
Similarly, there were few signs of popular involvement in the
exclusive dinner held in the town hall after the ceremony. However,
it would be hard to deny the popular element in this ceremony. Even
the mayor suggested that the park 'was one of those places where all
could meet both high and low, rich and poor, on what they called
common ground'.

Yet, what was this common ground on which high and low met?
For this ceremony, like all others, was used in different ways by
different people. The *Oldham Chronicle*, the bastion of the town's
Liberal establishment, argued that the park would stand as a
monument to the benevolence and public spirit of the largely Liberal
town council. After all it was they who had organised the project to

11   Ceremonial opening of Oldham's Alexandra Park, 1865 (Oldham Local Studies Library)

help those who could not help themselves during the cotton famine, just as it had been the mayor who had donated the fountain and councillor Bamford and alderman Riley who donated the stained-glass windows in the refreshment pavilion which were ironically inscribed 'Peace and Plenty' and 'Industry and Commerce'. Bamford, the principal organiser of the opening ceremony and chairman of the park committee, argued in his opening speech that the park was intended for the health and leisure of the inhabitants, it would help 'elevate the tastes and habits of the people', especially because the study of botany 'would teach them the lesson of subordination by proper training and discipline of the will of the Divine Creator – (Hear, hear)'. The National Anthem and the Jubilate Deo 100th psalm were sung, no doubt as a reminder of this need for subordination. However, Hibbert, the town's Liberal MP, had a more populist vision of the park; 'it was truly the People's Park – one for which the people themselves paid, which had been made with their own hands'. Other differences within the town's political elite soon surfaced. At the dinner, a toast to 'The Bishop, and Clergy, and the Ministers of all Denominations' prompted a long speech by a dissenting minister denouncing Anglican dominance within the town. Similarly, Hibbert denounced the absent county MPs, it was not an occasion 'to look to party... though they had there parties of different politics, he trusted all would agree with him, that whatever party was in power, no party would be permitted to live but for the good of the common country and the welfare of everything connected with it. (Hear, hear)'. Despite the best efforts of the organising committee to present an idealised image of the town as free of strife, latent political, religious, and social conflicts still emerged.

Where parks failed to cultivate unifying civic ideals, the erection of official statues might succeed. Although these statues were usually raised by public subscription, they served as official monuments to the locality's major political figures, and were consequently placed in the town's sacred ceremonial space. Thus in 1862 the statue of Herbert Ingram, Boston's Liberal MP (1856–60) and its most famous son as proprietor of the *Illustrated London News*, was erected in St Botolph's churchyard, facing the assembly rooms next to the town's market place; just as a statue of John Platt, Oldham's leading industrialist and Liberal MP (1865–72), was erected in 1878 outside the town hall. By enshrining these civic leaders in stone and placing them in such prominent sites, both the subscribers and the local

12   Statue of John Platt, 'the civic father' (Oldham Local Studies Library)

authorities, held them up as exemplars of civic virtue. As the president of the Acland Testimonial, the Earl of Devon, stated when unveiling the statue of Sir Thomas Acland, leading local landlord, aristocrat and MP for Devon (1812–18) and North Devon (1837–57), its purpose was

to commemorate and perpetuate the example of a worthy man, to commemorate all those virtues – all those qualities which have rendered the name of Sir Thomas Acland almost a household word amongst us...it is calculated to teach lessons of great importance to present and future generations. – (Hear, hear.) – No young man, passing this statue, and reading upon it the name of Sir Thomas Acland, can fail to see that this well deserved tribute was raised to his honour simply by the weight of his character (Cheers).[12]

Most of these statues depicted their subjects as men of action, modestly dressed and delivering speeches or, in the case of Herbert Ingram, holding objects of their life's work like a copy of the *Illustrated London News*. John Platt's statue went further, portraying the themes and achievements of his life in four female allegorical figures representing engineering, manufacturing, science, and art (see Plate 12). They alluded to his role as civic father; locally born and educated, principal partner of Platt Bros. and Co. engineering firm, chairman of the local railway company, mayor between 1861–2, founder and patron of the Oldham Lyceum, sponsor of two local papers. There is little to suggest his potentially divisive role as either Liberal activist and MP, or as the town's largest employer.

The erection of these statues often required the swallowing of substantial political differences, as at the inauguration ceremony of Herbert Ingram's statue in Boston during 1862 (see Plate 13). Representatives of all the town's social, political, religious, and military bodies were invited to join the procession and watch the unveiling of the statue. The sculptor, mason, committee, and subscribers all presented to the town's officials the statue of their hero, the local boy made good, Herbert Ingram. While the town's political, religious, and legal leaders were prominent in the parade and on the platform, the inhabitants were also part of the proceedings, parading and spectating. Even Ingram's political enemies, like the Tory Captain White, sang his praises and acknowledged his contribution to the town, expressing:

the deep sympathy he felt in the loss the town had sustained in Herbert Ingram. A more active energetic member it was impossible to obtain, and his efforts to benefit the town had been unceasing. For twenty years he had never flinched from his colours, which it was well known were opposed to that of Mr. Ingram... but he would ask his fellow townsmen to bury all their animosities and acrimonies in the tomb of Herbert Ingram... [so that]... his memories might have a soothing and beneficial influence on their future proceedings.[13]

Similarly, according to their chairman, subscribers to the Acland memorial were also 'men differing in political and religious opinion from each other, and men who will be found differing on important political questions from Sir Thomas Acland himself. – (hear, hear.)'.[14] The elevation of civic heroes like Acland and Ingram, seems then to have transcended social and political cleavages. It was

13   Ceremonial inauguration of Herbert Ingram's statue, Boston 1862
(*Illustrated London News*, 18 October 1862)

14   The public's uses of John Platt's statue (Oldham Local Studies Library)

the town that was celebrated as much as the individual, indeed the individual was celebrated as a product of the town. By erecting statues to these men the subscribers, the local political officials, and even possibly the inhabitants of the town recognised their achievements and qualities and sought to appropriate them as part of the town's official identity. Although, of course, not all so readily accepted this version of events, preferring instead to use the statue more practically as something to climb over to secure a better view of the hustings or some other official political event (see Plate 14).

This politicisation of the civic landscape extended beyond the construction of buildings, parks, and statues. Future work needs to address the potentially fruitful area of the naming of streets within towns and their use to convey an official political civic identity. Similarly, attention could be drawn to the increasing politicisation of time during this period by an analysis of the political uses of clocks on public buildings. It was surely no coincidence that the town halls which sprang up from the 1870s were often designed around the elevation of phallic clock towers. In Plymouth the lack of a clock tower on the municipal building led to the construction of Derry's clock next door to it in 1863. Municipal authorities were taking over the regulation of local time from the church, and by identifying themselves with the rhythms of nature sought to legitimate their secular power. Moreover, as we shall see below, the official timing of town and vestry meetings, as well as civic and electoral ceremonies, provided an important tool with which the local authorities could either reduce or maximise popular participation in these events.

Finally, while the 1850s and 1860s could rightly lay claim to have been the zenith of the construction of the civic landscape,[15] its different pace of development within the five constituencies reflected several factors. Presumably much was due to the different levels of wealth among local authorities, not to mention their different legislative rights to levy taxes, just as the increased use of public subscriptions from the 1850s no doubt reflected the improved standard of living achieved by some in those decades. There was also, of course, an important element of competition between neighbouring towns. Certainly the construction of Alexandra Park in Oldham was an attempt to emulate the opening of three parks in Manchester, which had greatly impressed the town's Mayor and MPs who had attended their opening ceremony.[16] However, the general flurry of activity during the 1850s and 1860s also testified to the need of the official institutions of local self-government to redefine themselves after over half a century of political change which had seen the politics of the parish increasingly superseded by those of the town. Local ruling elites sought to endow their institutions with new identities by inventing civic traditions which appropriated a selective past in order to emphasise the progress of the present. Political change was legitimated and given meaning by relating it to past struggles and glories. It was surely no coincidence that the construction of the civic landscape was most feverish in the decades which also witnessed the emergence of an increasingly organised and divisive party politics. Both Liberal and Tory local authorities alike were anxious to create new political arenas which they could claim lay above party-political proclivities.

This section has then endeavoured to show how local official political cultures expanded the political arena during this period in an attempt to develop new strategies for legitimating their power. Indeed, the creation of official civic landscapes also provided an important context for the performance of the developing symbolic repertoire of the parish, town, county, and nation. It is to an analysis of these symbolic practices that we now turn.

THE PARISH, TOWN, AND COUNTY

Of course, not all the symbolic practices of official politics were ceremonies in the formal sense, and this was especially true of the parish, town and county meetings I shall examine in this section. Although these events were legal they invriably exceeded their legality and yet remarkably, despite unsuccessful attempts by local officials to reimpose restrictive legal definitions upon them, these meetings retained official approval. No doubt officials realised that popular participation in these meetings provided the best means of establishing a meaningful, and yet largely unthreatening, political dialogue with the disenfranchised. Parish, town and county meetings therefore constituted another official political arena in which the exercise of power, both locally and nationally, could be legitimated and contested.

Although for many people parish, town and county meetings provided the most immediate experience of official politics, political historians have preferred either to ignore them or to portray them as riotous events with little political significance.[17] Yet the idea of these meetings as a noisy, drunkard, and cathartic exercise is misleading. For instance, meetings of the parish vestry were well organised and regular. Every year there was at least one meeting of the parish vestry, usually on Easter Monday, to discuss the churchwardens' accounts and their proposed church rate, as well as to elect the churchwardens for the following year. In the parishes of St Leonards, Shoreditch, and Oldham, Easter Monday continued to be used for the annual appointment of churchwardens, constables, overseers, and their assistants. In Oldham though, where the parishioners were always suspicious of the constables' accounts, vestry meetings were held every 3 months so that the accounts could be examined in greater detail. In Boston, Lewes, and the other parishes of Tower Hamlets annual vestry meetings were held at different times of the year according to local custom. However, the vestry was much more than just an administrative institution. Like town and county meetings, it could also be called to discuss any subject the parishioners wished, as long as the consent of the parish churchwarden or constables had been granted. National political issues were discussed as frequently as parochial issues or rather, as we shall see in chapter 5, parochial issues were used to address national problems. Thus in Boston much time was spent discussing the question of church rates, while in Oldham and Tower Hamlets the more radical parishes discussed the Peterloo massacre, the Police Acts, the Poor Law Amendment Act, the equalisation of the London rates, church rates, and the state of the silk and cotton trades. Certain national issues impinged upon most parishes; meetings were held and resolutions passed on the Queen Caroline affair, Catholic emancipation, parliamentary reform, the Poor Law, the Corn Laws, the People's Charter, not to mention the innumerable loyal addresses sent to parliament or, more usually, the monarch. Parochial vestry meetings therefore provided an official arena for public political debate, at which the inhabitants of the parish could come together and articulate their grievances to both local and national officials.

However, as the regularity of vestry meetings declined from the 1840s, their official political role was increasingly subsumed by the public town meeting. Certainly the regularity of these public meetings (as they were sometimes known), together with the range of issues they discussed, reinforced the pluralist conception of towns that local authorities were keen to project. According to *The Town Book of Lewes*, even Lewes, in some ways the least politicised of the 5 constituencies, witnessed 55 town meetings between 1808 and 1868, and this was by no means a definitive or complete record.[18] Of the 55 meetings only 16 (29 per cent) directly concerned local matters, a further 7 (12.7 per cent) were about national matters with direct bearing on the town, while 32 meetings (58.2 per cent) were solely concerned with national issues. *The Town Book* suggests that Lewes' town meetings first 'took-off' during the early 1820s, reaching their peak during the reform agitation of 1830–2, before levelling off for the rest of the period. The subject of these meetings became noticeably less contentious from the late 1830s; sending congratulatory addresses to the royals, discussing 'Patriotic Funds' and condemning tyrannical Catholics. Such a change in tone reflected not a waning of party-political proclivities, but the changing role of the town meeting as competing political groups increasingly organised their own meetings, festivals, and media events. As we shall see in chapter 6, there was a growing feeling in the 1830s that whatever the cause it was best served promoting its own meetings, rather than arguing its case at town meetings where it was likely to encounter stiff opposition.

As far as we can tell, the same trend was evident in Devon's county meetings, which seem to have suffered a marked decline from the mid 1830s.

Recognition of the often divisive role of town meetings alerts us to the ways in which they were used to invent, reaffirm or contest the political identity of the locality. Although parish, town, and county meetings were supposed to represent the interests of their inhabitants, ratepayers or freeholders, the legal ambiguities surrounding the right to attend these meetings meant that they invariably drew both speakers and audiences from surrounding localities, particularly as they were frequently held on market-days. This was evident at a Royton town meeting called in 1819 to petition parliament for a reform of the Commons.

The Resolution [to petition] was then put, and upon the shew [*sic*] of hands for its adoption or rejection, the numbers seemed equal... When Mr. Kay again addressed the meeting, and observed, that from the number of persons assembled, it was natural to conjecture that many who held up their hands were not the inhabitants of the Township of Royton, consequently their votes were not entitled to the same consideration as those who were about to adopt a measure which they would be called upon afterwards to be responsible...[19]

Clearly, while the unofficial organisers of the meeting welcomed any boost to the number of participants, it caused all sorts of problems to officials like Royton's town constable Mr Kay. Town meetings were supposed to articulate the interests of the town, their resolutions were supposed to represent the coming together of the community, the creation of common positions: the meetings were presided over by the town's constable; addresses and petitions were sealed with the town seal, advertised in the town's local paper, and sent to the town's MPs. It was then convenient for Tories, like the Home Secretary Canning, to dismiss the more radical town meetings as illegitimate because they were unrepresentative of the town, being organised by travelling agitators and attended by 'foreigners', 'there is no check upon the proceedings of each man from the awe of his neighbour's disapprobation...'[20]

The influx of 'foreigners' at these meetings was not the only obstacle to creating a 'shared' political identity for the locality. Few parish, town, or county meetings passed resolutions which satisfied all their participants, more often than not they merely served to accentuate the community's political differences. Such was undoubtedly the case at the Devon county meeting called in 1813 to petition the Lords against granting any concessions to Catholics. Those who supported such concessions came to the meeting armed with an amendment expressing their continued support for Catholics and the principle of religious liberty generally. The meeting was packed, the scene set for a show-down between the rival factions.

> Mr. Barnes (Under Sheriff) read the petition; and Mr. Tucker of Ashburton, followed by reading his amendment, which he did with great emphasis. – The Sheriff now put the question to the general whole of the meeting – first, desiring those who were for Mr. Tucker's amendment to hold up their hands; – and afterwards, those who were for the address, to do the same. The address was carried by a very considerable majority. – The Sheriff then desired such only as were freeholders, to come within the iron railing, where he stood [which, when they had done, they appeared to amount to less than half the numbers present] and here the question was again put; when the majority for the address seemed to bear a still greater proportion, than appeared in the general assemblage first divided. The Sheriff and Petitioners now re-entered the hall, while those who had divided against them assembled in the *Nisi Prius* court... Those who voted against the address, and subsequently retired to the *Nisi Prius* Court... proceeded to form their amendment in a Counter Petition.[21]

This technique of hijacking county, parish or town meetings, by groups opposed to the purpose of the meeting was common and, as we shall see in chapter 6, it was a problem which continued to afflict even partisan meetings from the 1830s. However, not all such meetings failed so totally in passing resolutions which satisfied all the contending factions within the community. Unity and compromise were often the key-words at these meetings, even if that unity entailed a recognition of differences.[22]

Both Royton's town meeting on reform and Devon's county meeting on the Catholic claims demonstrate the key role of those chairing these occasions, be it the sheriff, mayor or constable. It was these officials who were responsible for the final official interpretation of the meeting as embodied in the resolutions, just as it was up to them how strictly the legal rights of attendance were adhered to. Legally the right of attendance at parish and town meetings was invested in the community's ratepayers, while only freeholders were supposed to attend county meetings. Yet, as we have repeatedly seen, these restrictions were rarely enforced, except when the local political establishment feared an embarrassing defeat. When such attempts were made they varied from issuing handbills stipulating that none but ratepayers should attend, as at Oldham's vestry meeting to assess the constable's accounts in 1819, to the equally unsuccessful attempt made by the chairman of St Leonard's vestry, Shoreditch, to forcibly prevent non-ratepaying Chartists from entering the building during a meeting on the new police bill in 1839.[23] Yet, it was not just local officials who sought to enforce the exclusive letter of the law, there was a tendency for any group who felt that the mood of the meeting was slipping away from them to question its legitimacy. Thus at a Lewes town meeting in 1811, a Tory objecting to the success of a reform amendment argued that 'he supposed an address was to follow, that the constables were to go to London to present the same, and asked who were to pay the expense thereof? "Who" said he, "but the inhabitant householders paying scot and lot!" He therefore reprobated the system which had of late prevailed in the Borough, in calling meetings of inhabitants *generally*, instead of INHABITANT HOUSEHOLDERS *only*, and concluded by moving, "that the latter only should vote on the present occasion".'[24] The failure of these and many other attempts to restrict the official rights of attendance at these meetings testifies to the way in which official politics included culturally many it continued to exclude legally.

It should not be imagined that the culture of official politics was always more inclusive than its increasingly restrictive legal structure, for there were several ways in which local officials regulated and disciplined parish, town, and county meetings. The procedure of calling and holding these meetings enabled local officials to veto, or at the very least ensure the failure of, those meetings to which they were unsympathetic. To call an unscheduled vestry meeting, over 20 ratepaying parishioners had to present a requisition to the church-warden or constable for their approval. Even that could not guarantee success, as at Oldham in 1830 when the authorities declined to call a meeting on the need for a radical reform of parliament, despite a massive requisition of 250 leypayers.[25] Simi-larly, town meetings had officially to be called by either the constable, magistrates, or the mayor, and they too often used this power to prevent their political opponents holding meetings. Requests by Boston's Chartists for public town meetings were frequently denied, along with the use of the town hall and the town-crier, just as the town's old unreformed Tory corporation had prevented town meetings during the reform agitation of 1830–2.[26]

However, even when officials were unable to prevent meetings to which they were unsympathetic, there were other obstructive strategies they could use. Not least of which was the ability to convene the meeting at a time when most people were working and therefore unable to attend. This tactic always ensured a poor turn-out and was therefore also used by officials to pass unpopular resolutions without resistance. In 1843 at a vestry meeting of St John's parish, Lewes, held on a Thursday at 11 am, a mechanic 'complained of the time at which the meeting had been convened, and stated that he thought the ratepayers ought to be consulted as to what would be the most convenient hour for holding such meetings'.[27] While the year before, at a meeting of St Leonard's vestry in Shoreditch called to change the time of their meetings from 6 pm to 3 pm, a Mr Thomas of the local Parochial Reform Association spoke for over an hour denouncing the 'attempt to disenfranchise the poorer ratepayers, whose presence in such large numbers was found to be very troublesome to the gentlemen in power'.[28] Despite this type of protest local officials remained adept at pushing through their own meetings and resolutions in other ways. At Oldham in 1832, the local Tory authorities held a vestry meeting to nominate four Tory constables to the Salford court-leet 'without any previous intimation except the ringing of the church bells'. The turn-out was inevitably derisory and the constables were duly nominated without protest. However, two weeks later, at the meeting to discuss the constable's accounts, the radicals exacted sweet revenge by ensuring that 'the bell of the town crier having been called into requisition the day before, to give notice of the meeting, the attendance was much greater than usual on such occasions...'[29] The politicisation of this procedure in calling and holding parish, town, and county meetings clearly reflected the significance competing groups attached to these official political arenas.

Local political identities were then continually invented, re-affirmed, and contested at parish, town, and county meetings. These meetings also significantly expanded the arena of official politics by facilitating the participation of all the inhabitants of the community irrespective of their gender, or their status as ratepayers or non-ratepayers, electors or non-electors. The concerns of these meetings were in no sense parochial (in the limited sense) rather they addressed substantive issues in substantive ways, and in doing so were used to sustain an important political dialogue between the rulers and the ruled. They were not, as Baron A. de Stael Holsten recognised, 'empty ceremonies – a sort of empty saturnalia for the day without any influence on the morrow. These meetings have a real influence on the opinions of the many; they enlighten and confirm them; they keep up, among the people of England, a sense of their rights and of their strength, without which all written securities are vain; and a statesman must be destitute of judgement and foresight who does not lend an attentive ear to the wishes expressed in meetings of this kind.'[30]

THE TOWN AND NATION

It should already be apparent that the official political arena was far from the sum of its electoral parts. The construction of the civic landscape and meetings of the parish, town, or county could be used to expand restrictive official definitions of the public political sphere created by law, as too could the ceremonies which shaped the official political calendar. This section will examine the ways in which these ceremonies and other symbolic practices were used by local political officials to legitimate their authority. Yet, if local officials were the agents of this official political culture, they were conscious of their town's relationship to the nation. Ceremonies and symbols celebrating the nation were as plentiful at the local level as they were in the capital; using the same actors and landscapes as civic ceremonies, these symbolic practices looked beyond the boundaries of the town to the wider political community of the nation.

Invariably civic ceremonies were used to draw attention to a specific moment or event in the town's official politics, they were a means of shaping the political memory of the inhabitants. Consequently, one of the most frequently used civic ceremonies was the swearing in to office of a new mayor. In Boston, as elsewhere, the unreformed corporation spent much time and money on its 'Mayor's Day' ceremony, as was apparent from the 'customary festivities' of 1829.

Enlivening peals of bells ushered in the 'morn', and groups of loiterers assembled in the Market Place to witness the last remaining token of the ancient forms and ceremonies of the Corporation. At nine o'clock a numerous party of gentlemen of Boston and the neighbourhood assembled at the New Assembly Rooms, by invitation from the New Mayor elect, and partook of a sumptuous breakfast. After this meal, the civic body, arrayed in their robes, and preceded by the corporation band of music, playing a march selected for the occasion, and by their usual officers, bearing the Silver Oar and Maces, proceeded to the Guildhall, where the New Mayor was sworn into office and took the chair, with the usual honours. By this time the crowd had very much increased, and there might be seen the giddy boy, gazing at wonder on the parade, and the grey headed old man, thoughtful and silent... As usual, the children of the Blue Coat School strewed cowslips for the new Mayor to trample over.[31]

Unelected institutions and officials, like Boston's unreformed corporation, relied heavily on ceremonies like this to win popular support and legitimate their power and, consequently, they knew all the tricks of the trade.

Every year this ceremony was performed, without fail, on the May Day public holiday, thereby encouraging the 'carnival' feel as well as the largest possible turnout of the town's inhabitants. But, just in case they had forgotten, the church bells were rung in the morning to remind everybody that the day really was an extraordinary one. The procession itself took place on Boston's sacred ceremonial centre, between the assembly rooms and the guildhall, an ideal location for a gathering audience. Music and rich iconography were used to attract and maintain the audience's attention. The ceremonial robes and the silver oar and mace emphasised the wealth and power of the corporation, as well as the antiquity of its authority. No wonder the audience were struck with awe. But awe was not enough, the inhabitants had to be drawn into the performance, hence the obsequious final act, the strewing of flowers at the feet of the new mayor, which also conveniently incorporated two powerful symbols of purity and rebirth, children and flowers. In many ways, the ceremony's very structure, with the inhabitants watching a procession of unelected officials and their 'gentlemen' friends provided a perfect visual metaphor of the town's official politics. Thankfully, the inhabitants did not always perform their role quite so obediently. At the height of the 1829–32 reform agitation, the corporation was so unpopular that, following attacks on the homes of its leaders during elections, the ceremony was cancelled. No doubt the corporation feared that in these circumstances not even its dazzling finery would ensure an amenable audience.

Significantly, despite a satirical mock procession after Boston's first municipal election in January 1836 – in which 'bands of music, headed by men bearing an oar, not a silver one, two brooms, instead of silver crowns, with a procession of mourners, are parading the

15   Mayor's Day ceremony at Boston, *c.* 1910 (Lincolnshire County Council: Local
Studies Collection, Lincoln Central Library)

town, the bells ringing a dumb peal – all to lament the downfall of a
faction' – Boston's reformed municipal corporation continued where
its unreformed counterpart had left off.[32] Despite the reformed
corporation's claim to be at least partially representative of the
town's male ratepayers, there were no ceremonial innovations on
Mayor's Day, indeed essentially the same ceremony seems to have
been performed down to 1910 (see Plate 15). Such continuity
reflected the need for Boston's new corporation to 'borrow legitimacy
from the old by nurturing [its] old ritual forms, redirected to new
purposes'.[33] It is unsurprising that, when Oldham was incorporated
in 1849, the new municipal corporation quickly invented a Mayor's
Day ceremony all of its own. On the first Sunday after the election of
a new mayor, the aldermen, councillors, and other town officials,
were invited by the mayor to accompany him in worship at the
church. Having first met at the town hall they would march in
procession to the church surrounded by a crowd of spectators. The
procession always followed the same clearly prescribed marching

order, according to the official's place in the municipal hierarchy, with the only additions being the Anglican clergy and 'considerable numbers of the respectable inhabitants of the town'.[34] Here, as in Boston, the ceremony provided an indispensable opportunity for the town's male political elite to display itself and its authority, creating public awareness of the offices, personnel, and functions of the new municipal corporation.

Indeed, the persistent use of such ceremonies testifies to the continuing importance of public display and spectacle in the culture of official politics. To be imagined power had to be symbolised. Without the silver oar and mace or the robes of office at Boston's Mayor's Day it would have been difficult for spectators to distinguish the town clerk from the councillors, aldermen, or even the mayor. The lack of such iconography in Oldham's Mayor's Day ceremony may well explain the more regimented nature of the procession in distinct marching units so as to clearly demonstrate the officials rank and function. Similarly, the town's seals invested the authority of the town on those who used them. Symbols, like ceremonies, were used to create power, not just reflect it. Oldham's new municipal corporation had then also to invent its own symbolic repertoire. Consequently, when the Charter of Incorporation was granted it was immediately placed on display to demonstrate the legitimacy of its new found authority. According to Bateson, 'thousands of people feasted their eyes upon' the charter, as if it had to be seen to be believed.[35] As ever, the town's new symbolic identity had to be balanced alongside older ones, and so the new town council, like the police commissioners before them, retained the familiar coat of arms of the Oldham family. Once again the new and the old were combined to assert the legitimacy of the town's official politics, for if, as Lynn Hunt has suggested, 'legitimacy is the general agreement on signs and symbols', they had to appeal to as many people as possible, the young and old and the radical and the tory alike.[36]

And yet the use and meaning of civic ceremonies and symbols were often fiercely contested. Occasionally through the great mass of glowing reports of official ceremonies one catches a glimpse of the divisions that were never far from the surface. For instance, when in 1837 Boston's reformed corporation proposed to sell the town's corporation plate (used by its unreformed counterpart at ceremonial dinners) it aroused instant and popular opposition. A large meeting of inhabitants resolved that 'such a proceeding will for ever disunite this town and tend to increase that party feeling and animosity which is always injurious to the peace and quiet as well as to the peace and prosperity of the inhabitants at large'.[37] Similarly, at Oldham's Mayor's Day ceremony of 1872, the new nonconformist mayor, William Wrigley, shocked the town's Anglican community by refusing to stage the usual procession to St Mary's church, preferring instead to attend his Unitarian chapel on the aptly named Lord Street. 'This breach with the past scandalised all people to whom respectability was a synonym for convention and it angered lewd fellows of the baser sort. During the service a howling mob gathered outside the Unitarian Chapel. Headed by a donkey they set off in a mock processional formation and marched down Lord Street driving the donkey up the steps of St. Mary's Church'.[38] Such events reveal the tensions inherent in constructing a fiction of 'shared' civic interests around supposedly unifying symbolic practices. However, the reaction to Wrigley's violation of the Anglican conventions of Oldham's Mayor's Day also reveals the popular expectations associated with such official rites, thousands of people turned out to watch them and they felt cheated when they were changed or, worse still, not held. In no sense, then, can we imagine that these official political ceremonies served solely the interests of local elites, rather they were part of a process in which the town talked to itself and defined its identity.

This was equally true of those local ceremonies which celebrated national events. If, as Linda Colley has suggested, the late eighteenth century witnessed the apotheosis of the monarchy at the national level, then this period saw its dissemination to the local level.[39] Royal fever swept all five constituencies: celebrations for royal births, birthdays, weddings, visits, coronations, and jubilees all blossomed, while royal illnesses and deaths were mourned sombrely if not soberly. It did not seem to matter that this love-affair with the royal family was not always reciprocated. When in 1854 the royal family passed through Boston on the train to Scotland the town organised a lavish reception at the modest railway station, so that Her Highness would not have to leave her carriage. Yet, even this proved inconvenient. As soon as the mayor had presented the town's memorial to her 'the Queens impatience to resume her journey became evident. Truth compels us to say that Her Majesty appeared somewhat ruffled in temper. She repeatedly arched her royal brow, pursed her royal lips, and shook her head as if in displeasure. She beckoned to one or two of her retinue, and exclaimed loudly enough to be distinctly heard, "Where are the papers?" "Where is the *Times*?" and in a few moments afterwards "Why *don't you go on*?"'[40] Yet royal rebuffs like these were never taken to heart. All those that had crowded onto the platforms of Boston station were presumably pleased enough with the mere possibility of catching sight of an arched royal brow. For those who had not been so honoured, the local papers were sure to provide the latest instalment in the royal soap opera; not only paying careful attention to the royal wardrobe, but also reporting that the Queen had lost weight but looked healthy, while the Prince of Wales looked pale, thin and ill, his Royal Highness wore brown and never spoke, but the Princess Royal looked 'interesting', 'womanly' and 'wore a profusion of rings'. Thus even a less than successful visit could be turned into a public relations triumph. Normally, however, royals were rarely at hand to foul up proceedings and in any case most of the royal celebrations that punctuated the official politics of the localities were as much about the town itself, as about the institution of monarchy.

At the beginning of the nineteenth century royal celebrations had once again allowed local political elites to parade themselves in front of a massed crowd of spectators. Up to its reform in 1835 the mayor and mayoress of Boston's corporation always held a dinner for the town's 'principal inhabitants' on the monarch's birthday. By the coronation of William IV in 1830, the mayor, the corporation, and sundry other officials, were marching in procession across the town, their one concession to popular participation to allow 'a number of gentlemen, [and] inhabitants of the town' to join them (see Plate 16).[41] Similarly, at Oldham, William IV's coronation was marked by a procession which consisted almost entirely of the constables, the local militia and fusiliers, the lord of the manor and Orangemen, with the inhabitants and civil officers squeezed together, three abreast (see Plate 17).[42] Much the same pattern was evident at the proclamation of William IV's accession in Lewes when, after the town-crier and a 'flourish of trumpets' had captured the attention, the high constable, surrounded by the constables, headboroughs, and town clerk, read the proclamation outside county hall. While the attentive audience promptly gave 'four times four hearty cheers', the town's band struck up the national anthem and a procession was formed in the following order – town-crier – band – trumpets – constables – headboroughs – town clerk – inhabitants, four abreast –

16   The royal proclamation from Boston's assembly rooms, 1910 (Boston Guildhall
Museum)

which paraded the principal streets proclaiming the news, which was
apparently 'hailed by loud shouts from the assembly'.[43] In these
three constituencies at least, then, royal celebrations only afforded a
limited role to local inhabitants before 1830, even if they were
carefully staged to ensure the largest possible audience.

However, as early as 1830, with the gathering momentum of
reform sweeping the country, such events became increasingly more
inclusive, as was apparent at William IV's visit to Lewes. As soon as
the royal visit was announced a town meeting was held to appoint an
organising committee which consisted of the town's entire official
political establishment – chief officers, headboroughs, magistrates,
local clergy and notables, town clerk, and 20 of the town commissioners – as well as 3 members from each friendly society. As this was
the first time in over 600 years that any monarch had visited Lewes,
the inhabitants were allowed to help write the event through their
friendly societies. Consequently, on the day, the streets were packed
with spectators. Although the town's political establishment in-

17 The royal proclamation at Oldham Town Hall, 1910 (Oldham Local Studies Library)

evitably gave themselves pride of place, flanking the royal carriages as they moved down the high street, both sides of the street were lined with members of the following friendly societies under their respective banners: Lewes Friendly Society, Amicable Society, Stag Club with Carpenters, Dorset Arms, Pelham Arms, Fountain, Wheat Sheaf, Curriers, Veterans, Kings Arms, White Lion, Old Ship, Odd Fellows, Free Masons, and lastly the Mechanics Institute. Underlining the importance of maintaining this carefully designed order, the 'Delegates from the several Societies who were Members of the Committee were each provided with a Wand and managed the regularity and order of their respective Societies'.[44] No one was to let the side down. None the less, the participation of these voluntary groups, under their respective banners and with their own 'delegates' (how significant that word is), represented official recognition of their status within the town's political community. That these groups were presented as friendly societies, rather than as the trade societies they probably were, reflected simply the nervousness of the town's officials, they were only prepared to include them symbolically through their least threatening identity. Similarly, although women no doubt figured prominently amongst the 'thousands of spectators', they were notably absent from the procession and thus denied the right to assert their place in the official political culture of the town.

These ceremonies were then civic as much as national events – although they always privileged the symbols of nationhood – the monarch, the national anthem, and the Union Jack. Indeed, the repetitive use of broadly the same national ceremonies and iconography in all the constituencies created a unity of symbolic action which not only bound the localities together, but also tied the periphery to the centre. However, like the creation of civic identities, the cultivation of a national identity was often problematical, involving as it did drawing together disparate and often conflicting groups. Consequently, those who rejected the official version of the nation being propagated by local elites during these ceremonies frequently questioned the amount of popular support they received.[45] However, there were other, perhaps more effective, ways to challenge the interpretation of the nation advocated by these official ceremonies. At Queen Victoria's coronation in 1838 there was a procession in Oldham which included all the town's officials, clergy, quasi-military bodies like the veterans, volunteers, and militia, several bands, schools and friendly societies, the Temperance Society, Wesleyan Methodists, and inhabitants. Having paraded Oldham and its outlying townships this huge procession broke up into its constituent parts, each group retiring to different inns for lunch or tea-parties, or re-formed into separate groups such as the Operative Conservatives and the Owenites. Meanwhile the town's radicals held a public meeting to address a pointed memorial to the new queen 'praying for the dismissal of the Poor Law Commissioners, and to agree to a demand to the House of Commons for universal suffrage, annual parliaments, no property qualification for members &c.'.[46] In short, each group used the holiday and procession to express their own definition of the nation and their own interpretation of how the monarch should behave.

This ability to celebrate or criticise the town through the nation, and the nation through the town, was further manifested in local celebrations of military victories. These celebrations are worthy of much more detailed work. Here I can suggest only tentatively that they were subjected to less official regulation and were more spontaneous affairs than other official political ceremonies, although this was not always the case. The mayor of Exeter, for instance, held a dinner for 300 of the city's principal inhabitants to commemorate the peace of 1814, while the grand peace procession at Plymouth was also well organised by the town's officials. Even in these localities there were also illuminations, firework displays, and smaller trade and parish processions which allowed the inhabitants a freer role. On the second day of a week of celebration at Exeter in 1814

scarcely a house but was illuminated in the most tasteful and elegant manner – long rows of lamps emblazoning *Peace*; *Downfall of Tyranny*; *Louis the 18th*, with the name of *Bonaparte* upside down, under it – *Vive le Roi*; and a hundred other inscriptions, *Stars, fleurs de lis*, &c. were conspicuous at every turn...in Gandy's street, Mr. Tucker, cabinet-maker, had thrown a platform across the street, about fifteen feet from the ground, on which was fixed a very large cage, with the tyrant Bonaparte, remarkably well dressed in his uniform, and as large as life, enclosed in it – a chain fixed around his neck, which was held by the Devil (an excellent figure, the same size as the one within) sitting on the cage, outside, in the similitude of his keeper.[47]

Such inventiveness was not unusual. In Boston the illuminations of 1814 produced representations of lions, eagles, Union Jacks, Britannia, the Devil, angels, the military generals of both sides, rising suns, busy labourers, and large loaves to demonstrate the horrors of war and blessings of peace.[48] Even though some used these occasions to subvert official meanings (witness the illuminate busy labourers and large loaf) it seems that most acquiesced with the official interpretation.

However distasteful historians on the left may find these flag-waving, monarchy-loving, patriotic celebrations, it is difficult to deny their importance or their popularity. They provided occasions at which individuals right across the social, sexual, and political spectrum, non-voters and voters alike, were allowed to demonstrate their attachment to the nation, however variously defined. It is surely significant that those normally excluded from the official political nation were often able to contest the official national identity on these occasions. Here again it is evident that the official political culture allowed the restrictive legal definitions of the public political sphere examined in chapter 1 to be substantially redefined.

ELECTORAL POETICS

Nowhere was this ability to redefine restrictive legal definitions of the official political arena more evident than during elections. Then, as now, elections were so much more than psephologists allow, rather they ritually followed a sequence of events which spoke to the disenfranchised as well as the electors, and enabled both to voice their approval or disapproval of, not only the available candidate, but the whole edifice of official politics. While there is some evidence to suggest that these electoral rites were as common at vestry and municipal levels as they were at parliamentary level, I shall concentrate almost exclusively on the latter. Although, strictly speaking, not all the events I shall analyse are rituals, taken as a whole nineteenth-century elections constituted a ritual process through which constituencies talked to themselves, creating narratives which expressed their sources of unity as well as their sources of difference. It is possible to read the narrative of electoral rites as a melodramatic text(s) through which constituencies literally acted out the various generic plots of romance, comedy, tragedy, and irony.[49] Intriguingly, this is made possible by the remarkably similar symbolic practices of elections in all five constituencies.

After 1832, the approach of an election was heralded by the stylised courtroom conflict of the revising barristers. Their battles over the eligibility of registered voters were widely reported by the press, their theatrical courtroom debates billed as the warm-up act before the main event.[50] The community had been given warning of the forthcoming conflict, it had time to brace itself, to batten down the hatches, while at the same time whetting its political appetite. The suspense and tension mounted when the local inhabitants or voters issued requisitions to the prospective candidates. It was in effect a pre-canvass canvass, designed to encourage hopeful candidates to stand by showing them how much preliminary support they could muster. Although they were invariably the work of leading activists or agents these requisitions were always romantically dressed up as popular petitions, so that the candidate could present himself as a selfless hero, responding to popular demand rather than ambitiously soliciting support.[51]

The candidates then formally accepted the ritualised fêting of the requisition through an 'Address'. Usually a printed letter of no more than a couple of paragraphs, the address declared the candidate's reluctant decision, due to popular demand, to stand for election. John Platt's address to the constituency of Oldham in 1865, was a masterpiece of the form.

> The presentation to me of a requisition, originating from a large and influential meeting of my fellow-townsmen (to which the signatures are so numerous that I am assured my return is beyond doubt)...leaves me no alternative, whatever my personal feelings and inclination may be, but to afford you an opportunity of again proving, before the hustings and at the polling booth, your adherence to those great principles of Civil, Religious and Commercial Freedom, which are the foundation of all just government, and for which in times past you have made so many sacrifices. I therefore come before you as a candidate for your suffrages at the ensuing election.[52]

Published in the local press, posted on walls, and distributed as handbills, the address was clearly important. Quite apart from being one of the longest and most unmanageable sentences of all time, Platt's address portrays him as modestly bowing to the weight of his own popularity, while simultaneously providing only the most ambiguous outline of his political platform so as not to alienate any potential supporters. It was a romantic image, one which served hundreds of candidates very well indeed.

Moreover, the very language used in these addresses was as important as the genres in which it was deployed. Thus Platt, like many reforming candidates, directed his address to the 'electors and non-electors' in an attempt to include the disenfranchised within the constituency's political community, while also alluding to their influential role at the hustings. Platt also carefully dropped the phrase 'fellow-townsmen', a claim which, although it ignored the town's women, was always a boon to any candidature. 'Foreign' candidates were always at pains to emphasise their loyalty and devotion to the town, especially in response to attacks by competing local candidates.[53] This local dimension was critical. If candidates were to succeed they had to demonstrate that they recognised their constituents' many different interests and were prepared to promote and protect them. This included not just representing the interests of local trade in the Commons, but also, in some cases, guaranteeing the material well-being of local charities and institutions.[54] Constituents needed to be convinced that their candidates would look after the whole community, the poor as well as the rich, the non-elector as well as the elector. In this sense the requisition and address represented a dialogue between the different sections of the community and its potential parliamentary representatives. They provided a means by which the community talked to itself to establish the conflicting interests of its inhabitants and the possibility of reaching shared solutions to them.

Thus, right on cue, in stepped the local officials with a gilt-edged chance to remind people of their place in this narrative with the ceremonial reading of the writ. Officially the writ declared the start of the election and so entailed a full display of the constituency's political elite at its sacred ceremonial centre. Thus in Boston the mayor, as returning officer, read the writ from the balcony of the assembly rooms; while in Devon, the sheriff, as returning officer, held a special county meeting at Exeter Castle, surrounded by local notables and officials. At Tower Hamlets' first election in 1832, the returning officer created a still more elaborate ceremonial reading of the writ, one which persisted beyond 1868. Accompanied by no less than 4 deputies, the High Constable of the district, and nearly 50 parochial constables, he travelled around the boundaries of the borough reading the writ over 15 times.[55] Much the same happened in Lewes, where in 1832 the

Constables attended by the Headboroughs and the Acting Town Clerk and many of the Electors assembled at the County Hall where the precept for the Sheriff was read by the Town Clerk after which the Proclamation of the day was made by the Town Crier they then walked in procession preceded by the Town Band through the Borough of Cliffe Southmalling and Southover repeating the Proclamation [six times] ... The Band played the Old National Air of 'God Save the King' after each Proclamation and the Shouts of the Populace which followed shewed [*sic*] the highest degree of Exultation.[56]

Processions like these allowed the constituency's officials to parade themselves in their official robes, and with their other symbols of office. Their voice was added to the dialogue between the constituents and their candidates. In the fluid and potentially subversive atmosphere of electioneering they demonstrated the solidity and permanence of their civic and national offices – hence the frequent use of the national anthem and the omnipresent Union Jack. This national dimension should not be overlooked. The writ was in effect the monarch's proclamation, although the ceremony fused together the symbols of nation, constituency and locality.

The writ having been read, the melodrama of the contest proper continued with the carefully orchestrated, if premature, triumphal

27.] *Order of the Grand Procession, on the Entrance of JOHN WILKS, Esq., the Blue Candidate, into Boston, July 8, 1830.*

Sailors, two and two, bearing Union Jacks.
Two men with a banner;—motto, " Boston's Pride, and England's Hope."
Youths on horseback, bearing small bannerets, Nos. 1, 2, 3, 4.
Two gentlemen on horseback.
Man with large flag ; " Firm, Free, and United."
Gentlemen on horseback, with bannerets, Nos. 5, 6, 7, 8.
Band playing " *See the conquering Hero comes !*"
Single gentlemen on horseback, with a banner, " Welcome, Liberty's Champion."
Large new Flag,
On one side—" Boston and Freedom ;"—Reverse—" Wilks, Liberty, and Reform."
The CANDIDATE in his Carriage, drawn by FREEMEN.
Private Carriages.
Gentlemen on horseback, with bannerets, Nos. 9, 10, 11, 12.
Boston Colours.
Shoemakers, with their new banner.
Drums and fifes.
Gentlemen on foot, with blue favors.

N. B. It is particularly requested that the Friends of Mr. Wilks will not press upon the Carriage, but form lines for the procession to pass, and join the line after the Carriage.

To leave the Market-place precisely at Eleven o'clock.

(Bontoft.)

18   Lining up the troops: the order of procession at Wilks' public entry into Boston, 1830

'public entries' of the candidates. The timing was not always so precise. Some were held before the writ and regularly repeated throughout the campaign, especially before the nomination and poll, while Lewes' first public entry was staged by the defeated candidate the day after he had lost at the poll![57] Whenever they occurred though, public entries were always spectacular, as they were designed to demonstrate the candidates' popularity. Nothing was left to chance; the time, venue, and the order and route of the procession were advertised in the local press, on walls, by handbills and word of mouth. At the designated time and place the participants were marshalled into the correct order and given appropriate colours and banners (see Plate 18).[58]

At county elections public entries consisted of candidates and their landed supporters marching their tenants, and others under their 'influence', from their estates to the poll (see Plate 19). However, in an inversion of this ceremonial form, the procession of an urban public entry set out from the town in order to meet the candidate's

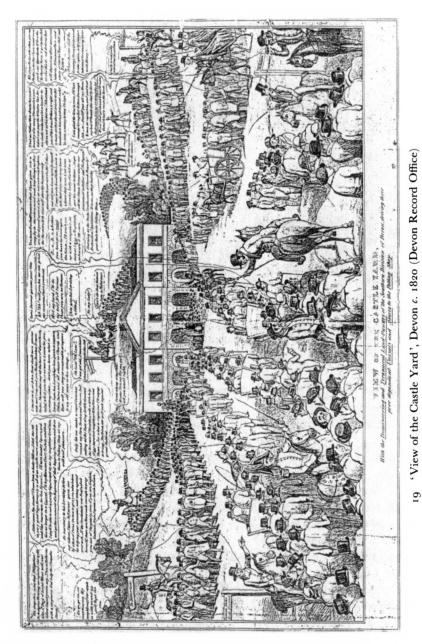

19 'View of the Castle Yard', Devon c. 1820 (Devon Record Office)

carriage outside the town's boundaries, before unshackling the carriage's horses and pulling it, complete with candidate, back into the town's centre, while the band played the proverbial 'See the Conquering Hero Comes'. The public entry of John Fielden and General Johnson, Oldham's radical MPs, before the 1847 election testified to the immense popularity of these events. 'Long before the hour named, large masses of people flocked to the spot; each vieing with his fellow to have the honour of offering a hearty welcome... Every available position from which a glimpse of the road could be obtained was thronged to excess, every window had had its full complement of occupants, and the tops of the houses contributed largely to the assembled multitude.' Reportedly there were no less than 18,000 present, the procession alone was a mile long and 15 people deep with 8 bands of music, so that flags and banners stretched out 'as far as the eye could reach'. When the candidates appeared and the initial applause had subsided, the bands struck up 'See the Conquering Hero Comes' and the women waved their handkerchiefs and ribbons. 'At this moment the scene was such as to gladden the bosom of even the most callous hearted', and the candidates dutifully 'appeared to be deeply effected... repeatedly acknowledging the congratulations of their constituents'.[59] As the public entry was supposed to demonstrate the gratitude of the candidate's supporters for his decision to contest the seat on their behalf, such a large turnout was by no means unusual.[60] Significantly, the town was laid before the candidate by a large proportion of its inhabitants – including those men, women, and children who could not vote – and by so doing they asserted their claims over the town and its potential representatives. The candidates themselves, however, were clearly not adverse to using the public entry as a vehicle themselves, to project the romantic image of themselves as the people's choice, bravely battling on their behalf.

The dialogue between candidates and the constituency's inhabitants continued with the canvass. In election etiquette the canvass, like the public entry, was not supposed to start until after the writ had been read. However, it was a difficult act to balance. Those who canvassed too early were accused of unnecessarily disturbing the peace of the constituency, while those who left it too late appeared over confident, guilty of the cardinal sin of taking the voters for granted. Especially as the central purpose of the canvass was for the candidate to fete and flatter the voters. As the Chester Poll Book of

1812 reported, the world was turned upside down during the canvass, 'rudeness is exercised as a privileged right, and while the great man bows in humble supplication for a vote, he is often treated with unceremonious effrontery'.[61] Such reversal of roles between leaders and led was also evident during Sir James Duke's canvass at Boston in 1837.

> At the shop of a respectable tradesman in the town the troop of canvassers encountered the mistress of the house, to whom they paid their respects in due form; but unluckily for him, Mr. Noble pushed forward to recommend the Sheriff, and immediately received a forcible intimation of the estimation in which he was held, for Mrs. A., taking the little man by the collar promptly served him with an Irish ejectment, by which his passage to the road was very greatly accelerated to the infinite amusement of the by-standers...[62]

At moments like these the story of the candidates' progress could turn quickly from romance to comedy. Yet, if the canvass literally allowed candidates to be brought back down to earth with a bump, it also enabled them to assess their support and possibly even to build upon it. As Lewes' Conservative candidate Bovill remarked of his door-to-door canvass in 1852, 'it is only by meetings like this... that we can show the electors that those who have their interests at heart are those who advocate our causes'.[63]

In the larger constituencies, this form of door-to-door canvassing increasingly gave way to mass meetings, where candidates were better protected from awkward questions or physical abuse and could address large numbers of voters simultaneously. Candidates in Tower Hamlets held a series of meetings in every parish, each chaired by a notable parishioner. According to the *Northern Star* the radical William Newton staged no less than forty meetings during his 1852 campaign.[64] In Devon, other forms of mass-canvassing were used as candidates relied heavily on a network of volunteers, usually members of the clergy or local notables, who canvassed freeholders in their respective parishes, no doubt bringing their 'natural influence' to bear. Even in these large unwieldy constituencies, whenever possible the personal touch of the candidate himself was deployed. Candidates had to be seen to be available, and therefore, when visiting towns or parishes, they would either extend open invitations for all to visit them at a specific address, or would conduct 'walk-abouts' on market days. Just a sight of a candidate seems to have

20   The hustings at Lewes outside County Hall, *c.* 1850s (Sussex Archaeological
Society)

been enough to create that fiction of personal familiarity which was
so important. Candidates ignored this at their peril, as Sir Thomas
Acland discovered in 1817, when his agent warned him that in 'the
Sothams [*sic*] you are not popular; amongst other things they say
they have never seen you, nor know anything of you personally...'[65]
However, barring such disasters, candidates issued an end-of-
canvass-address in which they expressed their surprise at the
wonderful reception of their canvass, thanked their supporters, and
exhorted them to maintain vigilance until polling when victory was
assured.

The sense of mounting tension generated by this ritual unfolding of
the campaign, not to mention the other innumerable speeches,
dinners, and processions, reached a crescendo with the construction
of the hustings in preparation for the nomination.[66] The hustings was
always located at the constituency's sacred, ceremonial centre. Thus
in Lewes the county hall provided the backdrop for the hustings at
both county and borough elections (see Plate 20), as the assembly
rooms did in Boston after the hustings were moved from St Botolph's

21   South Devon hustings at Plymouth, 1868 (Plymouth City Museums and Art Gallery)

22 Tower Hamlets hustings at Stepney Green, 1852 (*Illustrated London News,* 10 July 1852)

church in 1831. Oldham's hustings were built on what became the site of the town hall and then, from the 1847 election, beside the town hall steps. Devon's elections were held either inside Exeter's session-house, or in it's castle-yard, depending on the weather and turnout, at least until 1868 when South Devon's hustings were relocated outside Plymouth's Royal Hotel (see Plates 21 and 35). In Tower Hamlets the hustings stood on the central spot of Stepney Green, a traditional venue of popular events (see Plate 22). The location of these hustings reflected the significance attached to these sites in their respective civic landscapes; they were used as symbols of the localities' platform upon the official political nation.

Unsurprisingly the local officials used the hustings to associate themselves and their offices with this wider political authority. Indeed, the nomination had as much local as national significance. The local community was on display to itself; leaders to led, and led to leaders, leaders to leaders, and led to led. The hustings were essential to this process, as they literally elevated the local political elite so that all assembled below could see them. They were usually no less than 12 feet tall, and large enough to accommodate the returning officer, his clerks and officials, as well as the candidates, their agents, and committee, not to mention press reporters and sundry local notables (see Plates 20–22). Despite the length of this list, access to the hustings was jealously guarded and usually 'no person was admitted on the "political stage" without a ticket signed by the returning officer.'[67] Yet it would be wrong to assume that once on the hustings the local political establishment presented a united front. Those on the hustings separated into rival camps and were often seen squabbling and barracking each other, they literally acted out many of the conflicts which gripped their audience below. In the middle of all this, mediating between the competing factions both on the hustings and in the crowd, was the returning officer, whose central position upon the hustings was supposed to reflect his impartiality. To reinforce the *gravitas* of their exalted position some returning officers invented their own ceremonial public entry upon the hustings.[68]

Yet, if the constituency's political establishment could use the nomination, so too could its inhabitants who gathered together in one place to express their differences. Candidates were conveyed in procession to the hustings by their respective supporters who then separated and occupied opposite sections of the open space in front of the hustings, as at Boston in 1830 when the market place underneath the hustings on the Assembly rooms balcony was divided into two camps, the 'Blues occupied the end adjoining the fish-market, and the pinks that nearest the bridge.'[69] In some places, like Norwich, officials used posts and large chains to ensure that the rival factions were kept apart in front of the hustings.[70] As each candidate appeared on the hustings they were cheered or booed by different sections of the audience, like prize-fight boxers entering the ring. This dialogue of heckle and counter-heckle, chant and counter-chant, continued throughout the nomination (as indeed it did during the poll and the declaration) not only between different groups in the audience, but also between individuals on the hustings and in the audience.[71] The audience itself was by no means small. Nominations at Lewes and Devon consistently attracted between 1–6,000, although the nomination at South Devon in 1868 drew 10,000. At Boston turn-outs fluctuated between 1,500–10,000, while surprisingly nominations at Tower Hamlets were no bigger, attracting as few as 100 people in 1846, although usually numbers varied between 6–10,000. Oldham's nominations seem, therefore, to have been the most popular of all. As many as 12–15,000 people attended the borough's first nomination in 1832, and even 1,200 attended the uncontested nomination of January 1835. Yet the largest turn-out of all was at the nomination of 1868 when the audience was reported variously at between a staggering 20–40,000. Clearly the nomination was very much a popular event, one in which the disenfranchised asserted their rights to influence the course of the election and be included within the official political nation.

It was, then, at the nomination that the excluded and their champion could briefly taste triumph and remind voters, candidates, and, most importantly, local officials of their part in the electoral narrative. At times such shows of strength represented little more than tragic walk-on parts or pyrrhic victories, as when the Chartist Julian Harney stood against the new Foreign Secretary Lord Palmerston at Tiverton's nomination 1847. Having overwhelmingly won the show of hands he declined the contest, arguing that it would not be a fair fight because of the limited franchise and the use of influence and corruption. Yet in some cases a powerful popular performance at the nomination could force an unpopular candidate to retire without forcing a poll. Such was the case at Lewes in 1812 when Colonel Macaulay stood against the sitting member, Shiffner. At the nomination 'the friends of Mr. Shiffner, by getting complete possession of the Court, to the exclusion of those in the interest of the Colonel, by their noise and vociferation bore down all before them...the shew of hands, from the cause above stated, appeared greatly in favour of Mr. Shiffner. Colonel Macaulay, in a short and sensible speech...declined the contest...and soon after returned...to London'.[72] However, this technique of 'packing the hall', so common at unreformed elections, became increasingly redundant as the nomination and hustings were moved outside to accommodate larger audiences. Arguably, however, the larger the audiences became, the larger the influence of the disenfranchised. Certainly Benjamin Grime recalled how at Oldham 'both parties struggled hard to get the sympathy of the masses, though the franchise had not yet reached them. Their moral support was highly appreciated by Whig and Tory, and great pains were taken to secure their show of hands at the hustings on the day of nomination. It was believed that those who got a good majority when the show of hands was demanded by the returning officer were in a fair way of receiving a majority of votes on the day of election.'[73] Just as the nomination was used by the local elite to display themselves prominently, so it was used by the disenfranchised to avenge themselves upon the official political arena and to assert their right to be included within the story the local political community was telling itself. Significantly, the nomination ceremony, the singularly most important event during an election, seems to have afforded the excluded their greatest influence in shaping that story.

This was equally true of disenfranchised women. One cannot underestimate the scale and style of womens' involvement, not only at the nomination, but throughout the entire electoral ritual process. In some places like Ipswich, separate hustings were built solely for women 'who by their presence, to the number of about 400, gave interest and animation to the scene'.[74] As we have already seen, women were also a significant presence at public entries and other processions and mass meetings, even occasionally entering the very male arena of the electoral dinner. Candidates' wives were often used as canvassers, while the candidates themselves were always appealing to women to use their influence as wives, sisters, or daughters over the male voters. Although these entries in to the official political arena were no mean achievements in themselves, they were usually sanctioned by men. It is all the more significant that some women dared to exceed their officially defined role as supporters of men. We have already seen how a woman took her boot to the backside of John Noble during Boston's 1837 canvass, but at the very same election in Oldham, 'one of the Conservative canvassers was assailed ... by the hootings and hissings of a group of female radicals'.[75] Naturally, male reporters reserved their fiercest criticisms for women who sought to include themselves politically on male terms. At the 1868 declaration at Oldham 'one creature, in particular, whom we remember to have seen at the election of 1865, as a supporter of the Conservative candidates, was again present near the hustings, and she distinguished herself by the same unwomanly noises and fierce gestures. She was even worse than the wildest male partisan in the assemblage.'[76] Such vitriol testified to the relative ease with which brave women could transcend their allotted feminine role and claim their rightful place in the community's great melodramatic election saga.

The poll provided yet another chance for the disenfranchised of both sexes to flex their political muscles. During the poll crowds of non-voters gathered around each polling booth to monitor the votes of their enfranchised neighbours and, in doing so, to entertain themselves at their expense. Casting a vote was therefore a daunting experience, reminiscent of running a gauntlet. With her usual perception George Eliot perfectly captured this intimidating atmosphere in *Felix Holt*. The way up to the polling booths was variously lined, and those who walked it, to whatever side they belonged, had the advantage of hearing from the opposite side what were their most marked defects or excesses in bodily appearance... but if the voter frustrated wit by being handsome, he was groaned at and satirised according to a formula, in which the adjective was Tory, Whig or Radical... and the substantive blank to be filled up after the taste of the speaker.[77]

The sensible voter swallowed hard and accepted this treatment. Those less than sensible offered gestures of token defiance, like the Tory elector at Boston's 1831 election, who 'waived his hat in defiance' to the hisses and catcalls. What followed was horribly predictable. He had 'scarcely proceeded one step before the mob attacked him, knocked him down, beat him on the head, and finally his shoulder was dislocated'.[78] Here again the disenfranchised were able to turn the world upside down by pillorying those placed above them in the official political hierarchy. Like the canvass, polling turned a romantic electoral story into a carnivalesque comedy, it was the great leveller, and as such it formed an essential weapon in the armoury of the disenfranchised, at least until the introduction of the secret ballot in 1872.

Apart from those contests decided by the retirement of one or more of the candidates the declaration was usually held the morning after the final close of the poll. This allowed the returning officer to compile the results from the various polling booths, no small matter when they were as far apart as Exeter and Plymouth. It is hard to resist the feeling that in Boston and Lewes, the postponement of the declaration until the following day was used to heighten anticipation and the ceremony's impact (see Plates 23 and 24). Despite this, the declaration never drew the crowds like the nomination. Although turnouts varied from contest to contest and constituency to constituency, they were usually between 1–15,000. Once the returning officer had announced the result the candidates delivered their final speeches from the hustings. The victorious candidates always spoke first so that, like true 'Englishmen', the losers could end by thanking the returning officer for his impartial conduct. This time all the candidates' speeches exuded goodwill and emphasised the need for old differences to be resolved. As figureheads of the contending parties, the candidates symbolised the conflicts that had racked the constituency over the preceding days and weeks, and so it was critical that they did their utmost to calm troubled political waters. None

23　Waiting for the result, Lewes, 1892 (Sussex Archaeological Society)

24　The declaration at Lewes, 1892 (Sussex Archaeological Society)

took to this role better than Mr Scarlett, the defeated candidate at Lewes in 1816. Having spent his whole campaign branding his opponent a dishonourable liar, he had no qualms in saying that he hoped

all angry feelings would subside, and all animosities be forgotten. 'Although' said he, 'Sir John Shelley and I have differed in opinions as to the propriety of his being my opponent, I am happy now that the contest between us is over, to declare my conviction that you cannot be represented by a more honourable man and that he, as a man of honour, has only done that which he felt right... I have ever regarded and esteemed him: my feelings towards him are still the same: I still love him.' – Here Mr. Scarlett's feelings overpowered him: and those who were but a moment before politically his enemies, were now naturally his friends.[79]

Nowhere was this cultivation of consensus and the belief in 'fair play' more evident than at declarations. The sub-text suggested that the important thing was not winning or losing, but how one played the game. A game that had to be played hard, but fair. It was this belief in 'fair play' which allowed candidates to lose manfully, without regrets or recriminations, so that they could shake the hands of their opponents and thank the returning officer for ensuring that fair play had been done. Even when candidates broke these codes of behaviour, as they often did, the local press and pollsters were quick to assure everyone that justice had been done, that life could go on as before.[80] For some the declaration represented a romantic resolution of conflicting roles, while for others romance turned to tragedy and left those conflicts in the electoral story unresolved.

Either way the epic electoral tale was far from finished, rather it was merely preparing its characters for a fitting finale, a finale which was at once both romantic, tragic, comic, and ironic. This grand finale was the chairing, it was the ceremony that ended all ceremonies. The chairing represented the culmination of weeks, sometimes even months, of mounting tension and supposedly represented the constituency's symbolic acceptance of their newly elected representatives. The people elevated the new member above their shoulders and paraded him through their town. The chairing of Boston's victorious Tory Mr Cabbell in 1852 was typical, he

was met at the station at 12 o'clock, by the chief members of his committee... they proceeded to the Peacock, where the procession was formed, in the following order: – 1. About 250 horsemen, comprising many of the electors of the borough and a large body of the neighbouring farmers ... 2. The band and banners. – 3. The carriage of Mr. F. Cooke, Mr. Adams, Mr. White and other gentlemen, and graced with banners and a magnificent bouquet from Mr. Cooke's garden. This was followed by the private carriages of the members of Mr. Cabbell's committee and of the neighbouring gentry, and upwards of 100 phaetons, gigs, coaches and every other possible variety of vehicles, affording accommodation to about 700 persons, and all of them decked with banners and colours. To these succeeded a crowd of pedestrians, forming altogether a procession nearly a mile in length.[81]

The size of this chairing procession was not unusual. In 1830 the chairing of Boston's radical candidate Wilks attracted an estimated 10–12,000 participants and spectators, and the following year his procession alone included a thousand.[82] People travelled for miles to witness a chairing. Not only were the streets lined with people, but windows, roof-tops, and even lamp-posts were packed with eager spectators (see Plates 25 and 26).

No doubt part of the attraction was the elaborate decoration of the chairs – festooned with flags, banners, colours, and flowers they were spectacular sights. Such was their popularity in Devon that during the 1818 contest all three candidates used the chairs to be carried to and from the poll, each attempting to be the most magnificent, to out-shine the others.[83] Such details were clearly important, reporters often described the decoration of the chair in as much detail as the ceremony itself, while one of Devon's most popular orators based an entire speech upon Bastard's chairing in 1816, arguing that the style of the chair, its decoration and colours cast doubt on Bastard's manliness and patriotism – damaging charges for a Tory candidate.[84] The chair and its ceremony provided a chance for the constituency to show off to itself one last time; to show off the wealth and prestige of its new member as reflected in his chair's decorations; and last, but by no means least, to show off the supposedly re-established unity of the locality.

O'Gorman is therefore right to stress the communal dimension of the chairing and its official use to engender a sense of consensus.[85] Yet we must also be alive to the ways in which the official meaning of the chairing was subverted. Thus, just as the chairing could symbolise the adoring elevation of a new member, so it could be used to remind the candidate that the people had placed him where he was, and so they could also topple him from those dizzy heights at any time. For a candidate balancing precariously on the shoulders of his supporters

25 The chairing of Sir Ralph Lopes, newly elected MP for South Devon, 1849 (Devon Record Office)

26 'Chairing the Member' by William Hogarth, 1775

in a chair this was a forceful point (see Plate 26). Similarly, the chairing could equally be used to accentuate the differences of the constituency's rival groups, rather than uniting them. Thus, at the Devon election of 1816, Acland's defeated supporters distributed cards calling for manifestations of 'mourning':

> *BLACK DAYS:*
> July 1st and 2nd, 1816.
> Sacred to the 'Triumph in Devonshire of Fraud, Falsehood and Ebrington!'[86]

By hanging black crepe from their windows and closing their shops along the processional route of Ebrington's triumphal chairing they turned a celebration into a wake. Similarly, at Chester's election of 1826, supporters of the defeated Independent candidate refused to participate in the chairing of their Tory opponent, so that 'as soon as the cavalcade had passed through the Northgate, they found all the blinds down; in many places the shutters closed; and not a soul, maid, wife, or widow – man, woman or child, to greet them as they passed! A little further they encountered a lamp-post decorated with the INDEPENDENT colours, and hung with *crepe*. A label was appended, on which was written "NOBODY *is not dead yet.*" At this point the procession turned back...'[87] Such incidents were rarely reported in the press, indeed at the first hint of any trouble chairings were cancelled. As the chairing was supposed to symbolise the coming together of the political community after weeks of conflict, it was an obvious target for dissent and protest. Stones and mud were thrown at the chair and its occupant, attempts were made to topple the chair from the shoulders of its bearers and, if all else failed, 'mock' chairings were used to rob the official one of its legitimacy.[88] Clearly such dissent can not be read as simply serving as an official safety-valve. The great electoral story did not always have a happy ending.

This was reflected in the closing dinners, balls or other events which always followed the chairing. The competing groups retired, victorious or defeated, to the headquarters of their respective committees to listen to the final speeches of the candidates, committee members, and party activists, and to toast their cause and their own efforts in promoting it. The rival groups therefore recognised that they would remain divided to the bitter end. When attempts at reconciliation were made, as at Lewes in 1826 when the two candidates visited each others' dinners, disaster quickly followed:

Between seven and eight o'clock, Mr. Kemp paid a kind of congratulary visit to Sir John, and his friends at the Star, where he was handsomely received, and staid [*sic*] a full hour. Some little time after he had withdrawn, Sir John returned the compliment, by visiting Mr. Kemp and his friends at the Crown, where his *entre* was loudly cheered: but, ere the cheerings had lost their echoes, some of the most active of the Baronet's partisans made their appearance, when the '*Demon of Dischord*' took the command, and in an instant, set the whole room in an uproar...the tables were mounted, and...bottles, bowls, pots, and glasses were indiscriminately kicked from their stations...the force of which was soon felt by Sir John who was kicked, cuffed and bundled down the stairs into the street, where however, he luckily made his escape in a whole skin.[89]

These dinners were, therefore, partisan affairs, if toasts were made to the town, county or nation they were done so from a partisan perspective. Significantly, therefore, the electoral poetic closed with the recognition of differences not similarities within the community.

Thus far it has been argued that the ritual process of elections told a story complete with a central cast of characters, and a sequence of events which built an epic narrative full of suspense and excitement, not to mention romance, comedy, and tragedy. Through this narrative different groups sought to impose themselves and their interpretation of events. We must therefore be wary of too readily accepting the official meanings of this narrative. It is difficult to deny that officials usually had the upper hand in shaping the events and meanings of electoral poetics. How else can we explain why official electoral culture repeatedly facilitated the participation of the disenfranchised? Certainly it is important to recognise how local officials sought to regulate and discipline such popular electoral participation. Unfortunately, to do such a huge subject justice would require a book in itself, therefore in what follows I have ignored those forms of official regulation which have already been discussed by other historians, such as the legislation outlawing electoral corruption and the use of physical force.[90] I shall concentrate on those less well-known official techniques of regulating popular electoral participation, many of which were introduced by the supposedly Great Reform Act of 1832.

The creation of the electoral register with the 1832 Reform Act was just one such technique. After 1832 those who qualified as electors had to register in order to cast their vote. Compiling the register was a complex and lengthy affair. It began with the parochial overseers who alone knew which houses were occupied and who had paid their rates. Their list was then sent either to the clerk of the peace in counties or to the town clerk in boroughs who published them as provisional lists, any objections to them were then heard by the revising barristers. Such a time consuming, expensive, and potentially humiliating process undoubtedly disenfranchised many potential voters, especially in London where, as we saw in chapter 1, the problem was worsened by the use of compounding. In 1866 the Poplar vestry clerk believed 'that if all persons entitled to be put on the register were to make a claim and attend to establish it, the numbers on the Register would be increased three-fold, viz. from 1,450 to 4,350; but the usual reply I receive when I inform the claimants they will have to attend the revising barristers court is "Oh, I am not going to lose my time to go there. If you cannot put me on the Register I shall not trouble myself any further".'[91] The process of registration was for many simply too time consuming and expensive, entailing an unwelcome unpaid break from work with no eventual guarantee of success. We must then recognise that, just as the official political culture could encourage popular participation, so too could it serve to restrict and prevent it.

Registration was also used to regulate popular electoral participation in other ways. By registering electors before polling began, the 1832 Reform Act attempted to simplify a process that had caused considerable problems in the unreformed electoral system. Before 1832 the eligibility of electors had been contested on the hustings during the actual poll. As the ultimate arbiter in this process, the returning officer invariably appeared partisan and, therefore, to be violating that most sacred of English electoral codes 'fair play'.[92] If the returning officer was not perceived as an impartial purveyor of 'fair play' then the whole official electoral process was compromised. However unfair the electoral system was, it had to be *seen* to be fair. Consequently, in 1790 Devon's returning officer received strict instructions not to enter 'into loud disputes with advocates. He should not raise his voice or get in a passion, but, if the advocates are noisy, sit down until they will give him a quiet hearing.' Nor should he appear facetious by asking aristocrats and men of fortune if they qualified as 40s freeholders, or likewise to ask old men if they were over 21. 'Gentlemen are often displeased at these jokes, and they are often ill-naturedly misrepresented by the standers-by'.[93] The wit and partisan proclivities of the election crowd had to be contained, and the reputation and dignity of the official returning officer maintained at all costs. Once freed from these onerous duties the returning officer was better placed to project himself as the embodiment of the electoral systems' 'fair play'. After 1832 barely a moment passed at an election without the returning officer stressing the importance of 'fair play' and 'peaceable conduct'. For instance, at Boston's nomination in 1835 the mayor wound up his speech saying that, 'I have, therefore, but one more appeal to make, and I hope it will be complied with; which is that those gentlemen who appear here as candidates this day, and likewise their friends, may have a patient and fair hearing. Fair play is a distinguishing characteristic of Englishmen; the gentlemen now before you are entitled to it, it is their privilege, their right. Take then this motto "Peace, Order, Fair Play".'[94] Such appeals no doubt helped create the (mis)conception of an English electoral system characterised by 'fair play' and 'honour', as did the candidates' willingness to play along with this image (at least once the result had been announced). For many, however, the returning officer remained a partial official who could wield his considerable power vindictively, calling in the military and mis-reading the show of hands when things were running against his side.[95]

In many ways the 1832 Reform Act enhanced the power of the returning officer to discipline popular electoral participation and, thereby shape the course of the election. In the first place, because he was responsible for the timing of the nomination, the poll and the declaration, he could either encourage or prevent popular partici-pation by staging them either during or outside working hours. This power had been less important before 1832 as many contests ran over several days (even weeks) with polling possible from dawn to dusk (8 am to 8 pm), thereby giving those living in remote outlying areas more time to travel and cast their vote or shout their heckle. Therefore, when the 1832 Reform Act ensured that all polls were open for no more than 16 hours over 2 days, the timing of elections became crucial as mid-week polls often excluded many from voting, while mid-week, mid-morning nominations and declarations could also prevent thousands from participating.[96] Yet perhaps the most significant 'reforms' of electoral procedure in 1832 was the re-distribution of polling booths. In the unreformed electoral system each constituency had only one central polling place, whereas from 1832 the returning officer was legally obliged to provide a polling-booth for every 600 electors at geographically strategic locations around the constituency. Like all such clauses this one appears to have had a positive effect for electors, as they no longer had to travel great distances to cast their vote. However, for the disenfranchised it represented a considerable set-back, for by dispersing the crowd at the central hustings it significantly reduced their collective power to regulate and intimidate their enfranchised neighbours. As we shall see in the following chapter, this marked the beginning of a trend which culminated in 1872 when the introduction of the secret ballot finally ended the remaining influence of the disenfranchised over electors. Ironically, opponents to the Act argued that it was 'un-English' and 'unmanly' and would violate the principle of 'fair play'.[97]

Thus, before we too rapidly applaud the official electoral culture for its ability to expand the legitimate arena of politics, we must acknowledge the important role of the 1832 Reform Act in allowing popular electoral participation to be better regulated. It is impossible to deny that the cultural poetics of elections enabled disenfranchised men and women to assert their right to be included within the official political nation. That is not to argue that the official meaning of elections passed by unnoticed, far from it. Perhaps the most startling manifestation of its success is evident in the largely unchallenged hegemony of English parliamentary politics. After all, as long as the non-electors were still clamouring for the vote the official political process was still in business.

CONCLUSION

I have argued in this chapter that the culture of official politics considerably expanded the legal definitions of the public political sphere examined in chapter 1. It represented an attempt to convey the legitimacy of the official political nation to those legally excluded from it. Moreover, by creating new political arenas which culturally included the legally excluded, local officials ensured that they were better able to regulate popular politics. The culture of official politics also provided an important mouthpiece through which rulers and ruled could have a meaningful political dialogue about the nature and distribution of power within both the locality and the nation. And yet when all was said and done, it was a culture whose parameters were fashioned from above, and above all it told the story the official political establishment wanted to be heard.

It is, for instance, striking how similar the official political cultures of all five constituencies were. Thus, we find that despite their different social and political complexions, officials in all five constituencies used symbolic practices that were remarkably similar in form. That is not to argue that there were not differences in style, content and use. We have repeatedly seen how even within the same constituency one building, ceremony or symbol could be endowed with many contrasting meanings by different groups. This is significant not least because it may help to explain the continuing relevance and use of these official ceremonial forms. Far from suggesting a decline, the evidence we have points to the persistence, even elaboration of these symbolic practices. The construction of official civic landscapes continued apace from the 1870s with the great gothic revival which still dominates the skyscapes of towns and cities in the north-west. Mayor's Day ceremonies and royal proclamations also apparently continued largely unchanged in Boston and Oldham until at least the First World War (see Plates 16 and 17). Indeed, Oldham's corporation was busy expanding its ceremonial and symbolic repertoire, extending its town hall, and arming itself with mayoral robes, chains, and staves of office.[98] Similarly, official electoral poetics were in good shape in 1868 when they appear to have been adopted indiscriminately by newly enfranchised constituencies like Stockton.

However, if any part of this official political culture came under threat in the last quarter of the nineteenth century, it was that associated with elections. As we shall see in chapter 6, this was partly the result of the radical critique of it, large parts of which were adopted in the electoral reform legislation of 1832, 1872, and 1883. Ironically these 'reforms' did much to diffuse the power of individual or group actors in the popular political audience to shape the course of the electoral poetic. Ultimately, however, it was the emergence of new forms of mass party politics which most fatally undermined the official electoral culture. With their increasingly sophisticated political culture and electoral organisation, the Gladstonian Liberal party and its Conservative counterpart, appropriated many of the forms and functions of the official electoral culture. As will be apparent in chapter 6, party politics gradually took over its regulative and disciplinary roles, and were eventually better suited to create and manage popular political participation, even among the disenfranchised. The appropriation of these integrative and regulative roles by mass party politics, enabled officials to distance themselves from divisive electoral events so that they could instead concentrate on projecting the fairness of official politics through its 'dignified' ceremonial part.[99] Certainly the hegemony of parliament was never in doubt from the 1870s. It is arguable that it had never really been in doubt since the 1790s for, although radicals had flirted with alternatives before 1848 (albeit with very little popular success), they had long attached great symbolic and political weight to gaining the vote. One unfortunate and apparently unforeseen consequence of this was that they neglected other arenas of political power which were gradually being removed from underneath their noses. It is to a consideration of these that we now turn.

CHAPTER 3

The medium and the message: power, print, and the public sphere

INTRODUCTION

If, as we have seen, officials appealed to a public beyond the officially defined propertied political nation, then this chapter will examine the techniques by which this 'public' was in turn regulated and disciplined.[1] If property was no longer sufficient to ensure the legitimacy of the disinterested virtue and independence of the official political nation, then another set of criteria had to be found. Consequently, as we shall see in chapter 8, definitions of property were expanded to include the property of reason, which was increasingly seen as an alternative source of virtue for the aspiring citizen, providing, if not financial independence, then at least moral and intellectual independence. The language of 'Old Corruption' had been inverted to form a critique of a mass popular politics without virtue, whose only salvation was the possession of reason, hence the importance of print as an enabler of education, a vehicle for the restoration of independence and virtue.[2] Of course the danger was that this language with its appeals to a new rational public could be, as indeed it was, appropriated by radicals to demand that all those possessing reason should be included as citizens of the official political nation. Central to this discourse was the post-Enlightenment perception of print as the universal tool of reason, an ideal form for rational political debate that was available to all. However, I hope to show in this chapter that print was far from universal, instead it was used to reconstitute the public political sphere in an ever-more restrictive fashion, excluding groups believed to be 'irrational' like women and the illiterate poor from public political debate.[3]

It is necessary, given this increase in the political uses of print and its close association with reason, to examine the extent of popular literacy. While the study of literacy is notoriously imprecise,

something approaching a historiographical consensus has begun to
emerge about the levels of literacy in England between 1750 and
1914.[4] Although figures varied enormously according to region,
locality, age, gender, and occupation, it has been estimated that in
1840 something like 50 per cent of women and 33 per cent of men
were still illiterate. My own analysis of literacy levels in the five
constituencies based on the Registrar Generals' marriage registers,
indicate clear regional and sexual differences. Sixteen and 18 per cent
of men, and 27 and 33 per cent of women in Lewes and Tower
Hamlets remained illiterate in 1849, as opposed to 25 and 28 per cent
of men, and 37 and 41 per cent of women in Boston and Devon.
Oldham was far and away the least literate constituency with only 40
per cent of men and 15 per cent of women able to sign the marriage
register.[5] However, marriage registers tend to exaggerate the extent
of literacy, as there were not only always older sections of the
population with lower levels of attainment, but because the ability to
sign did not necessarily imply the ability to read or write with ease.
As historians have increasingly recognised, it is probable that many
unable to sign were functionally literate, in that they could read
rudimentary texts either by themselves or with other members of the
family, neighbourhood or workplace.[6] Therefore, however imprecise
these figures are, it is clear that, despite the gospel of self-improvement
and the increased provision of educational facilities, a significant
proportion of the population remained illiterate throughout this
period. This had important consequences for the way in which
people perceived and experienced politics.

For, in what follows I shall argue that oral, visual and printed
modes of communication afforded individuals within the popular
political audience different roles in the production and reception of
appeals. Although these modes always developed in relation to each
other so that they were never discrete hermetic categories, and, while
denying a linear chronology of the rise of print and the corresponding
decline of oral and visual media, I shall contend that this period
witnessed a marked increase in the political uses of print. It was a
development encouraged by a series of legislative measures which
privileged the uses of print in order to erode the public and collective
character of oral and visual politics with a conception of politics as
the private affair of (male) individuals. It was surely not coincidental
that many political groups, from the Chartists to Disraelian
Conservatives, saw increased educational provision and the spread of

literacy as an essential pre-requisite to an expansion of the franchise. Citizenship of the political nation was provisional upon the possession of reason, virtue, and independence, and therefore mass political participation had to occur within the private realm of the home, a setting conducive to rational political debate and thought, unlike the often passionate and emotive public arena of the streets. Therefore, despite all the legislation which historians have traditionally seen as heralding a brave new world of mass democratic politics – the electoral reforms of 1832, 1867, and 1884, the reduction and eventual abolition of stamp duties, the 'anti-corruption' legislation, the introduction of the secret ballot in 1872 – this period witnessed a marked decline in people's ability to shape the political appeals available to them as the official political subject was redefined in the image of print.

As we shall see, it is impossible to locate the exact date or even the decade in which this process began, and even more difficult to find its conclusive end. Ironically, this is not because the experience of the five constituencies was so divergent, indeed far from it. Remarkably, the modes of political communication deployed within the five constituencies were essentially the same, as were their trajectories of development and decline. Consequently, from my representative, rather than comparative, use of the constituencies, a common if uneven chronology emerges with the advent of many new modes of political communication and organisation during the 1830s, which were in turn supplemented by others in the 1860s and 1870s. When this process ground to a halt is less clear, partly because it lies beyond the confines of this study, deep in the twentieth century, and partly because the development of new technologies like television, radio, and satellite eclipsed it, providing new axes of tension and relationships of power.[7]

THE POLITICS OF SIGHT

Politics had long contained a strong visual dimension, and during the nineteenth century its persistent presence was plain to see. Few meetings were complete without a display of some sort, whether it was the sight of a procession, a speaker on a husting, a building or the seemingly requisite use of banners, colours, flowers, effigies, and other iconography. One cannot underestimate the scale and intensity of the politics of sight, or the power these forms of communication afforded to the individuals who used them.

Much of this sense of power and popular agency was generated by the melodramatic dynamic of public performance. The melodramatic qualities of ceremonies, meetings, and the use of iconography within them, not only attracted attention, but also encouraged participation in highly stylised roles. As we saw in the preceding chapter, the popular reception of these roles was crucial in the struggle to legitimate or contest power, but our concern here is how their inherent theatricality accentuated the uniqueness and poignancy of the occasion by generating powerful emotional responses. As in the theatre, the combination of light, sound, and movement was used to create an extraordinary world which was truly memorable. There can, for instance, have been few events as visually or emotionally arresting as a torchlight procession by several thousand people through the streets of a still largely unlit nineteenth-century town. Anthropologists like Victor Turner have long recognised the significance of this emotional dimension to public performance, arguing that we cannot reduce such events to the purely logical and cognitive, rather they work between two poles, the emotional and the cognitive, with both working upon and informing each other to make the message more compelling.[8] Yet this stimulation, even simulation, of an emotional melodramatic imagination also created a very marked sense of involvement and historical agency among participants and spectators alike. Thus the usually dour and unexcitable reporter, Edwin Butterworth, waxed lyrical when describing the nomination at Oldham's first election in 1832. Having set the scene from the hustings he watched the processions of different groups, complete with their banners, favours, and bands of music, and the responses to them by those hanging out of every window. 'No spectacle', he wrote, 'could be more pleasing than to observe the motions and feelings of this mighty multitude which amounted to 12 or 15,000 at the lowest computation... To view a vast powerful and industrious community concentrated in one mass for the purpose of exercising for the first time the privileges of freemen was certainly an imposing and a solemn sight, *calculated to excite impressions of wonder and stir up recollections of the great consequences of the moment*'.[9] The sheer size and spectacle of the occasion clearly made Butterworth feel that he was not simply watching history in the making, but actively taking part. The distinction between participants and spectators was a flimsy one – all took part in the performance both visually and vocally.

If all were actors in this dramatisation of history, then by regularly repeating such performances they generated a sense of historical continuity, linking past events and generations with those of the present, and even anticipating those of the future. Yet it was not just the form of ceremonial events that were repeatedly re-used, but the iconography itself. Again, we have seen how town halls, ceremonial dress, and the other insignia of public office were used year in and year out during official political ceremonies. Similarly banners, colours and other icons were often passed from one generation to another within and between popular political movements. Thus, at a Reform League meeting in London Fields during 1866, pride of place was given to a green banner with a red border and the inscription 'We require justice before charity; the People's Charter, and no surrender.' This banner, which had originally belonged to Tower Hamlets' National Charter Association, but was by then in the possession of the Silk Weavers Association, was clearly evocative to the huge audience at London Fields as 'when the banner was shaken out in the evening breeze, loud cheers burst from the people'.[10] The historical lineage of the struggle for parliamentary reform within Tower Hamlets, and the role of the Silk Weaver's Association in that struggle, was immediately made manifest. The remarkable history of Skelmanthorpe's 'Flag of Freedom' further illustrates this sense of continuity, as well as the flexibility of visual icons like banners. Originally produced by Skelmanthorpe's reformers during 1819 in response to the Peterloo Massacre, the banner was buried and hidden from the local constable to be re-used at reform meetings in 1832, 1839, and 1884, not to mention the celebrations at the end of the Crimean and American civil wars, as well as the opening ceremonies of both the Anglican parish church and Wesleyan chapel.[11] As this is the only surviving early nineteenth-century political banner for which we have a history, we must assume that the multiplicity of uses in its long and varied past was not untypical.

Just as the same banner could be used in different ways to inform various historical moments, so too could old banners be adapted and used for different purposes. At a public meeting in Lees on the rejection of the reform bill during May 1832 'a banner carried in the Lees Coronation Procession was exhibited, but not decorated with the words "God Save The Patriot King" which it formerly bore, but inscribed "God Save Our Patriot People"'.[12] The alteration of this banner reflected not just popular disillusionment with the new king, but the way in which such visual media allowed the past to be literally re-invented. Like the popular memory they represented such visual iconography was flexible and utilitarian, allowing a malleable use of the past in which the past was harnessed to the struggles of the present. As we shall see, this elasticity of the visual past contrasted with the increasingly sequential and teleological printed histories that emerged during the mid-nineteenth century. Visual uses of the past were, however, by no means immediately superseded by these new static printed versions, as there remained considerable symbiosis between the different visual, oral, and printed modes of constructing and transmitting the past. Orators frequently alluded to the iconography they saw before them at meetings, and this was in turn reported by the press and related to a possibly quite different audience.[13] None the less, visual (and oral) media did allow a sense of agency in the creation of histories which print increasingly denied.

Clearly the production of this media of visual iconography is central to any discussion of the power they afforded individuals within the popular political audience. Unlike their printed counterparts visual texts were not the result of a single author. Instead they were collectively produced by a complex web of organisers, designers, sponsors, users, and those to whom the ceremony, event or icon was supposed to represent. We have already seen how, although the nomination at Oldham in 1832 was organised for official purposes by the returning officer, those who were supposed to be an audience helped write the event. Butterworth recalled how 'long previous to the time *the lower classes had been busily engaged in preparing and making flags* to do suitable honour to the popular candidates'.[14] Everyone was reputed to have sported the favours and colours of their candidate while others went to greater lengths, like the 'old man of 84 riding an ass and bearing a radical flag inscribed "Primrose Bank", and a female fully equipped in the proper colours'. No political event was complete without eccentric displays of dressed dogs, painted faces, and all sorts of special attire. Yet individuals were also organised into groups by party activists and officials. Thus the members of Chadderton, Royton, Crompton, and Oldham Political Unions marched in procession from their respective townships to the hustings 'with twenty one elegant flags...innumerable bows and favours of the popular colours and three bands of music', while the officially organised group of special constables, complete with white wands, kept watch over them. In short then, the visual text of this event was written by many different individuals, groups, activists, and officials.

Perhaps what is most striking is the inventiveness with which familiar and accessible materials were used by individuals to construct their own visual icons. At the public entry of Fielden and Johnson into Oldham during the 1847 election, 'a large number of emblematic devices and various descriptions...were exhibited by a considerable procession of factory boys, who displayed specimens of the pod and raw material of the cotton plant'.[15] Similarly, while the popular political crowd in the port of Boston burnt readily available tar barrels, its counterpart in rural Devon dressed themselves, their houses, and their streets with flowers and other forms of vegetation as symbols of allegiance.[16] Just as Bradford's Chartists wore bits of green paper in their hats at elections instead of expensive ribbon or silk, and used tin cans to simulate regimental drums when drilling in 1848.[17] While the silk-weaving communities of Tower Hamlets and Coventry received much needed boosts to trade during elections, when huge quantities of silk ribbons were sold cheaply as party favours.[18] Individuals, including, it seems, even the poorest, were able to make their own icons with materials at hand – they could literally make their own visual politics.

Unsurprisingly this made both local and national officials distinctly uncomfortable, for they at least felt that these forms of visual iconography represented an autonomous popular politics. Such fears reached fever pitch during elections, when reporters, officials, and activists alike all used the prevalence of colours, banners, and other icons as a barometer of the level of conflict within the community.[19] Consequently, when officials feared a difficult and divisive contest, visual icons were banned so that 'party spleen had no index to affix its wrath'.[20] Such was the paranoia that visual iconography aggravated, even created, divisions which disrupted the delicate social and political equilibrium of both the town and nation, that legislation was passed to outlaw their use. This had long been on the official agenda, as Edward Thompson discovered an undated draft of a 'heads of bill' among Walpole's papers which was designed to prevent 'Evil minded and disorderly person...[assembling]...in a riotous and tumultuous manner' during elections, by prohibiting the use of 'any sort of Flags, Standards, Colours or Ensigns'.[21] Significantly, the bill was thought to be too controversial, 'beyond the limits of the possible' in Thompson's words. By 1827, when the Election Expenses Regulation Act banned the distribution and use of 'any Cockades, Ribbon, or other Marks of Distinction' for 6 months either side of an election, there were no such official reservations.[22] The statutes of this Act were reaffirmed by both the Corrupt Practices Acts of 1853 and 1883. Such a concerted legislative assault clearly reflected an official attempt to discipline popular politics by creating a restrictive definition of the political subject which prevented the use of these enabling visual modes of political expression. Significantly, the legislation had little effect. There seems to have been only one case of prosecution in all the constituencies, a young teenage girl sporting the radical colours during Boston's riotous 1831 election. No doubt it was an especially onerous offence for a young woman who should have been at home to be publicly active on the streets. Despite this vindictive prosecution, such forms of visual iconography continued to be used at elections – they were just too deeply engrained in English popular political culture. As Hudson Gurney had warned during the debate on the 1827 Bill, 'they could not break English custom, do what they would'.[23] This was not mere hyperbole, the materials and repertoire of many visual modes of communication drew not only on a long popular political tradition, but, as we shall see in chapter 6, on the religious, military, and folk beliefs and practices of popular culture more widely.

However, as the organisation of politics became increasingly formalised during the 1830s and 1840s, so the production, materials, and designs of visual iconography became more sophisticated, elaborate, and expensive. Although there is little detailed evidence on these points, it appears that the production of makeshift placards, banners, and favours by individuals and families for particular events was increasingly supplemented by the commissioning of more durable and permanent banners by formal organisations like factories, trade unions, and local political associations.[24] Silk replaced calico, sewn letters gave way to paint, words to elaborate images, supporting poles to ornate flagstaffs with guide ropes. Although this use of stronger but lighter materials enabled ever larger banners to be made, it also made them more expensive, beyond the reach of many. The commissioning of such banners came to represent an organisation's coming of age, a symbol of their popularity, permanence, and financial strength. Thus, in 1832 'a splendid new silk banner of the National Union, with the Union Jack in the corner, and appropriate mottoes and emblems...excited much attention' when displayed to Boston's newly formed Political Union.[25] No wonder the Hoxton branch of the Reform League were so keen to raise funds 'for the purchase of a banner for the branch' by holding a series of concerts.[26]

The production of these more elaborate banners was confined largely to the specialist. It is, for instance, clear from the accounts of Ebrington's election campaigns at Devon between 1816 and 1820, that the production of visual iconography was entrusted to a small group of men.[27] A William Presswell was paid for providing placard poles in 1816, while John Presswell (presumably William's son) was credited for printing handbills in 1818 and as a 'maker of standards' during the 1820 election. William Noseworthy designed and made Ebrington's triumphal car at both the 1816 and 1820 contests, as well as registering as 'a maker of standards' in 1820, just as Samuel Davy was listed as a 'decorator of placard poles' at both the 1816 and 1820 elections. However, the amounts these figures were paid (Noseworthy received the highest payment of all, £5 in 1820) makes it unlikely that they made a living by these means, particularly as their names are noticeably absent from the expenses of the other candidates. It would seem likely however that they earned their living in associated fields, either as printers, drapers, or sign-writers. Certainly as banners became larger and more ornate their design and production became monopolised by professionals and local political leaders. Such was clearly the case with the decorations for the 'Grand Conservative Banquet' in Boston's Corn Exchange in 1866, which were designed by the local Conservative party secretary and agent Mr Bartol Storr.[28] This account is reinforced by John Gorman who has argued that the banner-making firms of Tutills and Toyes monopolised the production of trade union banners from the mid-1830s.[29] Increasingly, both the design and production of visual iconography were taken out of the hands of the people they sought to represent.

This trend was not as clear-cut as it initially appears. As Huw Beynon and Terry Austin have reported, the designs of the larger more ornate banners were often the subject of collective discussion, as 'the banner and motif were seen to represent the lodge and the village. Great care was taken over the choice of image and the words and phrases used. These issues were the matter of debate, and disagreements were settled by votes at lodge meetings'.[30] Banners were deliberately designed to represent and unite, as well as to create, constituencies of support. This much was recognised in a letter from G. Staley Mosse to the Reform League secretary, George Howells, proposing a new banner for the Reform League. 'Standards, banners or colours have ever had a powerful influence on the human mind. All nations, all races, all great and united masses of people, have adopted them as *symbols of their unity* ... If it is an original movement, it ought to select a Banner distinct from every other, *and the Banner ought, to the minds of all those that are under it, to express the meaning of the movement and the causes of their unity*. If it does not do this, the Banner is without meaning.'[31] Here we are at the heart of the matter, banners both had to symbolise the unity of the group, while simultaneously expressing difference from other groups. If the banner did not have resonance with those it was supposed to represent it was 'without meaning'. The relationship between banner, designer, and its constituency was therefore an intricate and delicate one.

Consequently we should not assume that the meaning of every banner or icon was clear and stable. Rather they were invariably ambiguous and diffuse. As Epstein's analysis of the meanings of the 'Cap of Liberty' in nineteenth-century Lancashire has convincingly shown, visual icons often condensed many different ideas and associations, as individuals and groups appropriated them in contrasting ways endowing them with entirely different meanings.[32] The accent was on the individual's reception and use of them, unlike a printed text the reader or actor could change both the content and form of visual media. For instance, during the 1830s, meetings of Boston's Blue Club were traditionally opened by sharing a drink from the Blue Cup presented to the 'Independent' W. A. Maddocks to commemorate his election in 1806. However, by the late 1830s the 'Blues' were increasingly divided between those who supported temperance and those who did not. At one meeting in 1837 the *Boston Herald* reported that temperate Blues refused to share 'the enlivening beverage', preferring instead to pledge themselves verbally 'to support the cause of "Wilks and Liberty".[33] Yet this propensity of visual media to generate tension and differences among the like-minded was nothing compared to the fierce conflicts they provoked between rival groups. In this context visual media were supposed to represent differences and the necessity of taking sides in fighting the good fight. The very word 'standard' echoed military language, and certainly the military analogy was frequently used, as when Tower Hamlets' radical MP George Thompson, 'exhorted the Boston

Liberals... to keep their armour clean and their banners unfurled'.[34] As standards these visual icons were frequently attacked by rivals, as if destroying a flag would destroy the resolve of their opponents. It was then not surprising that at Peterloo the cavalry were instructed to 'Have at their flags!' while for Samuel Bamford, on the receiving end of this attack, 'the preservation of our colours... was a point of honour, worth any sacrifice'.[35] Yet, with a few infamous exceptions like Peterloo, the victims of such attacks were the flags and banners themselves, or the houses and committee rooms of the hated enemy. People were often threatened, but rarely hurt. The intensity of feeling obviously created by the use of visual iconography suggests that, despite their multivocality and ambiguity, they still generated certain set associations. After all it was the icons which were attacked, not those who used them and gave them meaning.

It was no doubt this recognition, together with their failure to prevent violent attacks on individuals and groups with rival colours, which prompted parliament to outlaw the use of these forms of iconography. Yet there was also more to it than that, for these forms of visual politics were also used to reconstitute the public political sphere. While Mary Ryan is correct to stress the collective dimension in the production of rites and symbols in her analysis of the American parade, she is surely mistaken to argue that they were restricted by the 'social constraints and political possibilities of their time'.[36] Rather, as we have already seen in chapter 2, ceremonies and symbols were used to redefine the public political nation and its agenda. Although they could be used to propagate restrictive definitions of the public political sphere, I have argued that the difficulty of preserving distinctions between audience, actors, and producers within the visual public performance meant that it was more likely for visual politics to expand the political arena rather than reduce it. It is worth re-emphasising that most of those parading the streets, waving flags, gathering in crowds to hear speeches, were disenfranchised men and women. As Benjamin Grime recognised during Oldham's first election, such actions represented a visual enactment of their right to be included within the constitution.

Gangs of youths were daily parading the streets with favours in their caps, on which were inscribed 'Vote for Cobbett and Fielden', and waving small flags in the air bearing the inscription 'Cobbett and Fielden forever; Bright and Burge never'. Whenever a meeting was held to forward the cause of the working man's candidates processions were formed, headed by bands of music, flags and banners, with appropriate mottoes, flying in the breeze. These demonstrations...favourably impressed the electors, and in a large measure served as the substitute for a vote to the unenfranchised.[37]

The presence of women alongside their disenfranchised male counterparts at political events, together with their role in commissioning, producing, and presenting banners, flags, and other visual icons was much more significant than historians have previously allowed. They were not used just as morale-boosting crowd fodder or seamstresses by men. Rather they testified to an assertion of a distinct female presence, one which was also not afraid to celebrate its skills. As the designers and makers of these home-made banners and flags they were able to express their right to be included within the exclusively male political culture of nineteenth-century England in a way not as easily achieved through either printed or oral media, in whose production they were largely excluded. However, from the 1830s as political organisations became more formalised, it was increasingly unlikely that women would be allowed to raise money for banners they were either making themselves or commissioning, as they had done in Carlisle during 1819.[38] We can safely assume that men took control of the production of banners once they had been liberated by professional banner-makers from the imperatives of sewing and painting. Women were more likely to be used as allegorical symbols upon banners, than to produce and use banners themselves.[39]

Visual media were more than just the ephemeral clothes with which the popular political crowd dressed itself. Their popular uses and official attempts to restrict them went to the very heart of the debate about citizenship and the struggle to define the public political sphere. As each generation discovers and uses new visual strategies for exercising and contesting political power, it is at least arguable that visual modes of communication remained central to English political culture after 1867. Such continuities should not obscure changes in the dynamics of visual political communication, as was the case from the 1830s when those visual media produced and used by individuals themselves were increasingly eclipsed by more formal and expensive media produced by professionals, organisations, and their activists. As we shall see in chapter 6, this trend was accentuated by the marked decline of 'traditional' visual modes of communication, such as burning effigies and illuminations.

THE POLITICS OF THE SPOKEN WORD

The politics of the spoken word, like that of sight, has often been neglected by political historians. This is somewhat surprising considering that political life was punctuated with innumerable speeches, heckles, ballads, songs, not to mention the incessant waves of rumour and counter-rumour by word of mouth. Although these forms of oral communication were closely related to aural media – bells, guns, and crucially music (after all a parade was not a parade without a band blasting out 'popular airs') – I have left their analyses to other historians.[40] The persistent presence of both word and noise suggests the centrality of an oral tradition within nineteenth-century English political culture. This is not to imply that this oral tradition was, or ever had been, hermetically sealed, free of the centuries-old influences of the visual image or the written and printed word.[41] However, I shall argue that despite this interrelationship oral media endowed individuals in the popular political audience with far greater powers to shape and create their own appeals than their printed counterparts.

Perhaps the most important political uses of the spoken word were the speeches that peppered the political life of every locality. They were delivered from any available platform, at all times of the day and night, whenever or wherever an audience could be found. And, as Thomas Carlyle lamented, found they certainly were. According to O'Gorman, Brougham reputedly made no less than 160 speeches during the Liverpool election of 1812.[42] People would flock to hear their heroes speak for half an hour or three and a half hours. To attract hundreds, and often even thousands, of people in this way and hold their attention for several hours when many of them could not hear a word, required more than a written speech read aloud. Like visual media, the power of oratory lay partly in the theatricality of its performance. The speaker was always elevated on a stage of some sort (a hustings, waggon, balcony or table), surrounded by props (colours, banners, clothes etc.) and usually an animated supporting cast (fellow leaders and activists on the platform) who would smile, laugh, talk to each other, acknowledge people in the crowd, put down or encourage hecklers, goading the speaker on with well-timed applause or a 'hear, hear'.[43] The successful orator would also provide a play-act himself: moving around, making gestures with his arms and legs and changing his facial expression as the mood of his speech dictated.

Although they were seldom reported in the press, these were not trivial details. Hence the inestimable value of Palmer Newbould's detailed account of the oratory of Manchester's veteran Chartist, William Chadwick, during the 1890s. Chadwick's oratory was exceptional for the 1890s, as Palmer Newbould recognised 'his Gamaliels had been Feargus O'Connor, Henry Vincent, and others of a school of oratory *now extinct*'.[44] During this period however, surprisingly many local and national political leaders possessed oratorical skills like Chadwick's. In many ways this was the golden age of political oratory.

In the early 1890s, Chadwick (then over 80 years of age) embarked on a campaign tour of Staffordshire and Monmouthshire on behalf of the Liberals. Like many others, he slept, ate, and travelled in a campaign van which also served as a platform from which to deliver speeches, Before each performance (which usually occurred at night after people had returned from work) 'two large carriage lamps, with wicks carefully trimmed, were lit, and fixed on each side of the platform facing one another. These lamps threw a powerful light on the orator, enabling him to read notes or newspaper cuttings, but threw hardly any light on the audience' (see Plate 27). Such skilful use of the stage and lighting was not unfamiliar to Chadwick; after his release from prison in 1848, he had both run a theatre and worked as an actor-cum-mesmerist, before marrying an actress and touring the country as a 'professional entertainer'. Certainly a sense of theatre pervaded Chadwick's oratory. Palmer Newbould recalled that he

knew the use of stage 'properties.' If he could have retained them, I believe he would have exhibited nightly the handcuffs and leg-irons which had been his portion in Kirkdale Gaol in that terrible year 1848. As it was he had to be content with lighter 'properties'... [like]... a model of the famous cat-o'-nine-tails. In several of the constituencies he visited the sitting member had voted against the abolition of flogging in the army. Chadwick would reconstruct the whole scene. He would erect the iron triangle, bind to it – in imagination – a son of the people – (which of them had not a brother or a son or a friend in the army which had made Britain great?) – and then fetch, like a conjuror a rabbit, the awful instrument as from nowhere, and whirling it in the air bring it down with frightful vehemence upon the imagined culprit.

The use of such visual props was an essential part of Chadwick's melodramatic style, and it reminds us that oratory is best understood

27   The last Chartist: William Chadwick speaking from a Liberal van, 1892 (from
T. Palmer Newbould: *Pages from a Life of Strife*)

as a performance in which sight, spoken word, and even print were combined.

This element of theatrical performance highlighted the distinction between the orator and his audience. Palmer Newbould makes much of the almost hypnotic qualities of Chadwick's oratory – the way in which he could mesmerise an audience with his 'wonderful eyes' and 'beautiful words'. While I would not want to deny the enormous emotional powers generated by good oratory, this sense of an orator performing to a passive audience can be misleading. To capture the attention of an audience entailed drawing them into another imaginative world in which they became part of the performance, as though they were not just passively hearing it, but actively living it. Melodrama was an ideal vehicle for this. Listen to this report of Chadwick's speech at a temperance meeting in Ipswich. He

rose to speak, and by a studied pause had the audience waiting upon his first word, he suddenly rent the air with an awful cry of 'Fire! Fire!! Fire!!!' Those in the body of the hall looked amazedly round and up to the gallery, but there was no sign of flame nor smoke there. Having thus captured the attention of his audience, Chadwick went on to explain: 'In the month of

January, 1873, those awful words rang out on the stillness of the night.' And he went on to depict the plight of those besieged by fire and in peril of their lives with hardly an outlet of escape. But there *was* an outlet. And there was an outlet – with God's help – to those besieged by the demon of drink.

This use of melodrama sucked the audience into a world both fantastic and real, distant and immediate, in which anything could happen as good struggled against evil; the choice lay between the hell-fires of damnation and the sweet smell of salvation. Chadwick portrayed himself as a victim of these great moral forces and flattered the audience by endowing them with the power to absolve or condemn him. His battle was their battle, his concerns their concerns. Such melodramatic conventions then endowed individuals both with a sense of agency and desire, it made the powerless powerful.[45]

Melodrama was not the only way of drawing an audience into the speech. Each orator was renowned for his own style, some ironic, some romantic, some comic, and some tragic. The Tory candidate at the South Devon election of 1837, Bulteel, was known for his comedy, invariably concluding 'with one of those playful touches of fancy, for which he is so celebrated in electioneering tactics, and which come home to the hearts of the Yeomanry and their fair partners, with so much relish'.[46] Audiences demanded to be entertained as well as exhorted to 'do their duty'. The popularity of the Chartist orator Henry Vincent also reputedly owed much to the comedy which infused his speeches. Certainly his performance at the dinner to celebrate the return of George Thompson as MP for Tower Hamlets in 1847 went down very well, thanks largely to 'an admirable imitation of an aristocrat Whig on the hustings. His mimicry was true to nature, and irresistibly droll; it created bursts of merriment'.[47] Audiences liked to feel included by sharing jokes, and seemingly encouraged the orator to pick up on heckles, comment on banners and, best of all, crack jokes at their own expense. Invariably the most popular orators were those best endowed with the witty wisecrack or disarming riposte. Audiences liked to be given as good as they gave.[48] Henry Ellis, prospective candidate for Boston in 1847, understood this well. 'To Boston, he had looked, as to his "first love", and up to this time he had actively endeavoured to ascertain their sentiments, (A voice: "Stick to it"). A friend required him to "stick to it"; and no doubt he did so with the hearty feelings of an Englishmen; but he must have something to stick to; let them show him the sticking place, and he would put on the plaster (laughter).'[49]

Yet, Ellis' comic aside also reveals the importance of the audience's role in showing the orator 'the sticking place'. It was they who helped the orator to select and shape his narrative. Most orators, including the most talented, had a limited number of narratives and genres at their disposal, although they were used to discuss all manner of issues. I shall discuss the content of these narratives in chapter 8. My concern here is with the forms and genres within which these were told, and what these in turn tell us about the relationship between the orator and his audience. The skills of an orator lay in allowing the audience to lead the speech in certain directions while keeping it within the parameters of his narrative. According to Hamer, Gladstone was masterful at this, placing 'more and more emphasis on those parts of his utterances which drew applause and popular acclaim and less and less on those which did not'.[50] This was not, however, an easy skill to acquire, and so when James Heald first stood for election at Oldham, the ex-radical Tory activist W. H. Mellor was appointed as his minder, to teach him the familiar narratives of his constituency. When Heald addressed an audience of 15,000 outside the town hall, Mellor was dutifully at his side, helping him strike and then orchestrate the popular chords.

His sympathies had ever been with the operative class; his origin was from their ranks, and he was not ashamed to own it [Mr Mellor: 'That's the sort, that's the stuff'] ... it was all very well for them to talk who were electors and persons of property, who had the influence with the government, but who was to take care of the unprotected, the non-electors ['That's the stuff'] ... There was another question in which he had taken a great interest, the new poor law [From the Waggon: 'That's the sort; that's the stuff'].[51]

With Mellor's guidance Heald hit the right notes, extolling the familiar themes of a virtuous people locked in an epic struggle against an evil but powerful foe, led by a leader who had risen from their ranks and yet shunned his new social position for their cause. As we shall see in chapters 7 and 8, these were well-worn and well-loved narratives assured a good reception. Audiences did not want to have to painstakingly follow the speech, straining to hear, and struggling to understand, instead, they demanded old narratives with the same plot, the same set of characters, and the same motifs, so that they could appreciate any changes of emphases within them.[52] Orators may then have delivered the speech, but its direction and tone was shaped by the dialogue between audience and orator. As Jan Vansina has argued, the orator 'tries to frighten, delight, worry, and put them [the audience] on tenderhooks, in turn and skilfully builds on the passages which move the audience most, expanding the exciting parts and condensing or transforming the ones where the attention of the audience lags'.[53]

This delicate relationship between audience and orator is exemplified by William Chadwick's speech in an 'out of the way North Staffordshire village'. I have quoted this passage at length in Appendix 2 because it shows the way in which the relationship between audience and orator creates the momentum of oral performances. The orator first tests the audience with a sensational start, and then gauges from their reaction which narrative to deploy, quickly changing tacks if they proved ineffective. We have already seen how Chadwick's oratory evoked a melodramatic world of moral absolutes, but his speech in North Staffordshire reveals the emotional pull of these oppositions. As Kenneth Burke has argued, the appeal of this form of argument is irresistible as once

you grasp the trend of the form, it invites participation regardless of the subject matter. Formally, you will find yourself swinging along with the succession of antithesis, even though you may not agree with the proposition that is being presented in this form. Thus you are drawn to the form, not in your capacity as a partisan, but because of some 'universal' appeal in it. And this attitude of assent may then be transferred to the matter which happens to be associated with the form.[54]

Max Atkinson has reached a similar conclusion in his analysis of contemporary political rhetoric, arguing that the use of oppositions is the singularly most effective way to extract applause from an audience, irrespective of the content of the appeal.[55] Yet he also identifies the appeal of the rhythmic qualities of oratory and the use of repetition and intonation. Again, this use of repetition, especially the deployment of three similar phrases (presumably with gradually rising intonation) heightened the anticipation of the audience's applause while simultaneously signalling to them the correct moment to applaud. Chadwick clearly had the measure of these techniques, as is demonstrated by the passages 'The Tories taxed your windows... They taxed your newspapers... They taxed your soap...' and 'I have always been on the side of the people – always on the side of the poor man – always for the weak against the strong – always for the poor against the rich.' However, the most skilful orators did not wait for applause, rather they talked through or over it, thereby increasing both the audience's desperation to clap and their sense of active involvement in the performance as they search for a suitable moment to unleash their approval. Such a technique also suggests that the orator neither expected nor deserved applause, a false modesty that in turn implied that the message was more important than his gratification.[56] Ultimately, however, Atkinson's portrayal of the charismatic and emotional pulls of oratory as simply the product of technical skills which manipulate the audience is misleading. Although this might well be the case for the highly regulated audiences of late twentieth-century party-political conferences from which Atkinson's book was researched, it was far from the case in the nineteenth century.

During this period, at least at those meetings which were not ticketed, audiences were able to wield considerable power, if only because they could always threaten to shout the speaker down. Music, heckles, and any form of noise were used to upset the rhythm of unpopular speeches and to prevent them being heard by reporters and audience alike. At the declaration of the Oldham election of 1865 both sets of supporters endeavoured to outdo each other.

When Mr. Platt began to speak an effort was made to put him down, which was effectually drowned by the hearty plaudits of his supporters. As he proceeded his opponents finding that they were too weak to hoot and groan him down, resorted to the still more discordant plan of singing, and for nearly the whole of the time he addressed the meeting, this organized effort continued ... When Mr. Cobbett began to speak the compliment was returned with fearful interest, and very few could hear a word he said.[57]

Orators exposed to these tactics were peculiarly vulnerable to the power of the oral audience. In a sense the real contest here was between the different sets of supporters. The very public nature of these events in which oral media were used, and the sense of participation engendered by oratory, was conducive to the audience establishing its own powerful oral dynamic.

The public and collective nature of these events imposed pressure on the audience to demonstrate their allegiances orally, as any visitor to today's football terraces will testify. Often, at political meetings, as at elections, the rival groups would automatically separate them-selves, assembling on different spaces. Each group of supporters then exchanged chant and counter-chant, heckle and counter-heckle, push and counter-push. The radical supporters of Edmond Beales even managed to disrupt an indoor election rally for the 'Constitutional' candidate O. E. Coope at Tower Hamlets in 1868. When someone resembling Coope appeared on the platform all hell let loose as

someone in the gallery displayed an 'Edmond Beales' bill, at the same time calling for three cheers for that gentleman. The three cheers were given amidst the howls of the constitutionalists; and the Radicals retaliated by giving three groans for Coope – groans that would do honour to Pandemonium. Mr. Disraeli's name was received in the same spirit by the Radicals and the Conservatives in turn growled at the name of Gladstone to a terrific extent... Matters were not rendered any better by the distribution of a number of cards with Mr. Coope's address printed on them. They were sent spinning through the air, and at one period of the evening the air was literally filled with cards flying about.[58]

Coope was so fiercely heckled throughout his speech that the reporters were forced to leave their table and sit on the edge of the platform to hear. Each statement in Coope's speech was cheered by the Tories and booed by the Radicals, who, at regular intervals, displayed their 'Beales' bill, sending '"hurrahs" ringing through the hall... [which]...were taken up by the Conservatives for their candidate'. When a new Conservative banner was displayed on the platform the Tory cheers were countered by the singing of 'Rule Britannia' by the Radicals. Finally, as a resolution was moved supporting Coope's candidature 'a person in the gallery threw several eggs towards the platform, bespattering the speakers, the reporters, and others in proximity to the platform'. In a very real sense it was individuals and groups within the audience who controlled the performances on the platform.

These continual oral, physical and visual contests between two rival groups within an audience were commonplace at those meetings which were not ticketed. Vociferous audiences were like tornadoes, sucking in those on the edges, involving them in a drama with which they had to react.[59] The open-ended character of an audience's cheers and groans (such as hoooraaay, boooooo, and even applause) encouraged collective participation, with some supporters joining in where others left off, thereby sustaining the demonstration. The language with which reporters described these responses was significant, cheers 'rose', 'ringed', 'subsided', and 'faded'. Even 'bursts' of applause had no marked beginning and end. The open-ended

28   Charles Wood, Lewes' town-crier 1844–71, in full ceremonial dress (*The Sunday Times* Reeves Collection, and Sussex Archaeological Society)

nature of these oral utterances invited collective participation which, judging by the size of many oral audiences, was quickly accepted by the disenfranchised. Their oral contributions, whether individual or collective, spoke of their fight to an official political voice, and if denied this voice they would deny others' theirs by heckling, shouting, and singing. At unticketed meetings, oral forms of political communication were unable to distinguish electors and non-electors, and so provided a means of contesting exclusive definitions of the public political sphere. It was not just that orality inadvertently included the disenfranchised in its appeals, but that it enabled them considerable power in shaping those appeals. Consequently, as we shall see in chapter 6, political organisations began to use ticketing

29 Statue of 'Blind Joe', Oldham's town-crier *c.* 1820–1860 (Oldham Local Studies Library)

from the 1840s and 1850s to regulate the composition of their audiences, and thus to reduce the power of disenfranchised men and women to orally shape the course of events.

However problematic the term 'oral tradition' may be in failing to recognise the centuries-old fusion of oral, visual, and printed media, it does usefully characterise the rich vein of orality in nineteenth-century English political culture. The significance of oral modes of communication was not lost on local officials who continued to use town-criers for important ceremonial events, such as reading electoral writs and royal proclamations, well into the twentieth century (see Plate 28). These proclamations and writs, which used many of the mnemonic and dramatic formulas – metaphor, proverb, assonance, epithet, alliteration, and repetition – typical of so-called oral traditions, were clearly aimed at predominantly oral audiences.[60] In Oldham, the town-crier, Blind Joe, was so much part of civic culture that a statute was erected in his honour in 1865 (see Plate 29). This is not to argue that nineteenth-century England constituted a pre-literate oral culture, but that it could be categorised as a residual oral culture in which, although many were incapable of writing, they could read simple slogans on banners or in ballads. For these barely literate people orality remained their favoured mode of communication, despite their proximity to print.

This was illustrated by the popular political uses of ballads. It was not insignificant that of the five constituencies the ballad was most conspicuous as a form of political communication in industrialising Oldham. Benjamin Grime recalled how at Oldham they reflected

more than any ordinary epistle can do the sympathetic and party proclivities of the period... They were too expressive of the struggles and emotions that animated the body of the people during these periodical conflicts, and they enabled the great untaught to give vent to sarcasm and turbulent passions which ardour and zeal aroused within them. These rhymes were an easy way for the masses to express their sympathies and their antipathies. Reduced to verse in the native language of the locality, and adapted to some popular tune, the populace sang aloud or hummed their hopes and aspirations.[61]

These oral uses of ballads were central to the political dialogue of the town. Paradoxically, our record of their existence is as the printed versions which inundated poll books, local newspapers, and handbills. Although the means of their oral transmission remain largely lost to us, Henry Mayhew has provided a rare insight into the centrality of these forms of communication to London's labouring poor, estimating that in 1849 there were 250 ballad singers in London alone and approximately 750 nationwide, stalking 'the streets singing the songs they sell'.[62] To this must be added the running and standing patterers, long song sellers, play-bill sellers, glee singers, and street vocalists who all sold and performed their material orally (see Plate 30). Significantly, although Mayhew has documented all of these forms of oral activity on the streets of London's East End, I have found very little printed evidence of political ballads in Tower Hamlets. If this was typical of the level of oral activity below the printed uses of ballads, then it seems safe to assume that the other constituencies would also have been inundated with ballads.

Clearly ballads were part of the residual oral culture which still pervaded the life of the poor. They were sung collectively (even ballad singers sang in pairs) and publicly in pubs, on the streets, and at work. As with oratory, they owed much of their appeal to their uses of a melodramatic imagination. They were songs of struggle and desire, dressed up in instructive, amusing or scandalous conventions.

30   Henry Mayhew's 'Long-Song Seller' (National Museum of Labour History)

The scandalous element was often paramount. Leading local political leaders were nicknamed, abused, and ridiculed, as the ballad singers and patterers suggested to their audiences that their goods provided unique insights into the private lives of public figures. 'Alick i' th' Hop 'Ole' was typical in this respect (see Plate 31). It concerned Alex Taylor, the Oldham radical who defected to the Tories with John Morgan Cobbett during the late 1840s and was subsequently denounced as a 'turncoat' and traitor. The ballad invites participation ('O, an yo yerd the lattist news,/If not, ol tell yo if yo chuse;') and suggests a dialogue between performer and audience ('So neaw aw will conclude mi sung;' and 'So dunnot other smile or laff') while simultaneously hinting at illicit information and intimacies revealed ('A secret aw will tell to yo'). Underneath the self-deprecating exterior ('But ere aw close this bit o chaff') the ballad is instructive

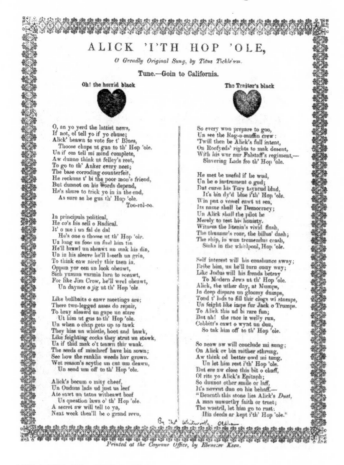

31 'Alick 'i'th Hop 'Ole', Oldham 1852 (Oldham Local Studies Library)

even moralistic in tone. The audience are warned not to follow the same deceitful, dishonourable path as Alick and, more significantly, reminded not to be taken in by the oratory of their leaders ('dunnot on his words depend' and 'when o chap gets up to tawk/ They hiss un whistle, hoot and bawk,/ Like fighting cocks they strut un stawk,/Us if thid mak o't teawn thir wauk.'). While the people are reminded of the pitfalls and dangers in their struggle for political emancipation so their leaders are reminded of the people's wrath if their trust is betrayed. The threat of popular revenge intimated by the mention of scythes, sinking ships, Judas, and 'Alick's Epitaph' proved prophetic. The following year Alex Taylor, beset by domestic problems and public unpopularity, cut his own throat. The shelf life of this popular ballad was cut unusually and tragically short.

Much of the power and appeal of these forms of oral media lay in the flexibility of their motifs, despite the persistence of remarkably similar genres and conventions. As with both ritual and oratory this persistent use of similar forms and genres reflected the audience's power over the performance. The performing ballad singer adapted his ballads to suit the tastes and requirements of his audiences. One ballad singer interviewed by Mayhew recounted how he had toured Cornwall for a year reciting different versions of the same 'cock' (false) love-letter ballad. The persistent use of similar genres and stylistic conventions reflected the performers' need to conform to the audiences' expectations. Often, within the space of days or weeks, the same ballad was used in different ways as rival groups sought to appropriate its success for their own purposes (see Appendix 3). Many political ballads were themselves adaptations of popular ballads like 'There's A Good Time Coming Boys', whose popularity in London during the 1840s facilitated its use in different forms at Oldham during the elections of 1852, 1859, and 1868. Similarly ballads were set to popular and well-known tunes which the ballad-singers 'picked up from street-bands, and sometimes from the cheap concerts, or from the gallery of the theatre', and later music halls. The ballad singers then 'went round the neighbourhood where these songs were being sung, because the airs being well known...eased the way for us'.[63] Certain tunes like 'See the Conquering Hero Comes' were endlessly recycled in an attempt to seek out and fulfil the demands of potential audiences.

However, one should not romantically overstate the power of the audience in the production and dissemination of ballads. While historians have tended to emphasise that the authors of these ballads were drawn from the ranks of the labouring poor this seems to over-simplify the position, especially in regard to purely political ballads.[64] This distinction between the commercial and political uses of ballads is critical, for the authors of the latter were often drawn from a much wider social constituency. They were usually local political activists and leaders like Boston's radical printers John Noble and Charles Barber, and Tory activist the Reverend Matthew Robinson, or Oldham's radicals William Knott (hat manufacturer and dealer), John Carrodus (barber), and Charles Pickering (cobbler). The 'New Loyal Constitutional Song' circulated during Devon's 1820 election was written by U. L. Radley, a surgeon and apothecary, while the pro-Ebrington ballad of 1816 'The Three Evergreens' was the creation of the Reverend J. W. Winclatt, Totnes' congregationalist minister. However, some writers clearly struggled to earn a living, such as the hand-loom weaver Joseph Lees, author of the hugely popular 'Jone O'Grinfilt' ballad, although he later became a schoolmaster. Similarly, in 1867 John Arnott, the by then impover-ished ex-Chartist leader, submitted a ballad to Edmond Beales, signing it 'A poor paralysed old Chartist'. It would then be wrong to caricature ballads as 'authentic' expressions of working-class political sentiment, for they obstinately refused to fit into such neat sociological categories. Like many visual media they were the products of complex mediations between authors, performers, and audiences of all social levels. Moreover, far from declining during this period, the political uses of ballads were still very much in evidence during the 1870s and even well into the twentieth century, albeit increasingly in printed forms.[65] Although print preserved many of the genres and conventions of ballads in their oral form, it redefined the relationship between author, text, and audience, however slowly and unevenly.

It has been argued that oral media of this period, much like their visual counterparts, afforded their audiences and participants considerable power in shaping the terms in which politics was articulated. This is not to argue that oral media could not be used in restrictive ways, but rather that generally their use facilitated more expansive and inclusive definitions of the political subject and the public political sphere. In the following section we shall see how the increasing use of print as a mode of political communication slowly began to eclipse the use of oral and visual media and, in the process, placed greater emphasis on the individual's private experience of politics.

POWER AND PRINT

Although the preceding two sections have endeavoured to establish the importance of previously much neglected oral and visual media, we must also recognise that although print had long been integral to English political culture its uses and influences rose rapidly during this period. From the 1830s print began to transform the public political sphere, changing the way in which people experienced and perceived politics, past and present. In what follows I have concentrated on two distinct, yet overlapping, forms of printed

32 The sight of print: commercial and political street literature at an Oldham
election, *c.* 1890s (Oldham Local Studies Library)

politics – namely the press and the 'street literature' that was
handbills, playbills, squibs, and ballads – beginning, sensibly
enough, with the latter first.[66]

The sheer volume and variety of street literature testified to its
central role within English political culture. Indeed, the ease and
extent with which it was used politically was remarkable. There is a
sense in which the popular genres and forms of street literature had
existed for generations and were part of the rightful inheritance of the
freeborn Englishman. Certainly it is hard to imagine nineteenth-
century politics without street literature. Amazingly, Frank
O'Gorman has reported that 'no fewer than 42,000 pieces of election

literature were circulated at the Carlisle by-election of 1816 while even at the 1812 aborted contest for Nottinghamshire county 500 election addresses were distributed in Nottingham and 2,000 in the county'.[67] Even at the unusually quiet Boston by-election of 1879, the billposter and general agent George Pinches accounted for half of the Conservative candidate's total bill-sticking budget for distributing 7,500 handbills. It is inconceivable that anyone did not experience this deluge of printed politics, for it was widely distributed and publicly displayed. As Henry Mayhew had made clear, political street literature was sold alongside its commercial counterparts (politics was after all good business) by 'running' and 'standing' patterers who used any device to sell their wares, 'either by means of a board with pictures daubed upon it, descriptive of the contents of what they sell, or else by gathering a crowd round them, and giving a lively or horrible description of the papers or books they are "working"'.[68] Here again the relationship between print, orality, and visuality was manifest. Indeed, handbills, squibs, and posters were displayed not only in the windows of print and book shops, but almost everywhere – on walls, rocks, street-lamps, doors, and even on moving objects like coaches (see Plate 32). Such public uses of print facilitated a collective experience which broke down the barriers between literate and illiterate, the former sharing their skills with the latter.

The visual appearance of street literature was of course central to its public and collective uses. So much is apparent from Benjamin Grime's description of the 'paper war' at Oldham's election in July 1852:

A few days before the election a large green poster appeared on the walls and hoardings, which contained the following sentence in good, bold type – 'Fox retains his brush! Why? Because neither Cobbett nor his friends have one word to say for themselves!!' The poster was immediately supplemented with a narrow slip of the same colour (green), on which was printed, 'But not the borough.' It will be seen that this was intended to be a continuation of the first portion of the poster just preceding the word 'Why' and it was accordingly posted across the originals through out the borough. The Foxites, not to be out-manoeuvred, returned to the charge with the following poster which was soon on the hoardings side by side with the foregoing. 'Mr. Fox does not retain the borough, the borough retains Mr. Fox! No dictation!!'[69]

33   Fox defeats the flighty Heald, 1852 (Oldham Local Studies Library)

Coloured posters on handbills were still at this stage rare outside the
metropolis, so the 'good, bold type' of this green poster would have
been visually very striking, just as the simple slogans and puns on
Fox's name made the poster's use of print accessible to many of the
semi-literate (see, for instance, Plate 33). However, such public and
visual uses of print were not simply eye-catching. There was a sense
in which the visual layout of street literature reflected its use of genre,
thereby creating an immediate contract of expectation with its
reader. As is evident from Plates 34–38 street literature derived much

34 'Oldham Races, 1847' (Oldham Local Studies Library)

35   'South Devon Election' horse race, 1868 (Devon Record Office)

of its popularity from its use of popular genres, imitating the conventions and forms of playbills, ballads, conversations, and popular sports like horse-racing. Politics was made at once accessible, concrete, and familiar. The visual appearance of these genres sought out an audience by promising to fulfil the expectations associated with the genre. However, despite the ability of individuals to read texts in different ways, the contract between a reader and a printed text was to some extent fixed, the reader was unable to alter the content, form or conventions of the genre in the way they could with visual and oral texts. Unlike print, there was, as we have seen, a sense in which the audience were not just receivers, but active producers of these more flexible oral and visual texts.

There was a similarly complex relationship between orality and print. Although print could undermine the uses of orality, it could also serve to strengthen and underpin them. Fast and cheap to produce and distribute, posters and handbills were perfect to advertise political meetings, especially in disparate areas like Tower Hamlets. For instance, at St Leonard's parish, a vestry meeting to address Queen Caroline was called at 'short notice' by the

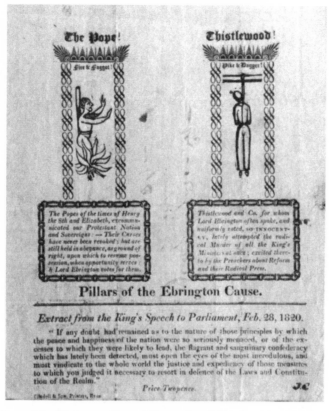

36 'Pillars of the Ebrington Cause,' Devon handbill, 1820 (Lady Acland and
Devon Record Office)

churchwarden, yet by quickly distributing 250 handbills announcing
the meeting he ensured a good turnout.[70] Similarly, a 'monster
placard' entitled 'SHALL LABOUR BE REPRESENTED?' was used to
announce an election rally for William Newton during the Tower
Hamlets election of 1852, a call 'responded to be at least five
thousand persons'.[71] Indeed, such was the effectiveness of these
posters and placards that they became legitimate targets for rival
groups to despoil and tear down.[72] If printed street literature could
generate audiences for oral and visual political meetings in this way,
so too could the press, which not only advertised such meetings, but
also reported them to often quite different audiences. Print
was often used to combat the problems of aurality at these mass
meetings, as at the huge torchlight meeting of the Reform League in

73.]THEATRICALS EXTRAORDINARY!

PINK OLD TOWN HALL, BOSTON.

By Permission and under the Especial Patronage of the Worshipful the Pink Mayor, J. S. B——y, Esq., being for the Benefit and immediate aid of a fund established by Corporations Usurping Power to prevent the abolition of NEGRO SLAVERY.

On Wednesday Evening, July 28th, 1830, will be performed, Misery's Popular Play of

THE SLAVE;

OR THE INTOLERABLE WEST INDIAN NABOB!!!

This Play is universally acknowledged to be the master-piece of Dramatic Tyranny. The uncontrollable sway of Negro Slavery in the West Index, having excited the indignation of the Friends of Freedom and Humanity, and the British Nation at large, notwithstanding the most determined opposition of the *Slave Drivers*. An order was immediately issued by the Nabob and Governor, to *Banditti*, to murder Liberty; they accordingly laid in wait and found him; but to their great consternation, were unable to kill him; they succeeded in landing him hand and foot, and put him ashore on what they thought was a Desolate Island, but where he was so fortunate as to find a large number of TRUE BLUES. At this juncture, the Slaves began to rise by themselves against their oppressors, being determined to regain Liberty, or perish in the attempt. They succeeded in gaining the island, and brought him back in great triumph, seated in a gorgeous Triumphal Car, most splendidly decorated with Blue, (the Blue Sky) resounding with the deafening acclamations of the liberators of these TRUE BLUES, they have placed him upon a Rock of Blue Heart Stone, firmer than Adamant, from whence he will dispense the glorious Sun, to the remotest parts of the Globe.

DRAMATIS PERSONÆ.

A West Indian Nabob possessing large Plantation and renowned for the ill-treatment of his Slaves........ OLD MACULLOM.

A proud (late) M. P. for Boston, returned to our Parliament and hoping for another, to Vote in favour of everlasting NEGRO SLAVERY.. YOUNG MACULLUM.

Athensian Screw Jack, Governor of the West Indies.......... J. W——n, Esq.

Squib, a Poor Convict in search of a Vicarage........ REV. M——a, Esq.

A Poor Lieutenant on Half Pay.......... E. C——

{ Slave Drivers in the employ of } 1st Slave Driver..... W——n, Esq.
{ Young Maculum and Old Maculum } 2nd Slave Driver..... T. B——, Esq.
{ WHIPS in their hands .... } 3rd Slave Driver..... G. H——, Esq.

LIBERTY, an avowed enemy to Slavery.... JOHN WILKS, ESQ.

Friend to Liberty, by a great number of.... TRUE BLUES.

{ A Banditti of Ruffians, engaged in destroying Liberty }
{ headed by a WISE Man and his SON .... } BY PLUMPER PINKS.

‡EPILOGUE, END OF THE PLAY.

The Rev. M——w R——n will for this night only, appear in his Friend B——y's Foolscap, (which has been politely given up for the occasion,) to eat a roasted Tithe Pig, a Tithe Goose, a peck of Peas, a quartern Loaf, three dozen of Penny Pies, and drink two gallons of Pink Punch, in the short space of ten minutes.

A SONG BY J. B——y, in his favourite character of Cantwell, Called "Common Councilmen are Substitutes for Men, as a Mockery of Power."

BY PARTICULAR DESIRE,

A Scotch Reel, by T. W—l—r, T. S——, and C. J. F——r,

by IN PINK FETTERS.

This Performance will enrich the microscopic eye; behold the weight of their Chains, T. T—k—r, H. F— x—n, loudly suffered in large iron links on the Big Throne, in the Tune of the SLAVES' HORNPIPE, with a Screw Hammer in one hand and a Thumb Screw in the other.

To wind off will be added, in ONE ACT, the unpopular Farce of

Taking up Freedom !!!

The Public are doubtless perfectly acquainted with the Plot of this OLD FARCE, it having been so frequently played by this Company; as Young Men even cannot obtain their Freedom so easily, as those who vote for the Pinks, and try any of a trifling Desire, half of them they have to pay are returned on their promising one vote, or if they promise a Plumper, the whole (about 30s.) is given.

Perpetual Mayor, when this occasion sits with a Burnt Brewer in his hand, H. R——k, Esq.
Deputy Mayor, J. S. B——y, Esq. Five Lord in Council, J. R. R——k.

Aldermen Treasellorum, G. H——y, Esq.
Common Men as Guests ..... B——y, Councillor Caleb, S. B——,
Common Magistrate.... S. B——y, F. C——te, Esq.
Sewel..... F. C——te, Esq.

CHIEF, CAD, and CANDLE-SNUFFER to the Performers, J. C——ke A——d.

Leader of the Band, J. T——gs, P. B——r, who solicits the indulgence of the audience, as he will be OBLIGED TO SIT WITH HIS COAT TURNED.

The Manager respectfully informs the Public that the Farce of Taking Up Freedom will shortly be REPEATED, unless Justice overtake the Performers, and the Law inflict its punishment.

W——n B——ry will be allowed to Work the Screw, by Selling at a very low price, about 100 SOAPED ORANGES to the on lend.

N. B. The Manager respectfully announces that as YOUNG NICHOL descended more degraded he would afford to offer the Play Bills will be forever distributed by A Pearl's son, one of the "Gentlemen" not carries the Silver Mace before the Pink Mayor.

Doors opened at 8, and to begin at 9, after the Blue Parade.

Tickets and Places to be taken of the Members of the C—— n, or of the Gallery Doorkeeper, by G. Portjwell, Kitt, Pump Square, Captain of the "Beacon Smack." (Noble.)

37 'Theatricals Extraordinary!', Boston 1830 (*A Sketch of the Boston Election*, 1830, p. 11)

WANTED IMMEDIATELY,

Many Thousands, to pay off OLD SCORES *and* NEW ONES,

FOR WHICH PURPOSE,

AN AUCTION

WILL BE HELD OF ALL THAT

INN *famous Concern,*

SITUATE IN BAMPFYLDE-LANE, AT THE SIGN OF THE

GREAT CANN,

In the Parish of *Spreyton*, for SALE of the undermentioned

Live and Dead Stock;

LOT 1. All the Tithes of the United Kingdom.
2. All the Taxes Assessed and not Assessed.
3. All the Sinecures of Great Britain, Ireland, &c. except such as may be reserved for the Noble Proprietor's own family.
4. About Twenty Barren Wethers, Naked.
5. Ditto, ditto, Clad in Purple and Orange.
6. A remarkable fine Hog, of the North Devon breed.
7. One Dog Fox with a fine litter of Cubs; to be viewed in the neighbourhood of Eggesford.
8. A large Lot of White Hats on *dirty poles.*
9. One Black Bull Calf, with a Shovel Hat of the *Manaton breed.*
10. Four Thousand and Ninety Asses in full bray from *God knows where.*
11. Several Thousand Geese, late the property of T. Northmore.
12. One Boat upon wheels, built for a *Steam Engine*, with the Oars; in which any one may take a *Trip*, the *safety* of which cannot be insured.
13. The Crew of the above Steam Engine; consisting of
   One Lord *stripped.*
   One Old Poltimore Cock, *without spurs*, having *Chicken by various Hens*, and one half-bred.
   One Prize Agent, *just* and *generous.*
   One Ex-Postmaster from Teignmouth.
   One Giant with *nine heads.*
   One Esquire *flogged.*
   One Sheep-faced Banker.
   One Nondescript from *North brook.*
   One Goodamoor Badger.
   One Harberton *Parrott.*
   One Black Steer from Yorkshire.
   One *Dawlish Spaniel Puppy*—takes readily to a new Master—would be a great acquisition to any Nobleman in want of such an animal—answers to the name of *Georgy.*
   One greasy foraging Cap, a little injured by a *pell-mell* rabble.
   One Jew Pedler's Box, lately found on the Barnstaple road, containing a few tarnished cockades, and some rat-traps, and a Bond of reciprocal Accommodation.
   One old Tawstock Hunter—the mark out of his mouth, but not the colt's tooth.
   One Port-rat as large as life, very high coloured—the Master *Dubious*, supposed to be *Peter's.*
   One old Nag ruefully given to *tripping*—wants *Bishoping.* To be sold cheap.

For further Particulars apply at *Castle Hill, Poltimore, Teignmouth, Ninehead, Arlington* and *Fuidge.*

Refreshment on Table at Six o'clock, consisting of *Big Loaves* and *Ashburton Pop.*

N. B. No admittance to Persons *without Shoes*, as the Duty on *Leather* will be Sold in the above Lot of Taxes.

.•. *The whole to be Sold without reserve.*

FLINDELL, PRINTER, EXETER.

38 'An Auction': selling Devon politics, 1820 (Lady Acland and Devon Record Office)

Tower Hamlets where there were no less than 6 bands and 3 separate platforms, and over 2,000 printed copies of the resolutions were distributed so that those who could not hear knew what they were voting for. Of course, meetings like this were also used as testing grounds for speeches, which were then edited so that the popular parts were printed and distributed as handbills. In 1826, a prospective candidate for Lewes delivered a speech to the Pink and Strong Club which 'seemed to rivet the attention of his auditors, and the thundering plaudits that followed, made the very sashes of the house tremble. Notes of this fascinating speech were taken, and being *arranged* during the night, it was the next day printed, and circulated to the extent, of 1,000 copies'.[73]

The portrayal of politics as melodrama in street literature also encouraged the collaboration of printed and oral audiences. Within the genres we have already discussed politics was personalised, battles between individuals were used to symbolise wider and deeper political struggles. Then, as now, disapproving reporters sneered at the way in which the frivolous obsession with personalities obscured the 'real' issues. Commenting on Oldham's election of 1835 Butterworth felt it

would be dry and uninteresting and in other cases wasting paper in frivolous jests, to launch out into a detail of the squibs, reports, bills and posters flying about in the hot days of electioneering strife. Calumny refuted by calumny, falsehoods heaped upon falsehoods, inconsistencies pointed out by those who are next charged with possessing them, committee slandering committee, Townsmen, Friends of Liberty, Haters of Deception, &c., calling on the electors to choose the right man and if they find him, to do their duty, to raise their name, and all such productions to serve party views.[74]

This was to miss the point that these 'paper wars' were designed to shock, for the shocking encouraged people to talk about the offending items and exchange the illicit information. And shocking they were. Each handbill competed with its predecessor for attention and, consequently, little was left to the imagination. During the Mile End vestry election of 1868 the Tories issued a placard accusing the Liberal chairman of the Parochial Reform Association, of being so mean and crooked that he used short scales in his grocer's shop.[75] Similarly, during Boston's 1831 election, the town's reformers accused one of the authors of Tory squibs, the Reverend Matthew Robinson, of having to write in order to support his mistress and bastard child – a damaging charge for an Anglican minister.[76] This was not harmless fun, although it was undoubtedly entertaining. Such handbills were used to set the political agenda by putting one's opponent on the back-foot, as at the Oldham election of December 1852 when the Conservative candidate spent much of his time denying the accusation that he had been a constable at Peterloo.[77] Some, of course, endeavoured to gain the moral high ground by refusing to rise to the bait, although this was a high-risk strategy.[78]

In many ways, therefore, print and orality were symbiotic, generating audiences and subjects for each other which invariably dissolved distinctions between those included and those excluded from the official political nation. As David Vincent has recently argued, the often 'impenetrable local references enhanced the sense of common membership of a local political community in which divisions between voters and non-voters and between the competing factions were mediated by a shared partly literate, partly oral discourse'.[79] Certainly Nossiter's assertion that street literature was simply an instrument of corruption is a long way wide of the mark.[80] The only way it was used to challenge the law was to articulate a distinct popular political voice which contested official definitions of the public political sphere. Consequently, as with visual iconography, parliament made frequent attempts to regulate and discipline the uses of street literature. The Seditious Publications Acts of 1798 and 1819 not only banned the publication of 'seditious' materials, but ensured that every handbill specified the name of its printer, so that the author and publisher could be traced and prosecuted if it violated the law. However, despite the prosecution of many of the local radical printers and newsagents in the immediate aftermath of these acts, much of the street literature produced and sold, especially during elections, persisted in making their 'seditious' and 'libellous' claims anonymously or, more usually, accrediting them to the mythical 'The Printer's Devil'. As with official attempts to regulate visual media, this legislation was largely a failure. Despite an award of £10 to informers, prosecutions were rare, and when they did occur it was invariably the result of rivalry between different partisan printers.[81] The failure of these Acts was officially recognised when the Corrupt Practices Act of 1883 reinformed their clauses and increased the fine from £20 to £100. Although street literature persisted in rude good health after 1883, the Corrupt Practices Act may have proved the beginning of its demise, heralding as it did the professionalisation of popular politics by national party organisations.

Certainly, this body of legislation reflected not just the desires of a coercive state, but the changing moral climate within English political culture. The views of moral and political reformers and disapproving autodidacts slowly began to predominate, and these forms of printed media were increasingly deemed inappropriate to a political system which placed a premium on 'rational' debate between individuals.[82] The proliferation of the penny press during the 1850s was essential to this invention of a mythologised political process in which intellectually independent men (not women) made enlightened and autonomous political decisions in private. Indeed, as David Vincent has shown, the reductions and eventual repeal of the stamp duty in 1854 represented an official attempt to drive both the scandalous and politically disruptive pauper press and street literature out of existence by market forces, rather than by repressive legislation which could prove politically damaging.[83] These measures, together with a range of technological developments, facilitated the creation of popular Sunday newspapers like *Reynolds' News* which provided the familiar combination of politics and sensational entertainment to a much larger audience.[84] In many ways, as officials had hoped, it was a quite different audience, for this new penny press was used officially to promote the rational and disciplined use of literacy within the family and its private home. As the Chancellor of the Exchequer had said of the reduction of stamp duty in 1836, 'he would rather that the poor man should have the newspaper in his cottage than he should be sent to a public house to read it'.[85] The 'ambition now was to place as much distance as possible between the oral and the literature, and between one politically conscious working man and another. The long-established tradition, prevalent in polite society as well as amongst the lower orders, of multiple readers of single copies was to be replaced by one individual, or at least one family per paper'.[86] As Joan Landes has argued of post-revolutionary France, the 'new print culture was a major factor in contributing to the constitution of a way of life that featured the restricted family domain and focused attention on the interior landscape of the privatised individual subject. In this setting, divisions between public and private life were strengthened'.[87] Slowly but deliberately the public political sphere and its subjectivities were redefined in ever more restrictive ways, as the accent shifted away from the public and collective political uses of print to those centred upon the private uses of individual men.

The press had long played a central role in linking a predominantly oral popular political culture to an official one increasingly dominated by print. John Wilkes' popular uses of the press during the 1760s was replicated by early nineteenth-century radical journalists in the pauper press who found larger, predominantly oral, audiences which belittled their circulation figures as the collective and public uses of the press persisted well into the second half of the century.[88] Until the widespread use of the electric telegraph in the 1860s, provincial communities relied entirely on the national press for their news of important national events and, consequently, the arrival of the London papers developed into a significant event in its own right (see Plate 39). Thus in Boston during the passage of the Reform Bill through parliament in 1831 'large parties assembled at the Red Lion Inn and Peacock Inns...awaiting the arrival of the Perseverance Coach from London, to learn the result of the important measure brought forward by Ministers'.[89] Just as in 1854 the 'rumours of the victory at Sebastopol...were confirmed by the arrival at noon of the daily newspapers..."The Child is but father of the man", and children of larger growth, now gray haired and garrulous, crowd the newsroom, reminding each other of forty years ago when the news came of the great victory of Waterloo'.[90] Inhabitants of the town gathered together to hear, or even read with their own eyes, the news emanating from London, thereby reflecting not only communal uses of print, but also the identification of London as the centre of national information and power.

Such public and collective uses of print were also evident in the often stylised rite of communal readings. People clubbed together to hire, or buy, a paper which was then read aloud to them by a literate individual either outside or in pubs, clubs or coffee houses. Grime recalled how his father sent him to buy a copy of the *Northern Star* 'which was the joint property of his father and a few of the neighbours. The paper would then be read in some retired place, on the grass if in the summer, or over a "tot of whoam-brewed"'.[91] Similarly, Joseph Platt, Oldham's radical 'auctioneer and occasional orator', and proprietor of the beer shop 'The Bird in Hand', was 'in the habit of taking in a daily paper [and] many newspeople resorted to his house to read it, and after they had read what they liked they

39   The public uses of literacy: the arrival of the news (*Illustrated London News*,
28 November 1868)

generally talked upon politics.'[92] One is struck by the evident importance of collective discussion, as well as the influential role of the literate reader. Increasingly, the uses of print brought with it new relationships and hierarchies of power within the popular political audience. Again, this was apparent from a testimonial dinner at Oldham for Robert Nield in 1853, at which he was presented with a pair of silver spectacles 'as a mark of their respect and gratitude for his kindness in reading the newspapers to them weekly, and at the same time assisting them to a better understanding of the position of affairs in the East by his able explanations.'[93] In the printed culture of politics literate young men invariably replaced the traditional guardians of oral wisdom, women and old men, just as the orality of rural districts were eclipsed by the predominantly urban culture of print.[94] Print was not just transforming the public political sphere, it was reconstituting the balance of power within and between communities.

Aware of collective oral uses of the press, journalists sought to satisfy the needs and tastes of their audiences in both style and content. The radical press was particularly adept at this, blending entertainment, sensation, and politics with a personal tone and melodramatic style, techniques which quickly filtered through to the broadly 'liberal' provincial press.[95] Even when reports were not written in formulaic 'oral' styles, the use of verbatim reporting meant that very often their reports of speeches reproduced 'a kind of frozen rhetoric'.[96] Although, ultimately, the press would displace orality at the centre of nineteenth-century English political culture, it was a long, protracted, and uneven process, in which print had first to use the dynamics of orality before it could supersede them. Consequently, much has been made of the emergence of the qualitatively new provincial and national press which apparently proliferated following the repeal of the stamp duties in 1854.[97] However, the evidence from these five constituencies suggests that, quantitatively at least, such claims are somewhat exaggerated, as the process of expansion had begun earlier, during the 1830s. Certainly that decade witnessed an increasing number of weekly local and provincial papers serving Boston, Lewes, Tower Hamlets, and Devon.[98] In Plymouth and Exeter no less than 17 papers started before 1855, with only 6 new titles being established after 1854. Although the repeal of the stamp duties increased circulation by making papers more affordable, it is doubtful whether it created new or wider audiences, for, as we have seen, papers had been used collectively since the eighteenth century. What changed after 1854 was the manner of the press' reception, which was increasingly private and individual, rather than public and collective.

This failure to develop substantially new audiences was also reflected in the similarity of the style and character of the provincial press following 1854. Here again the roots of change had been evident since the 1830s. There had been, for instance, a strong attachment to a fiction of impartiality from the 1830s, despite the clear party-political loyalties of each paper. The town, or region was portrayed as possessing its own interests which transcended party politics. Consequently, the deliberations of the local courts, vestry meetings, council meetings, town meetings, social, religious, culture, and political bodies were all recorded in exhaustive detail. It was no coincidence that the motto of Oldham's Liberal *Oldham Chronicle* was *Sapere Aude* (wise is he who listens). Whatever their partisan allegiances, local and provincial papers articulated a select version of the local past and present that masqueraded as a pluralist one. Theirs was a world in which reason triumphed over superstition, the advance of industry was matched by the progress of self-help and religious bodies, and the representative political institutions of the parish, town and county went from strength to strength.

This whiggish picture was also evoked by the panoramic reports of local politics which suggested a public political sphere that was at once pluralistic, representative, and responsive. It was a mythology lent further credence by reports of council meetings which self-consciously aped the procedures of the mother of all parliaments at Westminster. The language and behaviour of the council debating chamber, like that of parliament, was endlessly exalted and favourably compared to the politics of the street corner. As Olivia Smith has shown, this use of language to create a dichotomy between high and low politics was nothing new, but, significantly, it continued to be an important means by which the official public political sphere was disciplined and regulated.[99] The Conservative *Boston Herald* pulled no punches when reporting a speech by the distinctly aristocratic Blue candidate, Sir James Duke. It was, they claimed, worthy of him and 'the cause he advocates, and of the followers by whom he was surrounded; of course he was vulgar, abusive, coarse and violent'.[100] Similarly, an editorial of the Tory *Oldham Standard* in 1867 lamented the fact that at a meeting for reform of the franchise the 'oratory was that of that rough, uncultured, bombastes furioso style which is almost peculiar to Oldham demagogic. Never surely elsewhere was the QUEEN's English so murdered, common sense so outraged, and conceit so rampant, as on this interesting occasion'.[101] The connection between language, behaviour, and power could hardly have been made more explicit. Local dialect and the oratory of the mass platform were not becoming to those who aspired to belong to the official political nation. Speeches spoken in dialect were only printed once transcribed back into 'Queen's English', although significantly heckles were left in dialect form. This ability of the press to associate power with 'standard' or 'Queens English' reflected the growing power of print over oral media. Political meetings that lasted for 2 or 3 hours were condensed into a few column inches, the colour and spectacle inevitably edited out.

The culture of print, then, increasingly structured public perceptions of politics, language, and memory. Unlike the popular, flexible, and formulaic oral and visual uses of the past and present, print imposed fixed, verbatim meanings. In short, print transformed the whole process in which politics and memory was created and transmitted, how information was stored and the criteria used for judging its accuracy.[102] Therefore the issue of who was able to use and produce print becomes central to our understanding of the transformation of the public political sphere. While access to printed media undoubtedly improved from the 1850s and 1860s, it remained considerably more restrictive than its oral and visual counterparts. What is striking about the political uses of print from the 1830s, evident in the burgeoning ranks of town and county histories, almanacs, directories, newspapers, and even poll books, is the small group of people responsible for their production. In most towns the production of print was monopolised by one or two individuals who passed their knowledge, skills, and resources down through their own family. The Butterworth family of Oldham is undoubtedly the most well documented of all these families, although I could have equally focused on the Besleys of Exeter, the Nobles and Bontofts of Boston, the Baxters of Lewes, and so on.[103]

James Butterworth (1771–1837) started the family concern at the beginning of the nineteenth century when, working as a weaver, he dabbled in writing ballads and poems in both dialect and standard grammar, occasionally using the pseudonyms Tim or Paul Bobbin. He quickly diversified, turning occasional schoolmaster, publisher,

40 Continuing the family's printed knowledge dynasty: Edwin Butterworth,
c. 1840s (Oldham Art Gallery)

and stationer before landing the very respectable job of Oldham's
postmaster. Throughout these various careers he wrote prodigiously,
producing histories of local institutions, characters, trades, and
towns, most notably his history of Oldham in 1817. His more famous
son, Edwin (1812–48), was nothing if not a chip off the old block (see
Plate 40). Occasionally working in association with his two brothers,
Edwin set up a news agency providing reports as the Oldham
correspondent for several local, regional, and national newspapers.
Freelance journalism, however, failed to pay the bills or satisfy his

imagination. Working as Edward Baine's assistant, he was largely responsible for writing *A History of Lancashire* (1836), before going on to produce histories of several local institutions, characters, and towns, including *The Oldham Almanac* (1840) and his *Historical Sketches of Oldham* (1856). A bachelor to the end, the Butterworth knowledge industry finished with Edwin's death in 1848, when friends in the local printing and publishing trades (including Samuel Bamford) erected a memorial to him. The near monopoly of local printed media by families like the Butterworths afforded them considerable power in the construction of popular political memory.

Most were only too keenly aware of their role as self-appointed guardians of local knowledge and political history. In the introduction to their poll book for the 1847 Boston election, John Noble and Charlotte Bontoft were clearly conscious of the historic task afforded to them by print: the 'interest of a contested election, however absorbing at the time it is in progress, is soon dissipated; and its annals are in general speedily forgotten. Still even these records are not infrequently important links in the general history of the country, and the "fragments" collected in pamphlets like the present acquire importance long after the actors in the scenes they describe have passed away from the stage of humanity.'[104] Despite the often keen partisan allegiances of their authors, poll books were almost always prefaced by a statement of their objectivity, just as they were anxious to show that the end of an election marked the subsidence of party proclivities within the community.[105] Similarly, Butterworth's *Oldham Almanac* recorded the anniversaries of radicals, royalists, and tories alike. Alongside the death of William Pitt, George III, Charles I, and 'Prince Charles Stuart' sat the birth of William Cobbett, the formation of Oldham's Radical Association, and the anniversary of famous Chartist meetings. The authors of these printed versions of the past then aspired, like the press, to articulate a pluralist urban identity that aimed to be above social and political differences.

Increasingly, then, the culture of print redefined the public political sphere in its own image. Classically John Vincent argued that the first effects of the press on the organisation of politics was in 1858 when Bright gave a speech in Birmingham covered by fifty reporters 'which was really a press conference'.[106] Again this neglects the influence of the press in shaping the terms of political activity in the preceding decades. At elections reporters had long since been allowed access to the hustings so that they could hear the speeches and make their reports unhindered by the audience or the weather. During the 1830s when journalists were unused to such preferential treatment, reports of election ceremonies were often prefaced by thanking the returning officer for his foresight and kindness.[107] Increasingly similar arrangements were made at both partisan media events and town and county meetings, as at Devon's county meeting of 1829 when the *Devonport Chronicle*'s journalist reported that the 'High Sheriff in making his arrangements has not forgotten to provide for reporters, and in front of the hustings is placed a barrier, behind which none excepting the reporters are admitted'.[108] By the 1850s most political meetings included provisions for reporters, whether it was specially constructed galleries or strategically sited tables close to the platform.[109]

Certainly it was increasingly apparent that orators were aware that they were addressing larger audiences than those assembled in front of them. At a particularly raucous election rally held by the Conservative candidate for Tower Hamlets in 1868 Mr O. E. Coope, the chairman 'Mr. Charles Wigram came forward and in vain endeavoured to address the meeting, and he therefore addressed himself to the reporters, who unable to hear his remarks at the table placed for their use, were obliged to sit on the edge of the platform'.[110] During the same election when Hackney's 'Conservative and Constitutional' candidate was consistently barracked by radical hecklers he retorted, 'fortunately this effort to blind the eyes of the public would not succeed. The reporters would prevent it (three groans for the *Standard* were here given)'.[111] There was clearly a recognition that the press provided access to a wider audience, and that if the audience at the meeting could not be converted then the readers of the press might be. As politicians became more adept at using the press in this way it would seem likely that their oratorical techniques changed. Gladstone, for instance, was reputed to have developed an intricate system to deal with press reports of his speeches (see Plate 41). During these speeches if he used a word wrongly, or if he felt the audience had misinterpreted him, he gestured to the reporters to replace the faulty word or to ignore the reactions of the audience.[112]

Eventually, as politicians recognised, the growing influence of the press would change the character and organisation of the political meeting. As early as 1819, it was evident from a report of a Devon county meeting that it was usual for speakers to provide the journalists

41 Talking for the press: Gladstone at Blackheath, Greenwich, 1874 (*Illustrated London News*, 7 February 1874)

with copies of the speech they gave.[113] By the 1860s this trend was gathering momentum and it was apparent that audiences were increasingly divested of much of their power to lead and shape the direction of the speeches they heard. Similarly, the growing use of ticketed media events such as dances, dinners, and tea-parties at which speeches to sympathetic audiences would follow, left journalists to report the inevitable ' (Bursts of applause) ' and ' (Hear, hears) '. As we shall see in chapter 6, different political groups in the five constituencies introduced these media events into their organisational repertoires at different times, but generally by the 1850s they had become regular fixtures in local political life.

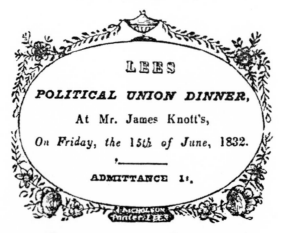

42   Ticket to 'Lees Political Union Dinner', 1832 (Oldham Local Studies Library)

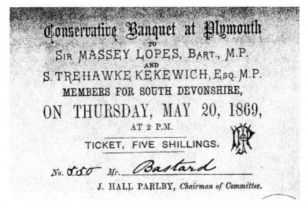

43   Ticket to 'Conservative Banquet at Plymouth', 1869 (Devon Record Office)

However, the political uses of print extended far beyond those we
have already examined – it was also used to ticket meetings and other
events, as well as canvassing and polling cards, and even to canvass
by post (see Plates 42–45). The introduction of these new modes of
printed communication reflected the emergence of a public political
sphere which was increasingly professionalised and restrictive. Just as
ticketing could be used to exclude the hostile and the disenfranchised,
so the use of the post to canvass by letter excluded non-electors by
targeting the enfranchised only, and even prevented them from
asking candidates difficult questions.[114] These uses of print allowed
politics to be confined to certain groups in a way which street

MR. FOX'S COMMITTEE.

———◆———

ORDER FOR COACHMAN
TO GO WITH THE BEARER.

Chairman.

To be delivered to the Chairman on returning.

TO POLL AT BOOTH **A**

INDEPENDENT SCHOOL, GEORGE-ST

No. on Register, _____

Name of Voter, _____
    t.

VOTES FOR

W. J. FOX, ESQ.

The Committee earnestly requests that you will Vote early.

CAPTAIN'S CARD.

No.			
		District,	
No. on Reg.	Voter's Name.		Residence.

When all the Electors whose names are on this Card have voted the Captain must deliver
it to the Chairman of his District.

44 Foxite canvassing cards, Oldham, *c.* 1852 (Oldham Local Studies Library)

literature and the press had generally failed to do, although attempts
were made. Just as candidates attempted to define the audience for
their electoral addresses to specific groups like the 'Independent
Electors', so *Flindell's Western Luminary* was pointedly subtitled 'The

SOUTH DEVONSHIRE ELECTION.

Conservative Candidates:
S. TREHAWKE KEKEWICH, Esq.
SIR MASSEY LOPES, Bart.

Conservative Central Committee Rooms,
Royal Hotel, Plymouth, 17th Nov. 1868.

The COMMITTEE for securing the return to Parliament of the above-named Conservative Candidates for South Devonshire, beg to inform you that the POLLING DAY is fixed to take place on

FRIDAY, 27th Nov. Inst.

The Poll will commence at EIGHT o'clock in the morning, and will close at FIVE.

The Committee earnestly desire the favour of your support on behalf of the above-named Candidates, and that their supporters will go EARLY TO THE POLL.

The Property upon which you qualify being situated in the Parish within the Polling District of Holsworthy, you will have to RECORD YOUR VOTE in

BOOTH No. 1,

At Cnows's Cabinet Maker, Lower Square, opposite the Stanhope Arms,

HOLSWORTHY.

At Holsworthy, apply to the District Conservative Committee there

BALDWIN JOHN P. BASTARD,
Chairman Central Conservative Committee.

Name of Voter ....

Parish in which Property is situated ....

Vote for KEKEWICH & LOPES.

SOUTH DEVON ELECTION.

VOTE FOR LORD AMBERLEY.

THE COMMITTEE FOR CONDUCTING THE ELECTION OF

LORD AMBERLEY,

Beg to inform you that the POLL will open on...... *Friday* ......
Morning at 8 o'clock, and will finally close at 5 o'clock on the same day.
Your description on the Register is

Number *1923*
Name *Baldwin J Pellesfor Bastard*
Your Polling Place is *Plymouth* ...... Booth *No. 5*
                                   Hampden Street
You are earnestly requested to POLL EARLY.

45   Canvassing by post: letters from South Devon's Conservative candidates, 1868
(Devon Record Office)

Family Newspaper of the Nobility and Gentry, Farmers and Traders of the Counties of Devon, Cornwall, Dorset and Somerset.' Yet the only way to ensure that these forms of print reached specific groups alone was to deliver them to the doorstep, as a candidate at Dorset did in 1831.[115] Such attempts to remove the political uses of print from the public arena to the private realm was officially encouraged with the introduction of ballot papers at parochial elections.

It is not insignificant that these immensely important changes in voting procedure were first introduced at the parochial level of vestry and board of guardians elections. As we saw in chapter 1, it was at this level that reforms were often tested before their implementation at municipal or parliamentary levels, much as Scotland is used today. The abolition of the traditional oral and visual poll – the show of hands – came with the introduction of the Sturges Bourne's Act of 1818. This Act decreed that all vestry decisions had to be settled by a formal poll and, as some votes were worth six times the amount of others, a show of hands would have clearly been impractical. Because the system was so complex and unpopular it was often simply ignored, although it appears that in many places, while most decisions were decided informally by a show of hands, the most contentious issues were formally put to a poll.[116] At these formal polls, votes were cast verbally to the vestry clerk who acted as returning officer, recording the votes and calculating their worth on the scale of one to six. The demise of this absurdly complicated system came when the Poor Law Amendment Act of 1834 introduced private polling, at which ballot papers were delivered to electors' homes, where they were filled in before being collected two days later and counted. As Brian Keith-Lucas has recognised, such a system 'assured that the elector should be able to complete his voting in the quiet and seclusion of his own home; and that there should be no public scene to attract the mob, and no hustings where every voter would have to brave the taunts and missiles of his political opponents'.[117]

Parliament thought the system so successful that the following year it was integrated into the Municipal Reform Act. Remarkably there seems to have been little reaction to the introduction of this system in any of the constituencies. Although it enabled many people to vote who previously had not been able to do so because of the pressures of work and home, or because they had been intimidated by the system of open voting, the system also generated plenty of its own problems. Not least of all, it assumed that the electorate was literate and capable

tepney Union.   No. of Votes._____

Voting Paper for the HAMLET OF RATCLIFF.

For the purpose of enabling each Rate Payer to give his Vote in the most free and deliberate manner, without the loss of his time, or the .truction of his ordinary business, or the other inconveniences usually incurred by attending to give his Vote at a polling booth, at a distance from home, this Voting Paper is directed to be left at the Voter's Dwelling for one clear day by the proper Officer, who will by order of the Com- sioners acting under the .authority of the Poor Law Amendment Act, attend on the Nineteenth day of December Instant, to receive back the :er on which the Vote must be inscribed hereunder as directed.

The Voter will write his Initials opposite the Name of the Persons for whom he Votes.

If the Proxy Votes he should sign his own Name, and state in writing the Name of the Person for whom he is proxy, thus :—M. N. for P. Q.

If the Voter cannot write, his mark must be attested by a witness, whose Initials must be placed opposite the Names of the Persons for whom Votes.

TAKE NOTICE, this Paper must be carefully preserved by the Voter, as no second paper will be given. When it is filled up, it must be t ready for delivery to Messrs. ASHLEY, HART, LEE, and SHILLCOTT, the Collecting Officers, who will call for the same on the eteenth day of December Instant.

No other Person can be allowed to receive the Voting Paper ; if it be not ready for the Collectors when they call, the Votes will be lost. They also be lost if more than Four Names be returned in the list, with the Initials placed opposite thereto. The Voter must therefore be careful in ing his Initials against those for whom he votes.

ials of the Voter the Names of Candidates.	Names of the Persons proposed as Guardians.	Residence and Calling of the Persons proposed.	Names of Proposers.
	John Hawes	Brook Street, Pawnbroker....................	Thomas Ratcliff, and others
	Robert Warton	Collingwood Place, Surveyor.................	Robert Johnson and others
	Daniel Cloves	Cock Hill, Coal Merchant	Robert Johnson and another
	Richard Hallett, Jun.	Broad Street, Slop Seller	Robert Johnson
	John Goodwin	Narrow Street, Coal Merchant	John Hawes
	Thomas Ratcliff.............	Brook Street, Baker	John Hawes and others
	Robert Johnson	Colet Place, Plumber	John Otter and another
	Edward Henderson	Cock Hill, Butcher	Allan Cleland
	Thomas Holt	Broad Street, Brewer.....................	Robert Johnson
	William Crew	Phœnix Place, Butcher	Lawrence Sallnow

I Vote for the Persons in the above List, opposite to whose Names I have placed my Initials ,

Signed this   day of December, 1836,

46   Stepney Union ballot paper, 1836 (Tower Hamlets Local History Library)

of reading the often quite sophisticated ballot papers (see Plates 46 and 47). Consequently, the illiterate and semi-literate elector required the help of a literate person to put their mark or signature in the right place, for, unlike ballot papers in societies with high rates of illiteracy today, there were no visual symbols as aids. Unsur- prisingly there was much room for corruption, as the publican James Rodwell's testimony to an inquiry into corruption at the previous election of guardians at Boston in 1854 shows:

A voting paper was left at my house by somebody. I can neither read nor write. I got a lodger to fill up the paper for me. He first read me the names; there was a lot of them. I said you may put me down for Gromm, Tewson *u 21*

ST. GEORGE IN THE EAST.

SOUTH WARD.

VOTING PAPER for VESTRYMEN
27th MAY, 1862.

SIX of the following to be Elected.

1. WILLIAM CLARK
2. THOMAS HERBERT
3. JAMES FRASER
4. ~~ALEXANDER LITTLEJOHN~~
5. ~~LUKE SEARSON~~
6. JOHN STEPHENS
7 GEORGE GRUMBRIDGE
8. ~~GEORGE SMITH~~
9. ~~JOHN BARNES~~
10. RICHARD COLLYER
11. ~~JAMES THOMAS~~
12. ~~JOHN PALMER~~

Voters are requested to Strike out the names of the Candidates for whom they do not intend to Vote.

N.B.—If this Paper when deposited contains the names of more than the number to be Elected, the VOTE will be LOST.

ST. GEORGE IN THE EAST.

SOUTH WARD.

VOTING PAPER for VESTRYMEN
27th MAY, 1862.

SIX of the following to be Elected.

1. ~~WILLIAM CLARK~~ —
2. ~~THOMAS HERBERT~~ —
3. ~~JAMES FRASER~~
4. ALEXANDER LITTLEJOHN
5. ~~LUKE SEARSON~~
6. ~~JOHN STEPHENS~~
7 GEORGE GRUMBRIDGE
8. GEORGE SMITH
9. JOHN BARNES
10. RICHARD COLLYER
11. JAMES THOMAS
12. ~~JOHN PALMER~~

Voters are requested to Strike out the names of the Candidates for whom they do not intend to Vote.

N.B.—If this Paper when deposited contains the names of more than the number to be Elected, the VOTE will be LOST.

47 St-George-in-the-East ballot paper, 1862 (Tower Hamlets Local History Library)

and Fricker. I suppose he did so but I could not read the paper. On Saturday morning, somebody said that Mr. Moreton's name was down on my paper. I really don't know whether it was or not, but I said I would not vote at all; and I did not give the paper in.[118]

In this system the possession of literacy was more important than the qualification to vote. The use of private voting within the sanctuary of the home was symptomatic of the increasing reliance on print within official politics and its use to redefine the public political sphere by placing the accent on the individual male's private experience of politics.

Yet the full implications of this for English political culture was not evident until the introduction of the secret ballot in 1872 transformed the cultural poetics of elections. The public nomination, which had been the occasion on which the disenfranchised exercised most influence, was legislated out of existence and replaced by written nominations to the returning officer. The provision of a greater

number of indoor polling booths also assured the dispersal of any
potential crowd of people, thereby reducing the risks of intimidation
and disorder. Indeed, the Act stipulated that not only should the
disenfranchised be refused admission to these new indoor polling
places, but that any person found misbehaving in or around them
would face immediate ejection. In short, many of the electoral events
which had previously afforded the disenfranchised their most
powerful role were eroded or abolished. No longer could the
disenfranchised vote at the nomination or hold a vigil beside the
hustings to intimidate the voters, nor could they deploy exclusive
dealing, for how were they to tell how the shopkeepers and tradesmen
had voted. Inevitably, the Act also precipitated the decline of a whole
range of electoral ceremonies like processions to and from the
hustings. The parliamentary select committee reviewing the op-
eration of the Act at the 1874 election was well pleased. It agreed
with the electoral agent who thought 'the present system is preferable
altogether, because it does away with the hustings and noise that
there is beforehand, and the noise that there is during the time that
the voting is going on, and the noise afterwards, and various other
things'.[119] Certainly, after 1872 the individual voter was less troubled
by the moral, physical, and economic influence of either the
disenfranchised or the employer, he and his conscience were left alone
in the polling booth, it was an entirely private affair.[120] The
contemporary critique of the Act hinged upon the claim of it being
'Un-English', a negation of the freeborn Englishman whose in-
dividualism and manliness allowed him to stand up and be counted.

   In this reading the Ballot Act did not herald the dawn of a great
new democratic era in which the politics of individual opinion
triumphed over the politics of influence and corruption.[121] Instead, it
has been read as part of the closing down of the public political sphere
by officials who sought to replace the public and collective experience
with an increasingly private and individual male one. Central to this
project was the official privileging of the political uses of print which
enabled appeals to be directed at private individuals. Although, once
again, it must be reiterated that this growing hegemony of the culture
of print was a slow and uneven process which did not provoke a
subsequently linear decline of oral and visual uses of politics.

CONCLUSION

This chapter has attempted to establish that the almost exclusive concern of political historians with printed text-bound politics has limited our conception of nineteenth-century English politics and the influence of individuals within the popular political audience upon it. Instead of concentrating solely on the production of political ideas and languages, I have sought to recapture something (but by no means all) of the manner in which they were transmitted and received by a rich texture of the oral, visual, and printed forms. In other words political media were not simply empty vessels waiting to be filled with discourses which they then conveyed to passive audiences, rather they actively shaped political languages and were used to redefine the public political sphere and its subjectivities.

However, although it has been continually emphasised that each form of oral, visual or printed political communication did not operate within discrete categories with lineal chronologies of development and decline, it has been possible to discern a decisive transition from an oral-cum-visual-cum-printed political culture to one in which print was increasingly dominant. Despite the formalisation of oral and visual media from the 1830s, these forms of political communication still enabled people to shape the terms of their own participation, publicly and collectively. Conversely, many printed forms of politics were products of a single author which were increasingly aimed at individual men in the privacy of their home. Therefore, by defining the political roles of individuals, these different forms of communication reconstituted the public political sphere. While the nature and accessibility of visual and oral media allowed different social, political and sexual groups to assert the legitimacy of their politics, the political uses of print increasingly served to distinguish the public from the private, the rational from the irrational, and therefore to create a public political sphere which not only excluded women and disenfranchised men, but which even disciplined the behaviour of those included within the political nation.

It would be misleading to suggest that print only served to create a restrictive and exclusive pubic political sphere, for it could also facilitate popular politics. National political organisations were dependent on print to break down the isolation of individuals within local communities through membership cards, rule books, correspondence, and, of course, the press. Indeed, it was these printed technologies which enabled the creation of a nationally organised mass political democracy with the Reform Acts of 1884 and 1918. However, I want to emphasise the disabling aspects of this apparently enabling trend for the person on the proverbial street corner. As politics became increasingly organised and national in character, ever greater distances were placed between the individual and their political leaders. Far from becoming a watchword of democracy and representation, political parties, as we shall see in the following chapters, were perceived as oligarchic cliques. Therefore, while much further work would need to be done on the crucial period 1868–1918, it could be tentatively suggested that, as ever greater number were included within the official political nation, the transformation of English political culture simultaneously limited their power to shape the political agenda. Far from representing a triumphant march towards the model parliamentary democracy, nineteenth-century English politics witnessed the gradual and uneven closure of the public political sphere. In short, the invention of democracy in England turned upon a broadly liberal conception of politics as private, individualistic, and rational which is still very much with us today and which is fast being exported to the nascent democracies of what used to be called eastern Europe and the Soviet Union.

PART II

The languages of organisation

CHAPTER 4

A language of party?

INTRODUCTION

The idea of party and its relentless rise has long been central to most narratives of modern British political history. While the role of 'party' in the eighteenth century is still hotly debated, the assumption remains that the period between the first two Reform Acts witnessed the birth of the 'modern' party system, as the Liberal and Conservative parties emerged from the shadows of their Whig and Tory counterparts.[1] Although this process briefly ran aground on the rock of the Corn Laws in 1846, it once again gathered momentum during the 1850s, before the 1867 Reform Act finally ushered in the classic age of two-party politics, symbolised in all text books by the rivalry between Gladstone and Disraeli. This enchantingly tidy and resilient orthodoxy owes much to the conception of 'party' as emanating from a central source at Westminster and, consequently, assuming a wide degree of national uniformity. This chapter will suggest a different approach by examining the popular perceptions and experiences of party in electoral politics. In no sense is it intended to be a definitive or complete account of the development of party politics during this period, rather it is an examination of some popular conceptions of party that have hitherto been ignored or neglected.[2]

We must be careful not to fall into the Whiggish trap of imposing anachronistic definitions upon party from a late twentieth-century bench-mark, ignoring changes in the popular experience of party and the different conceptions of its constitutional role. In the end it may not much matter how one defines party so long as we learn more about its popular perceptions and uses. To this end I shall argue in the following pages that Westminster's national party identities played a limited role in the popular electoral politics of the five constituencies. Instead, local political organisations identified them-selves with colours, individual leaders, and even particular symbols like flowers. The prominence afforded to these local political identities, and their constant revision and redefinition, suggests a deep-seated antipathy to the concept of party. Party-politics was perceived to be socially and politically disruptive, symptomatic of 'Old Corruption' and its oligarchic misrule. It is not then surprising to find the appeal of the eighteenth-century creed of electoral 'Independency' persisting well into the second half of the nineteenth century. This is not to argue that political leaders and organisations were not adverse to occasionally deploying party labels and identities when they stood to benefit from doing so. By the 1860s many of the factors working against the foundation of strong, nationally based, party-political organisations had begun to subside.

COLOURS, CLUBS, ORGANISATIONS AND LEADERS

We have already seen in chapter 3 how the propensity of colours, ribbons, and favours to empower people, to create and express their own politics, spurred successive governments to outlaw their use. And yet by the nineteenth century they had become so entrenched within popular political culture that these measures proved entirely ineffective. Right up to the 1860s elections continued to be dominated by the uses and languages of colours, not least in constituencies like Boston with long electoral traditions. When, at Boston's election of 1852, the local press referred to the competing groups as the Orange, Pink, and Blues there was nothing unusual, they were only using the candidates' descriptions of themselves. The reforming candidate, J. A. Hankey told the nomination that 'he relied solely on the merits of the cause with which he was identified, the "Old Blue Cause" (cheers)', while his opponent, G. J. Heathcote, 'rejoiced that the Old Orange Cause had still so many supporters in the borough'.[3] Colours often proved a more attractive rallying cry than Westminster's party labels, for their meanings were more ambiguous and therefore capable of appealing to wider constituencies of support. Yet, for all their multi-vocality, colours were also firmly rooted in local political histories and cultures. Heathcote's 'Old Orange Cause' was that of his Ancaster family's interest (his uncle had also represented the borough between 1826 and 1830), which his supporters could variously interpret as representing Peelite Toryism, Whiggism, or Liberalism. Either way his agent deliberately refused to pigeon-hole him, describing Heathcote instead as 'the advocate of civil and religious liberty, the improver of England's institutions not the destroyer, and a Protectionist ... he was a safe Liberal Conservative Whig'.[4] Similarly, Hankey's 'Old Blue Cause' alluded to over half a century of local political struggle against corruption and oligarchy, which united Hankey's campaign with those fought by an otherwise disparate group of candidates who embraced the whole spectrum of reforming opinion in these years from 'Independents', 'Radicals', 'Whigs' to 'Liberals'.[5] We should not then assume that colours were local shorthand for national party allegiances, rather they cut across those allegiances and created their own local constituencies of support.

However, although colours were clearly used to define and distinguish local political groups, they were also often informed with national concerns and preoccupations. Thus, while Boston's 'Old Blue Cause' had begun as an Independent campaign against the twin pillars of local political oligarchy – the corporation and the Ancaster interest – it quickly broadened its critique to include all forms of 'Old Corruption' at national, as well as local, level. Yet, despite these appeals to the wider national political context, little attempt was made to standardise the use of colours with similar groups in other localities. Apart from its use by reforming candidates in Boston, the colour blue was also deployed by the radical candidate William Newton at Tower Hamlets (1852), the 'Independent' campaign of Lord Ebrington in Devon (1816), as well as by Tory candidates in Oldham and Lewes. Similarly, at the 1868 election Liberal candidates fought under blue in Grantham and Cambridge-shire, red and green in Burnley, yellow in Nottingham, pink in Lewes, and orange in S. Devon.[6] Even at this late date national issues, campaigns, and parties were mediated by local political traditions. This much was clear from *The Morning Star*'s report of the 1857 election.

The enslaved tenant votes for his landlord, the independent freeholder votes 'blue' or 'yellow'. Unluckily the meanings of 'blue' and 'yellow' are not fixed in the eternal fitness of things ... Sometimes 'blue' means two different things in two neighbouring towns; sometimes it means one thing in the town and another thing in the country. We have heard of a free and enlightened voter under such circumstances always voting in one place for the Tory and

48   Boston's Blue Club admission medal, cost five shillings (Brighton Art Gallery and Museum)

in another for the Whig, and yet maintaining his perfect consistency because in both places he voted 'blue'.[7]

Appeals to local political identities were then evidently still more potent than Westminster's party identities.

Even within the same town or constituency the uses and meanings of colours were continually contested, as in early nineteenth-century Devon when the competing factions struggled to appropriate each other's colours and the standard of 'Independence'.[8] The Independent Lord Ebrington campaigned under 3 different colours within the space of 4 years: presenting himself as the true Blue candidate in 1816, he used blue and orange 2 years later, while by 1820 he sported purple and orange. These changes in colour did not reflect any change of political allegiance on Ebrington's part, but rather the struggle for a distinct identity and the mantle of the truly 'Independent' candidate. At all 3 contests his Tory opponent, the unfortunately named Bastard, used light blue as his colour, but at the 1818 and 1820 contests a third candidate, Sir Thomas Acland, also joined the contest professing his Independence and using scarlet and purple colours. As all 3 candidates contested the label of 'Independent', the choice of colours became increasingly significant, and therefore Ebrington was forced to differentiate his candidature by using ever more distinct colours. By the election of 1820, the identities of the contending candidates were so enmeshed and confused that flowers and plants were enlisted in order to emphasise their differences still further. While Ebrington's candidature became associated with the laurel plant, Acland used the oak of his family's coat of arms, leaving Bastard the ivy or evergreen.[9] Indeed, by the 1832 and 1835 contests for South Devon it was these symbols that had persisted as the mark of the candidates' allegiances, Lord John Russell using Ebrington's laurel and Montague Parker Bastard's evergreen. These uses of colours and flowers were not ephemeral decoration, they went to the heart of local political conflict.

The centrality of these local political identities was evident from their use in the names of political organisations in Boston, Devon, and Lewes. For instance, in Boston, sixty members of the corporation party founded the Purple and Constitutional Club in 1832 – a name which clearly referred to the club's roots within the town's unre-formed corporation whose parliamentary candidates had fought under purple colours before 1812. Similarly in Lewes, the language of Westminster's party organisations failed to register amidst the town's Roast Beef Club (1812–36), Porter or Blue Club (1826–47), Pink and Strong Club (1826), and Bundle of Sticks Club, (1831–60s) (see Plate 48). Likewise in pre-reform Devon where the two contending factions organised themselves into the Devon and Exeter Pitt Club (1824) and the Devon County Club (1816–34). In these three constituencies then the language of organisation appealed to long-standing local identities not to those of Westminster's Whig and Tory or Liberal and Conservative parties. That these organisations referred to themselves as 'clubs' rather than 'associations' was also significant. The language of clubs harked back to the sociable and informal organisational forms of eighteenth-century politics, rather than anticipating the more formal and representative language of as-sociation pioneered by late eighteenth-century radicals.[10]

However, such distinctions may not be as clear-cut as they at first appear. By 1832, in both Boston and Lewes, local branches of the nationally organised Reform Association and Political Union oper-ated beside both the reforming Boston Blue Club and Lewes' Bundle of Sticks Club without any apparent friction. As they supported the same candidates and shared the same leaders and activists, it seems safe to assume that they also shared many of the same supporters. Moreover, the often sophisticated organisational functions performed by these clubs suggests a considerable degree of symbiosis between supposedly 'traditional' and 'modern' organisational forms. Boston's tory Guardian Club, for instance, was established in 1833 to look after the claims of poor voters on the electoral register and, by 1835, its 200 members were not only holding regular monthly meetings and social events, but also nominating municipal candidates.[11] However, while these informal political clubs were gradually eclipsed from the late 1830s by Radical, Liberal, and Conservative Associations in both Boston and Devon, they remained central to the electoral politics of Lewes. Both the Porter and Bundle of Sticks Clubs met regularly up to the early 1860s, holding general political debates, hearing their MP's account of his stewardship, as well as attending to the register and selecting parliamentary candidates. Yet, despite all this partisan activity, both clubs were careful to maintain the fiction of independence from party-politics, as was clear from the reforming MP Sir Charles Blunt's presentation of a 'massive silver vase' to the Bundle of Sticks in 1831 for 'the disinterested, and independent part they took in the late election'.[12] It was not until the formation of the Conservative Association in 1865 and the Liberal Registration Society in 1866 that national party-political organisations existed in Lewes (see Plate 49).

Significantly, as we shall see, it was in those constituencies like Oldham and Tower Hamlets that had been newly enfranchised in 1832 that such national party-political organisations were most evident. In these constituencies there were no traditions of local electoral organisation through which national party identities and organisational forms had to be mediated. While Oldham's Tories were able to mobilise anti-radical support behind the Conservative Associations they formed in 1835, their radical rivals were endlessly revising their organisation to preserve unity.[13] However, in Tower Hamlets party organisations remained stubbornly and conspicuously absent, such was the size of the constituency that political organisations were effectively confined to the vestry, the trade, and the debating club.[14] Moreover, the lack of any Tory opposition within the constituency meant that, when cleavages appeared, they were between different reforming factions, not between competing national parties. Thus at the infamous 1852 election no less than five reforming candidates contested Tower Hamlets. It was not until the Conservative candidature of O. E. Coope at the 1868 election that Liberal party organisation sprang to life in the form of a Registration Society.

In all five constituencies, regardless of the presence or absence of national party organisations, there were unique local appeals to individual leaders which transcended those of party. In mid-

49 Guardians of the Cause: the worthies of Lewes' Conservative Association, *c.* 1870s (*The Sunday Times* Reeves Collection and Sussex Archaeological Society)

Victorian Oldham one was a Cobbettite, Fieldenite, O'Connorite, Foxite, Healdite, not a Radical, Liberal or Conservative. It was individuals who were as likely to command popular constituencies of support as party organisations. Thus the announcement of Donovan's candidature at Lewes in 1825 'caused some hubbub in the town; but... it appeared to have met the sanction of at least 300 persons, composed 'tis said of Shelleyites, Kempites, Stickites, and Lushites' who the following year cemented their alliance around Donovan by forming the Porter Club.[15] Individual leaders could then generate their own constituencies of support, uniting disparate groups under one organisational roof. Certainly this was the case with Boston's Liberal MP Herbert Ingram, 'for a long time disunion had prevailed in the Liberal camp, but this deplorable condition Mr. Ingram had fortunately been the means of removing, all sections of the Liberal party rallying around and coalescing under his standard'.[16] The problem with affording figures like Ingram such a powerful integrative role was that when they retired or died the popular alliances they had created quickly disintegrated, despite the best efforts of the succeeding candidate to claim the legacy. Thus, at the 1860 by-election caused by Ingram's death, Tuxford, his successor as Boston's Blue candidate, spent much of the campaign eulogising about the loss of his great friend. 'As a relative and a schoolfriend, I loved him; as fellow apprentices, we toiled in the same avocation, and leaving our native town together we pursued our respective courses, enjoying the sympathy and friendship of each other.'[17]

Of course, establishing one's closeness with the departed champion was so much easier if one was related to him. Hence John Morgan Cobbett's attempts to claim the political inheritance of his father in both Oldham and Coventry, and the requisition to John W. Malcolm in 1859 'induced, from the high respect still entertained in the Borough' for his uncle, Neil Malcolm, who had represented Boston between 1826 and 1832. To us this link may appear somewhat tenuous, but not to the inhabitants of Boston. The decoration at the 'Grand Conservative Banquet' of 1866 clearly alluded to the audiences' identity as followers of the Malcolm dynasty, not as members of the Conservative Association.

The chairman and principal guest [Malcolm] sat on a raised dais on the right hand side of the room. Over the chairman's head was the word 'MALCOLM' surmounted by a shield having painted thereon in gilt letters '646' the number polled by Mr. Malcolm at the last election. The vice-chairman and friends sat on a raised dais on the opposite side of the room and above their heads were two large banners, bearing the following inscription, – 'NEIL MALCOLM, 1826, 313– 1831, 337.' 'JOHN W. MALCOLM, 1860, 525– 1865, 646.' ... At the far end of the hall was a banner, showing the arms of Mr. Malcolm, surmounted by a large gas star.[18]

It was the achievements of the Malcolm family not the Conservative party that were celebrated here.

The ability of popular leaders to command their own constituencies of support irrespective of their allegiances at Westminster was apparent from the ease with which John Morgan Cobbett moved between Oldham's radicals and tories. He first stood for election at Oldham in July 1835 on the death of his father, portraying himself as the guardian of his fathers' radicalism which had triumphed in 1832. Yet his ambiguous statements over church reform and the rights of dissenters opened the door to Feargus O'Connor's candidature, thereby splitting the radical vote and letting in the Tory J. F. Lees. He returned in 1847 hopeful of victory, thanks to the active support of his father-in-law John Fielden. Together they campaigned under the old radical colours of green and white against the coalition of the radical Liberal W. J. Fox and the liberal Conservative John Duncuft. However, it was not until July 1852 that he was finally elected, this time having formed a coalition with Duncuft against Fox. Cobbett's populist platform in 1852 fused popular Protestantism with the traditional radical programme of universal suffrage, annual parliaments, and the secret ballot, together with a return to the ten-hour day, a reduction of general taxation, the abolition of the malt tax, and opposition to secular education. The common confusion over his party-political allegiances was reflected in a cartoon of a 'man half-blue and half green, the party colours of the Tory and Radical elements of this town'.[19] Although increasingly associated with the Conservatives during his unsuccessful campaigns at the 1857, 1865, and 1868 elections, he insisted on portraying himself as the independent working man's representative. Even at the 1868 election, when he eventually adopted the blue colours of the Conservatives and admitted that 'he had joined the Tories', he still asked:

Why then...should he shrink from being called a Tory? (Applause.) He did not shrink. He did not belong to any party at all, and he never would...he would not be a party man, nor would he attach himself to any party whatever. If they returned him to parliament they would send him perfectly independent, and he would vote as he imagined a working man would if he was sent there – (cheers) – that was to say he would vote as a man who had no object to serve, and who never wished to be in place (cheers).[20]

This movement across party boundaries by Cobbett reflects the fragility of party-political categories, demonstrating that they were not hermetically sealed categories with discreet ideological platforms. Indeed, in so far as politics was conducted along party lines, it tended to obscure rather than clarify the identity of national political parties. Few candidates were prepared to spell out their allegiances at Westminster to their constituents; election addresses were rarely anything other than a vague outline of political principles. Candidates sought to define themselves in opposition to their opponents, struggling to shape the public's perception of the use and meaning of party categories. It is then unsurprising that at Lewes' election of 1847, the 'Protectionist' candidate Godfrey Hudson branded his opponent Henry Fitzroy as a 'radical', even though Fitzroy had sat as Lewes' Conservative MP since 1837, because he had supported

Peel over the corn laws in 1846, and now described himself as a
'Liberal Conservative'. The *Sussex Weekly Advertiser* could not 'refrain
from protesting against...the practice so constantly resorted to by
the Tory party...of applying to their opponents the term "radical"
not only in an offensive sense, but with offensive intention. It is, in
fact, a covert mode of insinuating that of which common usages of
society prevent the expression in less ambiguous terms.'[21] Almost 20
years later during the 1865 election, the boot was on the other foot
and Fitzroy's (by then a Liberal) colleague complained that he 'had
studied the opposition addresses, and they were all very much the
same, for he could not find the word Tory about them. They were
now all Liberal Conservatives, a hybrid animal, and such men were
liberal to Liberals and conservative to Conservatives.'[22] Party-politics
consisted not of a battle between two clearly defined, ideologically
distinct, party groups, but rather a contest between competing
groups to ascribe their opponent a pejorative party label.

'INDEPENDENCE' AND THE SUSPICION OF PARTY

The persistent use of colours, clubs, and leaders to define local
political cleavages suggests a popular antipathy to the concept of
party. This antipathy is hardly surprising if we remember that party
was still a relatively new concept at the advent of the nineteenth
century, one whose role in the constitution continued to be hotly
debated throughout this period.[23] This was not just a debate about
the legitimacy of party in a properly balanced constitution, but about
the whole way in which political conflict was handled, both at
Westminster and in the country at large. For many, party retained its
eighteenth-century connotations, just as it had retained many of its
eighteenth-century identities, of oligarchic and factious cliques
dictating to, and misleading, the people. As party organisations
grew, so too did the perception of them as hierarchical and
unaccountable bodies dominated by sinister individuals and agents
lining their own pockets. The vilification of Meaburn Staniland,
lawyer, agent, and leading activist for Boston's Blues, exemplified this
fear of the manipulative self-serving party 'fixer'. Nicknamed 'Oily
Gammon', after the slang for cheat, he appeared in innumerable
ballads and handbills as 'THE FAMOUS POLITICAL JUGGLER' singing
'I've done my best/ To feather my nest/ With the gold I value so
dear.'[24]

Appeals to maintain the independence of the borough against a domineering MP, organisation, agent or patron then still struck a powerful chord with the electorate. When Oldham's radical champion John Fielden insisted during the 1847 election that he would not return to Westminster unless his son-in-law J. M. Cobbett was elected alongside him, he was soundly beaten amidst the popular cry of 'No Dictation'.[25] Yet this suspicion, distrust, and even downright hostility to party ran deeper still, it was perceived as a symbol of political conflict, an agent of social disruption. As a 'Working Man' reminded Oldham's electorate in 1852, 'No man is a true friend to humanity who allows himself to be the slave of any party. No man is a friend to the people who goes about opening old wounds, and spreading malice and revenge amongst them'.[26] Even Devon's partisan *Alfred* thought it necessary during the 1818 election to urge the 'Electors of Devon, amidst the jarring interest of contending parties, [to] aim at the preservation of social tranquillity...let them guard against the baneful influence of a party spirit...Let them not sacrifice to the spirit of party the charities of social life. Let them allow to others the same they claim to themselves. While maintaining the zeal, let them guard against the bitterness of party.'[27]

Such sentiments represented not so much a denial of party politics as a warning of its dangers and pitfalls. In this sense tories were uniquely placed to exploit these fears. In general their organisations were outnumbered by those advocating reform for, as we shall see in the following chapter, they were used to force the pace of reform by operating within the official political arena. Consequently, it was easier for tories, who had no such aims, to portray themselves as having risen above such sectarian forms of party-politics, representing instead the interests of the entire political community, be it parish, town or nation. As we shall see in chapter 6, their organisations reflected this belief, stressing the social and convivial dimension of politics, the politics of the 'good time'. It was to prove a popular and enduring appeal, one which was energised during the 1880s by its contrast with the dry procedural debates of the Liberal Caucus.[28] Yet if tories were uniquely placed to shun the formalised structures of party organisation, they were by no means alone in their attempts to exploit popular suspicions of party. Indeed, radical, Chartist, and Liberal objections to 'class legislation' can be read as a variation on the anti-party theme. Popular Palmerstonianism had, after all, fused this appeal with that of the nation to arrive at a creed which cut across party boundaries. The Palmerstonian campaign for administrative reform in Boston during 1855 rested on its appeal to 'lay aside party differences, and merge party distinctions in the common cause of the Fatherland'. The town meeting to support the campaign brought together 'Tory, Radical, Whig, Conservative and Liberal, uniting heart and hand in support of one common object... For the time we must endeavour to forget that we have party feelings or party motives, and to remember only one thing, that we are ENGLISHMEN.'[29] Ironically then the denial of party was often used for partisan ends.

And yet there was also a seemingly genuine belief that party proclivities could obscure the common interests of the parish, town or nation. Vestry and municipal politics were saturated with rhetoric denying the role of party. In 1834 a local Baptist minister reduced a vestry meeting at Boston to uproar by remarking that

'as this was a party matter between the Conservatives' – here a burst of groans and hisses, mingled with cries of 'no politics' 'no party', completely drowned the speaker's voice... The Chairman said it was his desire to act with the strictest impartiality, and he considered it highly improper that any individual should attempt to rouse political animosities on a question with which party had nothing whatever to do.[30]

Even as late as 1883, an Independent Political Association was established in Norwich whose aim was 'to contest only municipal elections on the grounds that local issues, especially of town hall spending, could be most fairly decided by an organisation that operated free from party spirit, national politics, and the corrupt influence of the Tory and Liberal mafias that acted in semi-collusion to line their own pockets'.[31] Clearly, the perception of party as an essentially divisive force, not suited to protecting the interests of all the people in the communities of parish, town, and nation, was hard to shake off.

This was apparent from the quite remarkable, and hitherto much neglected, persistence of the eighteenth-century creed of electoral Independency.[32] As Frank O'Gorman has argued, by resolving political cleavages into a struggle between oligarchic and independent forces, Independency transcended Westminster's partisan boundaries. Having originally concerned itself with the misuse of power and influence within local communities, Independency quickly broadened its appeal by embracing a critique of 'Old Corruption' at the national, as well as the local, level. Indeed, by the early nineteenth century in constituencies like Boston it was hard to distinguish between radical and Independent platforms. However, it would be wrong to associate the language of Independency with any one political group. Its anti-oligarchic appeal, with its emphasis on the individual's and locality's right to self-government, represented an assertion of popular liberty and the rights of the freeborn Englishmen very much in the vein of popular constitutionalist discourse which belonged to all parties and to none, and was appropriated by them all. I have argued elsewhere that, far from being squeezed out after 1832 by the twin pressures of electoral radicalism and nationally organised parties as O'Gorman suggests, the language of Independency persisted throughout this period as it was used and appropriated by the emergent Liberal and Conservative parties of the 1850s and 1860s. In short, the eventual triumph of party was based upon the reworking of the language(s) of Independency, not its displacement.[33]

The existence of Independent candidatures in the unreformed constituencies of Lewes, Boston, and Devon should not come as any surprise. During the first 3 decades of the nineteenth century all three constituencies witnessed the attempt by groups of Independent electors to throw off the oligarchic mantles of domineering patrons (in the case of Lewes and Devon) and a corrupt corporation (in Boston). However, what was striking in all three constituencies were the attempts by many of the candidates to appropriate the language of Independency for their own ends. At the Devon election of 1816, both the Whig candidate, Lord Ebrington, and the Tory candidate, Bastard, portrayed themselves as Independents in an attempt to broaden their constituencies of support. The debate about the true meaning of Independency raged. In a lampoon on Bastard's election address, 'A Freeman' had no doubt who was the real Independent candidate, nor could he resist the obvious pun.

And last of all, he calls on you, in his greatest manner, to do what – (what do you think my friends?) – 'to arouse and assert the sacred cause of BASTARD and REAL INDEPENDENCE'. You see my friends what sort of a cause his sacred cause is: – By his own account, it is a hotch potch of bastard independence and real independence; a very right noble cause, properly mixed. Let us my friends stick to real independence, and let him have his bastard independence; a sort of independence with which no man but a Bastard will have anything to do.[34]

By the contest of 1818 Ebrington and Bastard's struggle to claim the Independent label as their own was complicated when a third candidate, Sir Thomas Acland, joined in, asserting that it was his 'sole wish and ambition to be considered the Independent representative of independent constituents'.[35] These attempts by all sides to appropriate the discourse of Independency testified to its powerful political appeal. It was an appeal that persisted into the reformed electoral system, emerging in the most unlikely places.

We have, for instance, already seen how J. M. Cobbett attempted to project himself as the independent representative of the working people of Oldham during the 1868 election. In doing so he followed the example set by James Heald at Oldham's election of 1852 when he claimed that 'he was an independent man, and if he obtained a seat in the House of Commons, it must be as an Independent member'.[36] Despite their proximity to Westminster's central party organisations, the language of electoral Independency was evident even in metropolitan constituencies well into the second half of the nineteenth century. As Tony Taylor has argued, 'radicalism amongst London's MPs continued to be measured in terms of their distance from the court, the throne, and the largesse of governmental patronage, the basis of the old "Independent" position'.[37] As late as 1880 Independency was also alive and well in the Cornish borough of Liskeard, where an Independent Electoral Association was established by E. P. Bouverie to co-ordinate his support among both Liberals and Conservatives.[38] Despite the occasional appeals to the independence of electors by self-styled 'Private Members', this was increasingly exceptional as the grip of the two-party system gradually tightened during the 1880s.[39]

Alongside these continued appeals to electoral Independency ran an almost pathological popular fear of coalitions. Few elections seemed complete without the incessant rumours about coalitions formed between candidates to bully, cajole, and deceive the honest and independent electors. Thus, at the Devon elections of 1818 and 1820, Acland and Bastard were repeatedly accused of having formed an informal alliance against the reforming Ebrington. Handbills like 'The *Coalition* RENEWED: but *No Tricks upon Travellers*' by a South Molton 'Freeholder' gave vent to this suspicion, rounding upon Acland and Bastard for supposing

that the enlightened Freeholders of the County of Devon, are to be cajoled out of their Rights and Independence, by an assertion 'that no Coalition has been formed, or will be formed' when their actions give a direct lie to their statements? If the least doubt can remain on the mind of any man, that a *base and deceitful confederacy* has not been again formed, let him refer to the speeches of the supporters of the former Gentlemen, and he will discover the *trick* so flimsily concealed – Shall we be driven to the poll by a Junto? No! Let us again convince them that we are Englishmen, and will not be deprived of our Rights and Liberties by such UNPRINCIPLED COALITIONS, and let us (as it is our duty to do) withdraw every vote, which has been obtained under such deceitful representations, and give our undivided support to the Noble Lord, who has so manfully fought the battle for our Liberties and Independence.[40]

The message was clear. Coalitions ran against the grain of the freeborn Englishman, offending his sense of independence and 'fair play'. Again this hatred of coalitions of oligarchic 'juntos' fixing elections was by no means confined to unreformed constituencies – it was equally evident in Oldham and Tower Hamlets, especially at the 1852 election. It could be argued that popular hostility to partisan coalitions was stronger in those constituencies like Oldham where party organisations were strongest because the risk of dictation by oligarchic party cliques was greater. If these constituencies represented the vanguard of nineteenth-century radical politics they were by no means free from 'traditional' political appeals. Instead it was precisely the persistence of these supposedly 'traditional' appeals, rather than the emergence of supposedly 'modern' ones, that was most evident in these places.

THE RISE OF PARTY

The languages of party were, then, never new, rather they built upon those which already existed, often evoking centuries-old struggles, allegiances, and identities. At Lewes' election of 1818, one of the candidates declared that 'the love of those principles which had placed the Brunswick family on the Throne of this Realm, had been his constant theme and admiration. He confessed he was a party man and that upon the great constitutional principles of Mr. Fox.'[41] At the same election in Devon the *Alfred* recognised that more was at stake than the merits of the three competing candidates, it urged that it was 'not merely LORD EBRINGTON, but LORD EBRINGTON'S PUBLIC PRINCIPLES, – the principles of FOX, CAMDEN, and CHATHAM, that demand our support. Great as his Lordship merits and noble as is the sacrifice which he makes to stand in the gap, the CAUSE is more entitled to our esteem.'[42] These appeals to past struggles and identities were not made redundant with the increased use of Conservative and Liberal party identities from the 1830s. Rather, as with the language of Independency, the 'old' Whig/Tory, court/country cleavages were used to inform those of the emerging Conservative and Liberal parties. As late as 1865, Sir Lawrence Palk, the South Devon Conservative MP, claimed that 'he had always acted with what was called the "Country Party", whose principles he had taken up early, which principles he had maintained and should maintain without change to the last'.[43] This seemingly endless appropriation of centuries-old political languages and identities has important implications for our understanding of the rise of party.

Such emphasis on the importance of recycling political languages in the mid-nineteenth-century invention of party sits uneasily alongside the triumphant whiggism of the historiographical orthodoxy. This orthodoxy is still in large measure a product of John Vincent's seminal work on the formation of the British Liberal party.[44] Despite his subtle treatment of the construction of partisan 'communities of sentiment', not least through the language of leadership, Vincent ultimately accounts for the rise of party by the social and religious cleavages left in the wake of the forward march of British history. His famous 'broad church of Liberalism' was created and sustained by an increasingly assertive middle class through the vehicles of non-conformist religion and the provincial press, and it was in response to these forces that Disraelian Conservatism organised itself.[45] Increasingly this account is being questioned as political historians have recognised, somewhat belatedly, that parties actually created their own identities and constituencies of support, rather than reflecting the identities of existing social groups. None the less, even within this new analytical framework, Vincent's model can be recast around the creative discursive roles of religion and the press. In what follows I want to suggest that, because of the especial attention afforded to the industrialising towns of England's north-west by historians of party, the influence of these two agencies has been greatly overestimated. As a result it may be necessary to talk not of one rather sudden and dramatic invention of party between 1855 and 1867, but of a continuing process reinventing diverse and unstable party identities.

This is not to argue that religion played no part in the invention of party identities, especially in the north-west. At Oldham, for instance, the town's militant dissenters had provided both the personnel and the organisation that preserved radical politics during and immediately after the Napoleonic Wars.[46] It was the ambivalence of both William and John Morgan Cobbett to dissenting issues which first split the town's Radical party in 1835, before finally causing its disintegration in 1847. The re-emergence of J. M. Cobbett as Fielden's radical partner in 1847, at the latter's insistence, forced the radical dissenters to launch the counter-candidature of James Holladay, who in turn later yielded to the Unitarian W. J. Fox. With the death of Fielden, his Unitarian father-in-law in 1849, Cobbett was free to swim with the tide of popular Protestantism flowing through the north-west at this time, feeding, as it did, off the tributaries of the Orange movement and anti-Irish sentiment.[47] Despite Cobbett's insistence of his independence from party, there can be little doubt that his popular Protestantism, fused with the strong social dimension of his politics, quickly created an appealing tory populism. At the three elections of 1852, 1865, and 1868, at which another Tory stood, Cobbett made no bones about allying with them against the dissenting radical or popular Liberal opposition. With all the candidates advocating the traditional radical programme of universal manhood suffrage and vote by ballot at the 1852, 1857, and 1859 elections, religion was the only principal difference between the two factions, just as it was pivotal in creating the straight two-party contests of 1865 and 1868.

Elsewhere, however, religion played a less formative role in the invention of party. Although popular Protestantism was equally virulent in Lewes, it belonged to an older tradition which stretched back to the anti-Catholicism of the seventeenth century, rather than the ethnic divisions of the nineteenth century. Therefore, it was invariably a source of unity not difference, and was perceived as a pre-requisite for any candidature of whatever political persuasion.[48] During the 1850s this strand of popular Protestantism was used to transcend the town's partisan cleavages. Launching Lewes' Protestant Association in 1857, a Mr Foskett claimed 'that there was not a party, whether Whig, Tory or Conservative, who had not forfeited the confidence of the Protestants of England (hear, hear)...No politics would be introduced at their meetings, and if they joined the branch...they would be at full liberty to vote for whomsoever they please when an election for the borough took place.'[49] While Protestantism was truly popular in Lewes, it completely failed to register in the politics of Tower Hamlets. In a sense this is unsurprising as attendance levels at both Anglican and dissenting places of worship was notoriously low in the metropolis' poorest and largest constituency. On the other hand, Tower Hamlets had a large Irish population which was intricately involved in radical and Chartist politics. However, despite this potential for a Protestant, anti-Irish Tory backlash, none occurred. Even when a Conservative candidate eventually contested the borough in 1868 religion was not a central issue. Thus, although religion was critical to the invention of party in some areas, it was as likely to cut across partisan allegiances elsewhere.

Perhaps then, like Vincent, we should look to the emergence of the provincial press following the repeal of the stamp duties in 1854 to explain the growth of party-political identities in the constituencies. However, as we have seen from chapter 3, this argument assigns too great a role to the Repeal of the Stamp Act in 1855. Of the five constituencies, only Oldham was significantly effected by this Act, which inspired the creation of 6 local papers between 1855 and 1868, 2 of which became permanent fixtures in the town's life. Elsewhere, however, the 1850s and 1860s saw little difference in either the quantity or the political quality of the local and provincial press, which in any case had been highly partisan since the 1830s or, in the case of Devon, earlier still. From the early nineteenth century there had been fierce rivalries between Devon's whiggish *Alfred* and the tory *Flindell's Western Luminary*, a rivalry encouraged further by the establishment of the reforming *Western Times* in 1827. The *Western Times* quickly became a force to be reckoned with in the county's political scene, leading the campaign against Exeter's infamous Bishop Philpotts and supporting the reform agitation during 1831 and 1832. By April 1831 Sir Thomas Acland's agent wrote to him warning that 'the *Western Times* party... abrogate completely to themselves the power of returning the Members, and on whose sufferance your seat is stated to be held'.[50] The *Western Luminary* did not shrink from such a partisan challenge, openly reminding 'the Friends of Constitutional Reform, and our Civil and Religious Institutions; the supporters of the Interests of the British Farmer, and the Rights and Liberties of the People' to vote for the Tory candidates Buller and Parker at the 1837 election in the bluntest manner possible.[51]

Similarly, in Boston the town's political cleavages had long been played out by its local papers. While *Drakard's Stamford News* and the *Stamford Mercury* supported the town's Independent/Radical/Liberal

Blue candidates, the *Boston Gazette* represented the Whig/Orange interest and the *Boston Herald* those of the Tories/Pinks. All these papers contested each others' reports and promoted their favourite candidates and campaigns. No doubt the involvement of John Noble and Thomas Fricker in the production of these papers intensified the sense of partisan rivalry. As we shall see in chapter 7, Noble, who had worked as the *Stamford Mercury's* Boston correspondent, also occupied a central role within the town's reforming politics. Likewise, Thomas Fricker combined his jobs as editor and proprietor of the *Boston Herald* with the political roles of coroner, councillor, and, later, Alderman, all of which made him the self-acknowledged 'leader of the Conservative Party in Boston, the head that dictated its policy, and the strong arm that carried that policy out'.[52] Partisan rivalries had, therefore, always been created by the local and provincial press. It is at least arguable, that the press became increasingly de-politicised during the 1850s in an attempt not to alienate any potential readers in the pursuit of an ever larger mass reading public. We must, therefore, also look to the role of other agencies in the creation of party identities. Increasingly, historians have turned their attentions to the ways in which the state was able both to encourage the development of party organisations, as well as to create a more responsive discursive context within which to appeal to the electorate.[53] However, it is to the cultural space between those parameters defined by the state, and those defined by the people, to which we shall turn in the following chapters to understand more fully the way in which parties were invented at constituency level.

CONCLUSION

This chapter has endeavoured to question the centrality of party in the popular experience of electoral politics during this period. It has emphasised both the continuing importance of local political identities such as colours, clubs, and leaders, and the suspicion of party as expressed by the appeals to Independency, and the hatred of coalitions, agents, and oligarchic party organisations. This is not to argue that parties did not exist. Clearly party allegiances were very much part of politics at Westminster during this period, although even at this level there were periods of confusion and flux.[54] Despite the existence of party organisations in the five constituencies, national party politics were often undercut or mediated by local political allegiances and identities. Party affiliations at the constituency level were then uneven, volatile, and prone to disjunction, requiring constant invention and redefinition. Certainly, in the past it has been assumed too quickly that parties were discrete and unified ideological and social categories, ignoring the contingent and unstable nature of their identities and constituencies of support.

What sense can we make of the different experiences and perceptions of party in the five constituencies? It should not come as any great surprise that the older eighteenth-century political identities and organisational forms were most persistent in those constituencies which had had long electoral histories before 1832, namely Boston, Lewes, and Devon. These constituencies had evolved their own quite distinct local political cultures and identities which found expression in different symbolic forms, be it colours, clubs, or flowers. Conversely, it was easier for national party organisations and identities to establish themselves in Oldham and Tower Hamlets where they had no local electoral traditions with which to compete. However, even in these constituencies the invention of party invariably turned upon the popular appeals of individual leaders or the reworking of the language of Independency. Clearly, party-politics found its pejorative connotations hard to shake off. As we shall see in chapter 6, the development of distinct local party-political cultures at the constituency level increasingly began to conform to national party stereotypes as early as the mid 1830s. There can be little doubt that these party-political cultures increasingly assumed many of the roles and responsibilities which had previously been engrafted on the official electoral culture. It was surely not coincidental that each expansion of the electorate was prefaced and followed by the periods of greatest organisational activity. The new voters and constituencies had to be organised, their allegiances and behaviour regulated and disciplined. Increasingly, by the 1860s the culture of national party politics had begun to dominate, until by the 1880s it was these party-political cultures that defined the parameters of the public political sphere. Interpreted in this way, as part of the gradual closure of the public political sphere, it is possible to suggest that we have, perhaps, been too ready to accept the whiggish myth that the rise of party was necessarily enabling and emancipative. In what follows we must be equally alive to party's disabling and restrictive manifestations.

CHAPTER 5

Organisation as symbol

Principles alone, however true and holy, are not enough to
ensure adherence and respect for a popular movement.[1]

INTRODUCTION

Contemporary politics teaches us that successful political appeals can
not rely on rhetoric alone. The organisational structures and forms of
a group convey powerful symbolic messages about the sort of society
and political system it wishes to create or maintain. It is time to move
away from the conception of nineteenth-century political organisation as simply a practical response to the expanding electorate by
political parties anxious to mobilise and yet contain popular electoral
participation.[2] Such an approach has tended to reduce the role of
organisation to an institutional measure of the rise of 'mass politics'
and the forward march of party. In this chapter I will attempt to
understand organisation as a means of articulating symbolic political
appeals, a means by which radicals and reformers contested
restrictive and exclusive official definitions of the public political
sphere.

I shall begin by examining the representative structures of political
groups operating within the five constituencies, that is the ways in
which their parliamentary candidates were selected and held
accountable. This aspect of political organisation provided reformers
with the priceless opportunity of implementing their own theories of
representation, accountability, and popular participation, which
expanded official definitions of the public political sphere by
including and empowering the disenfranchised. Inevitably, the
organisational burden of proof lay with radical and reforming
groups, and consequently most attention is afforded to their modes of
organisation. Significantly, however, these often took very different

forms in the five constituencies because of the contrasting local electoral structures and political cultures with which they had to engage. These local political contexts also shaped the tactical strategies of reforming political organisations, the symbolic use of 'practical politics' to attract and mobilise popular support.[3] All political groups, but especially radicals and reformers, needed political power to gain administrative experience, a system of influence and patronage, political respectability and, above all, to practically effect peoples lives. Yet it is the way in which these practical political strategies enabled reformers to raise broad questions about the nature of authority and the exercise of power within their communities and, by inference, society at large that will interest us most in the following pages. As we shall see, the practical political strategies of reformers deliberately played upon the popular sense of political exclusion through the themes of anti-oligarchy, local self-government and popular representation. Here again, in their use of these issues reformers sought to create new political arenas by reclaiming old constitutional rights with which to contest restrictive and exclusive definitions of the public political sphere. Contrary to Derek Fraser's belief, local practical politics was not just a power struggle between middle-class political elites, rather it provided a platform upon which reformers mobilised the politically excluded in order to expand the official political arena.[4]

SYMBOLIC STRUCTURES

In this section I shall endeavour to show how reforming groups implemented their rhetorical demands for a fairer, more representative constitution through their organisational structures. Yet these organisational ambitions were confined by the local political contexts within which they operated. In those constituencies which had been part of the unreformed electoral system reformers had to negotiate with pre-existing electoral practices and organisations, unlike their counterparts in Oldham and Tower Hamlets.

Needless to say the representative structures of those Tory groups opposed to any reform of the constitution of 1688, owed much to eighteenth-century aristocratic political styles. Candidates were invariably selected by small groups of local leaders in conjunction with local aristocratic influence. Although the power of the aristocratic Ancaster and Pelham dynasties to nominate candidates in Boston and Lewes had largely collapsed by 1812, they retained considerable influence over the selection of candidates up to the 1850s.[5] In Devon the aristocratic yoke was even more resilient. Although no one family had the power to select or nominate a candidate, it was clear, right up to 1868, that no candidate whatever his political principles had any chance of success without the support of the leading local dynasties or, for that matter, the influential Anglican church.[6] We should not assume that when such aristocratic influences in local Tory organisations declined they were immediately replaced by some semblance of popular representation. Instead aristocratic oligarchy usually gave way to the oligarchy of local middle-class leaders or employers.[7]

This lack of popular representation in the organisation of Tory politics was reflected in their preference for the informal eighteenth-century organisational language of the club rather than the union or association.[8] These clubs invariably lacked any representative or consultative framework and were consequently easily dominated by small cabals of local notables. Although the often complex and dull business of organisation rarely interested your run-of-the-mill free-born English Tory, local Tory elites were occasionally prone to pressure from below. So, for instance, the Conservative freemen of Boston showed themselves anxious to maintain a fiction of independence, so beloved of freeborn Englishmen, when selecting a candidate in 1847. A Mr Appleby seemingly spoke for many of his fellow Tories when he argued that the

question for that meeting to decide was, whether the Freemen and electors would have a representative of their own choice, or whether they would consent to have a member thrust down their throats by others who had only risen from their rank as themselves, but who now presumed the right of dictating to them. He would ask, what right had any county gentlemen to tell Mr. Colquhoun, as he had heard they had done, that his return was secure. They might think so, if they pleased; but the old freemen would have a voice in the matter; and if these gentlemen thought proper to have a candidate, so also would the freemen.[9]

Local Tory leaders and 'county gentlemen' ignored such protests at their peril, and so at the election later that year their favoured candidate Colquhoun failed to stand, his place going to a compromise candidate, Mr Benjamin Cabbell. This type of open public revolt by Boston's Tory rank and file was unique among the five constituencies.

Either Tory leaders elsewhere took greater care to canvass the opinions of their supporters or their authority was unassailable.

The selection procedure for reforming candidates in Lewes was not dissimilar. Candidates were selected by influential local activists through the Bundle of Sticks Club, once the opinion of the members had been taken into account.[10] It is not clear whether the 400 members of the town's Liberal Registration Society were afforded any greater say in the selection of their candidates after its foundation in 1866. Conversely, there can be little doubt that the rank and file of Boston's Blue party played an increasingly active role in the selection of their candidates. Up to the late 1850s Blue candidates seem to have been invited to stand by an unelected individual or committee, before being subjected to a vote at a public meeting of the party.[11] This lack of any defined organisational procedure soon led to problems when no candidate could be found who united all wings of the party. While the radicals championed the rights of both the electors and non-electors to choose their own candidates, their more cautious colleagues persisted in imposing their own candidates upon the party.[12] It was not until 1860, when the death of Herbert Ingram threatened to split the party once again, that the Blues followed the example of the Independent Reform Registration Society by sub-jecting the candidates to a vote of the Liberal electors. Significantly, however, the disenfranchised were excluded from this process and therefore predictably by 1865 the whole system had broken down and the party's carefully nurtured unity shattered. By the contest of 1868, despite the arbitration of the Liberal's central organisation at the Reform Club and the appointment of an 80-strong committee by the local Liberal Association, the selection of candidates was effectively a free-for-all in which anyone adopted by a public meeting could stand for election on behalf of the party.[13]

Although Boston's radicals failed to impose their organisational model upon the Blues, their counterparts in Oldham and Tower Hamlets were more successful at implementing their theories of representation. Their organisations were designed to afford all the constituents (electors and disenfranchised alike) not merely greater power in the selection of radical candidates, but also the capacity to ensure that once elected they remained accountable. Contrary to the official concept of the MP as an independent *representative* of his *electors*, radicals believed that the MP was a *delegate*, returned to parliament by his *constituents*, the electors exercising their franchise on *trust* from the non-electors and not as a *right*.[14] Therefore, in order to be selected as a radical delegate the potential candidate had to accept the conditions of his *constituents*, namely pledge himself to advocate a series of measures; give them an annual account of his stewardship in parliament and be prepared to resign the seat if asked to do so by a majority of them; and lastly (if the least difficult to bear) be elected free of expense. In theory, therefore, radical organisational structures were designed to redefine the official concept of parliamentary representation and, in doing so, to expand the public political sphere by affording a central role to the disenfranchised.

Six months before Oldham's first election the town's Radical Political Union called a series of meetings at which the borough's constituents, not just its electors, established their pledges and nominated two candidates. Over 10,000 people, including a small proportion of women, regularly attended these meetings – a number which far exceeded the 1,131 officially enfranchised in 1832.[15] By the end of July John Fielden and William Cobbett had accepted not only the general radical terms discussed above, but had also specifically pledged their support for universal manhood suffrage, annual parliaments, secret ballot, reduced taxation, civil and religious freedom, an investigation into the national debt, as well as the abolition of the corn laws, tithes, monopolies, sinecures and pensions, and all forms of slavery. Yet if these meetings allowed the disenfranchised to shape the appeals available to electors of the borough, they also revealed some of the tensions which beset the use of radical theories of representation in Oldham. For Fielden's immense personal popularity enabled him to set his own conditions by insisting that he would only be returned alongside Cobbett, so that together they could concentrate on advocating the latter's fourteen propositions for financial reform.[16] Despite this elevation of a leader above the very structures designed to keep him accountable, the selection and election of Fielden and Cobbett at Oldham in 1832 represented a triumph for radical theories of representation and organisation.

It was however a short-lived triumph. The unprecedented degree of unity generated amongst Oldham's reforming factions by the Political Union and their pledges began to disintegrate almost immediately the election had finished.[17] Rivalry and mutual suspicion between the borough's radical Huntites and Cobbettites, Dissenters and Anglicans, deepened as both Cobbett and Fielden flouted their 1832 election contract. Not only did they fail to deliver their annual account until an election threatened in December 1834, but Cobbett's ambiguous attitude towards the disestablishment of the Anglican church had disillusioned many of his dissenting supporters. Cobbett's death in 1835 and the subsequent by-election only made matters worse. Although Fielden supported the campaign of Cobbett's son, John Morgan Cobbett (who was even more ambivalent to church reform than his father), he had also, disastrously, intimated support of Feargus O'Connor's candidature, which undoubtedly had the better radical and dissenting credentials. The resulting split in the radical vote let in the local Tory candidate, J. F. Lees, by thirteen votes. Although this defeat was quickly reversed in 1837 with the election of General W. A. Johnson as Fielden's colleague it remained a blot on the collective radical memory and symbolised the collapse of the supposedly model radical organisational representative structure.

When General Johnson retired in 1847, the old wounds and divisions reappeared, despite the deliberations of a Reform Committee specifically established to find a candidate acceptable to all factions. Having successfully drawn up a list of pledges remarkably similar to those of 1832, the committee failed to agree on the nomination of a candidate. They left the decision to a public meeting of the constituents at which they put forward three potential candidates, namely W. J. Fox, J. M. Cobbett and J. Holladay.[18] Although Holladay and Fox convincingly won the show of hands, John Fielden, fresh from his triumph with the Ten Hours Bill, raised the stakes by insisting once again that he would only accept re-election if his prospective son-in-law J. M. Cobbett was returned alongside him. With this endorsement the Cobbettites refused to admit defeat, promptly holding a meeting at which they nominated Cobbett as a candidate.[19] The town's old radical party was never to reunite. Fielden, the champion of 1832, had turned 'dictator' and was soundly defeated, with Cobbett, at the poll. By 1852 Cobbett had firmly embraced popular Protestantism which considerably eased his switch to the Tories during the fifties, while Holladay and his supporters joined forces with the Foxites and took on the mantle of a radical and popular Liberalism. The whole radical organisation lay in tatters and the representative standards initiated in 1832 never fully recovered.

In a sense the weight of Fielden's personal influence ensured that the representative theories of 1832 had always been an illusion. Although Fielden had adhered to the ritual of the annual account after his initial lapses in 1832–3, it was only ever a symbolic gesture. As Stewart Weaver has argued 'the outcome of the vote was probably never in question', and even if it had been it is unlikely that either he or his colleagues would have resigned their seats.[20] We should not be too ready to dismiss the attempts by radicals to redefine official notions of representation and the public political sphere. Both the use of annual accounts and the freedom of the candidate from the expenses of elections remained regular features of Oldham's political life right up to 1868. In Oldham, at least, these parts of the People's Charter that never reached the statute books during the nineteenth century had been implemented since 1832. Not only did these organisational practices preserve the radical notion of the MP as delegate, but they also continued to ensure that those officially excluded from the political nation were included within the political life of the constituency.

As at Oldham, the enfranchisement of Tower Hamlets in 1832 enabled the borough's reformers to implement very similar radical theories of representative organisation. If selecting representative candidates was problematic in Oldham, it was even worse in Tower Hamlets where no single organisation was ever able to unite the constituency's different reforming factions. Consequently, at every election numerous public meetings were held by different groups, each passing different pledges and nominating different candidates.[21] It was a problem exacerbated by the lack of any opposing Tory or Conservative organisation against whom the reformers could unite and, consequently, it was not unusual to have 4 or 5 reforming candidates competing against each other at Tower Hamlets' elections. This lack of a central, unifying organisation to pull together the different reforming factions meant that, in effect, candidates were selected by each faction's leading activists, although they were always careful to cover their tracks by presenting their candidates to public meetings.[22] These public meetings created a fiction of involvement among the constituents but, as in Oldham, it was a fiction which generated a sense of inclusion among the disenfranchised. Moreover, most radical candidates pledged themselves to annual accounts of their stewardship even if none of those elected, with the exception of George Thompson, ever accepted the possibility of resigning their seat if deselected by their constituents.[23]

Ironically, it seems that the somewhat impromptu electoral
arrangements made by reformers in Oldham and Tower Hamlets
during 1832 were the closest they came to ensuring the accountability
of their MPs during this period. As soon as attempts were made to
institutionalise these arrangements, something of their representative
nature was lost. The mass public meetings of up to 15 thousand
constituents held to select candidates and their pledges in 1832 were
soon replaced by more formal organisational structures of associations and their committees based upon a numerically very limited
membership. These organisational bodies were frequently accused of
junta-like dictation and proved easy targets for their opponents.
Listen, for instance, to J. M. Cobbett lampooning the Foxite Reform
Association during Oldham's July 1852 election. 'He understood
that he had forfeited the respect of the Reform Association by his last
vote and that that body, according to the newspapers, had censured
him. But forty persons were not the people of Royton. – (A voice:
"read them up; there's more than forty, there's fifty.") Well fifty. –
(A voice: "There's sixty.") Well sixty if you like, but at that meeting
nineteen only were present.'[24] Moreover, as political differences
polarised both within and between rival organisations during the
1840s and 1850s, the large public meetings of constituents were
replaced by smaller partisan meetings of one set of supporters which,
as we shall see in the following chapter, were increasingly ticketed.
Therefore a candidate's annual account ceased to be delivered to the
constituency as a whole, and was confined to the members, electors or
supporters of one political group or organisation. Increasingly, MPs
used the occasion of the annual account as just another opportunity
for politicking, delivering set-piece speeches rather than explaining
their votes in the House. In this form, devoid of its radical edge, the
use of the annual account spread into the older constituencies like
Boston and Lewes.[25]

However, while the advent of increasingly formal modes of
organisation from the late 1830s restricted popular forms of accountability, other arenas facilitating popular representation opened
up. Town and county meetings for instance had long been used to
censure MPs for their voting record in unreformed constituencies. As
early as 1816 an attempt was made at a Devon county meeting to
prevent Sir T. D. Acland from presenting a congratulatory address
to the queen because he had 'by his late parliamentary conduct
forfeited the confidence of the county'.[26] As we have already seen

from chapter 2, the use of town and county meetings for partisan purposes also began to decline from the 1830s as they were appropriated by party-political organisations and various pressure groups. In 1833 Oldham's Dissenters pointedly sent a petition advocating disestablishment and religious liberty to William Cobbett, whose opposition to such measures was well known.[27] As the number of political movements and pressure groups proliferated during the 1830s so candidates and MPs were often subjected to a bevy of questions, addresses, and deputations asking them to define their position on any number of issues. These ranged from general questions on the rights of Dissenters and trade unionists, the points of the Charter, temperance and moral issues, to quite obscure and detailed matters. At a meeting in Oldham to re-select W. J. Fox during 1852 a

young man named Horsfall (secretary, we were informed, to the Weavers Association at Royton) came forward and put a series of questions to Mr. Fox, reading them from a paper he held in his hand. The questions embraced Mr. Fox's vote on the Irish Arms Bill, the People's Charter, the African squadron, Mr. Henley's motion on a reduction of 10 per cent on all salaries paid by the government, and the motion for a repeal of the Malt Tax. – The honourable member replied to the several questions at some length, to the evident satisfaction of the majority of the audience, and the questioner ultimately retired amidst laughter and hisses.[28]

The use of such deputations and questions was not simply a technique by which rival factions disrupted meetings. Interest and pressure groups were capable of delivering a substantial number of votes to a candidature if their lobbying was favourably received.[29] Therefore, however well protected candidates were by their agents, committees, and organisations, they were still kept on their toes.

The press also played an important role in keeping MPs, and representatives at all levels of the political process, in touch with their electors and constituents. Quite apart from reporting the speeches of local MPs whether in the Commons or the constituency, the press also published detailed accounts of MPs' voting and attendance records. The 'Whig' Charles Butler felt the full force of the press during his 16 years (1852–68) as MP for Tower Hamlets. The *East London Observer* endlessly compared his poor attendance in the House of Commons with that of his more popular colleague, A. J. Ayrton. It was not just the behaviour of parliamentary representatives that were scrutinised by the press in such exhaustive detail. Every May the *East*

London Observer published a definitive record of the attendance and votes of local vestry officials, while almost all local papers gave thorough reports of all vestry and council proceedings. Some papers, like the *Sussex Weekly Advertiser* went further still, chronicling every cough and cold of its borough and county members.[30] Yet the press did more than simply keep constituents in touch with their representatives, it also kept the representative in touch with his constituents. Then, as now, any MP worth his salt assiduously read his constituency's local papers, always keeping a careful eye on the local political climate. As we shall see in the following section, the use of the press was central to radical strategies to keep representatives and representative bodies accountable to a wider public, a public which often included many of the disenfranchised.

The uses and forms of political organisation were then a central component of the repertoire of symbolic communication. Radicals in Oldham and Tower Hamlets, and to a lesser extent Boston and Lewes, were able to contest restrictive official definitions of the public political sphere by including the disenfranchised in their organisational structures to select and elect candidates and ensure their accountability. Such strategies effectively empowered the disenfranchised, including them within a political nation from which they were legally excluded. Similarly, the annual account literally enacted radical demands for annual elections, just as the election of representatives free of personal expense attempted to by-pass the exclusive property qualifications for candidates. Despite the radical uses of such organisational forms at Tower Hamlets and Oldham during the 1830s (and, to a lesser extent, in Boston and Lewes during the 1840s), there was a marked retreat from the radical idea of the MP as delegate by the 1850s and 1860s. The formalisation of political organisations from the 1830s seems to have made them more amenable to oligarchic control from above, even though they carefully preserved a 'fiction of consultative democracy'. Certainly, historians have emphasised the use of such fictions in the development of Conservative and Liberal party organisations from the 1860s, although there were echoes of radical representative theories in the 'caucus' of Joseph Chamberlain's National Liberal Federation.[31]

PRACTICAL POLITICS

This section will examine the tactical organisation of radical politics. Although the emphasis of radical practical political strategies changed over time I will concentrate on four campaigns which, for the most part, took place in Tower Hamlets, Oldham and Boston. As with the representative structures of their organisations, radicals used their practical political strategies symbolically, to define and yet expand the terrain of struggle.

Not unsurprisingly many of the most popular and successful radical campaigns were conducted at parochial or municipal level. In the first place, as we have already seen in chapter 2, the dubious legality of public meetings throughout much of this period meant that the officially sanctioned arenas of parish, town, and county politics became indispensable forums for public political debate. As we shall see, control of the institutions and offices of these political arenas empowered radicals to call and legally protect their own public political meetings. Secondly, as was evident from chapter 1, the ambiguous legal definition of the parochial franchise facilitated a degree of popular participation and representation unparalleled elsewhere in the official political arena. And finally, there were often simply no other practical alternatives for gaining power within this official political arena. The structure of the local political process was therefore vital in conditioning the probable strategy of radical action, as I hope will soon become apparent.

Reformers in Devon and Lewes, apart from their parliamentary exertions, were confined to chipping away at the edges of the local elite's political authority.[32] For the most part these elites controlled the politically important local institutions and offices and, consequently, reformers concentrated their efforts on capturing symbolically important offices, like the office of county coroner. So, for instance, when in 1824 Isaac Cox, secretary of the reforming Devon County Club, was elected as coroner for East Devon he claimed that it signalled a major triumph for the cause of reform because it was an office which

was of the few remaining landmarks which clearly pointed out the privileges once possessed by British freeholders; there was a time when they elected the Sheriff, Magistrates, and many other officers, but which their forefathers had lost through supineness; thank God this still remains, and long may it remain and be valued by them; for it is the duty of this officer ... to inquire into the cause of death of every person … so that no mans life … can be taken from him, be he high or low, rich or poor, without the circumstances attending it being strictly inquired into before a jury of his neighbours.[33]

Similarly, over 800 votes were cast at the election of the Sussex county coroner at Lewes in 1809, when the victorious popular candidate, the reforming Independent Mr Wheeler, was regaled like a new member of parliament. The *Sussex Weekly Advertiser* recorded that 'on quitting the hall the populace drew Mr. Wheeler home in a post chaise, where he had not long arrived before he was sent for to take an inquest'.[34] The event was commemorated with a celebratory dinner and the presentation of a poll book to all Wheeler's supporters.[35] Clearly, the capture of this once great office of the revered Anglo-Saxon constitution was an important symbolic victory, one which played upon the popular sense of political exclusion and lost constitutional rights.

Although Oldham's radicals were not reduced to this type of gesture politics, they too concentrated on the institutions and offices of the ancient constitution to emphasise the sense of popular political loss and exile. In a sense, of course, they had no alternative, as the town was not represented in parliament until 1832. None the less, the campaign for the accountability of the town's policing was redolent of the politics of the freeborn Englishman's ancient constitutional rights. Contrary to Foster's thesis, this campaign had more to do with upholding the ancient principles of local self-government and freedom of assembly than protecting the rights of trade unionists.[36] As early as 1812 the town's radicals seem to have captured control of the vestry, thereby enabling them to control the appointment of the strategically vital constables. Parochial constables were important primarily because they could both call and sanction public meetings, but they were also responsible for the recruitment of special constables and the appointment of jurors at local inquests. It was a strategy which quickly paid tangible dividends, as it enabled Oldham's radicals to stage a series of 'monster' meetings close to the town's centre on Bent Green during the reform agitation of 1816–17, despite the best efforts of the Tory magistrates to deter them by calling in the military and stationing them on nearby King Street.[37] Two years later the radical constables tested the town's Tory authorities still further, appointing sympathetic jurors at the inquest of the Peterloo victim John Lees, which was widely and embarrassingly reported throughout the country. Although the jurors were eventually dismissed by the Court of King's Bench before they had delivered their verdict because of alleged irregular proceedings, the inquest had already served radical purposes, it had kept the dreadful deeds of Manchester's magistrates in the popular eye a little longer and demonstrated once again the oligarchic nature of central government.

Enraged by these radical successes, the following year central government revived the powers of Salford's Tory court-leet to appoint Oldham's constables over the head of the town's popularly controlled vestry. The radicals however refused to lie down and die. At a time when the infamous Six Acts made any type of public meeting a hazardous affair, the town's vestry was especially important. Using their control of vestry meetings, Oldham's radicals rejected the accounts of the new constables, 'on the grounds that the person whose accounts were before the meeting, not having been elected by the inhabitants were not the legal constables of the township, and the leypayers ought not to recognise them or their accounts'.[38] Although this radical counter-attack was doomed to fail, as the Court of King's Bench unsurprisingly sided with Salford's court-leet, it proved an important symbolic victory for the radicals. Not only had they managed to keep the town's rates by forcing the court-leet to appeal to the town's wealthy inhabitants in order to defray the constable's expenses, but, by preserving the vestry as a critical political forum, they had also shown how partial and unrepresentative central government was. By refusing to settle the constable's accounts, which included the expense of erecting temporary barracks for the hated military, the people refused to pay for the instruments of their own oppression, for it was the military who were used to keep them in a state of political bondage. In an attempt to wrest the political initiative from Oldham's radicals once more parliament passed the Oldham Police Act in 1826, which established an unelected body of commissioners responsible for the town's policing and general administration. As we saw in chapter 1, despite the exclusive property qualifications, radicals gained control of the police commissioners by 1831, immediately dismissing all the town's watchmen in the interests of one-upmanship as much as economy. The scene was set for the battle to run and run.

From 1832 Oldham's radicals secured themselves necessary reinforcements in this battle with the election of two sympathetic MPs. This was timely indeed, for, just as John Fielden led the campaign against the introduction of the new poor law from the House, so he was able to echo his constituents' opposition to the proposal in the Municipal Corporation Bill of 1834 that all boroughs should be compulsorily incorporated, with each council having full control of local policing.[39] In 1839 he was called upon again to oppose the County Police Act which gave Oldham's Tory magistrates, rather than the more radical police commissioners, the power to appoint up to 21 rural policemen out of the county rates. It was no accident that this Act was introduced at a time when Chartism was at its peak, and there had been wide reports of Chartist drilling in Oldham which had left the radical police commissioner, Alex Taylor, protesting against his colleagues enrolment of 400 special constables.[40] Indeed, 9 months later Alex Taylor, who always had a good nose for a populist issue, moved the first resolution at a meeting of Oldham's leypayers, protesting against the introduction of these so-called rural police. The resolution argued that 'the evil arising from the said Act is the placing of such rural police under the immediate control of justices appointed by the government…irresponsible to the people (who provide the funds for the payment of such police), and accountable only to the secretaries of state'.[41] Once again, although the radicals were powerless to resist the Act, they used the issue skilfully, presenting themselves as guardians of both the leypayers' pockets and their ancient freeborn liberties against the encroachments of an unrepresentative and oligarchic government.

Certainly they did not let the issue drop. In 1843 the radicals rejected the constables' annual accounts on the grounds that they included the expenses of erecting a temporary barrack in 1842 for the military when there had not even been a breach of the peace.[42] Despite the censure of the town's magistrates 'for unfitness and over-officiousness', and the hiring of a sympathetic solicitor in the shape of William Cobbett's son, R. B. B. Cobbett, to represent their case through the courts right up to the Attorney General, the radicals were only ever able to defer the accounts until 1845. It was the increasingly partisan use of the rural police by the magistrates, particularly during the Chartist agitation of 1848, that convinced many radicals of the need to incorporate the town in 1849.[43] Indeed, the incorporation of the town effectively ended the radical use of the issue of popular local control of the police. In any case, the issue had served its purpose. The radicals had demonstrated their claims to represent the inhabitants of Oldham against oligarchic magistrates and central government, by defending the erosion of their ancient constitutional rights to local self-government, self-defence, and freedom of assembly. Perhaps, more significantly, they did so without alienating the ratepayers, always carefully dressing their rhetoric in appeals to economy and retrenchment. Finally, by 1849, not only was the right to public assembly more firmly grounded in Oldham, but the use of the mass platform as a means of agitation was in question. In this context the accountability of the police was eclipsed by other issues and concerns, although in Tower Hamlets where the Home Office used their metropolitan police force to suppress the right to public assemblies, the issue remained alive and well throughout the 1850s and 1860s.[44]

Conversely, between 1808–31 the right of public assemblies was much less of an issue in Boston because the town's reformers had always been able to hold public meetings for parliamentary elections. Indeed, up to 1830 Boston's reformers had concentrated their energies on the parliamentary level, consolidating upon the victory of W. A. Maddocks in 1802 by returning a reforming candidate at every election. However, with the swell of reforming opinion that swept the country between 1829 and 1832, Boston's reformers felt increasingly confident that they could carry the town, and so looked for new local grievances and targets for reform. The impenetrability of the unreformed corporation limited their options, turning their attentions to that other bastion of the town's Anglican ruling elite – the parish vestry and its power to set the hated church rate. Boston's reformers sought to open up a new arena of political debate, in which they could contest the balance of local power and project their own anti-oligarchic appeals for religious freedom and economy.

The church rate was an obvious target for a group of reformers dominated by dissenters.[45] Yet it was a campaign which also appealed to a wider constituency, playing as it did upon the well-worn principle of 'no taxation without representation' and the general need for retrenchment and economy by corrupt oligarchic authorities. However, before they could storm the Bastille of St Botolph's Anglican church the reformers needed to know when vestry meetings were held. Consequently, the first phase of their campaign focused on ensuring that the Tory churchwardens publicly announced the date and time of all future meetings of the vestry. By 1831 'considerable dissatisfaction was excited in consequence of the refusal of the churchwardens to comply with the order of a previous vestry meeting to *advertise* all future meetings of the parish in the *Gazette,* so that the parishioners who do not attend the church might know of these meetings as well as those who do'.[46] The following year, alert to the timing of the meeting, the radicals managed to elect George Hill and John Bontoft as churchwardens, both of whom were Dissenters and leading lights of the town's Political Union. These were the first positions of official political power held by any of Boston's reforming Blue party, and they wasted no time in using them well. Not only was the president of the Political Union (Meaburn Staniland) appointed as their legal adviser, but a successful application was made to the magistrates to inspect the county rates, from which the costs of policing and repairing the damage at the riotous 1831 election (when several Blue supporters were imprisoned) were defrayed.[47]

These were the first sweet tastes of power by Boston's reformers. The capture of these posts, at the very heart of the town's Anglican establishment, was itself significant – a harbinger of radical change. Certainly the town's Tory establishment did not enjoy the boot being on the other foot, as the reformers rapidly made up for lost time. In 1833 the dissenting churchwardens issued a handbill announcing a timber sale in St Botolph's church during divine service on Sunday. When, after much Anglican protest, the handbill was eventually withdrawn, it was replaced by another insinuating that the church itself was up for auction.[48] Consequently, throughout the 1830s Boston's Tories led an often vicious counter-attack upon their reforming rivals, regularly accusing them of profane behaviour at vestry meetings. Yet these attacks seem merely to have incited reformers and Dissenters still further. Thus, during a vestry meeting of 1839, the reformer C. F. Barber moved an amendment to adjourn the meeting while sitting 'with his hat on smoking a cigar on the steps of the baptismal font'.[49] As sweet as this revenge must have been it was only ever a side-show to the more important battle over the church rates.

Despite the election of reforming churchwardens in 1832 it took several years before the hated church rate was finally rejected. This was not for the lack of trying. In 1834 the tory *Herald* complained 'the Radicals of Boston ... [have made] ... the granting of a church rate a party question – a trial of strength between them and the friends of order.'[50] Despite all their efforts, the Reverend A. Perrey's 1834 amendment to postpone setting a rate until 1836 was still defeated by 396 votes to 340. Momentarily this defeat seems to have punctured radical momentum, at least on the church-rate issue. Over the following 3 years their attentions turned elsewhere, especially to gaining control of the town's newly reformed municipal corporation and, to a lesser extent, the poor law guardians.[51] It was not, therefore, until 1837, when the corporation was firmly under their control, that the reformers' energies were once again redirected to defeating the church rate. Having established a Church Rate Abolition Society and petitioned parliament, Boston's church rate was defeated in 1840 by 388 votes to 301. As ever the *Herald* complained about the reformers' zeal and energy:

As a specimen of the means resorted to by the opponents of the rate we may mention Mr. Noble, bookseller, employed a man to parade the streets, ringing a bell, and carrying a large placard of which the following is a copy; – 'The poll is now open in the Church vestry for a church rate. Those who are opposed to this unjust tax should proceed instantly to vote against it, or they will be saddled with a rate.' The old clique of agitators Messrs. Noble, G. Hill, Bontofts, and T. S. Cooke were prodigiously active in hunting up voters against the rate.[52]

Such was the effort expended on this victory that a few weeks later at the municipal election the reformers had to rest largely on their laurels. It proved disastrous as all six Tory candidates won, enabling them to wrest control of the council from the reformers for the first time the following year, appointing the Tory leader W. H. Adams as mayor. Although by 1844, with the church rates finally and totally defeated, the reformers regained control of the council once more.

The issue of the church rates in Boston then served as a vital staging-post in the town's reforming politics. As with the issue of police control in Oldham, it represented the first foray into practical local politics by local radicals and reformers. It provided a vital form of patronage and experience of local government that stood the radicals in good stead at the first municipal elections of 1835. Many of the individuals involved in this campaign went on to become the town's councillors, aldermen, mayor, and, in the case of Meaburn Staniland, MP. Yet, in many ways the issue chose itself. Between 1830 and 1835 it was the only practical avenue by which the radicals could gain any effective local political power. Moreover, as an issue it evoked the same symbolic resonances evident in the Oldham radicals' campaign for control of the police, of liberty versus tyranny, freedom against oligarchy, economy versus extravagance. This was a potent mixture which was also used to equal effect in the parishes of Tower Hamlets, where the campaigns against the church rate paved the way for the radical campaigns of parochial reform in the 1850s.[53]

As we have seen, the theme of economy, of reducing the burden of parochial taxation, was a continuous strand in the practical reforming politics of Oldham and Boston. If this appeal was subsequently played down by reformers once they had secured the control of their respective municipal corporations, it continued to dominate the terms of parochial political debate in Tower Hamlets up to 1868. This was no doubt partly due to the late start afforded to the radical campaign for parochial reform by Hobhouse's 1831 Vestries Act.[54] Before this legislation, the popular radical campaigns against London's infamous oligarchic Select Vestries, which had begun from 1818 in parishes like St Matthews (Bethnal Green), Christchurch (Spitalfields), Mile End Old Town, and St Leonards (Shoreditch), were in effect toothless, confined to passing resolutions of 'no confidence' and petitioning parliament for their reform. However, as elsewhere, the campaign provided an important and legitimate focus for radical energies in the difficult years following the notorious Six Acts of 1819, although, unlike Boston, the campaign for parochial reform in Tower Hamlets was conspicuously quiet during the agitation for parliamentary reform between 1829 and 1832. During the 1830s, despite the campaign against the church rates, much of the energies of Tower Hamlet's radicals were directed towards local trade or Chartist politics.[55] However, as the momentum of Chartism began to wane during the mid-1840s, radicals in Tower Hamlets redirected their attention to their own backyard and parochial reform.

Often, in parishes like Shoreditch and Stepney, this second phase of the campaign for parochial reform grew out of the anti-church-rate agitation of the mid-1840s, even though it was not until the mid-1850s that it really took hold.[56] Contrary to the received wisdom this was not solely a movement of the shopocracy, designed to reduce the burden of parochial taxation.[57] The undoubted rhetorical stress on parochial economy and retrenchment has tended to conceal the campaigns populist appeal of creating a demonstrably representative model for local self-government. The programmes of the numerous parochial reform associations that sprang up throughout the parishes of Tower Hamlets during the 1850s were designed to recover the purity of England's ancient constitution, with its accent on decentral-

ised power and local democratic accountability. For instance, at a
meeting of the Ratcliff Parochial Reform Association to nominate
candidates for the approaching vestry elections in 1858, the candidates pledged themselves

> to advocate the principles of the association: reform, retrenchment, open
> vestries, the admission of the representatives of the press and the ratepayers
> to the deliberations of the vestry and the Board of Works, publication of
> accounts and those measures of economy which the Parochial Reform
> Association had advocated since the injustice and oppression of the Board of
> Trustees had compelled the ratepayers to associate and meet for a redress of
> grievances.[58]

Economy and retrenchment was therefore one among many measures
advocated by the parochial reform associations, it was just one
consequence of achieving local self-government. This is not to argue
that protecting the ratepayers' pockets did not prove an attractive
appeal to the shopocracy, just as it also was to the thousands of
lodgers and compound householders who were effectively disenfranchised by the high level of rates in the metropolis. It was these groups
of mainly working-class people who stood to be enfranchised at both
parochial and parliamentary elections by a lower rate. As with
practical reforming politics in Oldham and Boston, the campaign for
parochial reform in Tower Hamlets represented an attempt to
expand the public political sphere by creating new arenas of popular
political debate and participation.

Securing a large and popular franchise was only one plank in this
strategy. Publicity was also important as it encouraged participation
and kept the vestries accountable to their wider public. Consequently, the press was central to these radical campaigns. *The
Parochial Expositor; Or Anti-Church Rate Payers Gazette* had led the way
as early as 1840, before transforming itself into the *Parochial Chronicle*
in 1852. By 1857 it had been joined by the *East London Observer*, which
quickly established itself as the king of the parochial campaigning
papers.[59] Its opening editorial was a manifesto, declaring its
objectives as

> dragging into publicity the doings of vestries and boards of Guardians,
> tearing the veil of secrecy from the conduct of officials who have come to
> consider themselves the *employees* of a central board rather than the servants
> of the people ... we do not overrate the importance of the work to be done,
> when we say, that upon its successful accomplishment rests the hopes of the

England of the future. If it be well done, not only will the funds of each parish be economised – its officials efficient – its rights preserved – its duties properly performed – and its inhabitants rendered comparatively prosperous, happy and contented – but the welfare of the whole state will be increased in proportion to the restored health and vigour of its members... Besides this, men, by acquiring a knowledge of their own local affairs, will become better citizens... The affairs of the parish furnish a school in which men are trained in the habits necessary for public business... At the same time, the parochial organization properly understood and used, is an instrument of political power for the redress of common grievances, more powerful than the leagues and associations which have sprung up on the ruins, and endeavoured to supply the place of, local self-government.[60]

It was an editorial which seemed to speak for a whole generation of London's reformers and radicals. Parochial reform was an idea whose time had come.

Happily, it was also an appeal capable of uniting the different strands of reformers in Tower Hamlets. In a sense the bases of this coalition had already been provided by the candidatures of T. P. E. Thompson in 1841 and his namesake George Thompson in 1847, both of which advocated the abolition of the corn laws and church rates together with the five points of the charter. William Newton's candidature in 1852 consolidated the trend, appealing to the working men and the shopocracy simultaneously upon the platform of 'The Rights of Labour'.[61] In many ways Newton, proprietor of the *East London Observer*, came to personify the campaign for parochial reform. After his defeat at the Tower Hamlets election of 1852, Newton turned to parochial reform, rather than the trade politics of the Amalgamated Society of Engineers from which he emerged, in the belief that only popular democratic local self-government could stop the concentration of power in the hands of central government. In this sense Newton drew upon a long tradition of radicalism which incorporated both the historical belief in the ancient constitution and the natural rights faith of republicans like Paine and Spence. Indeed, when the Chartists developed their own organisation during the late 1830s and early 1840s they drew heavily on many of the 'features of the age-old parish system of local government with its quarterly general meeting of the vestry.'[62] This radical belief in local self-government as a check against centralisation of power at Westminster manifested itself in many forms during the 1850s, particularly in the Anti-Sabbatarian Movement and the Anti-Centralisation Society, to name but two organisations which were especially strong in the metropolis. Certainly it was a strand of radical thought which had strong resonances for Tower Hamlets' Chartists, many of whom had not only participated in these organisations, but had also been subjected to the partisan policing of both unrepresentative vestries (in 1842 and 1848) and the Home Office (in 1848 and 1852). However, by the 1860s, with most parishes under the control of parochial reform associations and with the collapse of the equalisation of rates campaign, parochial politics were once again eclipsed by the renewal of radical agitations for parliamentary reform. Newton became an increasingly isolated figure in the radical politics of Tower Hamlets – his candidature at the 1868 election finished disastrously at bottom of the poll.

The campaign for parochial reform in the parishes of Tower Hamlets was, however, only one among many practical political strategies deployed by reformers during this period. The very disparate nature of the community within Tower Hamlets made the more focused radical campaigns of Oldham and Boston less likely to take hold. None the less, the parochial reformers of the 1850s seem to have had some modest success in drawing together the different parishes and the different reforming factions in Tower Hamlets. Again this owed much to the Janus-faced nature of the campaign, which could mean all things to all men. The appeals against the centralisation of power and against inefficient local oligarchies charging high rates appealed to the working class, shopocracy, and middle classes alike. This should not obscure the radical edge of the campaign, the use of pledges and the press, and the attempt to enforce popular accountability on the offices of local administration. The campaign served as a model to reformers and radicals elsewhere. In both Boston and Devon reforming ratepayers associations were established during the 1860s. They played on the same themes of cheap, accessible, and accountable local self-government versus a wasteful, oligarchic, centralising national government.[63]

Yet, although the radicals of Oldham, Boston, and Tower Hamlets used their practical political strategies to demonstrate the efficacy of their platforms, they were also politicians at heart, with an eye for the main chance. Politics at this level owed much to the revolving door of patronage, and radicals were not naive enough to think they could dispense with this. After all, what use was power if old friends could not be rewarded and potential allies and supporters enticed by material rewards? Thus we find the usually stringent Oldham police

commissioners appointing the radical veteran John Knight (secretary
to the Political Union) as salaried town treasurer a few months before
his death in 1838, just as the Boston radical churchwardens had
appointed Meaburn Staniland (president of their Political Union) as
their legal adviser in 1833.[64] The radicals of Boston and Oldham
seem to have excelled at building up a patronage system. According
to John Foster, the radical control of Oldham's massive poor-relief
budget gave them sone £16,000 to dispense as they saw fit, in jobs,
contracts, and, of course, relief itself.[65] Boston's reformers also used
their control of the newly reformed corporation's budget wisely and
effectively. As early as 1837 the town's Tory paper, *The Herald*,
complained under the heading '"Liberal" Liberality' that 'to so
ridiculous an extent do the Reformed Corporation of Boston carry
their party feelings that they positively refuse to advertise in this, the
only paper published in the town or within 30 miles of it, even those
matters that relate exclusively to the town'.[66] Twenty-five years later
at the 1860 election, it was still complaining that the Liberal mayor
'in the exercise of his privilege, has given three booths to be erected
by builders of his own party, and only one to his opponents.'[67]
However petty these examples may seem to the late twentieth-
century reader used to multi-million pound political scandals, it still
represented an important trend with the politicisation of public
funds. Practical politics was about more than putting rhetoric into
action, it was also about getting your hands dirty and oiling the
financial wheels of the reforming community.

All this was, of course, essential training for any aspiring politician,
and in many ways local practical politics provided the perfect
breeding ground for the politically ambitious. As the ex-Chartist Dr
Bowkett argued in 1858, 'In his opinion, the best possible way for
men to educate themselves to elect good members of parliament, and
take a part in general legislation, was by attending closely to their
own immediate parochial affairs'.[68] This was even more the case
during the first half of the nineteenth century when, as we have seen,
reformers had been excluded from power in many local communities.
Practical local politics therefore gave them the opportunity to learn
the tricks of the trade, or sharpen up their skills. Even from these five
constituencies the list of radical leaders coming of political age
through the ranks of parochial or municipal politics is long. Take, for
instance, Meaburn Staniland of Boston, whose involvement with the
radical churchwardens paved the way for distinguished careers as

councillor and alderman, during which time he served as the Liberal electoral agent before achieving the ultimate accolade of becoming an MP himself in 1859. Similarly, William Newton in Tower Hamlets and John Platt in Oldham serve as other examples of local politicians making good. As we shall see in chapter 7, the number of local radical leaders who commanded a sizeable following in the community because of their part in local practical politics was larger still. This dimension to practical politics should not be underestimated, for it was at this level that ambitious local leaders first came into contact with budgeting, council committees, and debating procedures.

Practical political campaigns were an essential part of the politics of reform. By resisting the impositions of unaccountable and unrepresentative bodies to control the police, impose the poor law, charge church or excessive rates, radicals and reformers demonstrated their own commitment to popular representative government to a much larger constituency than their usual body of support. Like the internal representative structure of their organisation, practical politics wedded radical discourse to practical action, expanding official definitions of the public political sphere.

CONCLUSION

This chapter has attempted to expand our conception of nineteenth-century political organisation, casting doubt on the notion that it was merely the institutional reflection of wider social and political structures. I have endeavoured to show how organisation was used creatively to construct constituencies of support and redefine the boundaries of the official public political sphere.

What is striking about the radical uses of the symbolic dimensions of organisation is the construction of oppositions evident in other modes of radical discourse. By enacting their creed of popular representation, accountability, and participation, Radicals provided a tangible and practical critique of the official political process, one which evoked 'an image of strength and conflict: a united (popular body), confronting the corrupt authority in power, and demanding a restoration of the people's rights'.[69] Both symbolically and practically, therefore, radical organisation endowed the politically excluded with a sense of dignity and agency denied them by the official political process. In no way was this a cathartic exercise, rather it enhanced the sense of exclusion, of a people stripped of their natural and historical rights, denied citizenship in their own land. Although the organisational forms of reforming groups differed in each constituency, they all evoked the same image of a strong and just popular body confronting an unrepresentative and corrupt political process. The different modes of radical organisation evident in the five constituencies owed much to their contrasting political cultures and electoral traditions. So, for instance, reformers operating within the unreformed constituencies of Boston, Lewes, and Devon, were forced to build upon existing electoral organisations and identities, whereas their counterparts in Oldham and Tower Hamlets were presented with a cultural clean slate in 1832. As we have seen, these different local political contexts were also critical in shaping the choice of practical strategies of reforming politics in the five constituencies.

However, despite these differences, local radicals and reformers seemed to have shared a special preference for practical politics at the parochial and municipal level. Local self-government was, after all, at the heart of radical theories of representation – it had been the touchstone of the freeborn Englishmen's natural historical democracy based on the mythology of an Anglo-Saxon past. In this sense local reforming politics were part of an ancient struggle against an encroaching central government. Each strategic campaign seems to have been carefully chosen to reinforce the image of radical and reforming organisations as popular and representative bodies pitting themselves against oligarchic and unaccountable authorities. Here again one is conscious of radical modes of organisation constructing, and playing upon, a series of symbolic dichotomies of good versus evil, liberty versus tyranny, economy versus waste, the people versus an elite, local versus national, that were echoed by other forms of radical discourse. The use of these oppositions were central to the attempts of reformers to contest and expand restrictive official definitions of the public political sphere. However, as we shall see in the following chapter, it was not just the organisational structure of the official politics that radicals wished to transform, but the whole cultural fabric of political life.

CHAPTER 6

The politics of culture

INTRODUCTION

Political historians have often lost sight of the critical role of culture in the construction of political identities and allegiances. Long ago, however, John Vincent reminded us of the seemingly intangible and emotional loyalties generated by the culture of Gladstonian Liberalism: 'For the nineteenth-century man the mark or note of being fully human was that he should provide for his own family, have his own religion or politics, and call no man his master. It is as a mode of entry into this full humanity that the Gladstonian Liberal Party most claims our respect'.[1] Similarly, Patrick Joyce has illustrated how central the culture of beer, Britannia, and *bonhomie* was to the style and appeal of popular Toryism in late Victorian Lancashire.[2] By the 1860s this Tory political culture increasingly defined itself in opposition to that of the Gladstonian Liberal party, with its moral earnestness and its emphasis on education, self-improvement, and temperate habits. Although such an account errs towards caricature, it does encapsulate something of the different personalities of the competing parties. This chapter traces the development of these rival political cultures from the early nineteenth century, stressing both the broad cultural similarities of different reforming and Tory groups across the five constituencies, and the essential continuity of styles in popular political culture.

Popular political culture was highly contested. Each movement or party sought to define its political style culturally, using its political culture to champion their own definitions of citizenship and the public political sphere. This often entailed a struggle to select, appropriate, and use specific cultural forms, making them one's own and endowing them with meanings sympathetic to the cause. Indeed, in such ways political groups created their own traditions, locating themselves historically, and emphasising the long genealogies of their struggle and its demands.[3] As we shall see, this contest to appropriate and use certain cultural forms and traditions suggests something of the reciprocal nature of the relationship between political leaders and their constituencies of support. It does not make much sense to categorise the politics of culture as a conflict between high and low, patrician versus plebeian, or classes. I want to suggest that this contest can be more usefully analysed as a *political* struggle to define the parameters of the public political sphere, that is the meaning of the constitution and citizenship. To characterise this conflict as part of the struggle to create distinct bourgeois or working class 'public spheres' is, I fear, to indulge in an exercise of historical wishful thinking.[4] What was at issue here was who possessed the independence and virtue to qualify as citizens, who should be included within the political nation and brought within the pale of the constitution. Although this debate could (and sometimes did) fracture along class lines, it would perhaps make more sense to analyse it as part of the construction of a distinctly gendered public political sphere. Certainly, as we shall see, although competing political groups sought to facilitate women's participation in the public political sphere, the terms of that inclusion were invariably restrictive, shaped as it was by a discourse of the 'social' created by men.[5]

THE LANGUAGE OF THE MEETING-PLACE

As we saw in chapter 2, the political uses of space played a formative role in the creation of official political culture. Similarly, therefore, popular political groups, especially radical ones, used public spaces as meeting places to define the style of their political culture. Political historians have tended to be deaf to this language of the meeting place, just as they have been blind to the ways in which competing groups used this language to contest each others' definitions of the political arena.[6]

Ever since the so-called 'underground years' of the late eighteenth and early nineteenth centuries, Oldham's reformers had held meetings on remote outdoor spaces. The 'terror' of Pitt's repressive legislation and the loyalist reaction during the Napoleonic Wars had forced the town's reformers to hold clandestine meetings at Tandle Hill and Buckland Castle Moor, several miles beyond the reach of both the 'Church and King' mobs and the local authorities.[7]

However, with the enclosure of much of the town's surrounding common moors and grounds in 1807, reform meetings, even on these remote sites, became illegal. As we saw in chapter 5, by concentrating their efforts on the vestry, the radicals were able to elect church-wardens and constables who in turn provided official sanction for reform meetings at Bent Green and Greenacres Moor during the agitation of 1816. By meeting on these previously common, but subsequently enclosed, lands, radicals denied the legitimacy of its enclosure and asserted the right to reclaim their freeborn rights to the people's land.[8] Significantly, it was in the rapidly industrialising urban areas of Oldham and Tower Hamlets that this emotive appeal to the people being exiled and excluded from their own land was most resonant.

The continued use of outdoor meetings throughout this period by Oldham's radicals testifies to the strength of this appeal and reminds us that, like so many industrialising towns, Oldham had grown over the countryside not beside it. During the 1830s the dramatic site of Oldham Edge became the favourite venue for mass outdoor radical meetings. In 1834 a series of meetings were held there at six o'clock in the morning by 20,000 'unionists' demanding the implementation of Fielden's plan for national regeneration.[9] When the authorities posted 26 soldiers at one of these meetings the unionists merely cancelled it, staging their subsequent meetings at ever more remote locations – like Beesom Hill, Broadsman's Edge, and Saddleworth's High Moor – all of which were at least 3 miles hard walking away from the town. Such meetings doggedly asserted their rights to be included within the political nation and its agenda, as well as to assemble on their own lands. Clearly, for the hundreds and thousands of men, women, and children who turned up to these meetings despite their distance from the town, they were important and evocative events. The sense of gravity and fellowship enacted by the ceremonial procession to the venue and the habitual recital of prayers and hymns was both off-set and complemented by the carnivalesque atmosphere generated by the ginger-bread men, beer-sellers, jug-glers, entertainers, ballad-singers, and hawkers of almost anything, who seem to have converged upon such events with amazing alacrity.[10] Contemporaries reported the heady atmosphere of fun and fear, politics, pleasure and pain when Oldham's Chartists set out to the famous Kersal Moor meeting with 3 bands of music and 20 banners flying. A carnival air pervaded the town and its vicinity, as

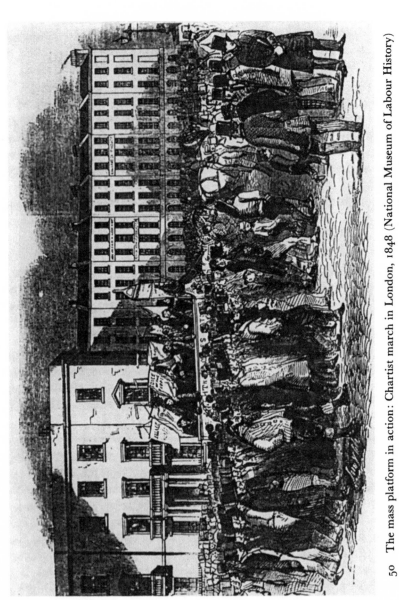

50   The mass platform in action: Chartist march in London, 1848 (National Museum of Labour History)

51   The mass platform in action: Chartists at Kennington Common, 1848
(National Museum of Labour History)

many of the shops and factories, deserted of their customers and
workforce, closed for the day (see Plate 50). Building upon such
successes, Oldham's mass Chartist demonstrations of 1842 were also
held on old common grounds or other remote sites, such as Shore
Edge, Wrigley Head Green, and, of course the old favourite Oldham
Edge (see Plate 51).[11] Significantly, it was not until the reform
agitation of 1866–8 that these types of meetings were once again
revived in Oldham by a new generation of reformers anxious to
emphasise their place within a long radical genealogy (see Plate
52).[12]

   Invariably the significance of these outdoor locations lay in their
geographic position. Often they were used because of their proximity
to a number of separate towns to ensure the largest possible turnout.
Tandle Hill was conveniently sited between Oldham and Royton,
Broadsmen's Edge between Oldham and Ashton, Beesom Hill
between Oldham and Saddleworth. And yet it was surely no accident
that so many of these sites were moorland summits, hills or edges, all
of which provided breath-taking panoramas of the surrounding
terrain. Of course, originally this fascination with high summits and

52   The mass platform in action: reform demonstration at Trafalgar Square, 1884
(Howell Collection, Bishopsgate Institute)

spectacular views may have reflected the siege mentality which
gripped many reformers during the Napoleonic Wars, just as it may
also have drawn upon the biblical parallel of *bamah*, high places at
which Jehovah was worshipped. Certainly, as I have indicated,
worship, prayers, and hymns were very much a feature of these
meetings.[13] Yet, perhaps most of all, such meetings drew upon the
popular mythology of the land, plundering Norman aristocracy
depriving the people of their freeborn rights as Englishmen,
dispossessing them in their own land.[14] The land remained a potent
symbol of a world that had been lost, a nostalgic image of a rural
England of small holdings and independent men; it highlighted the
blight of industrialism and the alienation of the freeborn Englishman
from his landscape. For radicals the land became a symbol of
regeneration and fertility. By marching and meeting on these hilltops,
they played out this belief as the low literally became high, masters of
the landscape for a few hours.

The political uses of outdoor spaces also had a long genealogy in
the metropolis. Radical political meetings had been held outdoors on

common recreational grounds like Stepney Green, Copenhagen Fields, and Kennington Common since the late eighteenth century (see Plates 51 and 52).[15] During the mid-nineteenth century it was a tradition kept alive by Tower Hamlets' radicals, despite the growing pressures of urbanisation and the introduction of the metropolitan police.[16] During 1848 and 1852 they regularly held mass meetings on Stepney Green, London Fields, and Bishop Bonner's Fields. It was the suppression of these Chartist meetings in 1848 and, more explosively, in 1852, which ignited the issue of the rights of public assembly and freedom of speech during the election campaign of that year. At a meeting in Bishop Bonner's Fields, attended by three of Tower Hamlets' most radical candidates, protesting against the police's dispersal of an earlier meeting on the same site, the chairman W. A. Hows argued that 'the birthright of Englishmen had been interfered with, the right of assembling for the free expression of their sentiments had been interfered with by an armed body of police, by instructions from the Home Secretary...They were not to be bludgeoned as they had been, and were prepared to prove that... those who had been so maligned by the Home Secretary were worthy of possessing the great right of Englishmen (cheers)'.[17] A resolution was immediately passed condemning this 'dangerous infringement on the right of public speech afforded by the common law of England...[as]...illiberal and *unconstitutional*.'[18] This was an emotive appeal on the very site at which the intolerant and oppressive Catholic Bishop Bonner had burnt his Protestant opponents as heretics.[19] The prevention of radical meetings on this public space therefore played upon this association, and in so doing heightened the sense of a dispossessed people, exiled in their own land. Not only were they denied the right to citizenship, but now they were also denied their ancient constitutional birthrights of freedom of speech and assembly. The choice of site, the large turnout, the presence of three parliamentary candidates (all committed to universal manhood suffrage), Hows' speech and the resolution, all testified that in thought, word, and deed the meeting strongly contested such exclusive and restrictive definitions of the constitution.

Even Marx was aware of the political significance of this struggle over the use and abuse of public spaces. Having witnessed the brutal attempts of the police to disperse a radical meeting in the capital's sacred space of Hyde Park in 1855, he wrote to Engels with the news that 'the English Revolution began in Hyde Park yesterday'.[20] The

Reform League also recognised the import of this constitutional contest over public spaces when, in the 1860s they revived the cultural forms of the mass platform. The initial popularity of Edmond Beales, the future president of the Reform League, owed much to his campaign to stage a public meeting in honour of Garibaldi on the contested ground of Primrose Hill.[21] This experience proved a useful rehearsal for Beales' presidency of the League, for, while its local branches in Tower Hamlets reclaimed the public right to use Stepney Green and London Fields for mass political meetings, the central leadership defied the Parks Regulation Meetings Act of 3 May 1866 by organising a meeting that July in Hyde Park. The furore caused by this meeting, as well as the one held the following May in defiance of the Home Secretary's ban, highlights the way in which radical uses of public spaces could challenge official definitions of the constitution. In turn both meetings were attacked as unconstitutional.[22] Some were so alarmed by the general radical control of the metropolis' public spaces that they established both the Open Space Movement (1870) to promote healthy outdoor sports, and the aptly named Constitutional Open Air League specifically to 'hold open-air meetings in place which were hitherto left to the Radical and Socialist demagogues.'[23] control of public spaces was therefore continually contested as different political groups endeavoured to articulate their competing definitions of the constitution and the wider public political sphere. Although these types of mass outdoor meetings were rarely held in Boston, Devon or Lewes, this does not mean that the use of public spaces or the constitution went uncontested. The contests in these constituencies were either less well documented or on a much smaller scale – in market places, pubs, or the streets of particular neighbourhoods.[24] Moreover, the pressure upon public spaces was considerably less acute in these less urbanised constituencies.

Alongside the outdoor meeting, the pub had also long been used as a political venue. For at least a century local political organisation had revolved around the communities of the street or neighbourhood and its tavern, debating club or pub.[25] The pub remained the centre of political organisation and information in most places until the late nineteenth century because they were places in which newspapers were read, ballads sung, gossip heard and conveyed, and political memorabilia proudly displayed. For instance, after the Napoleonic Wars at the heart of Oldham's most radical neighbourhoods of Bent and Glodwick, there stood in... West Street a public house which was known as the Reformers School, where Ab' o' Bunkers initiated novices into the principles of Radical doctrine ... During the following two years (1817–19) the Reformers met there in secret every Sunday afternoon'.[26] For contemporaries like Henry Vincent pub signs were an instant barometer of the political complexion of a locality. Touring Lancashire in 1838, he was amazed 'at the intensity of radical opinions here. You have an index from the numerous public house signs – full length portraits of Hunt holding in his hands scrawls [sic] containing the words Universal Suffrage, Annual Parliaments, and the Ballot. Paine and Cobbett also figure occasionally.'[27] Of course by no means every neighbourhood had its own designated radical or tory pub, many publicans deliberately kept aloof of partisan allegiances to stay in business. Invariably during elections pubs were hired out to the highest bidder for 'free and easies' or as committee headquarters, particularly in smaller constituencies like Lewes and Boston. In these places it was not unusual for the same pub to stage meetings for three rival political groups in as many nights.

However, since the turn of the century the intellectual influences of Enlightenment reason and the moral fervour of evangelical culture had led many reformers to shun the mental universe embodied in pub culture.[28] This was not only a morally bankrupt universe gripped by the superstitious fears of popular culture, but, worse still, the indirect taxes on beer propped up the very 'Thing' which enslaved them. Indeed, for some drink and the culture of the pub was all a horrible aristocratic plot designed to keep the poor in a state of subjugation (see Plate 53). Gradually, as E. P. Thompson has argued, 'the Radicals sought to rescue the people from the imputation of being "a mob": and their leaders sought continually to present an image of sobriety'.[29] In the wake of the disappointment of 1832 this project gained renewed urgency, as many radicals believed it had been their mobbish unrespectability which had caused the great middle-class betrayal – they were simply not perceived as 'fit and proper' persons capable of making independent decisions as virtuous citizens. Although pub meetings had been necessary during the early nineteenth century when the movement had been small and defensive (meetings and dinners held within pubs were amazingly exempt from the Seditious Meetings Acts of 1795 and 1819), in the new political climate of the 1830s this was no longer the case. By moving away from

53 The demons of drink: Oldham handbill, *c.* 1850s (Oldham Local Studies
Library)

the pub they would finally prove their political virtue and independence, and their claim for inclusion within the political nation
as citizens would be irresistible. Besides which many local tory
authorities had begun to use the licensing laws to control and
regulate radical meeting places.

   In these new political conditions many radicals became convinced
of the need for a more sober political style which would both broaden
their appeal and contest restrictive notions of what constituted an
independent citizenry. Crompton's Political Union was then not
unusual to stipulate in its rule book of 1832 that 'No person shall be
allowed to enter any meeting of the Union or its Committees who
may be intoxicated; and every member is fully expected to do all in
his power to promote temperate habits among his fellow-work-
men'.[30] These sentiments were even echoed in the habitually pub-
centred radical culture of East London when, in 1833, the Committee
of the National Union of Working Classes advised its branches not to

meet in pubs as 'nothing will more effectually contribute to the success of our cause... than sobriety and good conduct.'[31] Not least amongst the new constituencies of support radicals hoped to attract by moving away from the pub was women. Although women had always been prominent at radical mass meetings outside, they had long been conspicuously absent at meetings held in the 'masculine republic' of the pub. As late as the 1850s Sheffield's Chartist women complained that, 'while men continue to advocate or meet in pot-houses, spending their money... [they will exclude]... us from a share in their political freedom.'[32] Indeed, during the 1830s, the macho atmosphere of this radical pub culture had driven many women to embrace the Temperance movement with its portrayal of the pub as a centre of immorality which destroyed family life. Temperance literature was abundant with representations of virtuous but hungry women and children waiting in dark streets outside the bright lights of the pub on pay day, praying that their men would stop drinking and come home with what was left of their wages (see Plate 54).

The pub was so embedded in radical culture that any change in style had to be carefully and gradually negotiated as local leaders persuaded their supporters to wean themselves from it. Consequently, in each of the five constituencies radicals moved away from the pub at different speeds, depending on how embedded the pub was in local political culture and how committed both leaders and led were to the moral reform of radical politics. Typically, Oldham's radicals were the first to begin such a move, hiring their own rooms or chapels as early as the 1820s. The large temperance influence among Boston's radical leaders encouraged the use of 'dry' venues like the granary, guild-hall, theatre, town hall, and the grounds of private factories and shops for their meetings from the 1830s, at least outside election campaigns. However, the pub remained so firmly entrenched in Boston's electoral culture that it was not until 1847 that the reforming Blue candidate Sir James Duke was able to hold a meeting in the town hall rather than a pub. Even then Duke's agent, Meaburn Staniland, felt compelled to embark upon a lengthy justification when confronted by a thirsty audience.[33] Similar processes were repeated elsewhere. Despite the efforts of both Lewes' Reform Association and Bundle of Sticks Club to hold meetings outside pubs during the 1830s, it was not until 1847 that they successfully held their first 'dry' election rally at the local Mechanic's Institute. Similarly in Devon, the temperance influence was felt on the county's

54   Waiting for the wages: women outside a pub on pay day

political scene during the 1830s when Lord John Russell made liberal use of Plymouth's Mechanic's Institute and Exeter's Royal Subscription Rooms, rather than the customary venues of the Royal Hotel and New London Inn.

Predictably, the influence of temperance thought made least impact in Tower Hamlets where the pub's central role in commercial, cultural, and political life remained unchallenged. What challenges there were confined to the gallant, but unsuccessful, attempts of radicals like Charles Neesom, who established the doomed East London Chartist Temperance Association in 1840 and, a year later, the equally short-lived East London Total Abstinence, Charter and National Instruction Association.[34] Tower Hamlets' sheer size, together with the prohibitive cost of either building or hiring rooms in the metropolis, meant that, for the most part, politics continued to be organised through the customary convivial network of pubs and clubs and coffee houses.[35] Moreover, the influence of the brewing interest was particularly strong in Tower Hamlets. Although many of the brewers remained politically impartial during this period, the increasing association elsewhere of Liberalism with the temperance cause drove some brewing dynasties to the Conservative camp. Significantly, Tower Hamlets' first Conservative candidate in 1868 was the brewer O. E. Coope.

While reformers shied away from the pub with gathering speed outside the metropolis, it remained central to Tory political culture in all five constituencies. The strong association of Tory politics with the pub afforded it an air of sociability and informality increasingly at odds with the high moral tones of reformers. Oldham's Tories provide a case in point. The appeal of J. M. Cobbett's popular Toryism owed much to his identification with the pleasures of the people, particularly his campaign against the Malt Tax and his belief, echoed by the tory *Oldham Standard*, in the 'efficacy of home-brewed beer in improving the health and morals of the people.'[36] Several of Oldham's leading Tory activists were publicans, most notably John Nield, proprietor of the 'Crown and Anchor' and prime mover of the Operative Conservative Association. Not only was Nield's pub the headquarters of Oldham's Tories until the Central Conservative Club was built in 1874, but he was behind the town's Licensed Victuallers Association endorsement of the Cobbettite–Tory alliance in 1848. The central figures of this alliance, the town's Tory mayor William Jones, its Tory MP John Duncuft, and the Cobbettite leaders Alex Taylor and John Earnshaw, were all regular attendants at the Association's dinners during the 1850s.[37] This Tory association with beer and the politics of the good time became even stronger in the 1870s and 1880s when many of its characteristics were institutionalised in the club movement.[38] It was a political style sharply at odds with the increasing moral earnestness of their radical and Liberal opponents. The Tory's language of the meeting place spoke to a constituency that was truly independent, able to make up their own minds and indulge in John Bull's historic pleasures. It was they who protected the people's freeborn liberties and independence from interfering namby-pamby reformers.

Undeterred by such claims reformers continued to look for alternative venues to the pub. This was especially evident in Oldham where the strong links between the town's radicals and dissenting congregations were apparent from the regular reform meetings held in chapels and Sunday schools as early as the 1820s.[39] However, during the 1830s there seems to have been a growing reluctance on the part of these chapels' trustees and ministers to be too directly associated with radical politics. The first signs of this shift came in January 1832 when the trustees of the Primitive Methodist Chapel refused permission for William Cobbett to use their chapel for two lectures because they had failed to come to 'agreeable terms' with Cobbett's local managing committee.[40] The situation had clearly deteriorated 3 years later when James Holladay, a Dissenter himself, opened a meeting with 'a few remarks on the folly of working men contributing to the erection of Chapels over which they had no control – Mr. Knight stated that a Mr. John Ogden, one of the Wesleyan body, had refused the school room in which they should have met because to use his own words "he thought it might injure the school…"'[41] However, elsewhere dissenting congregations and their trustees were even less generous. It was not until 1860, when the Tower Hamlets Political Union met at Stepney's Wesleyan chapel, that the chairman was able to hail 'a new era in political movement that they were enabled to meet in a place devoted to sacred objects' and thanking 'the gentlemen connected with the chapel, for having so kindly, *free of expense*, placed it at their service' (see Plate 55).[42] Given the preponderance of dissenters among Boston's reformers it is surprising that they apparently made no use of the town's chapels, although the absence of such meetings in both Devon and Lewes where Anglicanism ruled OK is less surprising.

55 Ordering the audience: Stepney Temperance Society meeting in a chapel, 1844 (*Metropolitan Temperance Intelligence and Journal*, 27 April 1844)

Increasingly, then, radicals and reformers were forced back on their own initiatives and resources, hiring or building their own meeting places. This had the additional advantage that once a license for such a room had been granted by the authorities it was no longer necessary to obtain their permission each time a meeting was convened.[43] Unusually Oldham's radicals had secured a license for their rented 'Union rooms' in West Street by the early 1820s, rooms which quickly took over from Ab' o' Bunkers infamous pub-based reform school as the centre of the town's radical organisation before 1832. In January 1832 Oldham's Political Union opened up a new room in Yorkshire Street, which John Knight also used as a schoolroom during the week until he became a newsagent in 1834. This use of hired rooms for educational, as well as political, purposes emphasises both the importance radicals attached to education and their need to maximise the use of limited resources. It was not until 1840 that the Radical Association was again able to hire a 'spacious school-room in Rhodes Field, Oldham'. The success of Chartism in Oldham was symbolised by the hiring of yet another room in a more central location 2 months later.

Ironically, at the very same time Oldham's Owenites were discovering the problems associated with hiring rooms. Not only was it expensive, but the rent was lining an often unsympathetic landlords pocket rather than realising the useful financial asset of property. Moreover, hired rooms were rarely large enough to hold any sizeable meeting or to offer the sort of facilities that were needed in the new political climate of the 1830s, when the accent of reforming politics was increasingly on sociability, entertainment, and education. Eventually, in 1845, having hired no less than 3 different venues in the first 5 years of their existence, Oldham's Owenites resolved to build their own 'Hall of Science' by raising £900 from £1 shares.[44] For the Owenites this Gothic building – with its large lecture room (capable of accommodating 800 people), 2 ante-rooms, a singing gallery, a kitchen and, of course, a schoolroom – was essential to their attempts to liberate themselves from the culture of the 'Old World'.[45] Yet the grand designs of Oldham's Hall of Science had a chequered history. Almost as soon as it was built the hall had to be let as a very 'Old Worldly' casino, before finally being sold for half its original cost to the Temperance Society.

The failure of the Hall of Science owed much to its competition with the 'Working Man's Hall', built at the very same time in the very same street by Oldham's reformers. The Working Man's Hall outshone its rival in every way. It was classical not Gothic in design, and it was larger and more expensive. Despite its name it was to be used for no less than

the accommodation of *all classes* of society, the improvement of the manners, the refinement of the taste, the elevation of the moral character, the enlargement of the information, and preservation of the health, true enjoyment and social well being of the said inhabitants, through the following media: Lectures and discussions on Science, Literature, and Fine Arts, Theology, Morals, Social and Political Economy, and other subjects that are strictly legal and moral.[46]

It provided schoolrooms for children of 'all parties and denominations' as well as a 'News Room, Library, and a Depot for books, tracts newspapers and other periodical publications'. Inevitably such fine intentions did not come cheap. The hall cost somewhere in the region of £1,600, of which only £792 was raised in £1 shares, hardly an amount to encourage the financial participation of operatives as shareholders.[47] The deficit was reduced by hiring rooms for the 'accommodation of Benefit, Trades, Political, Temperance, Religious and other Societies at their regular meetings; and on days of festivity for public dinners, tea parties &c., balls, concerts, musical soirees, &c.'. This hall had not been built sooner because the town's police commissioners had previously allowed reform meetings to be held in their own recently completed town hall (1841–2). However, when in 1843 the Chartists were refused permission to hold a meeting at which Feargus O'Connor was the guest of honour, they resolved to build their own hall and, the following December, O'Connor returned to lay the foundation-stone in front of 5,000 spectators. In a sense the hall represented an alternative town hall, one that was not only truly socially, culturally, and politically pluralistic, but which also symbolised the power of working men to make their own independent political decisions. The building represented a stone memorial to radical endeavour, it reflected their growing self-confidence in their right to be included within the political life of the nation and the civic landscape of the town.

The prohibitive price of property and the high rates of the metropolis meant that, even had they wanted to, it would have been extremely difficult for radicals in Tower Hamlets either to hire or build their own venues. Such was apparent from the proud boast of Charles Neesom's East London Total Abstinence, Charter and

National Instruction Association that they had secured their own meeting place 'entirely under their own control' at 166 Brick Lane.[48] Despite the occasional success of venues such as the Owenite Hall of Science in Whitechapel radicals remained dependent on their network of pubs and the goodwill of vestry's granting the use of parochial buildings. Of course, for large prestigious meetings expensive venues were always for hire, such as the Eastern and Beaumont Institutions, the Manor Rooms (previously the Mermaid Tavern) at Hackney, or local theatres like the Pavilion and the Garrick. For quite different reasons radicals in Lewes, Devon, and Boston also lacked their own meeting places. In these less populous areas, radical support was simply not numerically strong enough to warrant building, or for that matter financing, their own hall. Here, as elsewhere, radicals were reliant on sympathetic employers and local authorities volunteering the use of their own buildings and spaces.[49]

It would be wrong to imagine that the attempt to liberate radical culture from the pub represented a mellowing of radical thought. As Sykes has shown, such efforts by radicals to distance themselves from the perceived brutality and saturnalia of the wider popular culture were not incompatible with political militancy.[50] Three members of Oldham's Working Man's Hall Board of Trustees were impoverished Chartists; the reedmaker Richard Haslam, the shoemaker Samuel Yardley, and the basket-maker Thomas Lawless. All three had been heavily involved in the town's Plug Riots of 1842, indeed Yardley was the only Chartist to be arrested for his part in the riots, while Haslam was still an active physical force Chartist in 1848. Equally significantly all three supported James Holladay's radical dissenting candidature at Oldham in 1847 against John Morgan Cobbett.

However, that is not to argue that these changes in the style of Oldham's radical politics, symbolised by the Working Man's Hall, represented the emergence of a distinct working-class public political sphere. Not only was the hall dedicated to 'all classes of society', but two of the hall's principal Trustees, Jesse Ainsworth and James Holladay, were wealthy employers. Jesse Ainsworth was a baptist and a landowner, a coal proprietor and a mill-owner, and in his own words 'an esquire by birth, a baron and knight, as well as Lord of the Manor'.[51] And yet, like Holladay, he also had perfect radical, dissenting, and temperance credentials. He had been chairman of O'Connor's election committee in the town during the 1835 contest,

and frequently put up O'Connor on his visits to Oldham. Ainsworth
was no pious or earnest middle-class radical, he was not adverse to
cracking heads and brawling at the temperance feasts he organised
for the miners who worked down his own pits. Similarly, the
dissenting mill-owner Holladay, who had embraced temperance
through his attachment to Owenism (he was Owen's host on his visit
to Oldham in 1838), had also been a leading member of O'Connor's
election committee in 1835. We cannot, therefore, explain the
emergence of new radical political styles by any simple social matrix.
This new, sober, self-improving, and independent radical politics
represented a moral and political assault on received exclusive
definitions of citizenship and the public political sphere. It sought to
prove that the politically excluded were virtuous and independent
proto-citizens with the moral right for a voice in the nation's affairs.
This language of inclusion was no appeal to working men alone, it
spoke to all those excluded, even, in its less macho tone, to women. It
was not simply the concept of citizenship that was enhanced by this
new radical language, but the very notion of what 'politics' was, and
how it could be conducted by whom.

This ability to use the culture of politics to redefine the public
political sphere was also evident in radical uses of ticketing at
meetings. In some ways ticketing was essential to the new radical
political style in that it helped to pay for the move into expensive
indoor venues. However, ticketing had been part of the culture of
radical dining since at least the 1820s as a means of defraying the costs
of hiring and decorating the room, providing the food, beer, and the
band, as well as the visiting speakers' expenses. Such events were
invariably organised by a managing committee of 'stewards', whose
duties included tabling the resolutions as well as balancing the books.
Because ticketing was subject to the laws of supply and demand, it
inevitably had the effect of regulating the social composition of the
participants. The greater the demand for an event the higher the
price of tickets and, consequently, the more socially exclusive the
audience. So, although the handbill announcing a dinner in Boston
to celebrate Henry Hunt's release from prison in 1822 appealed to the
'Friends of Freedom and the Public in General', it also added that,
'To prevent disorder, no person will be admitted without a ticket.'
Unfortunately the price of these tickets were not revealed, but it
seems likely they were prohibitive as only a select 300 people were
admitted, leaving 3 other parties of 'reformers, in humbler stations of

life' to meet the same evening in different pubs 'to drink the health of Mr. Hunt in humble ale'.[52] Early on radicals discovered the power of ticketing to regulate audiences.

The most exclusive of all radical dinners seems to have been those designed to raise funds by offering the chance to share a table with one of the bankable national leaders. Significantly, tickets for these events were only available directly from members of the managing committee, so that the audience was always informally vetted. Although I have no evidence for this, it would be surprising if political opponents and other 'undesirables' were not refused tickets or, at least in the case of the latter, seated at the back of the hall.[53] One such fund-raising dinner was held with Henry Hunt at Oldham in 1832. Both the time of the dinner – two o'clock in the afternoon – and the extortionate costs of the tickets – 14 pence each – ensured the exclusive tone of the event, and only 60 of the town's radical elite were admitted. As if to compensate, that same evening Hunt gave a speech to the town's 'general public' in the theatre, when 'everyone of his audience paid a small sum for admittance which is to be applied towards the expenses in his last election'.[54] However, tickets for many events were probably issued solely on a 'first come, first served' basis, simply designed to keep the numbers down to the room's capacity. The price of tickets for events like these fluctuated with the popularity of the speaker, the scale of the event, and its cost. At Oldham in 1835 tickets for a dinner with the little known Feargus O'Connor cost 1s., 6d., whereas a ticket for dinner with local hero John Fielden was 2s., 6d. On the whole though the price of tickets for most events throughout this period remained fairly constant at anywhere between 6d. and 2s. Significantly, even these cheapest tickets would have been beyond the pocket of most operatives, not to mention women. As we shall see, their Tory opponents did not waste the chance to ridicule the failure of radical action to meet with radical words – despite all their talk of the rights of freedom of speech and assembly they were not prepared to practice what they preached. Radical ticketing, it appeared, excluded the disorderly, the poor, and the unsympathetic from a voice, it sat uneasily alongside their apparently inclusive language of independent citizenship.

However, the uses of ticketing became increasingly sophisticated during the 1830s as more and more meetings were held inside, not least of all by the Temperance movement. It was they who appear to have first used cheaper tickets for women in order to attract their support. Sensitive to the difficulty of women attending public events without their male spouses, temperance campaigners designed special ticketing packages which facilitated the participation of entire family units. At Oldham's Temperance Feast of the 5th of November 1834 a single ticket cost 1s. compared to the price of 8d. for a double ticket, just as their tea-parties tickets were 1s. for men and 6d. for women throughout the 1830s.[55] It was clear from the handbill announcing a tea party in 1840 that Oldham's Chartists were quick to appropriate such techniques:

Three hundred tickets have been printed for the occasion; men's tickets 1s. each and women's 9d. each; and may be had in the following places Mr. John Wards...Thomas Taylor...Samuel Yardley...Thomas Smith...John Dodge...A public lecture will be delivered by Dr. P. M. McDouall, and those having tickets for tea will be admitted by showing the same; and those not having tickets will be admitted by paying 3d. each.[56]

Ticketing was therefore a double-edged sword, used both to include hitherto excluded groups like women, while simultaneously preventing the participation of others.

The overwhelming impression is that, from the late 1830s, ticketing increasingly became an exclusive, rather than an inclusive, weapon, used by Chartist and radical groups to discipline the popular political audience. Certainly any vulnerable radical meeting, like that 'of the Charter, Radical, Working Men's Democratic and Other Associations' at Trades Hall, Tower Hamlets in 1839, was always preceded by handbills which 'announced that no person should be admitted to the Trades Hall without the card of the Association to which he belonged, her Majesty's peace officers and the press excepted'.[57] The Anti-Corn Law League became particular masters in this field as they attempted to prevent the Chartists disrupting their meetings during the late 1830s and early 1840s, just as harried candidates fighting fierce electoral contests also rushed to protect themselves behind ticketed rallies. Benjamin Grime recalled how, during Oldham's acrimonious election of December 1852, the

Foxites held their weekly gatherings, but these were not held in the open air. The hostility of the Healdites would not permit it. They were held every Monday evening in the Working Man's Hall and, as it was often sarcastically said by Mr. Alex Taylor, Mr. Heald, and Mr. W. H. Mellor, the admission to these gatherings was certainly by ticket. The Foxites were necessitated to protect themselves from gangs of 'roofs' or, as they were well known as, 'Bendigo's Lambs'.[58]

Although Oldham's Tories loved to mock illiberal Foxite ticketing, their counterparts at Tower Hamlets had no qualms in using ticketing to stifle the often vicious disruption of their meetings by their radical opponents during the 1868 election. For most of their meetings 'admission was by tickets, which had been carefully issued through members of the Association ... and also bore the words "Any person using this ticket is bound to abide by the decision of the Chair".'[59] Indeed, so widespread was the use of ticketing by all sides during this election that Edmond Beales made its absence at his rallies a central part of his candidature, claiming he alone held 'free, open meetings to which every man that liked might come – open air meetings'.[60] Yet it was Beales who was swimming against the tide, attempting to reinvigorate the participatory politics of the mass platform in the face of the increasingly organised, disciplined, and ticketed culture of party politics.

However the popular political audience was never entirely tamed or disciplined, as ticketing itself was never totally successful. At times it seemed merely to throw down the gauntlet to one's opponents, like some type of organised sport. Not that the disruption or hijacking of meetings to pass contradictory amendments and resolutions was anything new. As we have already seen in chapter 2, these tactics had long since been deployed at parish, town, and county meetings. It had been the use of disruptive tactics which had eventually caused the decline of such meetings, or at least their eclipse by ticketed partisan versions. Yet even these proved susceptible to hijacking and disruption. The South Devon reformers could hardly have expected their Tory rivals to have been interested in the meeting they convened to express regret at Lord John Russell's defeat at the county's 1835 election. Yet the Tories packed the meeting and, rubbing salt into the wounds of the already defeated and dispirited reformers, passed an amendment ridiculing Russell's candidature.[61] If anything such practices became more, not less, sophisticated during the 1840s as the Chartists conducted their campaign of disruption at Anti-Corn Law League meetings.[62] By 1855 Ernest Jones was able to offer perhaps the most complete and classic advice we have on how to disrupt a meeting:

Rally every friend – be at the doors by twelve AT LATEST – fill the Hall – take possession of the front seats, so as to secure your friends a hearing – *enforce fair play and honourable conduct for all sides* – should you have to vote, vote with both hands, for our opponents always do so – don't be caught by

the clap-trap Democratic language of the names of 'great men' (WHO WILL
BE THERE) – be sure to maintain silence when the resolutions or amendments
(if any) are put, that you may not make any mistake in voting from want of
knowing what is being put to the vote – and do not divide your strength or
countenance any amendment or movement that does not emanate from
your Committee ...[63]

The uses of disruption, like the uses of ticketing, were deployed by all
political groups, they were not confined to radical hotheads or
drunken Tory brickheads as historical stereotype would have it.[64]
The politics of disruption was important because it was the means by
which competing political groups contested each others' rights to
restrict the freedoms of speech and assembly and, by inference, the
exclusive definitions of the public political sphere that ticketing
inevitably entailed. As the century progressed and the disciplines of
party politics hardened, so the tempestuous disruption of meetings
declined. They became increasingly newsworthy precisely because
they had become so unusual.[65]

This section has endeavoured to argue that the language of the
meeting-place was part of the political contest over the meanings and
uses of public space, which in turn defined the constitutional rights
for freedom of speech and assembly. The contest was not just about
radical groups attempting to expand the ever shrinking official
definition of the public political sphere by defending what they
perceived were their lost rights of public assembly on open spaces. For
this contest also involved the radical attempt to expand the political
arena and the notion of the virtuous, independent citizen by using
new meeting-places, like chapels, schoolrooms and their own
purpose-built halls. Despite their attempts to include women in this
less manly radical culture, this new cultural language of inclusion
and citizenship ironically often proved as disabling as enabling to the
constituencies it addressed. As Barbara Taylor has recognised, by
moving out of the pub in order to appeal to women, the new radical
culture simply imposed new *distinctly* female standards of temperance
which were 'inextricably connected with a wider re-definition of
female needs themselves'.[66] Far from liberating women from the
exclusive radical politics of the pub it actually served to enforce a
more restricted definition of feminine respectability and political
participation. This is not to deny that the new radical political style
of the 1830s facilitated women's participation, but rather to recognise
that the forms and terms of that participation were regulated by men.

The use of ticketing exemplified this contradiction at the heart of the new independent radical culture, it typified the move towards a more organised and disciplined political culture which would in the long term reduce people's potential to make and shape their own politics.

Of course radicals wanted to reform not just their own political culture, but also that of official electoral politics. Here again one is struck by the reciprocity between leaders and led, the way in which new codes of behaviour were always subject to negotiation, compromise, and, ultimately, even rejection. It will become apparent that these contrasting attitudes to the customary culture of popular politics formed the basis for the mid-Victorian invention of two competing party political cultures.

Reformers had long balanced their critique of the electoral system's structural flaws with an equally powerful cultural critique, one evoked by the demand for 'purity of elections'. If political reform was ever to be effective it had to be accompanied by the transformation of an electoral culture which relied upon the use of undue influence, bribery and treating. Although we now understand that in unreformed constituencies like Boston these cultural forms were often vital modes of popular political expression, for reformers they remained corrupt manifestations of a morally bankrupt system. Some, like Boston's radical MP W. A. Johnson, refused to 'comply with CERTAIN CUSTOMS, which appear to be indispensably necessary, to secure me again the honour of representing the Independent Electors of your Borough'.[67] It was not so much the result as the manner of the victory, which for many radicals made William Cobbett and John Fielden's election at Oldham in 1832 the model radical campaign. With his usual immodesty Cobbett was the first to make this claim, boasting that

not one single farthing's worth of victuals or drink was given to anybody for any service whatsoever...Not a man nor woman in this excellent town attempted to obtain from me either money, drink or any promise to do anything for them in their private concerns...Neither Mr. Fielden nor myself ever canvassed in any shape or form...Not a single disturbance of any sort; not a blow given in anger; not a drunken man to be seen about the streets; much singing; much playing music; much joy, much triumph.[68]

It was an example which reformers in Boston and Lewes at least tried to emulate. While Boston's Blues tried to hold their meetings away from pubs and dispense with the chairing ceremony, Lewes' reformers frowned upon, and avoided, their customary electoral balls.[69]

No group of reformers within the five constituencies went as far as Oldham's radicals in redefining popular modes of electoral behaviour. It was they who first abandoned the biggest symbol of the moral corruption of elections – namely the chairing ceremony. In 1832 they had bravely refused to be chaired, preferring to walk from the hustings to their committee rooms arm in arm with a poor weaver. In a joint letter to their new expectant constituents they had argued that the 'ostentatious show' of chairings were

contrary to our taste, and to the habits of our lives...Amongst the means which tyrants make use of, are those of amusing and diverting the miserable people with gaudy shows and pompous exhibits...Never was there a *chairing* in the United States of America: only slaves carry their pretended representatives on their shoulders...freemen leave their real representatives to walk on foot.[70]

Elsewhere few radical candidates had the nerve to follow suit. One of those who tried was Boston's John Wilks, who following his re-election in 1835 also used a letter to announce to his constituents that he wished to 'waive the unnecessary pageant of a chairing – to apply ere long the money it would have cost to the relief of the poor – and to rest satisfied that no such pomps and processions can increase your interest in my welfare'.[71]

It is significant that Wilks had to offset his bold initiative with the sop of a donation to the town's poor. So called 'corrupt practices' often had great significance within communities.[72] Thus when Wilks' commissioned a chair it could have represented his continued support of local trade, as well as his financial commitment to the borough. To replace it, therefore, he had to demonstrate this continuing commitment in other ways. Similarly, when Sir James Duke held Boston's first election rally outside the town's pubs it

excited a little murmuring among some of the advocates of 'vested rights' and a Charge of meanness was made against Sir James; but a munificent benefaction of twenty pounds to the General Dispensary, soon gave this cry its quietus, for even some of the strongest advocates of beer house meetings, acknowledged the superiority of this mode of expending money, on an object which would give to eighty of the suffering poor, medical relief for two months each, over the old custom.[73]

Radical leaders had to negotiate with their supporters when attempting to reform the official electoral culture. They could not simply impose their own models of radical behaviour from above.

As we have already seen from their languages of the meeting-place, it was not just electoral culture that radicals wanted to reform. Many were also disenchanted with the cultural politics of the mass platform, not least because, as Bamford recalled as early as 1819, they were continually 'taunted by the press, with our ragged, dirty appearance at these assemblages, with the confusion of our proceedings, and the mob-like crowds in which our numbers were mustered.'[74] Increasingly the cultural repertoire of customary radical street-theatre, with its attendant folk violence and saturnalia, became an embarrassment, something not becoming those aspiring to the vote. Just as many self-improving auto-didact radical leaders believed that Enlightenment reason had delivered them from the superstitious, irrational mental universe of popular culture, so they believed that radical political culture could only be morally and intellectually respectable and independent if the disorderly and the irrational were weeded out.[75] Not only would such a reform ensure that radical claims for citizenship were taken seriously, but in the process it enabled radicals to empower themselves as fully free and independent human beings.

In what follows we shall trace these changing attitudes to the customary cultural repertoire of radical street-theatre through the uses of fire and light in such forms as effigy burnings, torchlight processions, and illuminations. Of course such forms were neither new or unique to nineteenth-century radical politics.[76] By the early nineteenth century effigy burning was well established as a popular rite of reprimand for a variety of social, sexual, and political groups.[77] Radicals then drew on a readily accessible and popular cultural form, and significantly their uses of effigy burnings invariably fell around the customary calendar on the 5th of November. On that day in 1830 a group of Oldham's 'working people and others... having prepared an effigy of the Hero of Waterloo, they adorned him with a brown coat and finally blew him up with gun powder amidst a large bonfire, while a band of music encircled the group playing several lively airs.'[78] Similarly in Boston on that same night the following year, an Archbishop and the Duke of Wellington, the 'No Reform Statesman', together with 'a minor exhibition of dolls dressed up as Bishops, were hung upon a gallows, which bore the inscription "Anti-Reform"' and burnt.[79] Radicals had appropriated the forms of effigy burning and made them their own, complete with their own radical meanings which turned Anglican interpretations of the 5th of November on their head.

Clearly, the very appropriability of effigy burnings, as well as the persistent uses of other forms of fire and light, testifies to their immense popularity. Butterworth remembered how 'crowds of young boys and women from the factories *were drawn to the spot*' of a torchlit radical meeting as if by some magnetic power.[80] The attraction of fire to women has been somewhat obscured by its peculiarly masculine uses at political parades in Plymouth, Lewes, and Boston where men demonstrated their machismo by carrying flaming tar barrels on their backs. And yet the use of fire as a cleansing and purifying force was more likely to appeal to women. Such was the case when effigy burnings were used as a rite of reprimand in which a purifying fire consumed the effigies of darkness and evil. The often brutal folk-violence of these occasions does not appear to have deterred women. They were present at Bethnal Green in 1833 when an effigy of a police spy was paraded and summarily beaten, indeed a 'huge crowd applauded as the effigy was hanged, cut down, the head smeared with ochre and impaled on a stick, and the body cast into the fire.'[81] Similarly, 'to the apparent joy of a large multitude' an effigy of a Poor-Law Guardian in Oldham 'underwent successive punishments of suspension [and] burning' before being committed to flames.[82] It is surely not coincidental that women were most prominent in those campaigns – Queen Caroline and the Anti-Poor-Law agitations – which generated the greatest number of effigy burnings during this period. It has been argued that these forms of direct, informal, community-based politics facilitated, even relied upon, the participation of women, drawing as they did on women's traditional role within the moral economy of the popular political crowd.[83]

It is perhaps less surprising that the political uses of fire and light were revived during the early phases of Chartism, particularly, as I have indicated, with the Anti-Poor-Law agitation. The Chartists used fire at their meetings both as bonfires and torchlights to symbolise the cause itself; a light of hope amidst the darkness of corruption and evil; a vigil of light, an act of individual or collective devotion to the cause. Indeed, between 1838 and 1840 the torchlight procession became a Chartist stock-in-trade. Gammage, a once active Chartist and the movement's first historian, recalled it was 'almost impossible to imagine the excitement' generated by torch-light processions.

To form an adequate idea of the public feeling it was necessary to be any eye-witness of the proceedings... The processions were frequently of immense length... and along the whole line there blazed a stream of light, illuminating the lofty sky, like the reflection from a large city in a general conflagration... The very appearance of such a vast number of blazing torches only served more effectually to inflame the minds alike of speakers and hearers.[84]

For Feargus O'Connor the torches were 'worth a thousand speeches ... [they]... spoke a language so intelligible that no man could misunderstand'.[85] Of course that language had a variety of meanings, but the government heard a threatening language of physical force and promptly outlawed torchlight meetings. The failure of these uses of fire to win concessions from the government led many to question their very utility. In 1847 the Chartist leader Bronterre O'Brien criticised the cultural forms of the mass platform as incompatible with 'true Chartism'. He rounded upon O'Connor for ensuring 'that all the public should know of Chartism was through the medium of torchlight meetings, and senseless processions of three miles long, and demonstrations of tens of and hundreds of thousands of people, congregated they knew not why, and dismissed as impotent and ignorant as they came, and thousands of hard-earned money squandered upon flags and banners and coaches and triumphal cars, – and such like trumpery.'[86]

Certainly, as Dorothy Thompson has argued, by the 1840s Chartism's 'folk-violence of effigy burning and the direct action of the anti-poor law campaign gave way to disciplined organisa-tion... [and a]... more structured, less open and "spontaneous" politics.'[87] Although Chartism increasingly embraced a more formal culture of tea-parties and purpose-built halls, it is important to recognise that these new cultural styles never precluded the per-sistence of the so-called 'traditional'. Just as radicals continued to meet outside or in pubs at the same time as they hired and built their own rooms, so fire continued to be used alongside tea and dances. When O'Connor visited Oldham in 1841, there was both an orderly procession through the streets with 'numerous small paper lanterns as substitute for torchlight', as well as a tea party for four hundred men and women.[88] Despite the less menacing use of paper lanterns instead of flaming torchlight, such occasions remind us that in cultural politics the 'traditional' and the 'modern' were never mutually exclusive categories. The political culture of Chartism, like so much else of that movement, combined both the old and the new.

From the late 1840s there was a conspicuous absence of the political uses of fire in all five constituencies. It was not until the mid-1860s, when the Reform League breathed new life into the cultural forms of the mass platform, that effigy burnings, tar barrels, torchlight processions, and bonfires were once again evident at radical meetings.[89] Edmond Beales' election campaign at Tower Hamlets in 1868 was saturated with torchlight meetings on East London's customary public spaces, even if these were illuminated by naphtha lamps as often as by fire.[90] Similarly Mason Jones' campaign at Boston in 1868, associated with the Reform League, was responsible for staging a massive torchlight procession with no less than a thousand participants.[91] It would be foolish to suggest that the political uses of fire ceased at a certain date. Successive generations continued to deploy it well beyond 1867, during the Midlothian campaign, at the Tory 'jingo' demonstrations of the 1870s, and at the Social Democratic Federation's meetings in the 1880s and 1890s, not to mention the poll tax demonstrations of 1990.

Nevertheless I still want to suggest that radicals and reformers were quite deliberately distancing themselves from the cultural forms of the mass platform, like the uses of fire. Naturally this left a gap for the Tories to exploit, and exploit it they did. Thus, on the election of a Tory mayor at Boston in 1858, we find that 'a vast mob paraded the town bearing lighted tar barrels, flambeaux and flags, headed by a band of music, and the whole proceedings were wound up by a large bonfire on Bargate Green, where several barrels of ale were distributed gratuitously.'[92] Meanwhile in Oldham the political realignment of 1847 took place largely around religious and cultural lines; the dissenting radical wing embodied by James Holladay and W. J. Fox against the Anglican wing which coalesced around J. M. Cobbett's candidature. While the Foxites endeavoured to move away from customary political culture (it was they who were largely responsible for building the Working Man's Hall), the Cobbettites actively embraced it. This cultural cleavage was nicely evident at a meeting of the town's police commissioners during the 1847 election, when the Foxite radical dissenters, Quarmby and Holladay, pro-tested about the use of effigies of W. J. Fox and John Duncuft (Fox's unholy Tory ally against the dictation of John Fielden and J. M. Cobbett). These effigies, they complained, had not only been paraded openly around the streets, but had been threateningly thrust upon Foxite tradesmen without any response from the Cobbettite head constable, Alex Taylor. Taylor received vociferous support from his fellow Cobbettites, W. H. Mellor and John Earnshaw, who argued that the annoyance complained of was no worse or noisy than the daily parade of the boys of Blue Coat School each morning![93]

At the same time Tories in Lewes and Exeter had also begun to portray themselves as the defenders of customary popular political culture, not least of all on the 5th of November. From the 1830s, Lewes' reformers, encouraged by George Bacon's *Sussex Advertiser*, waged war against the town's infamous Bonfire Boys and their saturnalian behaviour on Guy Fawkes night. However, the popular Protestant reaction against such events as the Maynooth Grant (1845) and the 'Papal Aggression' of 1850 enabled Lewes' Tory authorities to endow the town's 5th of November celebrations with an, albeit informal, official licence, encouraging its often venomous anti-Catholicism. As Storch has recognised, in this 'No Popery version, the Fifth demonstrated against hostile external [and internal] forces supposedly threatening English liberties; the freedom to mark it became "a charter of the town, failing to preserve which Britons become slaves".'[94] Alongside the regular humiliation of effigies of the pope and Russia's Orthodox leaders, effigies of the town's 'ritualist' minister Reverend J. M. Neale and George Bacon (in the shape of a pig) were also committed to the flames. Here, too, the Tories were able to project themselves as the defenders of real independence, protecting the freeborn Englishman's customary popular culture from the enemy both within and without, radicals and Catholics alike. However, Lewes' 5th of November celebrations were never totally controlled by any one political, social or religious group. In 1862 the radical hero and Catholic, Garibaldi, was praised and honoured while all his enemies were burnt.[95] Four of the six special constables who refused to suppress the celebrations in 1848 were well-known dissenting reformers, while those arrested between 1806 and 1847 included respectable artisans, tradesmen, and even a solicitor and the town-crier.[96] Similarly, in Exeter, although the leader of 'Young Exeter' bonfire boys had long been a populist Tory coal-merchant, the town's reforming but fiercely anti-Puseyite *Western Times* even went so far as to suggest suitable candidates for effigies. By 1867 Exeter's Liberals were once again intent on suppressing the event.

The persistence of these customary cultural forms illustrated their firm hold upon the popular political psyche. Radical leaders soon realised that it was not enough to exhort their supporters to turn away from these supposedly corrupting cultural forms without providing counter-attractive events around the customary calendar of popular culture. Here again the influence of the Temperance movement was particularly strong, especially in Oldham.[97] Encouraged by the success of Joseph Livesey's visit to the town in February 1833, Oldham's nascent Temperance Society organised a 'Temperance Feast' on the 5th of November in the hope of distracting attention from the customary celebrations. The following year they concentrated their efforts on the town's Wakes by organising another feast, while on Easter Tuesday 1835 they staged a 'tea and Coffee Party'.[98] Although these events never attracted audiences of more than 200, they did include a large proportion of women. Women were no doubt attracted not only by the discourse of temperance and favourable ticketing arrangements, but also by the social nature of these events, their sense of fellowship and fun. These lessons were quickly learnt by Oldham's Owenites who held a 'social festival' during the town's Wakes in 1838 and a tea-party the following Easter Monday.[99] Before long Oldham's Chartists joined the bandwagon with their own 'festival' on Easter Monday 1841, at which 'a considerable number of persons of both sexes partook of tea and other refreshments, and were subsequently addressed on the importance of sobriety and the advantages of political knowledge', before 'a few popular compositions on political subjects were read and sung'.[100] On Wakes Tuesday of 1843 they held a tea-party and ball with Feargus O'Connor as guest-star. All the components of the great radical outdoor meetings were there: speeches of exhortation, famous champions, the sense of fun and fellowship, songs and prayers and, of course, liquid refreshments.[101] Such counter-attractive events were not the sole preserve of reformers, as Boston's Tory Guardian Club proved when they staged Morton's hugely popular play 'Speed the Plough' at the local theatre on Easter Monday 1834, the day of the town's annual fair.[102] Gradually, of course, as such events gained in popularity, local political leaders were able to move away from the customary calendar and develop their own commemorative calendar.[103].

Yet all this was about more than the usual contest over the meaning of the past, for reformers it was also about developing new political styles with new codes of behaviour which could more effectively challenge restrictive definitions of citizenship and the public political sphere. As I have already indicated, that this should occur after the disappointments of 1832 was hardly surprising. Neither should we be surprised by the anxious Tory attempts to attract new constituencies of support, enfranchised or not, by making their politics more entertaining and simultaneously contesting the claims of the new radical political style. Significantly, women were at the centre of this redefinition of radical and Tory political culture. Hitherto, women who had entered the political arena independently of men had been castigated as wayward, wicked women.[104] Feminine respectability belonged only to those women who did not step outside their clearly delineated private roles as wives and mothers – the public political sphere was an exclusively male domain. The redefinition of both radical and Tory cultural politics during the 1830s did not lessen the exclusive manliness of the public political sphere, rather it sought to facilitate women's public support of masculine political crusades by organising 'social events' which encouraged the participation of whole families. Women were, then, only politically enabled if they stuck to the social politics of the family. The culture of politics was not so much de-gendered as re-gendered in an equally exclusive fashion. The invention of the 'social' in politics may have blurred the distinction between women's public and private spheres, but it still proved restrictive and disabling for women.

Significantly these new social political styles were evident in all five constituencies although, as we shall see, they were less successful in tradition-bound Devon and Tower Hamlets. As early as 1833 even Lewes' Blue Party

entertained the voters wives and friends with a rural fete on Thursday last, in a commodious field...Upwards of 300 sat down to tea and other refreshments. A gingling match for a leg of mutton, a steeple race for a cheese, &c., afforded much amusement. Dancing, stoll-ball matches, and other sports were kept up till a late hour, and the day was spent with great harmony and satisfaction to all parties. At one time there was at least 1,500 persons on the ground.[105]

Two weeks later the rival Bundle of Sticks Society responded by staging their own outdoor festival with the seemingly obligatory

56 A family affair: a Conservative fete at Lewes, n.d. (*The Sunday Times* Reeves Collection and Sussex Archaeological Society)

'rustic games' and, 6 hours later, a procession to the Stag Inn (see Plate 56).[106] As one would expect in Lewes, these new social styles of politics were forced to meet customary popular culture half-way, as the manly rustic games and procession to the Stag Inn testify. It was not until 1866 that the town's newly formed Liberal party were able to go the whole hog. Their inaugural dinner and tea-party, held in a marquee within the priory grounds and 'tastefully decorated and festooned with flowers and evergreens', attracted 400 of the leading Liberal tradesmen and their wives. To avoid the habitual charge of dullness by their Tory opponents the meeting ended with a bang, the entertainment and spectacle provided by a 'grand display of fireworks'.[107]

In Boston, following the competitive uses of counter-attractive events at the town's theatre, the reforming candidate Handley staged an election rally in the town's Vauxhall Gardens which 'concluded with dancing, a band of music being in attendance'. It was a great success, even the Tory *Herald* admitted that 2,000 people attended 'comprising a great proportion of ladies'.[108] It was not until the radical John Noble organised the Boston Temperance Galas of the late 1850s that the town's political leaders recognised the political possibilities of entertainment and sociability. Noble combined the carnival feel of traditional outdoor radical meetings with the moral fervour of temperance oratory, fireworks, and rustic games. People flocked to Noble's Temperance Galas from as far afield as Sheffield and Hull to join the festivities, parading with the bands, listening to the speakers, or taking part in the 'rustic amusements, such as swinging, football, races, archery, quoits &c., but the most popular amusements appeared to be "kiss in the ring" and "tripping it gaily on the light fantastic toe" to the enlivening strains of various bands...'[109] Despite the success of these events, and the influence of Noble amongst Boston's reformers, it was the Tories who were first to exploit these new political styles. During the 1868 election, the Conservative agent and secretary, Bartoll Storr, staged a 'Conservative Ladies Entertainment'. The meeting was chaired by the constituency's only woman voter, and 'after a few short speeches, music and songs were introduced'. Mason Jones, the radical Reform League candidate, 'speedily followed suit, announcing a lecture to the Liberal ladies of Boston, on "The Wits of the Irish Bar"'.[110]

As we have already seen so often, it was in Oldham (where else?) that these new political styles were most evident and where they did most to define the character of nascent party political identities. Here, too, the Tories were not slow in realising the potential of politics' social dimension in attracting the support of women. In 1837 Edwin Butterworth lamented the activities of Oldham's Tory women who met without the supervision of their male spouses. He warned that:

Female conservative politicians are on the increase and it behoves the reformers to be on the look out incessantly as to their movements. During the past week the wives of the Oldham Operative Conservatives have been demonstrating their approbation of the conservatism of their husbands by drinking tea, taking comfortable glasses of liquor, and dancing to the loyal strains of the Church vocalists; on Monday at the Old Mess House, and on Tuesday evening at the Shakespeare Inn, Glodwick; about 120 females are said to have enjoyed these festivities for several successive hours very much to their own pleasure, *but it is doubtful whether to the advantage of their families.*[111]

The following week the reformers heeded Butterworth's advice, they held a retaliatory social event at the Grapes Inn, but typically the tea for 50 women was very much a sideshow to the lunch for 90 gentlemen which followed.[112] In Oldham, as in Boston 30 years later, the radicals were more reluctant than the Tories to leave women to their own devices. Certainly, it is difficult to imagine Oldham's radicals allowing the social mix evident at the Operative Conservative Dinner in January 1838 which included 'a number of ladies of Conservatives, both masters and operatives'. Only 2 days earlier 'a considerable number of females chiefly the wives of operative conservatives and several *respectables* of the fair sex were entertained with tea, liquor and a dance in the large room of the White Lion Inn'.[113] In the cultural politics of gender at least Oldham's Tories were more permissive than the town's radicals.

If Oldham's radicals had not learnt the lessons of the Tory culture of sociability, their Owenite colleagues had. Such was the success of Owenism in Oldham that much credit must go to their very full repertoire of social and educational activities. By 1840 Oldham's Owenites boasted not only their own choir, band, and dancing classes, but a comprehensive series of instruction classes on subjects ranging from the 'Physiology of the Brain' to Owen's 'Theory of Character Formation'. This emphasis on education and self-improvement no doubt proved attractive to the town's women, most of whom had been denied anything but the most rudimentary of educations. It also appealed to women as mothers by providing not only a Sunday school but also daily classes for children in female class-sewing, knitting and needlework, writing and arithmetic, science, mental improvement, and reading. And yet such an earnest pursuit of knowledge was offset by the popular Saturday dancing-class which was deliberately designed to inject a sense of fun and generate 'ties of communal fellowship'.[114] Such was their success that Richard Cooper, the local Owenite and Chartist leader, complained to a colleague that 'Our dancing class is attended to over-flowing, but I am sorry to say, that the greater part of those who attend have never dreamed of any philosophy but that of the fantastic toe.'[115] To their opponents, however, the sexual mix of these dancing-classes symbolised the Owenites' lax morals. Listen, for instance, to the tirade of a member of the local Anglican clergy against that 'promiscuous dancing shop, so pleasant with abominable amours' and 'a brothel', urging people 'to protect the chastity of young females' by boycotting the classes. Here again the feminine respectability of those women who entered the public political stage was questioned, even though their behaviour was 'social' rather than overtly 'political'. Indeed, it is hard to see how the social activities of Oldham's Owenite culture merited such hysterical attacks. The 'female class-sewing, knitting and fancy needlework' class hardly seems threatening to male definitions of femininity. Although, as Barbara Taylor has argued, Owenism valued womens' domestic roles as wives and mothers highly, sewing or child-care classes were not provided for men: 'Fatherhood was never the ground on which men entered political life'.[116] Despite this, Oldham's Owenites had shown how effectively a social political culture could be used to create an attractive political style and identity.

As we have already seen, Oldham's Tories were also not oblivious to using the different and unique qualities of their social events to help distinguish them from their opponents. As Oldham's radicals became ever more entangled with the improving doctrines of temperance and Owenite thought, the town's Tories provided a cultural counterpoint. They compared the liberality and social and sexual inclusiveness of their political culture with the prudishness and exclusivity of radical culture. Thus their Field Day in January 1839 boasted:

a dinner numerously attended and *gloriously excellent in those two necessary Tory requisites quantity and quality with an unlimited supply of liquids* was served in the Assembly Room ... which was elegantly fitted up – the apartment was hung with blue and white draperies, adorned by inscriptions, and several splendid flags ... The Dinner company was said to consist chiefly of operatives, but they were of the description that would be better designated by the word *professionals*, comprising many out pensioners of Chelsea Hospital, ex-members of the cavalry corps, petty officials of the church establishment, the particular friends and confidantes of Tory millowners, *and some few real operatives who aspire to the honour of mixing with gentlemen Conservatives.*[117]

This event served as a celebration of John Bull's good old English way of life, with its unlimited supplies of roast beef, plum pudding, beer, and *bonhomie*. This peculiarly populist notion of protecting John Bull's way of life had a classless appeal, it produced a Tory political culture in which the poor could rub shoulders with the rich. Of course the sub-text of all this was not simply that Tories had more fun, but that Tory notions of social and cultural inclusion were better than radical notions of political inclusion. Better not to be citizens but to have John Bull's independence and prosperity, than to be impoverished and reformed as citizens.

This clash of cultural styles in Oldham was crucial to the town's political realignment after 1847. J. M. Cobbett's candidature, together with the decline of the town's Chartists and Owenites during the 1840s, forced many radicals, especially those who were dissenters, to coalesce under W. J. Fox's standard of popular Liberalism. By the elections of 1852 the cultural personalities of the rival factions were clear. The Cobbettites daubed the Foxites as boring, effeminate, sober killjoys. Not only were the Foxites cowardly enough to hold

their rallies inside, behind ticketed doors but, worse still, Fox himself
was so unmanly that he had not got the 'bottom' to visit the town
during the campaign for the December by-election because of the
abuse he had received during the July contest. The Foxites, anxious
to disprove these charges, held a 'Tea Party and Ball' on Wakes
Monday in a lavishly decorated marquee. No expense was spared:
'The interior of the tent, the sides of which were wood, was tastefully
hung with coloured calico, and lighted with gas, the whole of the floor
being boarded for dancing. The sides were decorated with mottoes,
coupling the name of W. J. Fox with free trade, education, &c....'[118]
A double quadrille band, a master of ceremonies and 'a grand
exhibition of fireworks' were all laid on for tickets of 1s. for mean and
9d. for women. Despite a sobering heavy thunderstorm which
stopped the fireworks in mid-flow and caused 'little lakes all along
the benches of temporary seats', it was all apparently a great success.
Grand Balls were hastily arranged on the following two days.[119] Such
events sought to contest Tory notions of John Bull's cultural
inheritance – one could still have fun and food without pubs and
beer. It was in this way that John Bull would really inherit the earth
by proving he had the moral independence to reclaim his freeborn
rights as a citizen.

Certainly, Benjamin Grime recalled how the success of these balls
instilled a new-found confidence in Fox's campaign. The Foxites
began to hold unticketed outdoor meetings which, predictably,
quickly became a target for the physical and verbal assaults of the
Cobbettites. Although the Foxites complained vehemently to the
local magistrates about the violent and disruptive Cobbettite tactics,
there can be little doubt that the Cobbettites had played right into
their hands. Throughout both the 1852 election campaigns the
Cobbettites had portrayed the Foxites as sham democrats – advocating manhood suffrage, but by their ticketed meetings denying the
right of public assembly and freedom of speech; pretending to
represent the people, but really trying to reform and improve them
– and so the Cobbettite attacks on the Foxite's outdoor meetings
enabled them to turn the tables. These were the real attacks on
freedom of speech and assembly, they argued. The Tory roughs were
nicknamed 'Bendigo's Lambs'. A name which not only implied they
were un-independent flock like sheep, dependent on the leadership of
Bendigo, alias the Cobbettite leader W. H. Mellor, but also mocked
their very manliness, comparing them as lambs to the boxing legend

Bendigo. The Foxites produced countless broadsides and ballads, like the following 'Apostates Creed', which drove home this caricature of Tory political culture:

I believe in the enlightening power of beer (d—n education!); in the glory of guzzling; and in the steadiness of the British Constitution as based upon a beer-barrel. I believe in all blarneying, bullying and beating; in breaking windows and heads; and that brick-bats are better than the ballot. I believe in disorder above deliberation, in whistles and drums above reason and discussion; and in bloody noses above clear heads and eloquent tongues. Whosoever will not believe, as I do, shall be hooted belled, kicked and punced, till the breath be out of his body. This is my religious faith, and I will swear to it over a quart of Ale; and to twice as much over a quarter of Gin. Amen.[120]

These black-and-white characterisations of competing political cultures had a powerful political appeal, pulling the constituents into a world of moral absolutes much like that evoked by the best platform oratory or the symbolic uses of organisation examined earlier. However, we should be careful not to swallow these stereotypes too completely, although both parties in Oldham played up to them because they made them appear more worthy and more fun than they probably really were.

Certainly, the image of the regular Foxite closeted inside the Working Man's Hall, their head buried in books or engaged in earnest moral debates, was often wide of the mark. Even the Foxite Grime was forced to admit that 'the roughs did not appear to be all on one side. "Old Fox" began to have supporters who not only gloried in their physical development, and who gloried in showing their science, but also knew how to use their clogs, and consequently, it was now "punce for punce"'.[121] Besides this practical use of violence, Fox's popular Liberalism was also never prepared to sell itself down the river for the sake of the Temperance creed. The marquee for the Foxite wakes 'Tea Party and Ball' was strategically located next to the Spinners Arms pub, and it would have been very surprising if a few jars of ale were not discretely consumed between cups of tea. Even the emphasis on education and improvement can be over-stressed. When Fox's committee sponsored the staging of theatre at the Working Man's Hall during 1853, the first piece was strategically changed from Shakespeare's 'All's Well That Ends Well' to the more racy and accessible comedy 'The Honeymoon'. And, while the subsequent performances included other improving Shakespearian classics like 'Othello', 'Merchant of Venice', and 'Romeo and Juliet', none seem to have gone down quite as well as 'Mr. Egan's performance of ceiling walking; and the Ricardo family with their performing dogs', which the *Manchester Guardian* reported 'appear to give great satisfaction'.[122]

Neither were the Cobbettite popular Tories quite the fun-loving, bad-living, manly lot, they often portrayed themselves as. Patrick Joyce has argued that it is easy to misrepresent the convivial club culture of popular Toryism as simply institutionalised drinking, gambling, and bowling. To their members these clubs often 'represented an escape from and not an excuse for drink: the desire for "permanent instruction and amusement" and the hope of "social elevation and temperate regulation" found expression in the written histories of the early clubs'.[123] This was certainly the case at Hollinwood's 'Constitutional Working Men's Club' founded in 1868, whose only room was a well-stocked library.[124] The same history praised the 'splendid educational work' of Royton's first Conservative Club during the early 1860s. The stress was on the hand of 'fellowship, where rich and poor, employer and employee, could gather under the family spirit' of the clubs. Moreover, as the Primrose League demonstrated, entertainment and education were never mutually exclusive, and they did much to keep this Tory tradition of self-improvement alive throughout the late nineteenth century.[125]

Of all the five constituencies these new cultural styles and their role in the mid-Victorian invention of party were less marked in Devon and Tower Hamlets. The culture of Devon's county politics seems to have changed very little during this period. No doubt this can be explained largely by the Conservative domination of South Devon's politics following the 1832 Reform Act. Not one reforming candidate stood in the constituency between the unsuccessful candidatures of J. C. Bulteel in 1837 and Viscount Amberly in 1868. Radicals seem to have directed their efforts to their own boroughs, rather than wasting valuable resources on the organisationally unwieldy county scene. Thus, while Chartists in Plymouth and Exeter held tea-parties and social entertainments in Temperance Hotels, Mechanic's Institutes, and their own schoolrooms, it had little effect on the culture of county politics. Meanwhile the Tories contented themselves with appropriating the cultural forms of the radical mass platform. Their 'Great Meeting' of 1837, which was symbolically held in Totnes, the heartland of the county's radical community, included the presentation of a silk banner by the Conservative ladies of Totnes, and a procession 'with two bands of music, banners flying and walking twelve abreast' to meet the county's two Conservative MPs on the boundary of the town.[126] Although there was nothing new in all this, it does illustrate the more dynamic nature of South Devon's Tory political culture compared with that of their reforming rivals.

Radicals found it equally difficult to redefine the customary political culture of the similarly vast and organisationally unwieldy constituency of Tower Hamlets. For instance, as we have already seen, the East End's veteran radical Charles Neesom established the East London Chartist Temperance Association before he was imprisoned in January 1840. Neesom's influence, or that of his wife, was probably behind the attempts of Bethnal Green's Chartists to hire the Trades Hall for their 'first tea party, which was attended by more than one hundred persons, and to add to the novelty, a social tea loaf, ten feet long, and weighing forty pounds, was prepared for the company...A vocal and instrumental music class is formed.'[127] This success was short-lived. By October the East London Chartist Temperance Association complained that 'this society has met with enemies where it had certainly least right to find them – amongst those who profess Chartist principles'.[128] Undeterred, Neesom tried once again the following year to reform the culture of East London's radical politics by forming the East London Total Abstinence, Charter and National Instruction Association. This, too, sank without trace in the columns of the *Northern Star*. The failure of Neesom's ventures was nothing if not predictable. As we have already seen, radical culture in Tower Hamlets was firmly bound to the convivial culture of the pub. The persistence of this customary political culture was once again evident with the Reform League's dependency upon the pub and the cultural forms of the mass platform. It was left to influential, but isolated, individuals to sow the cultural seeds in the sands of their own branches. Some, like George Odger at the St Luke's branch, met with a modicum of success, staging a series of 'Social Entertainments' at Sanger's Lecture Hall during 1867 (see Plate 57). Yet generally these were the exceptions that prove the rule.

The contrasting cultural experiences of the different constituencies, and the opposing political styles adopted by similar groups within them, illustrate once again the pitfalls of a class analysis of cultural

NOTICE!

SANGER'S LECTURE HALL,

Opposite Bath Street, CITY ROAD, near the Eagle.

ADDRESSES

On POLITICAL and SOCIAL SUBJECTS, will be delivered

EVERY THURSDAY EVENING,

DURING THE AUTUMN AND WINTER MONTHS.

Evenings with the People!

SANGER'S LECTURE HALL,

207, CITY ROAD, opposite Bath Street.

The Saint Luke's Branch of the REFORM LEAGUE, under whose auspices these Meetings are being conducted, believing it to be desirable to combine Social with Intellectual enjoyment and instruction, have resolved that the FIRST of each Series of Addresses, shall consist of a superior class of Songs, Recitations, Readings, etc., and have much pleasure in informing their Friends and the Public that, their FIRST

SOCIAL ENTERTAINMENT,

Will be held

ON THURSDAY, OCTOBER 3rd, 1867.

When the following programme will be performed.

In making this announcement the Committee deem it but an act of justice towards the Talented Vocalists whose names it contains, to state that, the whole of their services are given entirely gratuitous and purely from a desire to further the object of these Meetings.

MR. GEORGE ODGER.

Has kindly consented to preside and will open the proceedings by the delivery of a short address.

Commencing at 8 o'clock precisely.

Admission 2d.   Reserved Seats 4d.

Tickets to be had of

Mr. G. HOWELL, Secy. to the League, Office, Adelphi Terrace, and the following

[list of names and addresses]

PROGRAMME.

1. "Base Oppressors"—CHORUS.
2. Miss CLARE, "Fly Little Bird"—SENTIMENTAL.
3. Mr. LE LUBEZ, "Donizetti"—SENTIMENTAL.
4. Mr. WARNER, COMIC MEDLEY.
5. Miss MURRAY, "Toll the Bell."—SENTIMENTAL.
6. Mr. YOUNG, SONG.
7. Mr. BROWN, "The Charge of Balaclava."
8. Miss BOLAND, SENTIMENTAL.
9. Mr. JOHNSON, IRISH COMIC.
10. Mr. R. RISEAM, SONG. BARITONE.

An Interval of Ten Minutes.

11. "To the Front." CHORUS.
12. Miss ODGER.
13. Mr. WOOLDRIDGE, "Gypsies' Tent."
14. CHAS. PEARSON, COMIC.
15. Mr. ODGER, READING.
16. Mr. and Miss YOUNG, DUET.
17. Mr. PIPER, "Fame." AN ORIGINAL POEM.
18. The Misses LOWRY, DUET.
19. Mr. LOWRY.
20. "Rally round the League," CHORUS.

HERR GLOCK, Pianist.

THE REFORM MINSTRELS,

Will attend to assist in making these Meetings interesting and instructive.

CHAIR TAKEN AT HALF-PAST EIGHT O'CLOCK PRECISELY.

Admission One Penny.—Females Free.

A SOIREE, or EVENING'S ENTERTAINMENT at the beginning of each series.

The BRANCH MEETS EVERY MONDAY, at the COACH and HORSES, Great Mitchell Street, Saint Luke's.

On Thursday the 10th, Dr. PERFITT, Subject: The Social Value of Democratic Institutions.

On Thursday the 17th, Mr. W. R. CREMER, Subject: the Necessity and Advantage of Reforming our System of Land-Laws and Tenures.

On Thursday the 24th, Mr. G. MANTLE, Subject: the Past and Future.—A Review and a Prophecy.

TREZISE, Printer, 4, Beech Street, Barbican.

---

57   Programme of a Reform League 'Social Entertainment', 1867 (Howell Collection, Bishopsgate Institute)

politics. The emergence of competing political cultures should be read as part of the struggle to define the parameters of the public political sphere and the qualities of the independent citizen. By the 1860s these competing political cultures had hatched two distinct party political identities. Although these cultural identities were especially evident in Oldham, they were present elsewhere, albeit in different ways. I have attempted to explain these local variations by the peculiarities of local political cultures and traditions, and the different speed of negotiations between leaders and led in the creation of new political styles.

CONCLUSION

This chapter has attempted to expand our conception of the political arena. By endeavouring to convey something of the rich texture of popular political culture during this period I hope to have put to shame that old political history which confined politics to the study of organisations and their ideologies. However, in no way has this been a complete or definitive study of nineteenth-century popular political culture. Rather I have attempted to deconstruct some of the constituent elements of that culture, and the way in which they were used to create political identities and constituencies of support.

The politics of culture is central to any understanding of nineteenth-century popular politics. It went to the very heart of the political process – the way in which power was created, legitimated, and contested. We have seen how radicals used the language of the meeting-place and their codes of behaviour to contest restrictive official definitions of citizenship and the constitution. It does not seem to me particularly fruitful to argue that these cultural contests to redefine the public political sphere represented attempts to create a distinct working-class or plebeian public political sphere.[129] As I have tried to establish, these were political, not social, struggles over the meaning of the constitution and the language of the independent citizen. Hence the participation of all social classes combined in the moral reform of radical culture and the notoriously pan-class appeal of Tory political culture. In any case, such an argument would have to assert that just as working-class radicals created their own plebeian public political sphere, so did working-class Tories. Equally, that is not to argue that these struggles to define the public political sphere were not occasionally ascribed with class meanings. Clearly, the language of the independent citizen could be given a class accent. However, it was the category of gender which most frequently made sense of the cultural contest to include or exclude the politically dispossessed.

Again and again we have seen how cultural politics shaped women's perception of politics and their ability to enter the public political arena. At first sight the feminisation of radical culture – by meeting outside the pub, as well as by using ticketing and social entertainments designed to attract family units – seems to have represented an enabling step forward, and yet it quickly became apparent that it was two disabling steps backwards. Far from expanding either the public political sphere or the definition of feminine respectability, it merely served to reinforce the primacy of their private roles as wives, mothers, and sisters. In short, women's public political presence was confined to supporting their husbands, sons or brothers in social, rather than overtly political, roles. The independence and political inclusion promised by the new improved and improving radical culture was certainly denied to women, indeed it was only their confinement to a domestic role which enabled men to prove themselves improved and independent proto-citizens. It was not until the 1880s that women once again began to re-emerge in the public political arena to reclaim their independence.[130]

Crucial to the imposition of this restricted definition of women's public political role was the reform and regulation of popular politics which proved increasingly disciplinary in character. This process had begun during the 1830s, as radicals sought to reform customary popular political culture in order to create a new independent political style which would finally establish their moral right for inclusion within the political nation. This disciplining of popular politics was critical to the mid-Victorian invention of party. As Robert Michels recognised, the growth of nationally organised mass political parties irrevocably shifted the balance of power in favour of the leaders over the led. The very hierarchical and centralised structure of party organisations meant that it was increasingly leaders, not their supporters, who shaped political appeals and defined the parameters of the public political sphere.[131] The invention of party was, then, far from the enabling and emancipative development of Whig historiography, rather it reworked the languages of the independent citizen in increasingly restrictive and masculine ways.[132]

This emphasis on the closure and disciplining of popular politics can be over-stressed. Consequently, I have also shown how many of the cultural forms of customary political culture were continually adapted and used throughout this period. These cultural processes of continuity, change, appropriation, and adaption are also suggestive of the relationship between political leaders and their constituencies of support. In the last two chapters we have seen something of the reciprocity of these relationships, especially during the first half of the nineteenth century, as new political styles and identities were only successful if they struck a chord with their popular constituencies. The age-old political imperative of maintaining the support and unity of one's popular constituency necessitated the equally ancient political skills of compromise and negotiation. However, as we shall see in the following chapter, leaders were themselves used by their popular constituencies, who, in treating them as icons, were able to endow them with their own meanings.

CHAPTER 7

The idol and the icon: leaders and their popular constituencies

The certainty of Heroes being sent us, our faculty, our necessity, to reverence Heroes when sent; it shines like a polestar through smoke-clouds, dust-clouds, and all manner of down rushing and conflagration.[1]

INTRODUCTION

During the 1980s, while commentators sought to explain the unique popular appeals of Ronald Reagan and Margaret Thatcher, historians were busy rethinking their understanding of the role of political leadership.[2] This chapter continues that task by analysing the narratives of political leadership in nineteenth-century England. Instead of studying the lives and actions of the 'Great Men' of Tory history, such an approach provides us with a history of leaders from the bottom up, as political icons whose meanings were created as much by their supporters as by themselves.

I must begin such an account by urging the late twentieth-century reader to imagine the immense significance of political leaders in nineteenth-century England. In a world devoid of the 'stars' of mass entertainment and organised sport, they occupied a (possibly the) central place in popular culture, at once revered and reviled, loved and loathed. Indeed, when football and the music-hall eclipsed politics in the hierarchy of popular interests during the late nineteenth century, politicians were well represented in the supporting casts.[3] This link with the world of entertainment is not as tenuous as it may appear. A sense of theatre was essential to any aspiring politician, not just as we have seen in their oratorical performances on the hustings, but to the projection of their whole political persona. Political leaders soon learnt that they had to present themselves in different guises and roles according to the peculiarities of their audience. Although the number of these roles

251

were theoretically infinite, in practice they turned upon a relatively small number of familiar and popular narratives.

The power of political leaders did not rest simply on their skills as cultural chameleons. At local level leadership was as much about practical organisation as symbolic meaning. Consequently, this chapter concludes by examining those local activists who, as 'culture brokers', shaped the terms of local political debate – writing hand-bills and ballads, organising meetings, delivering speeches, formulating resolutions and toasts.[4] They were the critical link between 'high' and 'low' politics, it was they who produced and mediated the political culture which is the subject of this book. What is striking from this analysis is the absence of class as the dominant or most meaningful category. This is significant, not least because the pan-class appeals of leaders cannot be read as simply cynical attempts to broaden their base of support or hold together fractious coalitions, for the images and appeals of the leader as icon were themselves a product of a complex relationship between leaders and led.

THE LEADER AS ICON

The veneration of leaders was not unique to nineteenth-century popular political culture. The leader as hero had occupied a central place in English popular culture for several centuries, although the nineteenth century could lay claim to be its golden age.[5] This section will examine the fascination with leader heroes and what it tells us about the relationship between leaders and led. That relationship, I shall argue, was mediated through the projection of a myriad number of roles and narratives upon leaders both by themselves, and also, crucially, by their popular constituencies.

Politics and its cultural forms were seemingly shaped around the central fact of leadership. The elevation of leaders on hustings and statues, as well as during chairing and public entry ceremonies, served to set them apart visually as if to affirm their superior status. Similarly, birthday anniversaries, releases from prison, electoral victories, or simply a local visit, were all sufficient reasons for a dinner to fête a heroic champion and shower him with gifts.[6] This language of devotion, reverence, and gratitude was also echoed in ballads, music, and songs. 'See the Conquering Hero Comes' was something of a theme-tune for this period, reverberated endlessly to ballads like

'Ebrington and Independence': 'Hail, faithful Leaders! of a Noble Cause,/ Well have ye earned our warmest – best applause./ Each heart exults, each bosom feels the fire,/ Your patriotic Services inspire.'[7] Oratory too, of course, encouraged the apotheosis of leaders. Those blessed with the gift of the gab appeared natural leaders, their commanding presence on a platform, their ability to keep audiences enthralled, conveyed the impression of men in control of their own destinies, shaping, not reacting to, the course of events.

Even print lent itself well to the canonisation of leaders. John Wilkes may have discovered the potential of print to project specific styles of leadership, but his example was soon followed.[8] Many nineteenth-century radical leaders recognised the importance of owning or editing their own paper or journal, using them (like Cobbett, O'Brien, O'Connor and Jones) not only to address their readers in highly personal styles, but also to report their sufferings and valiant endeavours to a national audience.[9] This sense of personal familiarity between leaders and led was also enhanced by printed portraits and cartoons. Such images enabled those, who otherwise would have never seen their champions, to make them an omnipresent figure in their life, hanging above the fireplace.[10] Few indoor radical meetings, dinners, reading or schoolrooms were complete without their pictorial pantheon of heroes on the walls. The *Northern Star* was especially adept at marketing images of Chartist leaders, their symbolic presence was felt at most local Chartist events, however remote or small. At a Chartist dinner in Tiverton during 1841 'the room was adorned with three handsome green banners, trimmed with white – one placed over the Chairman, with the inscription, "Feargus O'Connor, the Friend of the People" on which was emblazoned the "*Northern Star*" and on one side the portrait of Frost, and on the other that of McDouall...There were other portraits from the *Star* handsomely framed'.[11] Just as, over 20 years later, portraits of Gladstone, Bright, Mill, and Beales hung in the Clerkenwell pub where the local Reform League branch met.[12]

Of all political memorabilia it has been the visual images – the portraits, statuettes, and figurines – which have best endured, a testimony to both their popularity and the often sacred significance with which they were endowed. In Oldham several highly instructive visual representations of the borough's old political heroes have survived. A portrait of William Cobbett depicts him as a stout, handsome, but baby-faced man in his prime (see Plate 58). Dressed

58   The ideal image: portrait of William Cobbett (Oldham Local Studies Library)

like a gentleman, he wears an enigmatic smile and wide staring eyes that follow you. This can hardly have been the 'portly' old man of 67, with a large protruding nose and ruddy complexion, who Butterworth described before he was elected at Oldham in 1832. Even a retrospective portrait tried to turn the clock back for the 'Grand Old Man' of Oldham's politics (see Plate 59). Of course, not all images were so idealised. A statuette of W. J. Fox was far from flattering (see Plate 60). It portrays him as an earnest but ugly and

59 Retrospectively representing the grand old man (Oldham Local Studies Library)

squat man, uncomfortable with his body which is braced, upright, legs apart and arms crossed. A serious, scowling and disproportionately large face sits uneasily on his diminutive body. Underneath, on the pedestal, the words 'EDUCATION', 'REFORM', 'LIBERTY' and 'FREE

60   Statuette of W. J. Fox (Oldham Local Studies Library)

TRADE' are inscribed almost, conceivably, as an explanation or apology. And yet, as Wilkes and Nelson had demonstrated, such ungracious features could be turned to one's political advantage as the anti-hero writ large.[13]

Commercially, of course, the producers of these icons had to portray the image of the leader people wanted to believe in. Consequently, different images of the same leader proliferated upon the huge array of artifacts which made money out of celebrating the leader–hero. John Brewer discovered no less than 'thirty-one different engraved portraits, coffee and tea pots, spoons, jugs, figurines, snuff-boxes, pipes, tobacco, papers, buttons, and twenty six different coins and medals' on offer at the height of the Wilkite agitation.[14] Such techniques were not confined to famous national leaders alone. Even Alexander Donovan, the unsuccessful candidate

61   Medal commemorating Alexander Donovan, Lewes 1826 (Royal Pavilion Art
Gallery and Museums, Brighton)

at the 1826 Lewes election issued a medal to commemorate his first
canvass in the borough: 'On one side it exhibits the word "Donovan"
and on the other "Freedom of Election"' (see Plate 61).[15] Commercially famous national political leaders remained the biggest pull,
as the use of their names and faces on pub signs exemplified. John
Wilkes, Sir Francis Burdett, Henry Hunt, Daniel O'Connell, Feargus
O'Connor, Ernest Jones, Kossouth, Garibaldi, and Gladstone were
all honoured in this way, not to mention innumerable generals and
admirals.[16] Yet, the often short shelf-life of pub names like these
suggests something of the perilous fate of the leader as commodity. As
a portrait, figurine, or pub sign, leaders were the people's commodity,
deified and worshipped at times of success and spurned and rejected
at times of failure. Perhaps as interesting as the popular uses of these
types of iconography are the moments at which they were discarded,
pubs re-named, portraits taken down, figurines packed away.[17]

Leaders were not just icons or commodities; their significance was
also often highly personal. The *Morning Chronicle*, for instance,
reported that at Royton in 1849 the 'people have a fancy for
christening their children after the hero of the minute. A generation
or so back, Henry Hunts were as common as blackberries – a crop of
Feargus O'Connors replaced them, and latterly there have been a
few green sprouts labelled Ernest Jones.'[18] This practice reveals how
sacred leaders often became in the popular imagination. Association
with them seems to have conveyed the belief that their extraordinary
powers would somehow be passed on, a bastardised version of the

mystical royal touch if you like.[19] Amazingly, the sacred relics of leaders continued to be sold throughout this period. Alongside the thriving trade in porcelain statuettes of Garibaldi and the Tichborne claimant, there was the apparent obsession of visitors to Gladstone's country house 'Hawarden' to secure wood-chips from trees felled by the great man himself. This demand for less certifiable, but infinitely more personal, mementoes like wood-chips had a long genealogy: in their time, hawkers selling locks of Nelson's and Garibaldi's hair were reputedly common-place.[20]

The growth of literacy and the proliferation of print no doubt served to prolong such persistent idolatry. The serialisation of cheap, printed biographies and the profiles of leaders in the radical press took the stories of leaders' lives to ever larger audiences during the nineteenth century. Contemporaries like Thomas Carlyle were quick to realise the potential of this development. His theory that history was the story of the achievements of heroic men, elaborated in *On Heroes, Hero-Worship and the Heroic in History* (1841), struck a chord and received wide currency. Carlyle's heroes were set apart by their strength of 'character' which enabled them to shape events rather than react to them. They were moral heroes capable of uniting a fractious and divided society, role models for the modern age. This idea of men uniting behind one leader and shaping their own destiny had great popular appeal and spawned a mass of hagiographies.[21] Popular political culture, then, seems to have had an insatiable appetite for leaders and heroes. But what sort of political heroes did people want, and how did their leaders seek to satisfy these popular expectations?

The 'Gentleman Leader' was one such heroic role with an extraordinary popular appeal which leaders never tired of playing.[22] This was not, as is often assumed, a role confined to radical leaders alone; in many ways it was a product of the eighteenth-century creed of Independency. We find in Devon, during the 1816 contest, an 'Englishman' arguing that Edmund Pollexfen Bastard should represent the county because he had 'a good and honourable character; – an ancient Family; – an independent Fortune; – a total Freedom from all party shackles...a solemn Engagement already taken to adhere to his Independence...'.[23] Only wealthy gentlemen could be truly independent from the corrupting power of party, place, and patronage. It was an appeal which also worked well for Thomas Read Kemp, during Lewes' election in 1811. Kemp took the appeal of the independent gentleman leader further, emphasising the sacrifices he would endure as representative of his native town. 'Gentlemen, I have no selfish views in thus offering myself as a candidate to represent you in Parliament, I want nothing either for myself or my connections, within the power of a Minister to give; on the other hand I must sacrifice many endearing comforts; but the Independence and welfare of my native Town, are considerations in my mind, paramount to all others'.[24] This suggestion of a leader making sacrifices and suffering for his cause was a powerful and popular narrative, one which, because it gave voice to the reciprocity of interests and emotions between leaders and led, was used and appropriated by leaders of all political colours throughout this period. None the less, the appeal of this role, with its emphasis on the leader as a suffering and exiled martyr, was especially popular in radical circles – after all it was their gentlemen leaders who had most to sacrifice and their supporters who suffered most. As late as 1868, we find Edmond Beales arguing at an election rally in Tower Hamlets that 'he was there to serve no personal ambition, vanity or other purpose, but because he was invited by the electors... *Their cause was his cause; their battle his battle* (loud and continued applause)'.[25] This point was reinforced by George Howells, secretary of the Reform League, who had received a letter from Beales during this campaign pleading for money. No man, Howells wrote, was 'more fair minded, unselfish or more loyal... a true English, cultured, christian, gentleman... He lost his practice, his office, his voice, [and] his health in the people's cause.'[26]

Of all the figures who performed the 'gentleman leader' role, William Cobbett must rank alongside Henry Hunt and Feargus O'Connor as one of its most talented exponents.[27] Part of Cobbett's appeal was that his life demonstrated the possibility of transcending poverty and class boundaries – he had shown that with luck the labouring poor could play any role they wanted. Born into a family of poor agricultural workers he became a soldier before moving to London as a clerk. In London he tried his hand as a bookseller and journalist, trades which stood him in good stead when he emigrated to the USA. It was not until Cobbett returned from America in 1821 that he was able to establish himself as a farmer of some repute in Surrey. In Oldham he played heavily upon this image of himself as a landed gentleman farmer, an image reinforced by his style of oratory, his clothes, and his frequent use of snuff.[28] Twenty-five years after his death in 1860, the *Oldham Standard* evoked his memory simply by describing his clothes: 'There he stands as we were wont to see him in his life, at his lectures, with his blue coat and gilt buttons, white neck cloth, light linen waistcoat, and drab pantaloons, white hair, dead eyes and pudding face...'[29] That this gentlemanly image of Cobbett was popular among the notoriously unpretentious people of Oldham is somewhat surprising, and yet his following in the town was legion. Truly the stuff that legends were made of. According to Butterworth he was at times invested with the magical qualities of a 'demi-god'. Thus at 'the great man's' appearance in Chadderton during the 1834 election 'the large room of the public house, about 12 feet by 6 with a very low ceiling soon proved too small for the numbers who pressed in as much to get a glimpse of the notorious politician as to hear him ... [Cobbett] was cheered by the Chadderton clodpoles, who *looked upon him as a being who had not the flesh and blood of common mortals.*'[30] Ironically his death the following year, only 3 years after his election as the borough's first MP, was the making of the Cobbett cult. Happily, dead heroes cannot disillusion their followers like living ones can. And yet, as we shall see, for all his canonisation Cobbett's legacy to Oldham was far from straightforward. Foxites, Fieldenites, Cobbettites, Radicals, Liberals, and Tories all fought to inherit the mantle of this legacy – a tribute in itself to his popularity.

In this battle for the soul of William Cobbett his son, John Morgan Cobbett (see Plate 62), always had the upper hand. He shamelessly pushed home his natural advantage, alluding in practically every speech to his 'physical and political father'. Like his father, he too played the gentleman leader, setting himself apart from his constituents socially. He was not, he emphasised, 'a man of the people, but...he acted for the people'.[31] Yet, unlike his father, when he first contested the borough he was a dashing young man in his thirties who knew little of rural England. He therefore cast himself more in the role of the young urban squire, a suitable role for someone increasingly associated with John Fielden's Ten Hours Bill and other industrial agitations. However, when Fielden died in 1849 J. M. Cobbett was left politically isolated. He quickly embraced a strident Protestant Tory populism and reverted back to the anti-industrialism of his father, projecting himself as a landed gentleman dedicated to protecting 'Old England's' pastoral way of life. At the 1865 election Joseph Hilton was struck by J. M. Cobbett's rustic image, his 'knee breeches and green shooting jacket', which seemed to deliberately

62   The son of the father: John Morgan Cobbett (Oldham Local Studies Library)

63   The gallant general: W. A. Johnson (Oldham Local Studies Library)

emphasise his difference from the urban/industrial image of his rivals Hibbert and Platt, the town's largest employers.[32]

Appearance could be all. Certainly for the Chartist G. J. Harney a 'popular chief should be possessed of a magnificent bodily appearance, an iron frame, eloquence or at least a ready fluency of tongue... [he] ... should possess great animal courage, contempt of pain and death, and be not altogether ignorant of military arms and science'.[33] These were all qualities which came most naturally to ex-military men, and the narrative of the old soldier, who had been tested at war and now sought to fight the people's cause in parliament, proved particularly potent. Anyone prepared to make the ultimate sacrifice for his country would be able to endure the hardships involved in fighting the people's cause. Captain Marryat, a reforming candidate at Tower Hamlets in 1832, was always introduced as 'the "Gallant Captain"... a reformer, and the hero of a hundred fights'. Marryat made much of his military experience, projecting himself as an old soldier who only wanted 'a fair stand-up fight, and let the best man win (cheers)', one who was prepared to make the biggest sacrifice of all – 'he had shed blood for Reform having nearly been killed at an election (Great Cheering)'.[34] In fact 'Gallant Generals' and 'Courageous Captains' popped up all over the place. There was Colonel, later General, Johnson, Boston's MP in 1818–26 and MP for Oldham between 1837–47, hero of the Peninsular campaigns, who was known simply as 'The General' even after he had sold his commission in 1842 (see Plate 63). Major B. Handley, another 'Gallant Major' who had bravely done his duty and had been the 'hero of a hundred fights', was elected at Boston in 1832. Not surprisingly these military figures were also popular in that other port Tower Hamlets, where barely an election passed without the appearance of one. Captain Marryat in 1832, Colonel T. E. P. Thompson and Lieutenant-Colonel C. R. Fox in 1841, who, by the 1847 election, had become the even more gallant Major-General. Even those leaders like John Hibbert, Oldham's Liberal MP from 1862, who had no ostensible connection with the military, were not adverse to representing themselves in military garb (see Plate 64).

In many ways Giuseppe Garibaldi, the hero of the Italian *Risorgimento*, represented the ultimate military-cum-political hero. An immensely popular figure in England during the 1860s, he was afforded a royal welcome on his visit to London in 1864[35] (see Plate 65). His humble origins and shy, retiring character was transposed

64   Playing at soldiers: John Hibbert by Sir James Jebusa Shannon, RA (Oldham
Local Studies Library)

65   Everyman's military hero: Garibaldi arriving at Charing Cross (*Illustrated London News*, 23 April 1864)

against his courageous military tactics and dashing, gallant exterior. Contemporary portraits, figurines, and pub signs of Garibaldi portray an upright, plucky figure, resplendent in fine, showy clothes, a handsome, dashing man – undeniably playing up the element of machismo and (yes) sex appeal. Yet, if Garibaldi represented the zenith of a long popular political tradition, he did not mark its close. In 1899 a young Winston Churchill had begun his political career at Oldham with a heavy electoral defeat. At the by-election 18 months later he returned to Oldham a hero, having engineered a heroic escape from Pretoria during the Boer War. Met at the station by two brass bands playing 'See the Conquering Hero Comes', he was swept to victory on a tide of adulation.[36] As E. P. Thompson has suggested, this tendency to invest such leaders with almost superhuman powers reflected their followers own sense of political exclusion and powerlessness.[37]

If leaders were revered for their unique heroic qualities, those who had risen from the ranks were also relished for their very ordinariness – one thinks of contemporary examples like Chancellor Kohl and John Major. As a meeting of Tower Hamlets' electors and non-electors in 1852 resolved, if the rights and interests of labour were to be represented 'the same can only be obtained by sending men to Parliament who have risen from the ranks of labour, and who are acquainted with its wants'.[38] In this case it was the one time mechanic, now trade union leader and publican, William Newton who was proposed. However, Newton who 'had himself felt the insecurity of the working man's position' was not alone in projecting himself as a man of the people from the people.[39] It was a well-worn narrative used by both radicals and Tories alike. In mid-nineteenth-century Oldham for instance, W. J. Fox was known among his supporters as 'the Norwich Weaver Boy' while the mill-owning Tory John Duncuft countered with the nickname the 'Oldham Spinner Boy'. Fox's image as a man of the people was essential to combat J. M. Cobbett's portrayal of him as the employers' candidate (see Plate 66). Time and time again he emphasised that 'Trained to labour in early life, my strongest sympathies ever have been, and will be, with the Industrial classes. I am one of the million. I belong to the people. When I speak in their cause, it is as one of themselves and not as a Patron'.[40] Of course, the prohibitive property qualifications required of MPs meant that it was impossible to stand as a candidate and yet remain 'one of the million' in anything other than spiritual

66 Man of the people: W. J. Fox by Andrew Ashton (Oldham Art Gallery)

terms. Hence Fox's insistence that although 'from manual labour, I have passed into mental labour, still feeling the proud consciousness that I was not an idler in the world, [but rather] working for a good which is beyond all physical advantage or all external gain'.[41] Upwards social mobility did not, then, preclude projecting oneself as a man of the people. The important thing was not one's new-found wealth, but one's roots and the way in which one had risen in society. Fox, for instance, was adamant that he 'had not wriggled his way up in society by paying court to those above, or forgetting those below'.[42]

Of course, these 'men of the people' were often perceived as role models whose success could be emulated, even repeated. The popularity of this narrative should not be underestimated. Politics remained one of the few avenues through which working men could escape the snare of poverty. George Thompson certainly played upon such aspirations at Tower Hamlets in 1847.

He was born of humble parents (cheers). Those revered parents had not been able to give him any education (cheers). He could not point to Eton, and say he had been a 'fag' there. He could not boast of honours bought at Oxford, nor announce that he had graduated at Edinburgh, at Glasgow, or at Dublin. *Let all listen to him, and be encouraged to aspire to the highest honour which an Englishman could possess.* He had never had a quarter's schooling in his life (Great applause). He would not deny his parentage, or from a false shame turn his back on his ancestry. He wished the Commons of England to know it – he had sprung from the poor and the lowly (Renewed Cheers).[43]

Look at me, Thompson argued, born poor, uneducated, and yet risen to the heights of an MP, all in the good cause of the people. If the soundness of the cause helped, so too did the strength of Thompson's moral character. It was this unstinting moral might, not material might, to which all should aspire. As Fox had put it, improvement came from within oneself, not by sucking up to those above one. This was a radical, enabling message which gave people a sense of agency and control over their lives, for all could achieve such moral strength.

These leaders who had risen from the ranks of the working poor were not the only ones to represent themselves as men of the people. Industrialists and middle-class leaders claimed a natural affinity with those other productive classes who worked for a living. This appeal played upon a reworking of the enduring critique of 'Old Corruption', in which the lazy and parasitical aristocracy were presented as the natural enemy of the working or productive classes. Once again it was a narrative appropriated by all political groups. Thus we find O. E. Coope, the Tory brewer who stood as a Conservative candidate at Tower Hamlets' election of 1868, portraying himself as 'a working man, and therefore one of them, for he abhorred idleness, and looked upon industry as honourable (Cheers)'.[44] Similarly, Herbert Ingram, Boston's reforming MP and proprietor of the *Illustrated London News*, told a meeting of Boston's working men in 1859 that he was

67 'Honest' John Fielden (Oldham Local Studies Library)

proud to think that I have been a working man myself; nothing in my opinion so ennobles a man as honest labour (cheers). I believe that labour is the greatest blessing given to mankind (cheers). I have a son who is not ashamed to mount the fustian jacket, and I should be ashamed of him if he were (loud cheers) ... I myself am proud to be called the child of the working classes, and, as far as I can, I will be their champion (loud and continued cheering).[45]

This emphasis upon industry, productivity, and the dignity of labour created a community of interests between all those who worked for a living, however much they earned. It was a narrative which struck a powerful chord at the grass-roots level, as a working man made clear at the same meeting of Boston's working men:

There's my Lord Tomnoddy one of our hereditary legislators, when he gets up, he has to have a valet to assist him in putting on his clothes; and there's his lady requires two or three servants to titivate her up before she's fit to be seen; but the true hearted, honest working man and woman can do these things themselves (cheers)... What do men with handles to their names know of our wants our wishes, and our interests. We want men of business, men engaged in mercantile pursuits, men who will take care how the public money is spent.[46]

Like the gentleman leader this anti-aristocratic appeal seemed to transcend class cleavages; it informed essentially socio-economic categories with moral and political meaning.

Much the same was true of the personification of the leader as the 'Just and Benevolent Employer'. The popular appeal of this role was remarkable, especially in industrialising Oldham, where a large local employer was always elected. One of these, John Fielden (see Plate 67), owner of one of the largest mills in Europe and Oldham's radical MP for 15 years, was in many ways perceived as the classic 'Just Employer', even though his factory was attacked several times by workers angry about the introduction of new machinery.[47] Likewise the Platt brothers, the town's largest employers, also generated a remarkable popular political following despite the often brutal treatment of their workforce. When the freshly elected James Platt died prematurely in 1857 there seems to have been a genuine sense of loss in the town (see Plate 68). Certainly, reports emphasised the pluralism and diversity of his funeral procession, which was 'composed of all classes irrespective of political creed or religious differences; the conservative and the liberal, the protestant and the Roman Catholic, the churchman and the dissenter, walking side by side to testify that he who has been suddenly cut off from our midst was dear to us all'.[48] While his employees marched in the procession, some 40 thousand working people lined the streets to watch and pay their last respects. At a meeting of the Liberals that week a working man reflected 'rarely did it happen that men raised to affluence retained those sentiments common to them in more common life... yet they must rejoice when a man could be elevated in society

68 The just and benevolent employer James Platt: (Oldham Local Studies Library)

and sustain that character, and show towards the working men that respect which he believed had been generally manifested by Mr. Platt for those over whom he had the control, and whose interests were identified with his'.[49] It is difficult to detect any sense of latent class struggle in such sentiments.

If the narratives of leadership rarely accentuated a sense of class, they often celebrated a sense of locality and neighbourhood, as the role of the 'Local Lad (Made Good)' made clear. Radical jibes at 'absentee' representatives had long been a central and popular part of their critique of the electoral system.[50] Candidates who could claim to be natives, and better still residents, of the constituency had an enormous advantage over so-called 'foreigners'. When Hibbert replaced Fox as Platt's Liberal colleague at Oldham in 1862, much emphasis was placed on his status as a native lad.

> I stand forth as a candidate for the representation of this borough in parliament. I feel that to be a great honour. I feel it an honour because it is my native town – a town in which I have been interested since the day of my birth – (hear, hear) – a town in which I have been brought up – with whose growth I have had my own growth – with whose prosperity I have also had my own prosperity – and with whose distress I can also feel the greatest sympathy.[51]

At the 1868 election, the town's *Liberal Elector* contrasted the two local Liberal candidates with 'foreigners' put forward by the Tories. 'They do not reside in the borough: they never have resided in the borough, and only come amongst us for electioneering purposes. They have no property here, they contribute nothing to local taxation; they are not connected with us commercially, and take no interest in our local affairs'.[52] So powerful were these appeals that in Devon and Lewes membership of a distinguished (and preferably aristocratic) local family was a prerequisite of any candidature.

How much more potent the narrative of the local lad made good! However, although innumerable candidates cast themselves in this role, those who had 'improved' themselves elsewhere were recognisably more popular than those who had done so within their home towns. Herbert Ingram, Boston's prodigal son who returned to the town having made his fortune, was far more popular than W. H. Adams and Meaburn Staniland, both of whom had lived and worked in the town all of their lives. Clearly, one had more chance of stepping on other people's toes and putting your fellow-townsmen's noses out of joint if your money was made around them or, worse still, from them. Therefore, while William Newton played heavily upon the image of himself as a local lad made good during his comeback in Tower Hamlets at the 1868 election, it was all to no avail. A private report by Edmond Beales' electoral agent recognised that Newton's rise to 'comparative affluence' through his membership of the Board of Works had alienated his former supporters.[53] The moral being that if local lads were to make good they had to do so in ways which their constituents found acceptable.

If all these narratives relied on the immodesty of leaders, the role of the 'Honest but Reluctant Hero' did not, or, at least, not in the conventional sense. This essentially anti-heroic role was best typified by the rather sombre (even dull) personality of John Fielden. Popularly known as 'Honest John Fielden', Fielden seems to have deliberately played down his abilities and ambition to suit his limited skills as an orator. Perhaps his rather earnest and laboured style was adopted in contrast to Cobbett's natural flamboyance and egotism during their campaign for election at Oldham in 1832. We should not accept too readily Fielden's portrayal of himself as an unworthy second fiddle to Cobbett. Fielden was no donkey. He knew all too well how his anti-heroic style enhanced his popularity. Listen, for instance, to his speech at Oldham's nomination in 1832:

He had with difficulty allowed himself to be put in nomination because he had no abilities to fit him for being a member of Parliament. He had neither the quality of frightening by words or terrifying by substance – (laughter) ... As he had before observed there was no qualification for members of Parliament except what property gave – he had been favoured by circumstance to acquire a little property and thus he could qualify but independent of that he possessed no claims to their suffrage – he had neither talent, ability or industry (yes, yes) but if he had none of these things he had some good qualitys [*sic*] and those were a good heart and honest mind – (Loud applause).[54]

Fielden's modesty at once conveys the impression of humility. His wealth (merely the result of fortunate circumstances) had not given him any high-falutin ideas. He still possessed his humanity and those sound, solid northern credentials of a 'good heart and honest mind'. Fielden's brilliance lay in his ability to let his audience affirm his talent, ability, and industry. Not for him the exaggerated claims of invincibility that were the hallmarks of 'Gentlemen Leaders' like Cobbett and O'Connor.

Of course these roles were not the only ones which leaders used, just as they were not confined to dramatising one such narrative throughout their political careers. John Fielden, for instance, cast himself in a number of seemingly contradictory roles; including 'friend of the people', 'working man's friend', 'the operative's friend', 'local lad', 'man of God', 'just employer', 'urban squire', 'major manufacturer', 'the veteran radical', and 'Grand Old Man'.[55] Leaders could re-cast themselves in the roles and narratives which best suited the demands and expectations of the audiences they addressed. Gladstone was one who recognised the symbiotic nature of this relationship between leaders and led, realising that he, like all popular leaders, was 'cast in the mould offered to him by the mind of his hearers ... It is an influence principally received from his audience (so to speak) in vapour, which he pours back upon them in a flood ... He cannot follow or frame ideas; his choice is, to be what his age will have him, what it requires in order to be moved by him; or else not to be at all'.[56] As each audience would endow the icon of the leader with a multiplicity of meanings, the leaders' most enduring roles were those that made sense of most people's meanings. Figures such as Gladstone were popularly type-cast, maybe not unwillingly, first as 'Mr. Gladstone, the woodman' and then as 'the Grand Old Man'. Just as these roles generated different associations for every individual, so Gladstone's opponents appropriated them in often subversive ways, using his image as a woodman to portray him as a crazed reformer, bent on chopping down centuries-old institutions as though they were trees.[57] Here again the political contest was essentially over the meaning of these roles and their popular perceptions.

This is wonderfully illustrated by the battle over the meaning of William Cobbett, who dominated Oldham's politics like a colossus even after his death. It was his death and the subsequent collapse of the town's reforming coalition which ensured the construction of the Cobbett mythology. In the 30 years of fierce, bitter, and disruptive partisan strife which followed, all factions were quick to re-invent the past, and Cobbett's role within it, for their own purposes. In 1868 the Tory *Oldham Ensign* recalled the political crisis caused by his death.

William Cobbett, the soldier, the plough-boy, the eloquent and sagacious legislator, the friend of the poor, and the unflinching defender of the liberties of the people was soon to quit this sublunary sphere, and leave to others to reap the harvest from the seed which he had sown. William Cobbett died, on the 18th day of June, 1835, amidst the sorrow and regret of his warm-hearted constituency, and deeply mourned by every lover of freedom and progress in the kingdom. *And now begin the political troubles and disasters of the constituency of Oldham.*[58]

Such eulogies for a mythological Cobbett who probably never existed were commonplace amongst all of the town's competing factions, for they all needed to create an unassailable hero whose legacy they could claim to represent. Thus each group invented their own Cobbett and Cobbettite tradition. Each year his birthday was celebrated, first by the radicals and then, from the 1850s, by the Cobbettite Tories. Remarkably the Tories were still commemorating his birthday in 1868, 33 years after his death. A potent reminder, if any were needed, of the importance attached to the cult of William Cobbett.

Of course, by the 1850s the Tories had particular reason to foster this cult, as they sported J. M. Cobbett as their candidate. Much time and energy was invested by the Tories in drawing parallels between the politics of the father and the son. J. M. Cobbett himself seemed almost duty-bound to continually assure his audiences 'that if that man [W. Cobbett] were alive now he would pursue precisely the same course in politics as he was pursuing'.[59] This supposed hot-line between the heavenly father and his son on earth posed a considerable problem to the Tories' opponents. During the 1868 election, letters frequently appeared in the Liberal press from rehabilitated Cobbettites confessing 'that for many years I blindly and inconsiderately followed John Morgan Cobbett because of the name, as if there was some charm in it'.[60] John Platt, the Liberal candidate at this election, also repeatedly emphasised the differences between the politics of Cobbett senior and Cobbett junior, arguing that the 'people reverenced his father, and that was for the principles he enunciated; but how can they reverence the son, when he repudiated his father's principles? (Applause)'.[61] What was at issue, then, was the contest over the meaning of William Cobbett and his politics. The Cobbettite Tories saw him as a defender of Old England, a Conservative at heart. As the *Oldham Standard* put it in 1860, 'there are not many Conservatives who would greatly quarrel either with his doctrines or the spirit in which he worked ... the man was to his very heart's core an Englishman. He was positively the very type of the national character. He was called, indeed, William Cobbett, but his real name was John Bull.'[62] Meanwhile, for the radicals and Liberals the 'indefatigable Cobbett' belonged to their hall of fame which also included the 'noble Cartwright' and 'the honest Hunt'.[63] Or, as W. J. Fox put it, 'what is the worth, what the pride and the glory of William Cobbett, but that he was a man of the people, sprung from the people, felt with the people, wrote for the people; and even in his errors was true to his own perception of what the people needed?'[64] In short the ghost of Cobbett was perpetually re-invented as Oldham's competing factions used it to construct their different histories and different visions of the future.

Personalities were, then, part and parcel of politics. Indeed, we should not equate this obsession with individuals and personalities with antiquated or backward-looking modes of political expression. The personalisation of politics neither obscured nor simplified the hard political debate of often complex issues, rather it dramatised politics in terms of personalities. One cannot exaggerate the extent to which many related to, and identified with, their champions. When W. J. Fox was defeated at Oldham's July 1852 election, he complained to his daughter that 'my swollen hand is subsiding after the several hundred parting shakings on Friday – when many actually cried at losing me'.[65] Certainly it was not uncommon for several thousand to turn out to pay their last respects at the funerals of even quite obscure local political leaders.[66] Such occasions were marked by the sense that politics would never again be quite the same. And so it often proved, for political street literature was crammed full of oblique references to local characters that had been mercilessly parodied beyond recognition to the modern reader. This is why Benjamin Grime's vivid account of Oldham's politics during the first half of the nineteenth century is so invaluable; it provides a rubric through which otherwise impenetrable references can be deciphered. In what follows I make no apologies for drawing so heavily upon it.

In Oldham at least, local political leaders were rarely referred to by their name, instead, as Grime recalled, they

were represented under the most ridiculous and offensive characteristics that the imagination could pourtray [*sic*]. These ever-recurring effusions of the day certainly illustrated in a most forcible manner the turbulent passions that prevailed, and the ardent desires that struggled so desperately for political supremacy. They also delineated the striking characteristics and unmistakable peculiarities of the public men of the time. Though often times a little exaggerated, they, as a rule, conveyed the impressions which the public entertain of prominent men, and which are derived from natural individual peculiarities that cannot well be concealed from public observation... It seems that if men will themselves mix up in public matters they must become reconciled to bear sarcasm and ridicule.[67]

Thus John Earnshaw, quack doctor and Cobbettite leader, was known as 'the hobbling quack' because in 'his gait he had a way of stooping at every step'.[68] Similarly, Earnshaw's fellow partisan W. H. Mellor became 'Bendigo' after the famous boxer of the time because

he possessed a ponderous body, with every muscle developed, with irregular surface, as if it had been well battered with fisticuffs. His fists were continually clenched, as if he was always ready to give someone a cuff, and when on the platform, or the hustings, which he often was, haranguing the rabble, his fists were flying about like a butt-end of a drumstick, and everybody kept their distance, as if the battler had been in a boxing ring.[69]

And, as we have already seen, it was also an alias which characterised Mellor's often violent political style in disrupting Foxite meetings. This use of highly personal satire was, of course, neither new nor unique to Oldham. During Devon's 1820 election Lord Ebrington had been mercilessly mocked for his unmanly stutter and diminutive physique. At Boston one pollster felt compelled to explain that at 'Liberal meetings it was custom to refer by name, and in anything but complimentary terms, to various gentlemen identified with the Conservative Party. To this provocation the severity of several of the Election Squibs is due.'[70] Even Grime tells us he is only giving us an edited version.

Yet, edited or not, it is highly instructive of the importance of personalities in popular political culture. Nothing illustrates this better than the dramatisation of Alex Taylor's life. 'Known popularly as "Alick ut Mumps", he was a leading and immensely popular figure on the Cobbettite wing of the Radical party between 1832 and 1847 speaking at practically every public meeting between 1832 and 1847.'[71] Initially a power-loom weaver he established a grocer's shop in Mumps during the 1820s, although by the 1840s he described himself more grandly as a 'provisions dealer'. Many assigned this rapid upward mobility to the radical use of exclusive dealing during the 1830s and 1840s which reputedly amassed him a sizeable personal fortune. He was certainly not poor. By the 1830s he qualified as a police commissioner (at a rateable value of £60 a year), while on his death in 1853 his estate was valued at no less than £5,000 – a tidy sum by any standards. Despite his growing wealth, Taylor portrayed himself as a working man with strong anti-establishment leanings, an image reinforced by his appearance and personality. Grime remembered him as a 'tall, well-built man... an excited individual, quick on the foot, with head erect, and spectacles gazing earnestly and steadily ahead'.[72] Renowned for wearing shirt-sleeves come rain or shine, and the impressive muscular arms they displayed, he quickly became known as the 'shirt-sleeve orator'. For all this, cultivation of the manly working man image, it was Taylor's association with the pleasures of the people which did most to secure his reputation as their champion. Frequently associated with drink in Foxite ballads

like 'Alick 'i'th Hop 'Ole' – 'The Hop Pole' being the Tory's
headquarters the Crown and Anchor pub – Taylor also took part in
the annual pilgrimage to the seaside during the town's wakes week.

Whatever Taylor's popular appeal, his support for J. M. Cobbett
in 1847, and worse still in 1852, set him up as a symbol of Cobbettite
politics and therefore a legitimate target for Foxite abuse. His stand
against the town's incorporation was portrayed as self-seeking,
designed to protect the interests, place, and power of his dictating
faction on the police commissioners. A handbill addressed to Taylor
accused him of being 'an ignorant, a deceitful, and an expensive
leader', whose control of Oldham's Workhouse was 'a monument to
your ignorance, a convincing proof of your unfitness for leadership'.[73]
To Foxite writers Taylor came to symbolise the dreaded dishonest
and unmanly turncoat, a traitor to the cause, a lily-livered 'weather-
vane politician'. He was crucified in Foxite ballads such as '"No
Go" – The Sublime Watchword of the Mongrel Politicians of
Oldham' in which he was portrayed as 'that "shirt sleev'd *Janus*" –
the Mumps chameleon Devil,/ The Sovereigns rabble's mouthpiece,
progress in deeds of evil;/ May he gull them to their hearts content,
and may he keep them so,/ And when they find they're diddled, may
he wink and say, "No Go".'[74] The Foxites' eventual victory in this
ongoing battle with the chameleon devil came at the December 1852
by-election. The campaign had been long and vicious, and there was
none of the usual magnanimity at the declaration. John Platt used his
speech to launch a final stinging attack on Taylor.

He had no wish to say much in reference to that man, – let the people of
Oldham deal with him as he deserved. He had for years been a traitor to the
people of Oldham; but now that they had unmasked him, let him never
more have their confidence, but rather let him be held up to execration. He
(Mr. Platt) thanked God that he had lived to see the electors and non-
electors capable of distinguishing their true from their sham friends.[75]

Two months later Platt got his wish, Taylor was found dead in a
barn, having cut his own throat with a razor.

Clearly Grime's warning that 'if men will themselves mix up in
public matters they must become reconciled to bear sarcasm and
ridicule' was not misplaced. Romantic tales of leaders battling
heroically in the people's cause often gave way to tales of rejection,
loss, and tragedy. It was all melodramatic stuff, Mills and Boon
politics. Politics was full of stories of once indomitable popular leaders

dying rejected and broken hearted. In Grime's narrative, Taylor was in distinguished company. There was Feargus O'Connor who, 'bewailing the failure of all his schemes, became at least a wreck of what had been, and ended his life in a lunatic asylum'.[76] Similarly, John Fielden's defeat at Oldham's 1847 election 'was a sad blow to the old man... His friends believed he took his defeat to heart, and by continually brooding o'er the disaster he hastened his death, which took place shortly after, on the 29th of May 1849.'[77] By rights a life devoted to the people should be rich in spiritual, if not material, rewards, and these stories of once omnipotent men with broken wills and broken hearts were especially poignant. The people may have created their own leaders and endowed them with heroic qualities, but, as we have already seen with the chairing ceremony at elections, they always reserved the right to bring them back down to earth with a thump. This popular passion for unmasking heroes may help to explain the undeniable appetite for scandalously satirical street literature. Heroes were never allowed to live up to their expectations, for it was their failure and fallibility which reminded the people of their common humanity.

Not every local leader died so tragically, a reviled and rejected man. James Holladay, the radical Dissenter who stood as a candidate against J. M. Cobbett in 1847 before Fox announced his candidature, died a hero in the midst of a Foxite election rally in 1852. His life was portrayed equally melodramatically by the ballads and hymns which commemorated his death. The hymn sung at Holladay's memorial service stressed his saintly qualities, his ready acceptance at the gates of heaven. Images of heaven, happiness, light, and good are contrasted with earthly gloom and sorrow. 'O cheerless were our lengthened way;/ But heaven's own light dispels the gloom,/ Streams downward from eternal day,/ And casts a glory round the tomb.'[78] The Foxites were quick to make political capital out of Holladay's 'glorious death'. How, they asked, could the people now desert the cause of a man who had fought their 'battles, with his latest breath!'?

> Champions of Truth! cease not your noble strife!
> Tho' despots triumph, and deceit be rife,
> Tho' death have snatch'd away our honoured chief;
> Still, glorious patriots! fight in Freedom's van!
> Friends! ministering Angels! to your fellow man!
> Ye moral suns, without whose cheering light,
> The world would be one endless, dreary night;

Centres of Liberty round whom do roll –
Congenial Planets, sprung from your high soul!
Whence brilliant satellites again do spring;
Your god-like influence still widening,
Till the whole world shall in your radiance glow,
And tyrants have a final overthrow!
So work'd our much lamented HOLLADAY,
A *Star* among the Patriots of his day![79]

Here again the melodramatic struggle of the leaders' bright light against the forces of darkness and tyranny are evoked. The force of such narratives was that they endowed the audience with the power to redeem themselves. The success of the cause was not in their hands, they had to summon up the moral bravery that their 'honour'd chief' had shown during his life.

Religious motifs of suffering, sacrifice, redemption, and ultimately delivery were endlessly repeated in so many of these narratives of leadership. However leaders presented themselves, they always emphasised the immense sacrifices and personal suffering that they had endured in the people's cause – whether it was merely the classic sense of exclusion articulated by gentlemen leaders that they had been disowned by their own class and stripped of their personal fortune in their selflessness, or the more real sense of suffering created by imprisonment and transportation. Few radical meetings were complete without reference to those martyrs, past and present, who had suffered in tyrannical dungeons for asserting the people's rights. By the 1850s and 1860s radical leaders had to find new ways of evoking this sense of suffering and sacrifice. During the 1860s, for instance, John Bright made much play of his nervous breakdown, while local activists like Oldham's William Knott stuck to evoking the sacrifices of past generations.[80] Every leader had their own cross to bear. Whatever shape their suffering took it was essential for the redemption of their people.

The repetitive uses of similar roles and narratives suggests something of their very universal popular appeal. To argue that 'demagogic' styles of leadership demanded by these narratives were simply an unfortunate and unavoidable consequence of the lack of formal political organisations is, I believe, somewhat wide of the mark.[81] Although leaders were sometimes forced to adopt political personas which were capable of uniting often disparate constituencies of support, the obvious distaste for these forms of leadership by historians on the left has made them exaggerate these organisational functions. For instance, Chartism was the first nationally organised mass political movement, and yet it remained intricately tied up with the personal appeal of O'Connor, just as 30 years later the creation and fate of the Liberal party owed much to Gladstone's popularity, despite its even more sophisticated organisational machine. I would argue that the persistence of these narratives of leadership owed much to their romantic, tragic, and comic play upon the popular sense of power and powerlessness, inclusion and exclusion from the political nation. These, I have argued, worked upon cleavages that were essentially moral and political rather than social – categories which local activists were often uniquely placed to exploit in their roles as culture brokers. It is to an examination of these crucially powerful people that we now turn.

LOCAL ACTIVISTS AS CULTURE BROKERS

Those historians who emphasise the working-class nature of radical politics have sought to explain the predominance of petit-bourgeois shopkeepers and tradesmen among local activists as a practical necessity. There is clearly much substance to the argument that the lack of time, money, and literacy, not to mention unsympathetic employers, restricted the ability of working men to devote themselves to the rigorous demands of local political leadership.[82] From the 1830s, as political organisations became ever more sophisticated, these problems worsened for politically ambitious working men. It was hardly surprising that Chartists felt it necessary to introduce a system of paid lecturers and officials to their organisation, as well as demanding the payment of MPs.[83] Although these pressures undoubtedly prevented some from assuming politically active roles, historians seem to have often ritually invoked them in order to avoid asking uncomfortable questions. There has been no attempt to explain the popular appeal of petit-bourgeois leaders to radical and reforming political movements during this period, an omission which this section will endeavour to put right.

Clearly some local political activists wielded more influence and power than others. Although working men could speak at meetings, attend dinners and other events, they were rarely the culture brokers who shaped the terms of local political debate by organising meetings, dinners, and processions, tabling resolutions and toasts, as well as writing street literature. In the following pages I review the political careers of three such culture brokers. These men were not selected by any scientific criteria, rather they chose me by virtue of both their dominance of local reforming politics and their well-documented lives. Despite the very different political contexts in which they operated, all three were remarkably similar. All conformed to the role of the local lad made good, becoming shopkeepers and, eventually, tradesmen and merchants from humble beginnings. At their deaths all three left behind sizeable personal estates; and yet, despite their wealth, they remained outsiders socially, belonging neither to their new, nor their old, social setting, and yet knowing the forms and expectations of both. They were therefore the mediators between the politics of the 'high' and the 'low', the 'polite' and the 'vulgar'. They were the agents of popular political culture.

William Knott (1803–92) stood alongside John Knight and Alex Taylor as the most influential of Oldham's local political leaders.[84] In Grime's account of Oldham's politics Knott is a central figure, not least because he wrote many of the Foxite ballads and handbills upon which the book is based. As a Wesleyan lay preacher, Knott was known on the streets and in the ballads and squibs as 'The Reverend'. During the period 1830–68 there seem to have been few political meetings at which 'The Reverend' was absent – his presence pervaded the political, cultural, and economic life of the town. During the last 10 years of his life he was known affectionately by the children of his neighbourhood as 'Mr. Gladstone'. In many ways this was a fitting nickname for the grand old man of Oldham's radical politics. The flags of the Liberal club and the town hall flew at half-mast on his death, and everybody that was anybody turned out for his funeral which boasted a cortège of no less than seven coaches as well as a 'large number of sympathising spectators'.

First emerging on the town's political scene during the reform agitation of 1830–2, he was elected to the council of Oldham's Political Union in 1831, and Cobbett and Fielden's election committee in 1832. However, like many other Dissenters, Knott resigned from this committee during 1834 in protest against Cobbett's attitude to disestablishment. When Cobbett senior died in 1835, he allied himself with Feargus O'Connor's candidature against Cobbett junior, and was a leading figure in the former's election committee alongside John Knight and James Holladay. During the mid to late 1830s he reunited with his former colleagues in numerous local campaigns against the introduction of the Poor Law 1834–46, the incorporation of the town (1834 and 1839), and the county police (1838), as well as for the abolition of the church rates (1830s), Corn Laws (1840s) and the official policies in Ireland (1834 and 1848). He was also heavily involved in the campaigns for short-time (1831–2), national regeneration (1834–5) and factory reform, not to mention Chartism (1838–43). At parliamentary level, this renewed co-operation between Oldham's different radical wings was marked by Knott's membership of the Radical Reform Association and its election committee for Fielden and General Johnson between 1837 and 1847. However, the re-emergence of J. M. Cobbett as a candidate in 1847 saw him break away once more to support the candidatures of James Holladay and then W. J. Fox. He was a leading member of both election committees, and by 1852 chaired Fox's committee – a job he held until Fox's acceptance of the Chiltern Hundreds in 1862. Although he supported the Liberal candidatures of John Platt and John Hibbert down to 1868, Knott was primarily a Foxite, and increasingly his attentions focused on council, not parliamentary, politics. Having come round to sup-porting incorporation during 1848–9, as a means of both ridding the town of the county police and of improving the town's public facilities, he was elected as councillor between 1857 and 1860 and 1863 and 1865, before becoming Mayor in 1865. Although he retired as an Alderman in 1871, he retained a prominent role in the town as a Magistrate from 1867 to his death in 1892. His obituary recorded that 'Right to the last he was true to his Radical principles.'

The length of Knott's political career was unusual, a testimony to his enduring popularity – a popularity which derived from his unique social position within the town. For much of his life Knott seems to have existed in a kind of social limbo, neither 'in' nor 'out'. Certainly, until the 1860s Knott was never a member of Oldham's social and political elite – that network of industrial aristocrats which largely ran the town's institutions, who were linked by religion, birth, and marriage.[85] In contrast Knott was very much the self-made man. From the age of 10 he had worked with his father as a weaver, before being apprenticed to the hatting trade at 14. It was during this apprenticeship that he remarkably managed both to educate himself and to save enough to establish a shop selling hats and drapery during the 1820s. Throughout his life he remained a keen advocate of education, helping to establish both of Oldham's twin temples to self-improvement – the Working Man's Hall and the Oldham Lyceum. An original trustee of them both, he became a director of the Lyceum in 1848. It was no coincidence that his political career was most closely associated with the 'great educator' W. J. Fox. Meanwhile business continued to go from strength to strength, and by the early 1830s he moved his shop to the prestigious location of Oldham market-place. However, his upward social mobility and new-found wealth did not prevent him from appealing to his 'fellow operatives' during the reform meetings of 1832. Indeed, by the mid to late 1830s Knott expanded his business still further, becoming a manufacturer and wholesale dealer. During this period he travelled the north of England extensively on business, an experience which was no doubt politically useful as it brought him into contact with the politics, personnel, and publications of other industrialising towns. His frequent absences from Oldham, during which time his Greek wife and only daughter ran the business, inevitably made him lose touch with his fellow townsmen and, more importantly, his employees. By 1843 he caused a strike by reducing the wages of his factory's hat-dyers. The strike, which secured the support of the Hat Finishers and Dyers Union, spread quickly throughout the hatting factories in the surrounding area and lasted for several months. It was a painful experience, both spiritually and materially, which led him to specialise in manufacturing high quality silk hats until retiring in 1871.

Increasingly, therefore, Knott was from the people, but no longer of the people. His notoriously blunt, 'sledge-hammer' political style (apparent in both his oratory and street literature), together with his marriage to a Greek, ensured that he was never totally accepted by the town's social elite. It was this very social isolation which made Knott such an invaluable political leader. He knew the forms and expectations of both high and low politics, and could mix with both the people and the elite, while at the same time not being afraid of offending either, as his speeches, ballads, and handbills amply bear witness. From this socially and politically independent position he was ideally placed as a culture broker. He was the ideal mediator, a supreme Mr Fixit.

Henry Browne (1803–77), Lewes' leading reformer during this period, was cast in a very similar mould to that of William Knott.[86] Like Knott he was both a Dissenter and a draper, just as he was the leading culture broker of the town's reforming politics from the 1820s to at least the 1850s, and possibly beyond. He was, his obituarist noted, 'a fluent speaker [and] was always regarded as a "tower of strength" to the party'. Although by the time of his death he had not lived in Lewes for over 20 years, his obituarist thought that 'this announcement will be received with very much regret by a very large circle in this town, where he was widely known and esteemed'.

Born 'the son of an old inhabitant', he first emerged on Lewes' political scene in 1820, at the tender age of 17, as a signatory of a loyal address supporting Queen Caroline. No doubt helped by his oratorical gifts, he quickly rose to prominence. By 1825 he was a member of the provisional committee which established Lewes' Mechanics Institute, and at the 1830 election he nominated the reforming candidate Alexander Donovan. His interest in self-improving education and his role in the town's reform politics led him into a brief and unsuccessful experiment in the printing trade during the 1820s. Whether he had established the Browne and Crosskey partnership before or after this failure, what had begun as a simple drapers shop grew rapidly beyond recognition. Browne and Crosskey became one of the largest stores in the town, describing itself in the 1867 directory as 'warehousemen, clothiers, outfitters, general drapers, cabinet makers, carpet and furniture warehousemen, and agents to the Royal Exchange Fire and Life Insurance Co.'. By 1851 he was in a position to retire from active business, and 26 years later left a personal estate of no less than £12,000.

Despite his new-found wealth, Henry Browne remained one of that most rare breed in Lewes, a radical reformer. Alongside Henry Blackman he led the town's agitation for reform during 1830–2, commanding respect for his insistence on the full radical complement of annual parliaments, universal suffrage, and vote by ballot. Although he was elected as vice-president of the reforming society the Bundle of Sticks in 1831, as soon as the wave of reform hysteria had subsided by the mid-1830s, Browne's politics were too immoderate for much of the town. Although he continued to play an active role within the Bundle of Sticks, speaking at many reform meetings up to 1865, his attentions seem to have been focused elsewhere. Quite apart from the pressures of business and self-improvement, Browne seemed increasingly consumed with running the Mechanics Institute and his own scientific interests. In 1836 he was accredited with having invented the oxy-hydrogen microscope, whatever that may be, and during the 1840s he delivered a series of lectures on subjects ranging from the chemical properties of atmospheric air, the principles of electricity and chemistry, to the principles of political economy. His interest in the promotion of 'the mental and intellectual improvement of the working class' led him not only to ensure that the Mechanics Institute bought the theatre as their regular venue in 1840, but also the following year to support attempts to suppress the town's infamously raucous 5th of November celebrations. As if to prove he had not lost his sense of populism, he was out there with the best of them denouncing the vile papacy and its aggression in 1850. Perhaps it was this radical populism which set him apart from Lewes' social and political establishment, and meant that he was never even selected a director of the Mechanics Institute for which he had worked so hard. It is surely surprising that a Lewes lad, born and bred, was so ready to leave the town on his retirement in 1851. Like Knott he was an outsider, a local lad made too good.

John Noble (1788–1866) was in many ways the archetypal local radical political leader and culture broker.[87] A printer by trade, he was at the heart of the production of Boston's radical street literature. During the first half of the nineteenth century there was scarcely a reform meeting at which he did not take a leading role. His skills as a chair were legendary, his 'tact in the conducting of a public meeting was never equalled'. An 'indefatigable worker in the interests of the Liberal party, [he] was always on the look out for an opportunity to demonstrate the superiority of Liberal principles to all others. He was one of the foremost workers at every Parliamentary contest for half a century.' Moreover, as the unpaid correspondent for the reforming *Stamford Mercury*, and as the publisher of many Boston pool books, he has left an indispensable chronicle of the town's reforming politics. As his obituarist noted, 'his public career…has been the history of the progressive movement for half a century'.

Noble's political career is interesting, not least because it closely reflected the politicisation of the borough at large. He seems to have first become politically active during the unconducive atmosphere of the Napoleonic Wars when he supported Major John Cartwright's candidature at the Boston elections of 1806 and 1807. Cartwright's derisory performance at the poll no doubt convinced Noble to work with Boston's Blues, a group promoting the Independent W. A. Maddocks (1802–7, 1812–18), and it was from the radical wing of this group that Noble continued to practice his politics down to the 1860s. A keen supporter of Henry Hunt nationally, he was a leading member of the radical candidates' Colonel Johnson and John Wilks election committees during the 1820s and 1830s, and a founder member of Boston's Political Union. Following the disappointment of the Reform Act, Noble switched his attentions to municipal matters, leading the campaign against the town's church rates until their eventual abolition in the 1840s. It was this campaign, together with that to reform the town's corrupt corporation during the early 1830s, which brought him closest to martyrdom for the cause. The unreformed corporation twice arrested and charged him under the provisions of the Seditious Literature Act during the reform agitation of 1831–2, and prosecuted him for libel in 1833 for exhibiting insulting placards in his shop. He waged an ongoing war of words with the Tory Corporation and its mouthpiece the *Boston Herald* through the columns of the *Stamford Mercury* and in the handbills and ballads he produced. When the corporation was eventually reformed in 1835 Noble was one of its first councillors.

He soon became absorbed into the town's political establishment. By 1847 he was mayor, and 4 years later the town's chief magistrate. From these positions Noble seems to have exercised an unparalleled influence on Boston's social and economic development. An influence which, in the best traditions of local government, he was not afraid of using to line his own pockets. Thus he was an original shareholder in the town's gas, water, and steam-packet companies, later becoming director of the first. Yet Noble never lost the radical edge of his politics, supporting the Chartists, the Anti-Corn Law League and the Reform League, not to mention his presidency of Boston's Peace and Temperance Societies. As a prominent local Baptist, he was instrumental in founding the town's first Baptist school. However, ever anxious to dispel his opponents criticism of him as solely promoting the interests of the town's dissenters, he also established the town's only non-sectarian school. Like many self-made men, education was immensely important to his politics. He was the driving force behind the creation of the town's 'Library of the People' and Mechanics Institute, becoming vice-president of the Athenaeum in which capacity he was a fierce anti-Sabbatarian. He was also a member of the town's charity trustees and a Poor-Law Guardian. All of which seems to justify his obituarist's claim that 'few men did more for his native town'.

This energetic public life began humbly enough. His father's occupation is not known, in any event he died prematurely when

Noble was still a boy. His mother clearly struggled to support her three children and Noble had to develop his entrepreneurial skills and energy quickly. By the age of 13 he had begun selling children's books from a table in the market-place, a business which soon enabled him to hold a regular market stall. Never entirely secure, he kept his day job as usher at the local Unitarian school. By his late teens he had taught himself book-binding and opened a shop in his mother's front room. Through hard work and thrift (he used to get up at 3 am to finish his binding before opening the shop) he was able to move the business to a shop in the market-place, where it remained until his retirement in 1852. He was in 'every sense a self-made man'. And yet it was Noble's very uniqueness which made him, like Knott and Browne, the perfect culture broker. His upwards social mobility could not obscure his humble origins or the auto-didact culture from which he emerged. His life within the printing trade necessitated keeping an ear to the popular cultural and political ground which ensured an awareness of popular styles and subjects for squibs and ballads. This knowledge of the whims and tastes of his customers and audiences, coupled with his involvement within the commercial, political, and cultural life of the town, not to mention the consequent knowledge of personalities and issues, must have made him an indispensable culture broker.

These three individuals are not intended to be representative of all local reforming culture brokers, yet they did possess qualities and characteristics which were typical of many others. They were all self-made men who had risen from the ranks of the labouring poor, and consequently all valued the political importance of education, and recognised that knowledge was indeed power. One cannot under-estimate the importance of that dictum in the politics of radical reform. Most leading culture brokers worked in what may be termed the knowledge industries. They were printers, publishers, journalists, booksellers, newsagents, and schoolteachers. It was the skills of these men which allowed radical politics to be co-ordinated both within and between localities. It was they who corresponded with each other nationally through the press and post; it was they who provided the cultural framework upon which radical politics was conducted locally. By selling journals, ballads, producing street literature, and teaching children, they provided local radical communities with the cultural and intellectual tools with which they could contest the political and social status quo. Some, like Oldham's Joseph

Quarmby, radical activist, schoolteacher, and author of much street literature, followed William Cobbett in devising a new system of grammar which it was hoped would challenge exclusive notions of knowledge and language.

The scarcity of such intellectual and cultural tools meant that the power of culture broking was often handed down from father, or even mother, to son. For instance, in Boston, politics was very much a family affair. The same surnames appear again and again. Thus, just as the Butterworth family dominated printed production in early nineteenth-century Oldham, so the Noble and Bontoft families monopolised culture broking among Boston's reformers. John Noble's eldest son, active in Boston during the 1830–2 reform agitation, exported his communicative skills to Hull as secretary of their Political Union. Similarly, Noble's younger son followed in his father's footsteps even more closely, eventually earning himself a substantial reputation as a radical in London and an entrance in the *Dictionary of National Biography*.[88] The Bontoft family also passed the torch of radical politics and publishing from generation to generation. James Bontoft's (pollster and member of the Political Union's managing committee) wife, Charlotte, carried on the family printing-cum-publishing business after her husband's premature death, before passing it over to her three sons. One of these, Jason, proved a real chip off the old block. He was a committee member of the Liberal Association from 1855 to 1868, when he became corresponding secretary to its council of management.

It is hoped that this section will help explain the predominantly bourgeois leadership of nineteenth-century radical politics. For the function of local activist/leaders as culture brokers was to mediate between the cultures of high and low politics. As wealthy tradesmen they had the financial means necessary to perform the role, and invariably as members of the knowledge industries they had both the intellectual skills and the means of communication. Tory leaders were, of course, qualitatively different. Not for them the namby-pamby world of education. Rather their culture brokers were predominantly publicans, shopkeepers, or members of the Anglican clergy. Here again these people were able to straddle the worlds of rich and poor, high and low, just as their work also required the power to communicate. These figures were no less mediators than their radical counterparts. Just as literate, articulate, and knowledgeable self-made men commanded respect with the popular radical constituency, so the publican or tradesmen (like Alex Taylor) were the bulwarks and role models of the popular Tory constituency.

CONCLUSION

Politics, then as now, was about people. Historians, dazzled by the power of impersonal social and economic forces, have sometimes tended to lose sight of this. Certainly nineteenth-century politics was perceived in highly personal terms and projected through the personalities, roles, and narratives of leadership, just as much as through dry technical debates or organisational structures. Leadership was an indispensable mode of political expression, and leaders, aware of this, were peculiarly adept at evoking a sense of agency and generating powerful moral and political sentiments by performing certain roles. Of course, these roles and the narratives that shaped them rested, in part, on the leader's own life-history, personality, appearance, and self-image. Leaders also defined themselves in relation to the needs and expectations of their audiences, and these invariably came in the form of well-rehearsed roles and narratives. To a remarkable extent, therefore, people created their own idols and icons, certainly they led as much as followed. The popular mid-Victorian notion, still much in vogue today in some circles, that leaders became heroes by strength of character and that the world was divided into natural 'leaders and followers' was some way wide of the mark.

Thus, if leaders were partly created by their popular constituencies, the way in which they projected themselves gives us an important insight into popular political culture. And popular it certainly seems to have been, for there is little evidence here of leaders playing to distinct class galleries. The narratives of leadership may have played upon the melodramatic imagination of struggle and conflict, but these tensions were primarily moral and political in nature, the social languages and categories of class being conspicuously absent. Even when this political conflict was endowed with a class accent, by the anti-aristocratic appeals of 'men of the people' like William Newton, it was still based upon a sense of political, rather than economic, exploitation, demanding the political inclusion of the excluded, but productive, classes, alongside the already included, but idle, aristocracy. The familiar litany of the 'ins' versus the 'outs' created a community of interests among the politically excluded, one that was given further expression in other narratives and roles like the 'Just Employer' and the 'Gentleman Leader'. This political transcendence of class categories was also evident in the analysis of the roles of three radical culture brokers. It seems that their abilities as culture brokers and their appeals as leaders rested on the perception of them as outsiders. All had risen from the ranks of the working class to be successful and wealthy men, and yet in many ways they remained outside the social and political establishments of their communities. They were the agents of a genuinely popular politics, a politics which reflected their own transient social positions.

PART III

Narratives of the nation

CHAPTER 8

The nation and its people: the discourse of popular constitutionalism

INTRODUCTION

All individuals and societies make sense of the world by telling themselves stories, by constructing narratives which represent themselves to themselves. So natural is this impulse to narrate, to tell ourselves stories which transform chaos into order, that Roland Barthes has claimed that narrative 'is simply there like life itself... international, transhistorical, transcultural'.[1] Contrary to historians' concept of narrative as a sequence of events which tell themselves, literary critics have long since recognised that narratives are not neutral discursive forms, but are themselves charged with meanings. It is the content of the narrative form which intrigues them.[2] For it is the narrative form which enable texts and their agents to imagine, search out for, and ultimately create their own audiences. Conceived in this way narrative forms can be read allegorically, as attempts to endow events (real or imaginary) with a coherence and moral significance that they would not otherwise possess. For Fredric Jameson the imagination of an idealised, utopian future from a mythical golden age is central to the moral coherence of narrative, for it is a self-justifying form which seeks to demonstrate how this vision of an idealised future might be achieved. Narrative is a socially symbolic act which plays upon the political unconscious, simultaneously imagining and justifying a utopian future like 'a wish-fulfilling fantasy that, like all such fantasies, is grounded in the real conditions of the dreamer's life but goes beyond these to the imagining of how, in spite of these conditions, things might be otherwise'.[3]

In this chapter I shall endeavour to show how these narrative forms and functions dominated the nineteenth-century debate over the meaning of the English constitution, that is the discourse of popular constitutionalism. Indeed, I shall argue that this constitutionalist discourse represented the master narrative of English politics in this period. That is to say that competing political groups sought to construct their constituencies of support by appropriating and using the 'shared' language of constitutionalism in different ways. According to one's interpretation of the constitution, the nation's golden age either existed before the Normans' infamous invasion of Anglo-Saxon England in 1066, or was ushered in either by the Magna Carta of 1215 or by the Glorious Revolution of 1688. Despite the continued historiographical debate about the consequences of these events, their central place in the mythology of English political culture remains unquestioned. There is, of course, nothing new in all this. It is a debate which has continued for centuries as various individuals and factions have attempted to define England's notoriously slippery unwritten constitution in different ways in order to include or exclude various groups from the political nation.[4] Of course the various interpretations of the meanings and origins of English liberty were central to this debate about the constitution's libertarian past, present, and future; a debate which represented a master narrative through which England's political identity and destiny were defined.[5]

However, echoing the work of E. P. Thompson, historians of the left have argued that the discourse of popular constitutionalism, based as it was on nostalgic historical arguments about the freeborn Englishman's lost rights, restricted the radical potential of English popular politics.[6] For these historians the French Revolution of 1789 represented a watershed in radical thought, as English reformers finally abandoned constitutionalist languages for the republican Paineite language of natural rights. However, this chronology has recently been revised as historians have recognised the often incoherent and contradictory nature of political discourse, the ways in which, for instance, Paineite language drew on both rationalist and historicist theories, just as it could combine deism with religious restorationism.[7] John Belchem and James Epstein have argued it was the very diffuseness of popular constitutionalism – its ability to integrate the often contradictory languages of independence, political economy, Christianity, and natural rights – which enabled it to dominate the language of radical politics until the collapse of the mass platform in 1848.[8] Building upon these analyses, I shall seek to revise this chronology still further, arguing that popular constitutionalism remained the master narrative of English politics right up to 1867, and probably well beyond. However, unlike recent work which has emphasised the continuities within radical libertarian politics from the late eighteenth to the early twentieth century, this account will be attentive to the differences and tensions within this language, however it was appropriated and used.[9] It is, therefore, all the more important to recognise that, by reading the discourse of popular politics as one text, I have inevitably tended to collapse some of those differences between the five constituencies.

Much of the most recent work on the discourse of nineteenth-century politics has resolved itself into a discussion about the extent to which it constituted a language of class.[10] Several historians have recognised the populist appeal of constitutionalism, the way it spoke to the great mass of the politically excluded, including even those 'beer-swilling, male chauvinist, xenophobic, flag-waving workers whom historians are no longer allowed to forget.'[11] No doubt it was this recognition which led many to emphasise the influence of Paineite language, equating it with a proto-socialist, class-based, politics. Rethinking this approach, James Epstein has argued that different classes could appropriate popular constitutionalism's 'shared forms of rhetoric and symbolism from a particular class position' so that class is seen in terms of 'opposed discourses' competing with each other 'within the general unity of a shared code'.[12] Although, by avoiding idealised economic definitions of class, this approach has much to recommend it, it seems merely to create an equally idealised notion of class, one in which any discourse used by 'the working class' represented a language of class. Such an approach would seem to lead us back up the conceptual cul-de-sac from which we have just emerged. This is not to deny the place of class readings in nineteenth-century English politics, but rather to unveil some of the other hitherto hidden social and political identities given meaning by the discourse of popular constitutionalism, identities which, as we shall see, are not done justice by Patrick Joyce's 'family of populisms'.[13]

THE CONSTITUTION CONTESTED

For Freedom's battle once begun,
Bequeathed by bleeding sire to son,
Though baffled oft, is ever won.[14]

If there was unanimity about anything in the world of nineteenth-century politics it was that the English constitution was, or, at the very least, had been, the best in the world, it set them apart from the rest of the world, the most sacred symbol of Englishness.[15] Paradoxically few could agree why the constitution was the best in the world, it was all things to all Englishmen. As with so much of English political life, the answer lay in its glorious past. Although each group imagined the constitution's history in very different ways, all stressed the continuity between past and present struggles, and their implications for the future. If nothing else, the discourse of popular constitutionalism provided a strong sense of historical agency to those who used it.

To the Tories the events of 1688 neither restored lost political rights nor established any new ones. Rather they believed it enshrined the broad political principles that had existed, tried and tested, since the Norman Conquest of 1066. Listen to Sir Thomas Acland, Tory MP for North Devon, speaking at Totnes in 1837.

On what principles was erected the great charter of our liberties? The Barons of England said at Runnymede that they did not want new institutions – they would not have the laws of their country changed. The principle which animated the constitution was so elastic, so capable of expansion, that it might be suited to all wants and circumstances without ever being destroyed (Loud cheers.) Great Britain had never changed her laws. The miscalled revolution of 1688 was no change whatever of their fundamental laws of the British constitution, but rather a protest that the existing laws should not be changed (Cheers).[16]

Advocates of 'conservative' readings of 1688 could well take heart from such sentiments. Yet if the constitution had not been altered, what had 1688 all been about? Why did it remain such a potent foundational myth for Tories throughout the nineteenth century?

The answer, of course, was that it represented 'the great and providential deliverance that rescued England from popery and arbitrary power and rendered Englishmen's liberties, constitution, and religion permanently secure'.[17] It finally consolidated the nation's Protestant libertarian constitution against the encroachments of the 'Other', the ambitious, absolutist (and Catholic) states of continental Europe. It represented the culmination of a centuries-old religious crusade to establish a constitution which permanently enshrined a Protestant state, it was about deposing the Catholic James Stuart and settling the throne on the Protestant William of

Orange, it was about the Act of Settlement and the impeccably Protestant Oath of Coronation. One cannot underestimate the popularity of this appeal to England's unique historical mission as a free and Protestant nation. There are obvious parallels here with Sean Wilentz's work on the mythologies of America's providential Republic. Both stressed a sense of the nation's unique religious and historical destiny – the libertarian mission of Protestant parliamentary England which set itself apart from Europe's Catholic and absolutist states, just as America's democratic Republic set itself apart from the rest of the monarchical and oligarchic western world.[18]

The Tory nation was then one divinely appointed to defend the Protestant faith and the liberty and prosperity which they had earned as God's elect chosen people.[19] That this connection between Protestantism, liberty, and prosperity was critical was evident by the speech of a Tory activist at a meeting to establish a Protestant Association in Lewes during 1857:

If they did not adhere to and support Protestant principles, the country would soon cease to flourish, and the crown fall; but he firmly believed that the English were a Bible-loving people, and that the great Protestant cause of this country would not be lost sight of (hear, hear). God always recognised his truth, and would only support that nation which obeys his command... In this country four hundred years of rapine and bloodshed followed the conquest; but the Reformation... brought peace and prosperity, and the Queen of England withstood the influence and power of the greatest of monarchs, Phillip of Spain, when he near'd [*sic*] our shores with what had been called an Invincible Armada, which, by the hand of God, was cast on the rocks and shores, and removed England, without even a struggle, from the grasp of what might be fairly called the whole world (hear). After her reign we again got into trouble, being subject to the intrigue and corruption of Popery... but in the time of Oliver Cromwell, though a usurper, he was a protestant, and under him England gathered strength. Charles the second was also weak. Next came James the Second and his reign was one of bloodshed, which called forth the Prince of Orange, and he (Mr. Peters) need not tell them that England was prosperous in the reign of William the Third (hear). For forty years England enjoyed such prosperity as she had never enjoyed before, because she was truly protestant (applause).[20]

Here a sense of the Protestant crusade is evoked, with its battle against the dark forces of popery and despotism, a battle to preserve the liberty and prosperity of the freeborn Englishman. By evoking that distinctly Tory notion of a lost Eden, a golden age when Old England was truly Protestant and John Bull enjoyed roast beef, beer, and plum pudding every night, it not only suggested the possibility of recreating this utopia, but also contrasted it with the fate of those fallen from the crusade. Although Tories denied the need to reform a constitution which had been so perfectly balanced since 1688, they emphasised that all good Protestant men and women were integral to the nation's libertarian crusade, whether they were electors or not. Why should the people be legally included as citizens if they were already culturally included as Protestants? As we saw in chapters 2 and 6, it was a point reaffirmed by the inclusiveness of many of the ceremonial and symbolic practices of both official and Tory political culture. Tory readings of the constitution therefore emphasised the people's *duty* to protect its Protestant libertarian nature, not, as in radical readings, the *rights* they expected to flow from it.

This appeal to the unity of 'The Nation', to a people united by their Englishness in some primordial organic way, was also central to Tory attempts to deny the possibility of, or transcend, class tensions as well as political exclusions. The interests of the nation, they argued, were the interests of all, from the king in his palace to the peasant in his cottage. As South Devon's Tory MP Samuel Kekewich argued in his electoral address of 1868, 'I have never advocated class interests, because we all, from the richest to the poorest in the land, are so united as one family that we must depend on each other for our mutual prosperity.'[21] This emphasis on social consensus was the principal theme of his political life. Ten years earlier, while canvassing at Totnes, he had claimed that 'Nothing is more common to say "You are a man of class;" but I say to you that I am a man of no class interest, and I cannot bear the man who is the advocate of class interest (hear, hear). – For, gentlemen, the great social chain that links us all together cannot be broken without damage or destruction to the whole nation (cheers).'[22] The rural landlord, tenant, and labourer were united in one common bond, just as the urban employer, shopkeeper, and operative were. This organic sense of the nation was equally at home in Kekewich's rural homeland as in Reverend J. R. Stephens' native industrial Lancashire. It was a creed which provided the possibility of transcending the factional forces of class, for it was the duty and destiny of every freeborn Englishman, whether in his cottage, on his throne or behind his altar, to protect the nation's Protestant constitution. As ever, this language of inclusion excluded many from its call, for the constitution had to be protected from the 'Other', be they Jews, Infidels, Catholic French or Irish, and all those other busy-bodies bent on destroying 'Old England' like moral reformers, dissenters and *laissez-faire* industrialists. Consequently, in places like Oldham, where there was a sizeable Irish/Catholic community, popular Toryism took a distinctly racial turn, defining one ethnos against another, boasting clear links to several Orange Lodges and implicitly legitimating the horrendous anti-Irish riots of 1861.[23]

Ironically, these Tory languages of social and political inclusion, however illusory they may have been, had immensely radical implications, implications that had to be hurriedly closed down during the early nineteenth century. For, if all the people were included in the nation's Protestant crusade and had a common duty to protect its libertarian constitution, then why not enshrine that duty in law by including them as citizens in the political nation? Although, as we shall see, reformers had pressed this case for some time (at least for a variety of less generously defined 'people'), it was the fears and pressures unleashed by the foreign, unconstitutional, and unchristian creeds of the French Revolution of 1789 that finally compelled the Tories to construct a more exclusive definition of the people. It is in this light that Pitt's 'reign of terror' should be seen. The suspension of Habeas Corpus in 1794, and the notorious Treasonable Practices and Seditious Meetings Acts of the following year, constituted no less than an ambitious attempt to redefine the nation's common constitutional law and the rights of freedom of speech and assembly in ever more restrictive ways. Not for the first time, or for the last, the genius of Tory politics was not only to dress this exclusive redefinition of constitutional law as a patriotic defence of liberty but, worse still, to use those who would most suffer from such a redefinition to enforce it at popular and local levels; for many of those involved in the Reeves' Associations and Church and King mobs were non-electors. Ironically, despite the periodic re-enforcement of this repressive legislation, the Seditious Meetings Act was, for instance, re-introduced in 1812 and 1817, it was largely unsuccessful at preventing the growth of the radical mass platform with its demand that, as all men were part of the people, all should be legally included within the political nation.

Consequently, in the years immediately following the Napoleonic Wars, Lord Liverpool's Tory government took fright at such expansive radical definitions of the people and their constitutional rights. In the words of Sidmouth, they felt it necessary 'to create a fence around the Constitution; and a bulwark to protect it against those spurious rights which were foreign to its sober genius'.[24] This fence took the form of the infamous Six Acts of 1819. As Jonathan Fulcher has compellingly argued, the Six Acts should be read as the most comprehensive attempt by the government to date to enshrine its own official definition of the constitution, and, crucially, of the people's role within it, in law. Unlike the earlier Acts, the Seditious Meetings Act of 1819 did not confine itself to restricting the numbers of people allowed to attend meetings to fifty. It sought to define who those people were, declaring that only inhabitant 'Nobility, Gentry, Clergy, and Freeholders' were allowed to attend those public meetings sanctioned by the local authorities. Canning was careful to spell out the meaning and purpose of this exclusive legislative definition arguing that the 'people, as synonymous [*sic*] to a nation, meant a great community, congregated under a head, united in the same system of civil polity for mutual aid and mutual protection, respecting and maintaining various orders and ranks, and not only allowing fair and just gradations of society, but absolutely built upon them. That was a "people".'[25] For Canning and the government, as for all Tories, the people were merely the electorate, an electorate which was rightly established on hierarchical principles. In short, the great mass of the unrepresented had no legitimate claim to citizenship. These were, he claimed, the rules established in 1688. Moreover, it was radical definitions of the category of the people, not his, which were most exclusive, because they were 'first stript [*sic*] of the government, then stript of the aristocracy, then stript of the clergy, then stript of the magistracy, then stript of its lawyers, then stript of its learning, then stript of everything which ornamented and dignified human nature – in such a mass he could [not] recognise the people... without the grossest perversion of terms'.[26]

However, as we have already seen in chapters 2 and 3, these legislative attempts to impose restrictive definitions of the constitution were, to a large extent, simply ignored at the local level. Inhabitants who were neither nobility, gentry, clergy or freeholders regularly turned out at parish, town, and county meetings, not to mention parliamentary elections, to claim their voice as the people in the nation's affairs. This was of course all grist to the radical mill. Their demands for constitutional reform and universal manhood suffrage were, they claimed, merely based on England's historic common law, citing such authorities as Blackstone as their proof. All they wanted was to restore their lost rights, not to create new ones. After all, as Cobbett argued, 'The Bill of Rights declares that the Laws of England are the birthright of the people. It does not say, of the rich, of the nobles, of the priesthood, the yeomanry cavalry, the members of corporations, the borough-voters, but of THE PEOPLE.'[27] Radicals like Cobbett then turned exclusive Tory definitions of the people on their head, including all those the Tories wished to exclude, the dispossessed and disenfranchised. It was a language of inclusion ritually invoked at radical dinners up and down the land as they toasted 'The People the Source of all Power'. Take, for instance, Hume's invocation of this toast at a dinner for Tower Hamlets' two prospective reforming candidates in 1832, when he felt bound to

remove the erroneous impression that had gone abroad as to the real meaning of the toast ... In proposing the toast he felt it right to state, that in certain quarters there existed objections to the toast, as if it only included a portion of the people, while, in fact, it implied the whole people, high and low, of the nation, and from these certainly all power ought to emanate.[28]

It is important to recognise that this radical language of political inclusion was not in any sense backward looking, a discursive remnant from the eighteenth century. It continued to strike a powerful and popular chord throughout this period, as for instance when Boston's Reverend T. Matthews pressed the claims of David Wire's radical candidature in 1849 by arguing that the 'representative of the people should come from the people ... they required a representative of the unrepresented people – for the masses who had no voice of their own'.[29] By making the people synonymous with the unrepresented in this way, radicals continued to highlight and emphasise the popular sense of exclusion, of powerlessness and dispossession. As Henry Vincent told an adoring audience at Plymouth in 1842, you the people 'are now a degraded race, fallen away from your destiny! Spoilators, vagabonds, – (great cheering). None knew better than the aristocracy how much they owe to the people – (cheers) – who made the country what it is – from when William the Conqueror placed his foot on their gallant Saxon forefathers, down to this day.'[30] Such an appeal directly challenged restrictive Tory notions of the people's constitutional role past and present, it sought to empower the powerless by endowing those who the Tories had excluded with a sense of agency.

Of course the Tories were not alone in resisting such radical definitions of the people's constitution. For all its varieties Whiggism was busy searching for the discursive middle ground, providing a reading of the constitution which contested both Tory tyranny and radical mobocracy.[31] Like the radicals, they too disputed the Tory's foundational myth that the Norman Conquest of 1066 was the source of all the nation's political institutions, arguing instead that it represented the triumph of Norman autocracy over Anglo-Saxon democracy. It was not until the Glorious Revolution of 1688 that the lost political rights of Anglo-Saxon England's ancient constitution were finally restored, despite the best efforts of the Barons of Runnymede and the Magna Carta.[32] However, with the increasing political stranglehold and corruption of the (ironically) Whig oligarchy being worsened by the corrupting influence of rising commercialism and the consequent declining interest in politics, it soon became clear that the Glorious Revolution of 1688 had been hijacked. Inspired by the writings of James Harrington, the largely Tory opposition drew up a 'country programme' which aimed to restore the nation's moral and political virtue by rehabilitating the ideal of the classical citizen as an independent freeholder, one whose property afforded him (not her) the independence necessary for leisure, self-mastery, virtue, and active citizenship. This language of the independent, propertied citizen, with its appeal to restoring the purity of the constitution by using the people out of doors as a check against the corruption of centralised power, had radical implications, implications which radicals and reformers spent much of the eighteenth century attempting to make explicit. The ambiguity lay in how to define the independent propertied citizen, who were the 'people' who should be included in the political nation to restore the constitutional balance between monarch, parliament, and the people. The Whigs, seeking to maintain a fairly restrictive and limited definition of the people as propertied freeholders, found reassurance in the work of John Locke.[33] The problem was that they not only celebrated his connection between property and politics, but also his assertion of the people's right to resist corrupt and tyrannical government, hence their toasts to the revolutionary heroes of 1688 – Hampden, Sidney, Russell, and Milton – and this too, of course, was vulnerable to radical appropriations.[34]

As we saw in chapter 1, it is in the light of this Whiggish critique of 'Old Corruption' with its attempt to fix limits and parameters upon the category of the people that we should read such early nineteenth-century electoral reforms as the Sturges Bourne Acts of 1818 and 1819, Hobhouse's Vestries Act of 1831, the Reform Act of 1832, and the Municipal Corporations Act of 1835, not to mention the Poor Law Amendment Act of 1834. Despite the often contradictory results of this body of legislation, it was united by similarly Whiggish impulses to restore constitutional balance by ensuring that the people were legislatively defined, for the very first time in English constitutional history, as propertied men. Not only did these Whiggish reforms contrast nicely with the repression of earlier Tory governments and radicalism's more inclusive definition of the people, but it allowed the Whigs to resuscitate the belief in the aristocracy's traditional role as governors, nobly serving the people and protecting their rights and liberties, instead of lining their own pockets in the politics of commercial self-interest.[35] It was a skilful, discursive strategy backed up by the force of the law, but its inclusive connotations were hotly contested by radicals who sought to expand the categories of independence, property, and the people in an all together more comprehensive fashion.

We would be wrong to imagine that this debate over the meaning of the constitution and its category of the people did not intersect with other narratives or discourses. We shall later, for instance, see how the discourse of political economy combined with the language of popular constitutionalism just as easily as that of popular Christianity. Certainly, religious realignments during the eighteenth century were critical in shaping the different appropriations of the discourse of popular constitutionalism. Although rabid Protestantism informed Wilkes' radical opposition during the 1760s as the bedrock of English constitutional liberties, it was a language challenged by both French support of the American War of Independence during the 1770s and the growing influence of Enlightenment reason and secularism.[36] Increasingly, as some radical leaders, especially Dissenters, distanced themselves from the languages of Protestant libertarianism during the late eighteenth century, they allowed Tory loyalists to make them their own. The publication of Thomas Paine's *The Rights of Man* in 1791, and the French Revolution of 1789, therefore provided radicals with a further opportunity to dispense with the constitutionalist narratives of the freeborn Protestant

Englishman. Indeed, Paine provided radicals with no less than a new indigenous secular, rational, and republican master narrative of the English nation. To Paine, the revered English constitution was a myth, an illusion that had never existed. Political rights, he argued, were derived not from historical precedent, but from the laws of nature and reason, although he himself never entirely escaped the historicist Norman Yoke theory. Therefore, for Paine, the people consisted of all men (not women), whatever their propertied status. All men were entitled to citizenship of the political nation because they were all born free and equal.

There can be little doubting the impact of Paine's work on early nineteenth-century radical culture. It is now a historiographical common-place that his *Rights of Man* was the most well read and accessible plebeian text of this period. As Iain McCalman has shown, Paine's republican and deist ideas inspired a devoted set of disciples in London's radical circle around figures such as Thomas Spence and Richard Carlile and their followers.[37] This Paineite tradition remained a strong influence in the pubs and clubs of the metropolis, particularly during the 1850s and 1870s, finding new figureheads in the shape of free-thinking secularists like G. J. Holyoake and later republicans like Charles Bradlaugh.[38] However, outside the metropolis Paine's influence was much less marked and, arguably, even within London his influence has been exaggerated by his colourful and well-documented supporters. It is, for instance, significant that these figures were generally most prominent at times of radical retreat such as the 1790s, 1820s, 1850s and 1870s. It seems that radicals were only ever able to address a truly popular constituency when they spoke the constitutionalist language. We find that, at radical dinners outside London, Paine was only every toasted as one among a host of other radical heroes, heroes who certainly could not be accused of being Paineites. At a Chartist dinner in Plymouth, for instance, they drank to 'The memories of Paine, O'Connor, Hunt, Emmet, Cobbett, Washington, and the rest of the illustrious dead who advocated the rights of man.'[39] As this toast makes clear, Paine's legacy was a confused one; as recent work is showing, it increasingly makes more sense to talk of his legacies.[40] Just as his deism could become displaced or (con)fused with Judaism and popular Christianity, so his rationalist language was often combined with the historicism of popular constitutionalism. In Plymouth, the champions of the constitutionalist mass platform, O'Connor, Cobbett, and

Hunt, were deemed by the town's Chartists as advocates of the rights of man. Similarly in Boston, at a dinner in 1822 to celebrate Hunt's release from prison, the town's radicals toasted, 'The Rights of Man whispered by the Barons of Runnymede in 1215; talked of by the Parliament of England in 1688; boldly proclaimed by the Congress of America in 1776; and gloriously achieved by the People of the United States'.[41] It is possible that Paine's place within the pantheon of radical heroes owed more to these constitutionalist appropriations of his thought than to any commitment to his conception of a new rationalist and republican master narrative of English politics.

This is not to play down the significance of the 1790s as a critical decade whose experience of the French Revolution and the Napoleonic Wars did much to shape the course of nineteenth-century politics. However, contrary to received wisdom, this was not as a consequence of a major discursive shift, but because of the failure of any such shift to occur. I am arguing that the reason radicals failed to provide any feasible alternative to popular constitutionalism during the nineteenth century can be found largely in the political conditions of the 1790s. For it was then that Paine's republican and deist ideas became irretrievably associated with the 'foreign and unchristian' creeds of the French Revolution in a way which meant that the language of patriotic loyalty was largely lost to Paineite radicals.[42] As a result of both Pitt's terror and this popular loyalist reaction, radicals were forced underground and lumbered with equally damaging images of illegality and marginality, a perception hardened by such clumsy and clandestine conspiracies as Despard's in 1802. Once again we are reminded of the importance of the state's use of the law in structuring the shape of political languages by limiting the choice of discursive strategies. In the end it does not really matter whether radicals believed in the constitutionalist languages they spoke or not, or whether they merely used it to legitimate their activities both to the state and the popular constituencies of support they hoped to attract. The point is that it was the language they invariably used, and the language which proved most popular.

Oldham's veteran radial leader, John Knight, is proof positive of this, for if anyone in the five constituencies was receptive to Paineite languages it was him. If this apparently most radical language could not appeal to this most radical of men, in this most radical of towns, it seems safe to assume that they had little leverage elsewhere.

According to John Foster, Knight began his political career as a 'Tom Paine Jacobin' in the 1790s (he was arrested and imprisoned for two years in 1794), and by 1801 he had become a member of the United Englishmen's county executive. In 1812 he was arrested again for administering secret Luddite oaths to weavers in Manchester, as he was again in 1817 for allegedly being a ringleader of the Blanketeer march which was organised to petition against the Suspension of Habeas Corpus Act. Despite this caricature of Knight as a revolutionary Jacobin, he was equally committed to constitutionalist tactics. As editor of the *Manchester Political Register* (1816) and *Manchester Spectator* (1818) he had much contact with Major John Cartwright, and seems to have played a leading role in the formulation of Lancashire's Hampden Clubs (1816–18).[43] He also played a leading role in Hunt's mass platform agitation in Manchester leading up to, and including, Peterloo in 1819, and was once again arrested for his pains. On his release he laid low until the late 1820s, becoming secretary to Oldham's Political Union in 1831 and finally the 'venerable social father' of the town's Owenites in 1838, the year of his death. For at least the first 20 years of his political life Knight was exposed to, and influenced by, Paineite languages. As the impeccable constitutionalist credentials of the last 20 years of his life exemplify, his relationship with these languages was never as unproblematic as Foster suggests.

For Knight, as one suspects for many decentred others as well, Paineite and constitutionalist languages did not exist in discrete categories. For Knight the political rights of man were enshrined not only in the laws of nature and reason, but also, and perhaps more powerfully, in history and scripture (see Appendix 4). Moreover, far from developing his ideas, or adjusting them to the changing conditions of industrial life in Oldham as Foster suggests, Knight's public political language remained remarkably consistent. As he himself repeatedly stressed, his enduring 'motto has always been do as to others as they would that others should do unto you'.[44] For Knight, it was the lazy, land-plundering, rent-happy Norman aristocracy, who, by their political monopoly waged unnecessary wars and levied unjust taxes, had done most to violate this homespun, biblical principle. It was honest Anglo-Saxon labour which alone was the source of the country's wealth, a wealth which was squandered by the conspicuous consumption of parasitical kings, dukes, lords, bishops, priests, and lawyers. By 1838 Knight had added to this list of parasites the 'canal-lords, cotton-lords, railroad lords, gas and water-works, and other sorts of lords... [who contrived]... to obtain an income from capital, by substituting capital for some sort of labour'.[45] It was these groups who, because they consumed more than they produced, kept the labouring poor in a state of degradation, producing wealth for others' consumption.

One is aware here in Knight's language of a third narrative, that of popular political economy, combining with constitutionalist and Paineite ones. Like all such discourses, the genealogy and uses of this narrative were rich and diverse, arising from the moral economy of the crowd and the Scottish Enlightenment – including its appropriations by English Whigs – but, most directly, from the so-called 'new ideology' of Owenism and both the Ricardian and Smithian socialists.[46] It was the echo of such languages by Knight which led Foster to credit him, rather over-sympathetically, with developing a proto-marxist theory of surplus labour.[47] Although Smithian socialist political economy had developed a theory of labour exploitation as intrinsic to the capitalist mode of production, it was rarely pressed into service by radicals and, by the mid-1830s, its already marginal influence was disintegrating, living on only as a minority strand within Chartism.[48] Arguably, Smithian socialism failed to take hold of radical discourse because it was difficult to incorporate within the categories or analyses of constitutionalist language. Whereas in contrast, those versions of the 'people's science' of political economy, like Owenism, which emphasised the inequities of exchange and distribution instead of the mode of production, reinforced, rather than undermined, the constitutionalist critique of 'Old Corruption'. As John Belchem has argued, 'Alongside the fundholders, sinecurists, pensioners, and other tax gorgers, there now sat the cotton lords, millocrats, and other capitalists, parasitic middle-men whose privileged and tyrannical position of unequal exchange stemmed from the monopoly of political and legal power possessed by the propertied governing classes.'[49] Certainly, Knight's language, both in the preceding paragraph and in Appendix 4, managed to combine constitutionalist language with that of popular political economy, and even (another layer here) popular Christianity.

It has often been argued, however, that the very presence of the categories of popular political economy were tantamount to decidedly new class appropriations of the discourse of popular constitutionalism. That is to say that, for radicals, the people become synonymous with the working class. The battle between the people and the aristocracy was resolved into a battle between the productive working classes, the idle aristocracy and the equally corrupting and parasitic middle-men, Knight's 'other sorts of Lords'. It was the unequal distribution of political power which enabled the unproductive to oppress the productive with their class legislation. At a Chartist meeting in Shoreditch during 1842, a Mr Dyson complained that

the evils of the country arose from class legislation, which studied the interests of the few, to the prejudice of the many. As Parliament was constituted, it represented the Aristocracy, and in a few instances the manufacturers, while the labouring classes were deprived of all legislative protection – (hear, hear.)...In conclusion he moved a resolution which declared that all the evils and the distress under which this country laboured arose from bad laws and wickedly mismanaged legislation – that trade could only be established, property secured to the producer, and profit to the capitalist, by a full, fair and free representation of the people – (cheers).[50]

As is evident, such sentiments can not be read simply as a sign of (to paraphrase Patrick Joyce) the consciousness of a class, for this language of the productive versus the unproductive would seem here to include many of the industrious middle class in the category of the 'labouring classes'. Certainly, Tory populists like Oldham's James Heald were able to use this language in their own inimitable way, claiming that he too 'was opposed on principle to all mere class legislation...he regarded it to be the special duty of the legislature to watch over the interests, to redress the grievances, and multiply the comforts of the industrious classes'.[51] Of course, Heald, a mill-owner, included himself as a member of the industrious classes. One should not, therefore, be misled by the use of class categories, for defined in this way the labouring classes spoke of a community of interests between all those who worked for a living, whether they were owned or operated factories.

Yet this language of the productive versus the idle could, with a very little leap of the imagination, be endowed with class meanings. The stress on productivity, on working for a living, gave rise to what can only be called a language of labour. Meetings of the 'honest hard-working working classes' and 'industrious weavers' were frequent throughout this period. Their honest, manly, hard work was contrasted against the artificial, namby-pamby idle aristocracy.

Work was honourable, for it signified the individual's attempt to secure independence, to benefit rather than burden the community, be it parish, town, county or nation. Thus a man (not a woman) denied work was denied his honour, independence, and, in a sense, his manliness. For this was very much a man's world of labour, tied to the ideal of the male provider and breadwinner.[52] William Newton's campaign at Tower Hamlets in 1852 was certainly of this mould. As leader of the Amalgamated Society of Engineers, Newton was well placed to voice the needs of labour.

The labourers of this country do not require charity, but the independence of honest labour – and while there are in this country the two great sources of all wealth – land and labour – both idle, both ready to be brought into contact, and to produce necessaries and luxuries for millions, I cannot conceive that these trading classes of this country can be fairly called upon to pay for the support of those who are not willing and able to provide for themselves.[53]

Despite Newton's mastery of the language of labour it is wrong to see him, as Gillespie has done, as the first proto-socialist Labour candidate.[54] Certainly, he was capable of inflecting this language with class meanings, as he did when declaring that the infamous Preston Strike in 1854 'was a nation's battle between capital and labour'.[55] Neither was Newton alone in such class analyses. Fourteen years earlier the Oldham Chartist, Henry Smethurst, had claimed that the 'working classes were oppressed by the manufacturers as well as the aristocracy, for the former were year by year augmenting the tasks of the operatives without an increase in wages'.[56] However, despite the use of such class inflections on this language of honest, manly, and independent labour, it is equally easy to imagine the extra-class meanings of this language. For there are no specific class languages – as all political language is multi-vocal so a seemingly class language could be given a populist edge, just as apparently populist languages could be read and used from a specific class perspective. Others within Newton's campaign team, like the Chartist working man William Davis, were anxious to stress the pan-class appeal of his language of labour, arguing that, 'Mr. Newton aspired not only to represent the working men, but all who were anyway concerned in industrial pursuits. (Hear, hear.).'[57] For Newton, the assertion that the 'interests of the small shopkeepers and the working men were identical' was no contradiction.[58]

The importance of this constitutionalist language of labour was that it enabled radicals to contest exclusive definitions of the people by expanding the discursive category of property to include the skill of honest, manly labour. This was a battle that had long been fought out in the workplace as workers, particularly skilled male artisans, sought to protect the status of their skill and craft from the 'unfair' competition and de-skilling machinery of the emergent capitalist market.[59] Once again John Knight's speech in Appendix 4 shows us something of the way in which this battle was transferred onto the political stage. By arguing that 'Industry and frugality are known to be the original sources of all Property' Knight claimed the right of working men to be included within the political nation, so that they too could protect their property of honourable labour from the ravages of corrupt aristocratic government. Indeed, for Knight and his fellow radicals, the property of labour was far superior and more honourable than the landed property of lazy and unproductive 'Princes, Prelates, Priest &c.', stolen from the people as it had been during the Norman Conquest. Significantly, Knight used several discursive strategies to justify these claims, drawing on arguments of natural, divine, and historical right without apparent contradiction. It is often difficult to see where these discourses do not intersect. If, then, all those who possessed the property of honourable labour deserved citizenship as the people, who was left excluded from this seemingly beguiling language of inclusion? Certainly, one is struck most forcibly by the heavily gendered nature of this language of labour as Knight cast his withering aspersions on the manliness of the unproductive; 'let us look to the conduct of several descriptions of *men*, yes men, for Princes, Prelates and Priests are *but* men'. Women are absent from Knight's thoughts, despite their critical role as both domestic and public labourers. In this Knight echoed the language of his male radical colleagues, who sought to protect men's jobs and skills from the 'unfair' competition of cheap female labour in an attempt to uphold the ideal of the independent, male, breadwinning artisan.[60]

However, as Anna Clark has recently argued, this deliberate emphasis on sexual difference and the masculinity of labour and political rights may have also represented an attempt to contest Malthusian critiques of the self-inflicted misery of the over-populated world of plebeian life.[61] By asserting the dignity and honour of manly labour, plebeian men sought to project themselves as fully human, trying to support their families independently, not breeding irresponsibly like animals. Listen, for instance, to one William Thompson speaking at a Silkweavers' meeting at Mile End in 1826. 'He concluded by expressing a hope that the sun of prosperity would break through the clouds that hovered over them; and they would again see brighter days, when the industrious weaver should once more enjoy a fair price for his labour, and be able to maintain his family in comfort and noble independence.'[62] In a sense this language of manly independence was increasingly in tune with the evangelical redefinition of manliness as moral and intellectual independence during the early nineteenth century.[63] For the exclusion of women from the manly worlds of work and politics could be presented as the moralisation of men in their domestic duties, their recognition of the need to save women from the morally corrupting influences of industrialism and the largely aristocratic public sphere by restoring them to their domestic roles as wives and mothers of men. Such a discursive move not only enabled radicals to contest the *laissez-faire* language of political economy, but to rework, once again, the language of the independent propertied citizen in a more inclusive way; to demand in Knight's words 'the filling of the House of Commons with WISE and VIRTUOUS labourers'. For, as we have already seen in chapter 6, this moralisation of radical men as wise and virtuous, with its emphasis on temperance, self-improvement, and education, allowed radicals to redefine the category of property to include their new-found moral and intellectual independence. It was, they claimed, this type of moral and intellectual property, not the more narrowly conceived Harringtonian notion of freehold property, which ensured their virtue and independence as citizens. Here the language of virtue intersected with the language of manners, paving the way for the Gladstonian language of character with its insistence on the moral right of the dispossessed to membership of the political nation.[64]

Of course, the Tories did not take such radical redefinitions of these categories of property, virtue, independence or manliness lying down. Although the rash of constitutional reforms between 1828 and 1835 had exploded Tory claims that the Revolutionary Settlement of 1688 was sacrosanct, they still attempted to endow their restrictive readings of the constitution with credence and legitimacy. Listen, for instance, to a local Tory activist pillorying radical definitions of the people at Totnes' Conservative Banquet in 1837:

What did the Radicals mean by the talking about the people? Did they mean to term their late miserable display in this town, where they mustered about 500 persons – the people? Yet if they did we who treble their numbers (a voice 'four times') are not to form any party in the state: we are not to be included in the Radical category of the people! (Loud cheers.) And in the list which these liberal philosophers have drawn up, who do they call the people? They excluded the lords, the clergy, the landowners, the merchants, and even their old companions, the Whigs... They, the yeomanry of England were also not to be considered the people... [so] ... who were the people? By what names, he again asked, were they to designate that influential, that amiable class?... They were those who wished to destroy the rights of property as well as its legitimate influence. They were those who desired the subversion of the Established Church and Peerage; who could not, or would not pay their taxes: and those who clamoured senselessly for the Ballot, that un-English, that unmanly (cheers) – mode of voting. These and such as these, according to the Radicals, ought to have a Representation in the Legislature; and arrogate to themselves the exclusive title of the British people (Enthusiastic cheering).[65]

The ferocity of this attack surely suggests that the Tories felt they had been forced on the defensive by the radical constitutional narrative. They sought to contest its redefinition of several key-words upon which the category of the people turned. Firstly, there was the questioning of the Englishness of radicals and their attachment to Protestantism (as represented by the 'Established Church'). Most importantly, the Tories contested radical definitions of property which they claimed destroyed the rights and influence of the propertied, be they yeomans or aristocratic landowners; while, for good measure, they also ridiculed radical notions of manliness, virtue, and independence because of their support for the secret ballot and their inability to pay taxes.

Perhaps, partly as a consequence of this Tory counter-attack, radicals were never entirely successful at redefining the category of property and the notion of the virtuous citizen. They continued to contest the whole concept of private property with the idea of the land as the communal or public property of the people.[66] Here again radicals used several discursive strategies to make their point. They drew upon the Spencean notion of communal stewardship of the land, which combined arguments based on natural, historical, and biblical rights to disallow the legitimacy of private property. We find John Knight arguing in Appendix 4 that the land was the peoples' birthright, a right ensured by God's creation of nature and affirmed by both the scriptures and the history of Anglo-Saxon England before 1066. Having convincingly made his case for the 'popular claim to the land', he set it aside, 'admitting it to belong to those who now claim it'. Here he drew on the other strand in the radical language of the land, that championed by such figures as Cobbett and O'Connor, which did not contest the legitimacy of private property, preferring instead the concept of 'responsible ownership' and 'reasonable size'; or, in Knight's words, 'are they doing as they would be done unto'. Even this strand, with its emphasis on the historical rights of popular usage and access to the land, provided a suitably expansive definition of private property to justify the claim for universal manhood suffrage. Clearly, even for radicals, property was an exclusively male category, despite single women's legal status as property owners and the inclusive, gender-neutral logic of natural law given such forcible expression by Mary Wollstonecraft.[67] It was the difficulty of integrating such rationalist arguments for womens' inclusion as citizens within the historicist language of popular constitutionalism which no doubt partly explained its marginalisation within nine-teenth-century radical politics.

Critical as this attempt to redefine the category of property was, the language of the land was also important for its aspirational and utopian education of desire. For Knight the land symbolised the possibility of emancipation, not only from the aristocratic Norman Yoke, but from the degradation of industrial work. It offered the chance of natural regeneration as against the unnatural destructive forces of industrialisation. For the labouring poor the land provided an opportunity to free themselves from the slavery of factory work, and to reassert the independence of their labour. This was a powerful utopian appeal to restore a lost Eden of rural innocence and independence that had both radical and Conservative implications; informing both the Spencean and Chartist land plans as well as more conservative utopias such as Cobbett's idealisation of Old England's rural life and the Reverend J. R. Stephens' evocative organic natural community of cottage, throne, and altar. Moreover, such appropriations of the language of the land continued long after the so-called collapse of the constitutionalist mass platform in 1848. Significantly, the rights of the unemployed to cultivate uncultivated land, and the rights of public assembly on London's open spaces, were central planks of William Newton's campaign in Tower Hamlets during 1852.[68] Both were themes taken up by Edmond Beales and the

Reform League during the 1860s. With the disintegration of the Reform League in 1868, Beales and J. S. Mill established the Land Tenure Reform League to demand the abolition of the law of primogeniture, the promotion of co-operative agriculture, state acquisition of land to let to small cultivators, and the cultivation by small-holders of public, crown, and waste lands.[69] In Tower Hamlets where these issues often dominated political debate, the Tories had also established their own Conservative Land Society in 1860, its two objectives 'to give its members a secure investment for their money [so that they could acquire] a stake in the country... [and]... to give the franchise to its members'.[70] By 1868, O. E. Coope, Tower Hamlets' Tory candidate, was opposing the enclosure of forests and promoting the construction of public parks, promising that 'if they returned him to Parliament he would do his best in order... that the people might be able to enjoy the country, and the Lord of the Manor would not be able to encroach upon what he believed to be their rights (loud cheers)'.[71] The language of the land can not, therefore, be dismissed as an anachronism, rather its use and appropriation was central to the debate over the meaning of England's constitutional past, present, and future, and its ability to restore the liberty, prosperity, and independence which the manly freeborn Englishman had once enjoyed.

The narrative forms of this language, with its emphasis on the loss of a golden age and the struggle to restore and redeem it, seem to echo throughout the discourse of popular constitutionalism, whoever and however it was appropriated. Listen, for instance, to Ernest Jones' speech at London's St Martin's Hall in 1856. Having cursed the Norman aristocracy for plundering the people's land after 1066 he pleaded with his audience to:

Join with me for the re-conquest of the land. It is the task of the age – the mission of the century. You talk of unchaining yourselves; unchain the land, and your chains will fall. The franchise is the bond that binds your hands; but land monopoly is the dungeon that surrounds your bodies. I proclaim a new crusade – a great crusade – the greatest ever known; not for the mouldering tomb of a buried God; but the fresh green altar of the living Deity. Not for the invasion of a distant Palestine; but for the re-conquest of your native Canaan. Arise! Sojourners in the wilderness – the desert man has made around the fields of Paradise. Mount me with the Pisgah of your wrongs – and gaze, look down from the great height upon the Promised Land. There flows the river that keeps you from it; the name of our Jordan is aristocracy. There towers the Jericho that guards the prize; its name is parliament; its ramparts are monopoly. Come, sound with me the signal note tonight, which small makes those ramparts rock on their foundation. The peoples land shall be the peoples own. (Loud cheers.)[72]

One is struck by the obvious play upon biblical tropes and metaphors of loss, struggle, and redemption. The narrative forms of popular Christianity continued, it appears, to have great popular resonance. Just as Protestant libertarianism was central to Tory narratives of the nation and its constitution, so it also dominated radical narratives, providing a readily accessible and familiar language of desire with its sense of moral purpose and utopian destiny.[73]

Once again we can turn to Knight to demonstrate the enduring appeal of popular Christianity in radical narratives of the nation's Protestant libertarian constitution. His speeches and letters to the press were loaded with religious tropes, metaphors, and analogies, displaying an often bewildering familiarity with the Bible. This letter to the *Manchester Observer* a few months after Peterloo was typical, and is I think worth quoting at length:

Never was oppression, in any age or nation, fit to be compared to that which is systematised here... that suffered by the children of Israel, in Egypt, which we are told made them groan and cry till the Lord heard them, and sent Moses, with superhuman powers to deliver them, was evidently not fit to be compared to it... If this then be true, that our situation is worse than the children of Israel, in Egypt, and that the Omnipotent Being endued [*sic*] Moses with miraculous powers to deliver them, can we doubt that God will speedily raise up a deliverance who shall overwhelm the powers that be, as the Egyptians were destroyed? When through the famine, Joseph had brought for Pharaoh all the cattle and all the land of Egypt, we read that Joseph furnished them with seed, and bid them go and sow the land, and bring one fifth of the produce to Pharaoh, and keep the four-fifths for their own use: the fifth of the corn, appears to have been all that was required of the Egyptians for rent, taxes and tithes: whilst here the Priest, King and Peer, take more than the value of all the corn grown in the kingdom.[74]

Once again, as with Ernest Jones' call for a crusade to reclaim the land, the parallel with the suffering of the dispossessed Israelites, exiled in their own land, was instructive. They, too, were the elect chosen people, who would be redeemed and delivered to the promised land despite, or because of, their suffering. The powerless were transformed into the powerful because they knew that providence and destiny were on their side. Their lives and their lack of political power were given a moral purpose and a sense of agency.

There can be few better examples of this process of empowerment by these narrative forms than the notorious political sermons (how instructive that very phrase is) of Ashton's Reverend John Rayner Stephens. His speeches opposing the poor law were hugely popular in Oldham, they lulled (no, it was more violent and melodramatic than that), they pushed their audiences into a sharply polarised world, in which God and the Devil were locked in an endless titanic struggle.

Oh yes My Lord Russell it is too late, it is too late, it is too late, thank God, it is too late! Put me where you like me and keep me there as long as you like, as long as God and my poor body will allow you. You may do just as you like with me, it is too late, it is too late, it is too late, it is too late; the blood is up aye! it tingles in your fingers it is ready to spurt out at your fingers ends, and to blow the skull cap off. Your fathers blood is up; your mothers milk is flowing round, and round, and round; you are beginning to be women you are beginning to be the offspring of men and women; thank God for it! He has poured a new language upon the people, it is too late, it is too late.[75]

On paper one is aware of how subtly one is drawn into a whole religio-moral universe in which the Devil (Lord John Russell) is pitted against a weakened messiah (Stephens himself) bolstered only by a burgeoning force of goodness (the people). However, try and imagine the terror and the elation such a performance could generate. Stephens empowered the people, he gave them a role, a mission to enable himself as the messiah to lead them out of the valley of darkness and persecution. Should they fail in this their moral duty, he also invoked the fires of hell, horror, and damnation with the disturbing images of blood spurting out of finger-tips and blowing heads off. Such melodramatic images were amazingly not uncommon features of popular political discourse. Ghouls, hydra-headed monsters, fiendish vampires were summoned up by radicals and Tories alike. At Exeter in 1849, even a usually timid and sober free-trade dinner boasted a banner 'with a spirited pictorial representation of St. George's victory over the infernal Dragon, which might be taken as allegorical of any political conquest over the powers of evil'.[76] Moreover, as Gladstone was to prove, these religious and melo-dramatic narrative forms were highly versatile and persistent; the moral crusade against evil was very much a part of Gladstonian Liberalism.

As well as the horror and the struggle given force by these narrative forms there was hope: the hope of better times, hope of a golden age revisited. Such a utopian education of desire empowered people by giving them a glimpse of a future they longed for and the possibility of achieving it. There was nothing new in the use of such utopian narrative forms by radicals, after all millenarianism had played a significant role in English libertarian politics since the sixteenth century.[77] We have repeatedly seen how radicals evoked a utopian future by appealing to the possibility of restoring a lost, but mythical, golden age, when all men were citizens of a constitution headed by a benevolent monarch and worked independently and prosperously on the land. As though this was not enough, radical audiences were continually reminded that, in the words of the hugely popular ballad of the 1840s and 1850s 'A Good Time's Coming Boys'. The end of George Thompson's speech at a dinner to celebrate his election as MP for Tower Hamlets was not untypical, 'he would remind them of that portion of the Scripture history relating to the walls of Jericho, and entreat them to go on, sounding their horns and blowing the blast of liberty, and never ceasing until the Jericho of corruption had crumbled into dust. (Tremendous cheering)'.[78] Even the Owenites imagined their own rational and secular utopia, when, as one of Oldham's Owenites boldly declared in 1838, 'We, socialists, mean to put a final end to exploitation and oppression; to feed all the hungry, clothe all the naked, and remove all complaining from our streets.'[79] Utopia was the new moral world.

Perhaps it was the absence of these narrative forms in the Paineite language of republicanism which helps to explain its relative failure. Predicated as it was on rationalist arguments of natural rights, republicans were at a loss to evoke a golden age which could once again be transformed into a brilliant utopian future. Even Knight, the so-called 'Tom Paine Jacobin', was no republican. Although he often criticised the cost of the civil list the blame was always placed at the feet of scheming, unrepresentative royal advisers. Indeed, at a meeting of Oldham's 'working people' in 1827, he even argued that,

Under an absolute monarchy, with a liberal and kindhearted King, such as his present Majesty, who was well known to feel the sufferings of the people, he would not allow his people to starve. He would not shut his ears against their cries, nor lay his own head on the pillow till he had given them relief. (Applause). With such a Monarch they would be much better without a House of Commons (Loud Cries of 'Aye, we would!' 'We dunnat want em').[80]

For Knight, as for so many other radicals, the monarch was an essential component of England's ancient constitutional golden age, after all it was the 'Great and Immortal King Alfred' who had created the cornerstones of that constitution – trial by jury, manhood suffrage, and annual parliaments. It was only by getting rid of the borough mongers in parliament that both the constitution and the monarchy could be restored to their original purity. Hence the popularity of petitioning the monarch, instead of the Commons, so that, as the Shoreditch vestry resolved in 1841, 'the Queen might be put in possession of the real feelings, and understand the wants of her suffering people'.[81] The veneration of the monarch often came from the most surprising of sources, including Spitalfield's unemployed silk-weavers.[82] This idea of a good monarch siding with the people against the borough-mongering aristocracy turned upon the utopian desire for the restoration of the lost Eden of Anglo-Saxon England, when kings and queens were uncorrupted and people free, happy, and prosperous. As Dorothy Thompson has argued, 'anti-royal feeling was much more likely to take the form of an attack on a particular monarch than an appeal to republicanism as such'.[83] Quite simply, the institution of the monarchy was too deeply embedded within the master narrative of English constitutional politics to be ever seriously threatened. Republicanism remained little more than a minority creed of the *cognoscenti*, championed by a few at times of radical retreat, but never able to command a mass platform.

Popular constitutionalism, then, remained the master narrative of English politics throughout this period, because not only were there no viable alternatives, but because it drew its strength from the enduring appeals of its religious and melodramatic narrative forms. Far from abandoning popular constitutionalism with the collapse of Chartism, radicals continued to identify themselves as part of the great historical struggle for English liberty as Ernest Jones had done in 1847. 'Liberty is a tree of long growth in England. It was planted at Runnymede; it was sunned by the fires of Smithfield; it was watered by the blood of Marston Moor, and the veins of Charles; it was fanned by the prayers of the puritans and dewed by the tears of the Exile – and now it is beginning to bloom beneath the fostering of the Charter.'[84] During the 1850s and 1860s even those who had been on the periphery of Chartism began to claim it as one of the great epics in the radical narrative of constitutional struggle, particularly in London where the Charter remained an important rallying cry for radical politics.[85] At Tower Hamlets in 1859, when George Thompson was wheeled out of retirement for a reform demonstration in his old constituency, he received much applause for arguing that 'The Charter can stand by the Declaration of Independence in America, by Magna Charta, or the Bill of Rights'.[86] Of course, as we have already seen in earlier chapters, the emphasis of radical constitutional politics shifted during the 1850s, as radical and Chartist groups resolved to protect their ancient constitutional rights of freedom of speech and public assembly, or attempted to check the unconstitutional centralisation of power at Westminster through vestry politics. All this at a time when the secularist movement testified to the continued strength of Paineite narratives in London's East End. Yet it was the standard of Palmerstonian Liberalism which provided the most forceful reworking of the discourse of popular constitutionalism.[87] Palmerston skilfully managed to combine the concerns of both radicalism and Liberalism by posing as a champion of constitutional liberty at home and abroad, welcoming Kossuth and Garibaldi, and releasing imprisoned or transported Chartists. England became once again the land of the free, and the exiled were welcomed home.

Just as during the 1850s popular constitutionalism had pervaded the politics of the Paineite stronghold of Tower Hamlets, so when the reform movement gathered pace again during the 1860s it was to the constitutionalist critique of 'Old Corruption' to which they turned. Matthias, an ex-Chartist and committee member of Tower Hamlets' new Political Union,

could not help expressing his complete disappointment with the Reform Bill of 1832. There was no denying the fact that the Constitution of the House of Commons was continually growing more corrupt; and we have now the most corrupt House of Commons and at the same time the most insolent House of Lords we ever had. The Reform Bill had only the effect of placing the Whigs in a position of place, patronage and power. They had certainly studied their own interests, but had as certainly neglected that of the people.[88]

Proclaiming their manifesto in 1860, Tower Hamlets' Political Union demanded the restoration of the purity of the ancient Anglo-Saxon constitution – a constitution whose representatives 'were not only elected by the people but [also] paid by them'.[89] It was a platform which could still command a mass following, as was demonstrated by the revival of the Reform League during the 1860s.

We have already seen how Beales first rose to prominence in 1864 by defending the people's rights to public assembly at Primrose Hill to honour Garibaldi. It was Beales' campaigns and pamphlet on the ancient constitutional rights of assembly which seems to have secured him the presidency of the Reform League.[90] Considering the new generation of radical political leaders – figures like J. B. Leno, George Howell, W. R. Cremer, Benjamin Lucraft and Charles Bradlaugh – which gathered under the Reform League's standard, it is striking that the League couched its appeals in the language of popular constitutionalism. For instance, at one of the League's rallies in London Fields during 1866 J. B. Langley asserted that 'They came there to assert their right to be within the pale of the constitution – (cheers) – and because they had been hitherto excluded from their rights (Hear, hear.).' It was resolved that 'we the working men of the Tower Hamlets, protest against the present system of representation, whereby the people are compelled to obey the laws in making of which they have no voice, which is opposed alike to the spirit of the ancient constitution and our sense of justice'.[91] These constitutionalist sentiments were even echoed on the League's membership card (see Plate 69). Below the eighteenth-century dictum (used by both Wilkites and supporters of the American War of Independence alike) 'Taxation without representation is tyranny' stood a figurine with a sword in one hand and the scales of justice in the other. This idea of popular justice, of fair play to the rich and poor in the making of laws, had long been central to the discourse of popular constitutionalism. It was a theme which Gladstone played upon heavily in the language of popular Liberalism, and from it sprang the idea of the people's moral right to the franchise.

The use of Gladstone's creed of moral entitlement by the Reform League emphasises the common ground shared between the enduring popular radical tradition and Gladstonian Liberalism. Significantly, the reform movement now argued, citizenship was the moral (not the natural) right of those working men moralised by the language of virtue, manners, and character, those with '[s]elf-command, self-control, respect for order, patience under suffering, confidence in the law and regard for superiors'.[92] The constitution rightfully belonged to them, and it was Gladstone's crusade to bring them back within its pale so that they in turn could restore the constitution to its ancient purity. Naturally, this notion that the people were morally entitled to citizenship of the political nation accentuated the popular sense of exclusion in order to empower those dispossessed with a renewed sense of moral worth and destiny, just as earlier radical uses of

THE

REFORM LEAGUE.

"TAXATION WITHOUT REPRESENTATION IS TYRANNY."

"Every Man who is not presumably incapacitated by some consideration of personal unfitness or of political danger, is morally entitled to
come within the pale of the Constitution."— *R! Hon. W. E. Gladstone.*

№ 49735

THIS IS TO CERTIFY

That

Is enrolled a **MEMBER** of the **REFORM LEAGUE.**

Edmond Beales, Esq. President.
J. A. Nicholay, Esq. Treasurer.
Geo. Howell. Secretary.

69 Membership card of the Reform League (Howell Collection, Bishopsgate
Institute)

constitutionalist discourse had.[93] As with these earlier languages of
inclusion, this language of moral right was also based upon exclusions.
Clearly, for Gladstone, those working men without the independence
of moral 'character' joined Bright's 'residuum' and women in being
excluded from 'the people'. It was a language which was vulnerable
to even more undemocratic appropriations, as was forcibly shown by
Robert Lowe's infamous remarks on the immorality of the working
class and their unfitness for the franchise.

Of course, this sense of a moral right to inclusion within the
constitution drew much of its inspiration from the still potent force of
popular Christianity. At times it is difficult to separate the notion of
religious rights from their more earthly moral counterparts; the
moral voice of the people often resolved itself into the voice of God,
extending far beyond the demand for 'fair play' and justice. Listen,
for instance, to Beales' address to the new electors in 1868.

It was to the poor especially that Christ came to preach glad tidings of Gods
love and man's salvation unto a heavenly inheritance of glory, joy, and
immortality; it may yet be reserved for the poor to teach the rich and rulers

of the earth to be Christians, not in mere name and profession, but in truth and practice and to give democracy its noblest triumph in securing not only freedom, but the peace of the world.[94]

This language of moral Christianity was, as Beales demonstrated, a populist language, ideally suited to emphasise the superior virtues of the poor against the moral and political corruption of the rich. The same address continued in similar vein. 'Let the rich, and what are called the upper and educated classes, treat honesty as a myth, and sneer at patriotism as a dream – let them, if they will, still dishonour themselves, their class and their country, by continuing their attempts to make a seat in Parliament the subject of corrupt traffic, demoralizing expenditure, or lawless intimidation'.[95] Beales was by no means alone in using the categories of the rich and the poor, indeed their prevalence in popular political discourse makes it tempting to assert that they, and not class, were the dominant social identities of the time. One reason for this was the ease with which these identities had been woven into constitutionalist narratives long before Gladstone and Beales. 'The Poor Voter's Song', current during South Devon's election of 1835, portrayed a poor voter manfully resisting the bribes of the rich and powerful:

> What though these men be rich,
> And what though I be poor;
> I would perish in a ditch
> Ere I listen to their lure;
> They may treat me as prey,
> But their vengeance shall be braved,
> I've a soul as well as they,
> To be saved, boys, saved![96]

The honour, independence, and moral character of the poor voter ensured his ultimate redemption and deliverance, whereas the corrupted and corrupting rich man proved that it was easier for a camel to pass through the eye of a needle than for a rich man to enter the kingdom of heaven.

Very often the patent moral and religious overtones of these categories of rich and poor belied simple class appropriations. They were categories which seemed to suggest the possibility of transcending class identities. Sir Charles Richard Blunt, the reforming candidate at the Lewes election of 1831, argued that his guiding principle was 'to take the burden off the poor man, and place it upon the rich, whose broad shoulders are better able to bear it, so that the poor man may be once more able to raise his head in society'.[97] Of course, that is not to deny that the poor could become synonymous with the working class, after all their experience of poverty was acutest. However, even William Newton claimed in 1852 that he 'would not take from the rich to give to the poor; he had no desire to reduce the middle classes to the condition of the poor, nor the upper ranks to that of the middle classes; but he sought to give the poor man an opportunity to support and elevate himself by his own industry. (Loud Cheers)'.[98] By using this language, Newton seemed to both deny and accentuate class cleavages, appealing both to the rich middle classes and upper ranks, but also to the labouring poor (including presumably some of the middle classes) with the idea of meritocracy. Naturally, for the Tories any identity which offered the opportunity of populist readings was indispensable. It came as no surprise that when Conservatism eventually emerged in Tower Hamlets, under the auspices of the Metropolitan Working Men's Conservative Association (1868), its declared objective was 'to oppose the spirit which tends to set class against class... by welding together rich and poor in defence of Conservative and Constitutional principles'.[99]

I want to suggest that this desire to transcend class identities in the wider interests of the nation was not unique to Tory politics, but that it was also a major theme within radical and Liberal narratives of the nation's constitution. Even within these narratives the politics of class was often perceived as the politics of selfishness and factionalism, a language of exclusion which denied the sense of moral agency and community generated when speaking of the nation and its historic destiny. Here again, in this demand for a classless politics, the utopian forms of these constitutional narratives were evident. If Chartism represented the apex of working-class politics, it did so without demanding the triumph of the working class. They believed, like their Exeter branch, that 'class legislation is the source of all the miseries afflicting this country, and that we pledge ourselves to struggle unceasingly for its annihilation'.[100] This hatred of class legislation was echoed 20 years later by Gladstonian Liberals like John Platt, who told a meeting during Oldham's election of 1868 that he 'wanted not to put class against class, but for all to work unanimously together'.[101] A year earlier Oldham's Reform Association had similarly resolved that only universal manhood suffrage 'would destroy class legislation, and ultimately place the government

of the nation in the hands of the people'.[102] Ernest Jones, the
principal speaker at this meeting had set the theme early on,
preaching his new classless Chartist creed. Although claiming he

> was as much a Chartist as ever he was... It was the opponents of reform who
> raised the class cry. Instead of England being one nation, it was divided into
> many nations, and they talked of the representatives of the aristocratic
> classes, the middle classes, as if afraid that one should become more powerful
> than the other and like Kilkenny cats, tear each other to pieces (laughter).
> He protested against that; they should not speak of classes, but only of men
> – (applause) – and when one stood before them and said the aristocracy
> ought to have one share, the middle classes another share, and the working
> classes another, ask them how much the entire nation ought to have.[103]

The interests of the nation and its constitution remained uppermost
in radical minds, for once they spoke on behalf of a class they would
lose the moral advantage of speaking on behalf of the nation's
wronged, but morally just, people.

Unlike the people in Tory narratives of the constitution, radical
libertarian definitions were not confined to a dominant English
ethnos. In both Oldham and Tower Hamlets, where there were
respectively significant Irish and Jewish communities, radical and
Liberal politics often gave these ethnicities a powerful voice.[104]
Chartist demands for the restoration of Ireland's lost rights of self-
government and freedom of worship to prevent coercion and poverty
did much to secure the support of the Irish constituency in England.
Arguably, in places like Tower Hamlets and Oldham, Chartism was
primarily an Irish movement by 1848, certainly the majority of those
arrested in 1848 were Irish.[105] Yet, it was radical and Liberal uses of
the language of religious liberty which did most to include such
ethnic groups within the category of the people, instilling them with
the same sense of agency and moral destiny which gripped the
English *ethnos*. For, as we have repeatedly seen, it was radicals who
appropriated the narratives and tropes of popular Christianity from
the hegemony of the clergy and the established Anglican church,
opening up the language of religious liberty to people of all nations
and creeds. It was Gladstone, after all, who wanted to help all those
people struggling to be free, just as it was he who made disestablishment of the Irish Church and later Home Rule the cornerstones of late nineteenth-century Liberalism. This same inclusive
language of religious liberty had great appeal to Tower Hamlets'
Jews. Since the late 1830s a commitment to Jewish emancipation had

been an essential part of any radical candidature in the borough, even with the proviso as 'long as their services and loyalty to the state remain the one unquestioned, the other unimpeachable'.[106] Most radical or Liberal candidates deliberately wooed the Jewish community, staging meetings like Ayrton in Jewish Free Schools and printing Yiddish handbills, or like Beales and Newton pledging themselves to unsectarian education. Both the secularist and constitutionalist narratives of radical and Liberal politics contested the Tory exclusion of other ethnicities besides the English from the political nation.

Of course the most obvious (and historiographically least remarked upon) exclusion from the constitutionalist master narrative of English politics was women. We have already seen, both in this chapter and others, how patriarchal popular political culture was, but this should not blind us to the attempts of women to include themselves within the political nation. Anna Clark has recently shown how Chartist women resolved to break out of the discursive culs de sac of both Wollstonecraft's plea for their natural rights to inclusion in the public political sphere as rational individuals, and what she calls the bourgeois, evangelical language of domesticity.[107] They spoke a language of 'militant domesticity' which justified their public activities through their identities as mothers labouring to feed, educate, and offer a better life for their children.[108] However, although this language enabled women to win substantial concessions from the state through their campaigns in the anti-slavery, factory reform and anti-Poor-Law movements, it eventually entrapped them, subsuming their political rights under their husbands, and imposing a new rigidity on family life. One is struck by the parallel with Denise Riley's work on the suffragettes, who, by abandoning their femininity to assert their equality with men, lost their sense of sexual difference, a difference which feminists have, ever since, struggled to regain. As Riley ruefully notes, the 'history of women's suffrage gives rise to the less than celebratory reflection that categories often achieve their desired ends by subdued routes, not gloriously and triumphantly, as if at the end of an exhaustive, rewarded struggle to speak themselves, but almost as by-products in the interstices of other discourses'.[109] Certainly, it is surprising that, following the closure by men of both the language of militant domesticity and natural rights, women like Harriet Martineau continued to rely so heavily upon them during the 1850s and 1860s.[110] Perhaps it was less surprising

that the cause of women's suffrage made greater leaps forward when
it used constitutionalist languages and categories to contest the
exclusively masculine definitions of property.[111] The discourse of
popular constitutionalism was certainly vulnerable to such gendered
appropriations by women.

I have attempted to establish that the discourse of popular
constitutionalism represented the master narrative of English politics
up to, and possibly beyond, 1867. This is not to deny the place of
other narratives, but rather to argue that all were used as discursive
strategies to gain the upper hand in the debate over the meaning of
the constitution. Neither is this intended as a criticism of the
limitations of radical and Liberal politics. I have tried to stress the
ways in which the tropes of popular constitutionalism, with its
utopian emphasis on a just people struggling to restore a lost golden
age, struck a strong and immensely popular (and populist) chord. For
radicals to have abandoned either these tropes, or the constitutionalist narratives which gave them force, would have represented
a retreat from the powerful force of this 'shared' master narrative.[112]
Thankfully, such a recognition frees us from the teleology of much of
the historiography of that illusory beast 'working-class radicalism'.
For, once we acknowledge the plasticity and multi-vocality of
political languages, their ability to be appropriated from different
perspectives and endowed with conflicting meanings, we are free to
investigate the myriad of other identities besides class that radical
politics spoke to. The genius of the constitutional master-narrative
was that it enabled political groups to make this great mass of diverse
and often conflicting identities coherent, and thus empowered its
subjects with a sense of agency.

CONCLUSION

If we imagine the discourse of popular constitutionalism as the
master-narrative of nineteenth-century English politics, we are able
to examine not only its different appropriations by competing
political groups seeking to inform the constitution with their own
interpretation of the nation's past and its future destiny, but the
shared tropes and forms of these competing narratives. Central to this
struggle to interpret the constitution were the competing definitions
of the category of the virtuous people and their role in the battle to
include or exclude various groups from the political nation. However,

critical as these different interpretations of the constitution's past, present, and future were, they should not obscure the shared uses of either key foundational texts and moments – one thinks of the Norman Conquest, Magna Carta, the Revolution of 1688, Locke's *Two Treatises*, and Blackstone's *Commentaries* – or the melodramatic narrative forms and utopian tropes of loss, struggle, and redemption.

It is no coincidence that historians are increasingly aware of the importance of these melodramatic narrative forms, particularly that utopian vision of dispossessed but virtuous people struggling for redemption and the restoration of a lost golden age.[113] We have seen how such tropes provided a readily accessible and resonant structure to a whole kaleidoscope of possibly contradictory political languages, and helped feed those languages and their analyses back into the constitutionalist master-narrative. The force and resonance of these tropes relied, like the melodramatic genres of the stage and popular literature, on their ability to provide their subjects with a sense of agency and a coherent moral purpose, of rightness in an evil world populated by tyrants.[114] This was a radical and enabling message for one and all, but how much more so for the otherwise 'helpless and unbefriended', the powerless, those excluded from the political nation. It was they, surely, who most acutely felt the need for reassurance that beneath the chaotic helplessness of their predicament there was a moral order and they were on its right side. Therefore the melodramatic tropes of constitutionalist narratives empowered the powerless and politically excluded, by promising them not only the utopian earth of inclusion within the constitution, but also an active role in writing their own historical epic.

It is possible to read both the shared forms and the different appropriations of the contents of the constitutionalist master-narrative as a dialogue or political drama about power and powerlessness, not only within the political unconscious, but in the more tangible sense of who was included and excluded from the historical mission of the nation's constitution. The attraction of such a reading is that it acknowledges the complexity and richness of popular political discourse, the way in which it incorporated a whole series of sometimes conflicting, sometimes complementary, narratives and identities. No longer is it necessary to reduce all political languages to a consistent whole, just as it is no longer necessary to reduce radical narratives to the anticipation or realisation of proto-socialist or class identities. I have tried to show the homogeneity of different Tory, Whig, radical, and Liberal appropriations of the constitutional master-narrative and the pluralism of the identities they articulated. It is simply not sufficient to assert that any discourse used by a class reflected their consciousness as members of that class.[115] Such an approach is fraught with problems, neglecting, as it does, not only the diversity of supposedly homogeneous social classes and political groups, but also the plasticity of political language. Are we to take seriously an approach which implies that working-class Tories could appropriate Tory narratives in such a way as to articulate their identity as a class? In short, such a position inevitably entails denying the validity of any identity other than class. And yet neither does the category of populism make sense of the diversity and instability of political languages and identities, albeit with Patrick Joyce's proviso of insisting on the existence of a 'family of populisms', radical, Liberal, Conservative or classical.[116] Such a formulation should be welcomed, as it has rightfully checked the primacy of class readings of the constitutionalist master-narrative by emphasising the moral, religious, and political character of its identities. Just as it tends to privilege a rather strict reading of class in purely economic terms, so the category of 'classical' populism suggests some form of *a priori* populism, an inherently popular discourse prior to its use and appropriation by individual or collective actors. Ultimately, we need to ask whether these often unwieldy categories do justice to the indeterminacy and ambiguity of the myriad of identities voiced by constitutional narratives. In the end we really do not have to, and can not chose between class and populism – it is the instability of texts and their readings which we must hold paramount.

Conclusion: New narratives in the history of English politics?

This book has been about the meaning(s) of nineteenth-century English political culture. It has attempted to analyse not only the form and content of political appeals, but also the ways in which, through both their production and reception, they were used to create constituencies of political support. The dialectic between the form and content, and the production and reception of English political culture, has informed this book throughout. An analysis of the various modes of political communication has been central to such a project. Historians' current fascination with the paradigm of language has tended to privilege readings of the printed or spoken word and, consequently, equally important symbolic modes of political communication – the uses of iconography, ceremonies, space, and organisation – have been largely lost to view. In compensating for this trend I have attempted to expand our concept of political language by including many of these neglected oral, aural, visual, and practical modes of communication. In doing so I became increasingly aware of the significance of the melodramatic forms of political languages, forms which, for the most part, pervaded the politics of sight as much as that of the spoken and printed word. In a very real sense melodrama was the key in which the whole epic of nineteenth-century English politics was played out.

We have, for instance, repeatedly seen how melodramatic conceptions of the world shaped the culture of politics in all five constituencies. The melodramatic form of the political imagination provided a readily accessible and resonant language of feeling and desire, which instilled the subject with a sense of agency by evoking a world larger than life in which the forces of good would always triumph over those of evil, and the damned would always be saved. As we saw in chapter 3, such forms structured the dynamics of oral, visual, and, to a lesser extent, printed modes of political communication. Just as in other chapters, they were also evident in the romantic aspirations of official civic landscapes, in the projection of the lives and characters of royalty and popular political leaders, in the poetics of election campaigns, in the symbolic uses of organisation, in the politics of culture, and last, but by no means least, in the discourse of popular constitutionalism. It was the universality of such melodramatic forms which was most striking – they seemed truly popular, belonging to all political groups and to none, although they were, of course, used and appropriated in different ways.

These melodramatic forms of the political imagination owed much to the persistent influence of religious narratives.[1] Contrary to J. C. D. Clark's emphasis on the personnel and institutions of the Anglican church, I have emphasised the longevity of popular Christianity as a way of seeing the world. That is not to deny the existence of more formal links between politics and organised religion, be it church or chapel. (For, clearly, just as Anglicanism infused Tory politics, so radical politics were steeped in the traditions of Protestant dissent – as illustrated by their use of both outdoor camps and chapels as meeting places, not to mention the uses of the Bible, hymns, Sunday schools, and the like.) However, it is to point to the more suggestive presence and force of familiar religious tropes and themes in both radical and Tory politics, and their uses in articulating their contrasting languages of inclusion and exclusion. While radical leaders played upon images of themselves as suffering martyrs, their supporters imagined themselves as a virtuous people in struggle, who, like the Israelites, were exiled in their own land. Meanwhile Tories sought to overcome this sense of dispossession by including the disenfranchised as Protestants in the nation's historical crusade against the tyranny of Rome and her allies. It will be apparent that both readings revolved around creating constituencies of support with a sense of agency, not least of all by employing the utopian forms of popular Christianity with its stress on the guiding hand of providence and redemption.

This attention to the content of the political imagination's melodramatic forms is instructive, not simply because such forms dominated the constitutional master-narrative of nineteenth-century English politics, but because they also pervade the subsequent historiographical representations of it – whether marxist, liberal or tory – which I began the book by discussing. As we shall see, in analysing both these historical and historiographical narratives, this book has also taken on and appropriated these melodramatic forms. But first things first. For, whatever their continuing historiographical force, by now I hope it is clear that the central conflict of nineteenth-century English politics, the contest over the meaning of the constitution, was informed by (built upon) such melodramatic forms and tropes. Time and time again, in chapter after chapter, we have seen how this melodramatic debate about the meaning of the constitution permeated all areas of English political culture. The people's constitutional struggle for freedom of assembly, association, and speech, for a voice in the nation's government, and the state's attempt to deny those rights and suppress that voice, was manifest in the mass of 'reforming' legislation, in the politics of space and culture, the symbolic uses of organisation, and the discourse of popular constitutionalism. It was in these ways that the constitution was contested and definitions of the public political sphere expanded or restricted.

Having identified this contest over the meaning of the constitution as the master-narrative of English politics, it is also necessary to examine its different uses and appropriations. Although the structure of the book has assumed that the state's 'official' definitions of the constitution were in competition with their 'popular' counterparts, I have tried to show that such an opposition obscures many of the differences within these categories, not to mention the similarities between them. It is, for instance, difficult to talk of a uniform or static 'official' definition of the public political sphere for, as we saw in the first three chapters, official political discourse often pulled in several directions at the same time. While Sturges Bourne's reforms of parish politics and the parliamentary Reform Act of 1832 enforced an exclusive definition of the propertied male citizen, the persistence of historic local official structures and ceremonial practices, together with Hobhouse's Vestries Act, provided altogether more flexible and inclusive definitions of the constitution. Similarly, although a body of legislation bent on 'reforming' corrupt practices and enabling the individual's rational and independent pursuit of politics were dressed up as great liberal concessions, they tended to discipline and regulate popular politics, as much as emancipate it. Moreover, just as the more exclusive official definitions of the constitution commanded a considerable degree of popular support from Tories throughout the five constituencies, so official attempts to reform corruption and empower the literate rational individual won support from many reformers.

Clearly 'popular' definitions of the constitution were just as protean, diverse, and contradictory as their 'official' counterparts. Tory readings of the constitution elicited their own notion of inclusion within the political nation through the narrative of England's Protestant mission, a mission which included all social and sexual (if not ethnic) groups, propertied and enfranchised or not. It was a narrative which played upon Tory notions of liberty and the freeborn Englishman; notions which were powerfully fused together in their cultural politics of the good time which, with its beer and *bonhomie*, evoked images of Old England's Protestant golden age when John Bull's cup ran over with beer, roast beef, and plum pudding. In contrast, those reformers unhappy with the Revolutionary Settlement of 1688 – whether Independents or Chartists, Radicals, Whigs or Liberals – demanded the restoration of England's ancient Anglo-Saxon constitution whose principles had been reaffirmed in 1688. Of course, as we saw in chapter 8, there were many different uses and interpretations of this narrative, which in turn drew upon, and intersected with, many other discourses and consequently various definitions of the virtuous 'people' who should be once more included within the political nation's constitution. As we saw in chapter 6, the cultural politics of reform tended to stress the virtue, independence, and moral worth of those dispossessed, claiming that their interest in sobriety, education, and self-improvement proved that they were fit and proper persons, ideal citizens ready for the franchise. And yet, just as the Tory language of inclusion was founded upon the exclusion of the ethnic/Catholic 'Other', so the reformers' language of inclusion was invariably (and arguably increasingly) based upon the exclusion of women.

Therefore, on closer inspection, the whole idea of a 'popular' politics disintegrates into a series of different competing narratives with their own tensions and contradictions. It is deeply significant that the category of the 'popular' does not fracture into an incoherent cacophony of discourses, a sort of political tower of babel. As I argued in chapter 8, however diverse and protean these popular constitutional narratives were, they all drew upon the same master-narrative of England's libertarian constitution and its melodramatic tropes. Therefore, despite its various uses and appropriations by competing political groups in different contexts, it is possible to talk of a peculiarly English libertarian political tradition. It has been suggested that the strength of these narratives of England's libertarian constitution was their ability to endow their subjects with a sense of agency, by making their fractured decentred identities seemingly stable and coherent. The point is not that the nineteenth-century political subject had confounded the postmodern critique of the autonomous, rational, centred individual, but that it pretended it had, addressing people as though their identities were stable and coherent. Of course that was, and still is, the business (even the purpose) of politics. It is not just that we need politics to make sense of the often very chaotic world around us, but that it is arguably impossible to create a politics capable of attracting popular support which does seek to transcend differences both within and between decentred individual and collective actors with some kind of unifying identity. In this sense the melodramatic constitutional narratives of nineteenth-century English politics were about empowering people by creating order out of chaos, by imagining them as stable, coherent, acting subjects. Of course, such a conclusion immediately suggests the need for two supplementary studies. Either one which traces the history of those narratives with which people came to be as political subjects.[2] Or, one which examines the ways in which politics fails to narrativise the world for us, how politics speaks to our still decentred and fractured selves in such a myriad of contradictory ways that we remained overwhelmed and disabled by our differences.

If this book has tended to privilege the unity and coherence of those identities created by the constitutional narratives of nineteenth-century English politics, then it has done so mindful at least that a broadly national political culture contained significant local and regional differences. We have seen, in all five constituencies, the value attached to a sense of locality, of place and belonging. This was evident not only from the importance of parish, town, and county meetings, and the projection of leaders and parliamentary candidates as local lads, but also from the very marked persistence of local partisan identities. Of course the local context and sense of place also did much to shape the organisation and culture of politics, not least because of the diversity and local heterogeneity of the official structure of politics. Such differences were in turn complemented by the social peculiarities of each constituency. In Oldham and Tower Hamlets, with their large Irish and Jewish populations, the debate over the meaning of the constitution had to embrace questions of ethnicity – whether these groups were suitable citizens of England's constitution – in a much more sharply focused way than elsewhere. That is not to deny the autonomy of politics by asserting the determining influence of social forces, but rather to emphasise that one way in which the 'social' was understood (made 'real' if you like) was through political discourse. Take away constitutional narratives' languages of citizenship and we would be left with a very different understanding of the 'social' peculiarities of Oldham and Tower Hamlets, one which, say, excluded those who had blond hair or were 6 feet tall.

Such a cultural history of politics has enabled me to challenge the teleologies of liberal and marxist narratives of English political history, with their insistence on the triumphant role of the middle and working classes in the invention of England's democratic constitution. I have proposed a new narrative which has told a story about the fall of political man, and the closure, not the emergence, of the constitution's radical libertarian democratic potential. Despite the 'reforms' at parochial, municipal, and parliamentary levels which (to some extent at least) increased the size of the electorate, and a number of other Acts seemingly designed to encourage the politics of individual opinion at the expense of the corrupt politics of influence and the market, definitions of the constitution and its propertied male citizen became ever more restrictive and exclusive. This process was accompanied by, and built upon, the gradual, but marked, decline in the power of people to create their own politics. As more and more people were included within the political nation, they were ironically disabled as political subjects. The invention of democracy in England was then a sham.

Integral to this newly invented culture of democracy was the privileging of print as a mode of political communication. Eventually the perception of print as a medium which facilitated rational debate between enlightened individuals undermined the melodramatic, emotive, and collective uses of customary oral and visual media. Citizenship of the new model democracy entailed duties and responsibilities which could only be fulfilled through the virtuous independence afforded by reason and education and their natural vehicle print. In short, print allowed politics to be taken off the streets, it transformed the popular public and collective experience of politics to one centred upon the primarily male individual as head of the private family home. As we saw in chapter 3, it was a trend which received much encouragement by legislation restricting the uses of customary oral and visual modes of political communication, and encouraging the disciplines of the rational and private uses of print. The introduction of private ballot papers at vestry and municipal levels, and the secret ballot at parliamentary elections, were both central to, and symbolic of, the way in which print was used to invent this new democratic political culture. The previously rowdy and unpredictable nomination ceremonies, which had afforded non-electors such a central role at elections, were scrapped, and the 'crowd' dispersed and replaced by a series of discrete, private polling booths where the elector made his pact with God and/or his conscience, not with the non-electors.

The invention of party was also central to this closure of the public political sphere. Instead of interpreting the invention of party as an enabling and emancipative step forward on the road to a liberal democratic constitution, as most narratives of English political history have done, I have concentrated on the ways in which it disciplined, regulated, and disabled popular politics, closing down, rather than opening up, the radical potential of political subjectivities. Significantly, print was pivotal to the invention of party, for it enabled the construction of national party organisations, organisations which, together with the political cultures from which they emerged, became increasingly formal and disciplinary in character, placing ever greater distances between leaders and led. It was unsurprising to find in chapter 4 that the popular suspicion of party, with its dictating, oligarchic clique of leaders, agents, and activists, remained so prevalent throughout this period. It was a distrust born of experience. For, as we saw in chapter 6, the use of ticketing to regulate audiences, the use of counter-attractive events to distract attention from supposedly unsuitable events in the customary calendar of popular culture, and the attempt to fashion politics into a family affair by including women only as the spouses of men, were all innovations integral to the emergence of party. The culture of party politics gradually subsumed the regulatory functions of the official political culture, just as partisan meetings assumed the roles of town and county meetings. Increasingly, if individuals were to matter as political agents, they had to succumb to the disciplines and subjectivities of party politics, and therefore parties shaped the terms of their political participation.

Whatever the role of party in the closure of the public political sphere, we should not be blind to its empowering and emancipative qualities. Just as national party organisations broke down the isolation of local political groups, so the languages and identities of party politics had to resonate with individual or collective subjects in order to construct constituencies of support. Consequently, and again contrary to Whiggish notions of historical change, the mid-nineteenth-century invention of party was based upon the reworking of the constitutional narratives' languages of independence, albeit in more restrictive fashion. As we saw in chapter 6, such discursive strategies crucially depended upon negotiations between leaders and led. It was apparent in chapter 7 that such a dichotomy between leaders and led is in many ways misleading, leaders always existing as much in the imagination of the beholder as individuals in their own image. Despite this persistence of people's ability to shape their own politics, it is difficult to deny the logic which points towards the closure of the public political sphere, however gradual and uneven that process may have been. Although it was a process which was by no means complete by the end of this period, the book's central thesis remains that the expansion of the electorate was predicated upon ever more restrictive definitions of the political subject as citizen, definitions which closed down not only the radical potential of a libertarian politics, but also the parameters of the public political sphere.

This, of course, leaves me open to the accusation that, by turning the triumphant teleologies of the dominant narratives of English political history on their head, I have simply provided a different, if equally dogmatic, narrative which also closes down other interpretive possibilities – the closure of the public political sphere merely replacing the forward march of labour and the triumph of Liberal democracy. Clearly, I can not deny the possibility of such a reading, although I may want to add the obligatory academic qualifications and caveats, stressing the slow uneven and incomplete nature of the closure of politics. Or, more truthfully if less properly, I could claim that it was never my intention to close down other readings, but that in subjects as well studied as nineteenth-century English politics only the most novel and bold (some would say foolhardy) of narratives can break the interpretive log-jam, opening up the space for a multiplicity of other readings. The important thing is that now in the late twentieth century when, despite its crises in the west/north, Liberal democracy is fast being exported to the developing east/south, we rethink and problematise its politics at one of its founding moments. Therefore I make few apologies for the often audacious and melodramatic nature of this book. Perhaps my own narrative can be seen as a reworking of the forms and tropes of its subject, just as Rosaldo has suggested that by reclaiming the struggles of the English 'common people' E. P. Thompson's radical populist narrative was itself part of the very tradition he sought to describe.[3] One does not have to struggle to find the similarities. There is the romanticisation of the 'people' and their struggle to retain a radical libertarian politics; the hint of a golden age before the erosion of a 'genuine' popular politics; the celebration of all that was local, popular, feminine, fluid, and opened as opposed to the denigration of all that was national, official, masculine, static, and closed; the melodramatic portrayal of the struggle of people versus the state, radical versus tory, men versus women, the English versus the 'Other'; and finally, of course, the desire for closure with a new narrative of English political history, and even, perhaps, the utopian suggestion that if only people could build upon the radical libertarian politics we have lost and redefine the constitution once more...

Main occupational groups among the electorate as a percentage, 1808–68[a]

Lewes		Boston	
Lewes, 1812		*Boston, 1818*	
Carpenters	8.8 (29)	Butchers	6.1 (28)
Labourers	5.2 (22)	Tailors	5.4 (25)
Shoemakers	6.7 (17)	Bricklayers	4.3 (20)
		Cordwainers	26.3 (80)
Lewes, 1830		Joiners	9.8 (45)
Gentlemen	4.5 (34)	Mariners	8.9 (41)
Tailors	4.5 (34)		
Carpenters	4.4 (33)	*Boston, 1830*	
Cordwainers	5.3 (40)	Tailors	6.3 (32)
Labourers	10.4 (78)	Carpenters	6.9 (36)
		Cordwainers	17.7 (89)
Lewes, 1835		Mariners	8.3 (42)
Gentlemen	5.1 (38)		
Tailors	4.5 (34)	*Boston, 1852*	
Carpenters	6.1 (46)	Merchants	4.0 (38)
Shoemakers	5.8 (44)	Grocers	4.1 (39)
Labourers	4.5 (39)	Carpenters	3.6 (34)
		Shoemakers	5.5 (53)
Oldham, 1832		Farmers	10.2 (97)
Innkeepers	3.3 (27)		
Publicans	6.7 (56)	*Oldham, 1852*	
Shopkeepers	10.7 (89)	Beer-sellers	6.3 (134)
Cotton-spinners	10.0 (83)	Grocers	6.8 (146)
Hatters	3.8 (28)	Innkeepers	6.3 (136)
Weavers	4.9 (41)	Cotton-spinners	12.2 (262)
Farmers	19.6 (163)	Farmers	8.2 (176)

[a] Figures in brackets represent the actual number of voters listed as members of relevant occupational group.

Extract from William Chadwick's speech in North Staffordshire, c. 1890

'Mr. Chairman' he commenced ... Then followed an impressive pause, as though the venerable orator was anxious to see whether his resonant voice had reached the uttermost limits of his enormous audience. 'Mr. Chairman', he resumed, 'forty years ago I went to gaol with handcuffs on these wrists and leg-irons on these ankles'. (Sensation in the audience.) 'And why? And why, I ask you?' (Embarrassment in the audience. How should *they* know? Was he going to blame *them*?) 'Because I dared to say that in a land of plenty no man should starve. Because I dared to say that from the Common Fatherhood of God sprang the Common Brotherhood of Mankind. Because I dared to say that no man should earn less than a pound a week' – (a general illumination of countenances) – 'and should have a pound laid by for a rainy day'. ('That's reet, maister.') 'We Chartists said that the earth was the Lord's and the fullness thereof. But the Tories said the earth was the landlords', and the fools thereof ... The Tories taxed your newspapers to keep your minds in the dark.' ('Shame.') 'They taxed your soap to keep your bodies dirty – and then called you the Great Unwashed.' (Rising indignation.) 'We said every man should have a vote – and no man more than one. Toryism in the past has been brutal. Toryism in the present is dishonest. Mr. Chairman, I am proud to stand on this platform – the platform of historic Liberalism – the platform of William Ewart Gladstone.' (Applause.) 'I am proud that all through a long life I have always been on the side of the poor man – always for the poor against the rich.' ('' 'Ear, 'ear, guv'nor.' 'Go it, old boy.') 'The Tories would give to them that have, and take away from them that have not even that little which they have.' ('Giv it 'em 'ot, guv'nor.').

Palmer Newbould, *Pages from a Life of Strife*, pp. 4–6.

Variations on a theme: recycling the sound of ballads

OLDHAM ELECTION, OR 'NO GO, FOX'.

(A New Song to an Old Tune – 'With Wellington we'll go, we'll go.')

Electors all within this place,
There soon will come a day
When you'll be called to join the chase
To drive the Fox away.

    Chorus–
    With Duncuft we will go, will go,
    With Cobbett we will go;
    We'll wear the cap of liberty,
    But Fox will be 'no go'.

From Chadderton will be a run,
They'll come to poll in flocks;
Round Whitegate End, you may depend,
They'll vote against a Fox.

Chorus – With Duncuft, &c.

And Hollinwood is staunch and good,
With reservoir and 'docks:'
If he goes there, they loudly swear
They'll surely drown a Fox.

Chorus – With Cobbett, &c.

Now, many barbers in this town
Would like to cut his locks;
They say his nob requires the job,
And so they'll vote for Fox.

Chorus – With Duncuft, &c.

Then Crompton folk, with hearts of oak,
Will give him some hard knocks,
And men from Shaw and Crompton Ha'
Will never vote for Fox.

Chorus – With Cobbett, &c.

About Springhill some asses still
Are stupid there as blocks,
Among the drones at Culver Stones,
Are kennels for a Fox.

Chorus – With Duncuft, &c.

But Fulwood men will muster then,
And firm as Greenfield Rocks;
And sholver poots are fast as roots,
And will not vote for Fox.

Chorus – With Cobbett, &c.

Some Tailor Pats and Grub-street flats
Are stupid as an ox,
And one mad Jesse, if not two,
Will surely vote for Fox.

Chorus – With Duncuft, &c.

Some rotten saints in our big streets
Do well deserve the 'stocks;'
If men profess, and don't possess,
They are sure to vote for Fox.

Chorus – With Cobbett, &c.

But sturdy farmers all around,
Who keep their hens and cocks,
Have all declared they are prepared
To come and kill a Fox.

Chorus – With Duncuft, &c.

Though Royton has got Sandy lanes,
And Holdens, too, in 'flocks',
He'll get some thumps from some good trumps
That will not for Fox.

Chorus – With Cobbett, &c.

But let the day come when it may,
We'll put him in a box,
Cut off his tail, send him by rail,
And then we'll bag the Fox.

Chorus – With Duncuft, &c.

Grime, *Memory Sketches*, pp. 95–6.

OLDHAM ELECTION, OR 'NO SEAUR PIE'.

An Old Song 'Fettelt Up Gradely'.
Tune – 'With Wellington We'll Go'.

Electors all both great and small,
The time is near at hand
When you'll be called to drive away
The tyrants of our land.

　　　　Chorus –
　　Come rally, lads, both Whigs and Rads,
　　And lay the Tories low;
　　We'll wear the cap of liberty,
　　And Fox is sure to go.

From Chadderton you'll have a fly;
They'll come to poll in flocks;
They'll shout 'Free Trade', and 'No Seaur Pie',
And give three cheers for Fox.

Chorus – Come rally, &c.

And Hollinwood is staunch and good,
They care not for some knocks;
If Heald goes there again, they swear
They'll put him in a box.

Chorus – Come rally, &c.

How many barbers in this town
Admire fine flowing locks?
Heald's close cut nob's not worth a bob,
And so they'll vote for Fox.

Chorus – Come rally, &c.

The Crompton folk, with hearts of oak,
Are feeling some hard knocks;
The men from Shaw begin to thaw,
Their hearts are changed to Fox.

Chorus – Come rally, &c.

About Priesthill some asses still
Are stupid there as blocks,
For Tory jink, sour crumbs, or drink,
They'll bray against a Fox.

Chorus – Come rally, &c.

Millbottom men are true again –
Are firm as rugged rocks;
The sholver 'Poots' are fast as roots,
And swear they'll fight for Fox.

Chorus – Come rally, &c.

There's Nield's queer lips, and Bullock's slips –
Both stupid as an ox –
And one 'Cracked' Mellor, if not two,[a]
That cannot vote for Fox.

Chorus – Come rally, &c.

The canting saints, who stamp and stare,
Do well deserve the stocks;
No man can bless what they profess
Who rail against a Fox.

Chorus – Come rally, &c.

The sturdy farmers all around,
And wives that scrub with mops,
Have all declared they are quite prepared
To come and work for Fox.

Chorus – Come rally, &c.

Brave Royton has got Sandy Lanes,
And Holdens, too, in flocks;
Here 'Jack Of Trumps' will get some thumps –
They'll win or die for Fox.

Chorus – Come rally, &c.

So let the day come when it may,
We'll curl his hoary locks,
Put on his tail, and trim his sail,
And give three cheers for Fox.

Chorus – Come rally, &c.   Grime, *Memory Sketches*, pp. 170–1.

[a] Brother Jonathan is off the new register, and Bendigo is a non-elector – one of those men that Mr. Heald tells us is too ignorant to vote. Printed by No Seaur Pie & Co., Old Yeeld Street.

FOX IS SURE TO GO.

(Tune: 'Henry Hunt'.)

We guess you heard the song of late,
Named 'Fox, it is No Go;'
Then let us all, both great and small,
A contradiction show.
For Fox he is the poor man's friend,
He keeps the taxes low;
He feeds the poor, at every door,
Then Fox is sure to Go.

Chorus –
With William Fox we'll go, we'll go,
With William Fox we'll go;
We'll show the blue daub Tory crew
That Fox is sure to go.

A red-haired fool, just come from school,
Who dwells within the town;
He now declares, and often swears,
He'll chase our good Fox down.
One British pound we'll lay the hound,
If he will make a match;
A polling race shall be the chase,
To try our Fox to catch.

Chorus – With William Fox we'll go, we'll go &c.

A bully great, who has of late,
Turned all his green to blue,
Now gives his votes to those cut-throats
Who were at Peterloo.
Then, Oldham Folks, don't take such jokes,
But on the polling day
Let this blue coat in vain cry out,
'Come deal exclusively.'

Chorus – With William Fox we'll go, we'll go, &c.

You Quakerman who lives at Mumps,
And spelks unbroken limbs;
See how he daubs his daddy's robes –
His green with blue he trims.
Then keep your bones from blue-dipt stones,
All you that for Fox,
For if you to this doctor go
He'll give you painful shocks.

Chorus – With William Fox we'll go, we'll go, &c.

In Oldham town there are such lots
Of Foxites to be found,
That won't give way, on the polling day,
But firmly stand their ground.
The Tories all, both great and small,
Have pates like wooden blocks;
Then who will vote for loggerheads,
While we have such a Fox?

Chorus – With William Fox we'll go, we'll go, &c.

The thinking men of Oldham town,
Who labour for their bread,
Say, by a host of dirty blues
They never will be led.
The King of Mumps, and all his trumps,
Need no longer preach;
No more we'll send a Tory fool
Who cannot make a speech.

Chorus – With William Fox we'll go, we'll go, &c.

Grime, *Memory Sketches*, pp. 143–4.

FOX IS SURE TO GO.

(Tune: 'Henry Hunt.')

I once met with a fancy beau – from Billingsgate he came –
His name was Lawyer Cobbett, a man well known to fame;
A smart M.P. he wished to be, so keen at legislation,
He swallowed all the Chartist points, just to gull the nation.

    Chorus –
    Come, rally lads, both Whigs and Rads, the Fox is sure to go,
    We'll wear the Cap of Liberty, and lay the Factions low.

The universal will of man he loudly did invoke,
The people laughed at all his talk, and thought it was a joke;
For Church and guts stuck in his throat till he was almost foaming,
Some thought he was a Puseyite, so sent him out a-roaming.

Chorus – Come, rally lads, &c.

He's often tried a silly dodge, thinking to catch a Fox,
But people saw his impudence, and gave the fool a box;
The Whigs and Rads united true, and soon put him in a flutter,
And left him freezing on the poll, to watch him stamp and stutter.

Chorus – Come, rally lads, &c.

So the Bishop's man looked pale and wan, his pluck began to fail,
They hissed him for a mongrel, and bid him turn his tail;
He's here again, just watch his pranks, he'll make a pretty show,
With blue and green he'll dance a jig, and jump Jim Crow.

Chorus – Come, rally lads, &c.

With Fox, the champion of our rights, we'll fight with might and main,
In spite of Alick's humbug we'll send him in again;
With Free Trade laws that give cheap bread, and freedom of the mind,
That Fox shall proudly cock his tail, and leave the hounds behind.

Chorus – Come, rally lads, &c.

Grime, *Memory Sketches*, pp. 141–2.

'NO GO', OR RADICALS TURNED TORIES.

(Tune: 'With Henry Hunt', &c.)

Come, Jack and Ned, let's have some talk
About these Oldham men;
It seems they've gone stark staring mad,
And jumped Jim Crow again.
I always thought that men of sense
(Alas! it is not so)
Would never waste their time and pence
To bawl and shout 'No Go'.

> Chorus –
> With Cobbett we will go, we'll go,
> For Duncuft we'll declare;
> When two-legged asses walk the streets,
> Lord, how the people stare.

Lord Derby sent his minions out
To sound the nation's will,
So Oldham lads joined in the rout
With voices loud and shrill.
To help the base 'Protective Band'
To tax again our bread;
To raise the rent of barren lad,
To fleece us till we're dead.

Chorus – With Cobbett we will go, we'll go, &c.

With canting cry and base intent,
A fox must be the chase;
A host of knaves whose hearts are lent –
Are seen to head the race.
When will the world just learn to think,
And prejudice o'erthrow?
Men of firm minds will never shrink,
Or fear the words 'No Go'.

Chorus – With Cobbett we will go, we'll go, &c.

When Hunt and Cobbett led the van,
With hearts and souls inspired;
When Paine preached up the 'Rights of Man',
And truth our bosom fired.
Repeal the laws that tax our bread,
Give human rights to all;
Our cause was then by patriots led,
Not by a noisy brawl.

Chorus – With Cobbett we will go, we'll go, &c.

Clogs with stumps then knew no Mumps,
Reform came from the heart;
And honest men, not Jack o'Trumps,
Then played a noble part.
The game is up, the world recedes,
And factions grind us low;
Lads with caps, and such like chaps,
Now bawl and shout 'No Go'.

Chorus – With Cobbett we will go, we'll go, &c.

'No go', ye little patriot band,
Who, in your country's cause,
Fought and struggled heart and hand
For just and equal laws.
'No go', the Tories rule the town,
And laugh your deeds to scorn;
'No go', the honest hearts have flown,
Your banners left forlorn.

Chorus – With Cobbett we will go, we'll go, &c.

Must science shed its lucid rays,
And genius spread its wings;
And Oldham's weather out its days
In Alick's leading strings?
It cannot be, the mind is free,
And this the world shall know –
That faction's claws and tyrants' laws
Henceforth shall be 'No Go'.

Chorus – With Cobbett we will go, we'll go, &c.

Grime, Memory Sketches, pp. 123–4.

John Knight at reform dinner, Manchester 1819

The great fundamental Principle of Christianity and also of Equity and Justice, is, 'do unto others, as ye would that others should do unto you'. The universal observance of this one rule, would put an end to all our disputes and contentions, and we should henceforth dwell together in unity. No one would attempt to be an extortioner, exacting more than was justly due, and whatever was justly due, no one would designingly withhold. No one, (like the Egyptian Task Masters) impose heavy Burdens upon other Men's shoulders, which they themselves would not touch with one of their fingers. No one would attempt to evade the performance of his share of the task; nor require any indulgence or gratification for himself, which he would not allow to every other; Industry and frugality are known to be the original sources of all Property. Those, and those alone, who produce more than they consume, can accumulate property; but we need only look at our buildings, our roads, our canals, our fences and our various machines, implements, utensils, furniture, &c. to be convinced that more, much more, has been produced than has been consumed: notwithstanding, the vast numbers who never applied themselves to productive labour, some of whom have by luxury consumed the produce of our the labour of *many*: besides the vast quantity of property consumed by War; Hence we clearly see, that if Mankind lived economically (not starved or half fed) their task of manual labour would be easy, and their burden light. When then is reason, that the task of English labourers is so very hard, and their supplies of Food, Raiment, &c. so very scanty? The reason is simply this, there are so many who produce little or nothing, and consume so much, for whatever any man *consumes* more than he *produces*, whether he be a King, a Duke, a Lord, a Bishop, a Priest, a Lawyer, or whatever else, must be produced by others; and consequently increase the daily task of the remainder.

What reason can be assigned why all these classes should, thus live in *ease* and *luxury*, at your expense? how can you have been so blind or infatuated as to permit such a state of things to take place? or how could they, being Christians, ever attempt so unchristianly to impose on their fellow creatures. How could they, being Christians, forget, that it was their duty to 'do as they would be done unto'. When the Scripture says, 'six days shalt thou labour', are Kings, Princes, Lords, or any other denomination exempted from this obligation: Again when Christ says, 'Take no thought *what* ye shall eat, or what ye shall drink, or where withal ye shall be clothed.' Does he here add, except Princes, Prelates, Priests &c. you find no such words annexed; and therefore there is no Scriptural Authority that gives them these exclusive Privileges; And when Christ says, 'Whatsoever ye would that men should do unto you, do ye even so unto them', does he here make any exceptions in favour of those gentry? we find none.

With these principles in view, let us look to the conduct of several descriptions of *men*, yes men, for Princes, Prelates and Priests are *but* men; and equally subject to the precepts and commands of God, as other men.

In the very first chapter of our sacred Scriptures we read that God (not man) created the Heaven and Earth. And God said, 'let the Earth bring forth Grass, the Herb yielding Seed, and the fruit tree yielding Fruit'. And God made the Beast of the Earth, and Cattle and everything that creepeth upon the face of the Earth. And God created Man, male and female, and said unto them be fruitful and replenish the Earth and subdue it. And have dominion over 'the fish of the Sea, the fowl of the air, and over every living thing that moveth upon the Earth. Behold I have given you every herb, upon the face of the Earth, and every Tree yielding fruit, to you it shall be for meat.

And to every Beast of the Earth, to every Fowl of the air, and to everything that creepeth upon the Earth, I have given every green herb for meat.' And in the 9th chapter of Genesis we read that God Blessed Noah and his Sons, and said unto *them*, (i.e. to all of them, and not, like Parson Malthus, to the rich only) 'be fruitful and multiply and replenish the Earth. Every moving thing that liveth, shall be meat for you: even as the green herb I have given you all things.' Thus we see that the Earth with all the minerals therein, and cattle and vegetables thereon, were made and given to mankind, without money and without price, long before either our *feudal* or Borough mongering systems were thought of. We are further informed 1 Kings

4ch. 25 ver. that Judah and Israel dwelt safely every man under his own Vine and under his Fig-tree, all the days of Solomon, whose death is stated to have taken place 3029 years after the Creation, and only 2794 years ago: so that it is plain as words can make it, that the Earth, or the Land, was not then engrossed by a few individuals, who relieved themselves from labour, and enabled themselves to live in luxury, and even heap riches at the same time, by *letting* for money or rent portions of that land, which God had created and given to all, without exception, for their common benefit. Therefore we need not be surprised at the saying of David, Solomon's father, 'I have been young and now am old, yet I never saw the righteous forsaken, nor his seed begging their bread.'

If then God be the Creator of the Earth, and whatever is therein and thereon, and also the common parent of mankind, what can exceed the presumption of those individuals who lay claim to large domains, *engrossing* the gifts of nature, and of God; and thereby depriving their fellow creatures of their just and necessary share; and what says the Scriptures to persons? 'Woe unto him that addeth House to House', and Field to Field, till there be no place. If any man was to leave a large estate and many children, and should bequeath this estate to all his children equally, what would be thought of any one of them who should say to the remainder, you shall have none of this land unless you will pay me such or such sum: would he not be deemed a rascal; and would he be doing unto his Brother as he would wish to be done unto? Can any one consciously say yes? I think not. Besides which of our engrossers of land, would, with his own hands, reap a crop of corn for the crop itself? and if not, with what face can they require any man to plow [*sic*], sow and reap; and pay them a sum for the use of the field besides; or would they, in such case, be doing as they would be done unto? I think you will answer not!!

Further history informs us that in the 11th century, the lands of the Kingdom, were all taken from the King, on condition of furnishing, arming and maintaining, Soldiers, in time of War, in proportion to the lands they held in this way they were to furnish (when required) about 62 thousand men. Shortly after all this, these military tenants grew weary of the service, and agreed with the King to pay him a certain Sum of Money in lieu of this military service, and the King was thenceforth to pay the Soldiers himself: this agreement was solely confined to the King and landholders, no one else had any hand in the contract and therefore they had no right to be injured by such contract. At this time those who held no land, had nothing to do with military service, and no contract made between the King and his tenantry, had a right, to throw the burden of the Army upon those who held no land to support it. If the King made an imprudent contract with his Nobles, so that it was impossible for him to fulfil it, this ought only to have nullified or set aside that contract, and the service should again have fallen upon those who had the means of supporting it, namely those who held the land. But setting all things side, and even giving up the popular claim to the land: admitting it to belong to those who now claim it, are they doing as they would be done unto, in EXACTING for the use of this land, thousands of tens of thousands of pounds per annum, thus enabling themselves and families to lead idle, useless and luxurious lives, being clothed not merely in purple and fine linen, and farring [*sic*] sumptuously every day, but clad in silk, in every costly, exotic of Fur, Feather, &c. and also riding in carriages. In order to maintain which extravagance, their fellow creatures are subject to double labour and reduced to half a comfortable maintenance. Supposing those men to be stewards, as our Clergy sometimes represent them, how will their accounts stand when they come to appear before the judge of all Earth, who is no respector of persons, from whom no secrets are hid, and who will reward every man according to his works, according to the deeds done in the body. Again, I will ask, how will our Members of the House of Commons answer when they are asked WHY they have granted thousands and sometimes tens of thousands of pounds annually for the service and maintenance of individuals, when at the same time they have turned a deaf ear to the application of workmen for protection and relief, whose individual earnings have not been £30 a year. How will our Bishops and superior Clergy answer, when they are called upon to show, why they have recommended submission to such an Iniquitous state of Society: and why they themselves have exacted the last farthing from the poor, to make up their hundreds of thousands per annum.

How will the Magistrates answer, for sending men to prison, for attempting to advance their wages, until they could earn 12s per week, when some of those Magistrates were taking £30 a week, from the impoverished public, for their own services. All these evils, and many more arise solely from having a House of Legislators composed of great Landed Proprietors, and their influence forming a great Majority in the Commons. The Ministers are the Agents or Tools of

Landed Proprietors, the Bishops, the Priests, the Judges, the Magistrates, and all the inferior Peace Officers, and also the Military are merely their instruments.

On the purification of the House of Commons, by the restoration of Universal Suffrage, Annual Parliaments, election by Ballot, and filling the House of Commons with WISE and VIRTUOUS labourers, depends the future welfare of the commonalty of Great Britain and Ireland.

Taken from *Wardle's Manchester Observer*, 6 January 1819, p. 20.

Notes

A NOTE ON SOURCES

It will be evident from the notes that I have found the Butterworth manuscripts at Oldham Local Studies Library an especially rich source. These manuscripts represent Butterworth's personal diary of events in and around Oldham, from which he culled many of his reports to the local and national press. However, not only are the manuscripts often illegible, but the entrances are irregularly dated, consequently it has not always been possible to provide an exact date for references. In these cases the month and year alone are cited.

ABBREVIATIONS

OLSL   Oldham Local Studies Library
EDRO   East Devon Record Office
WDRO   West Devon Record Office
BPL   Boston Public Library
BBMA   Boston Borough Municipal Archives
ESRO   East Sussex Record Office

INTRODUCTION

1 See, for example, Jean François Lyotard, *The Postmodern Condition: A Report on Knowledge* (Minneapolis, 1979); Francis Fukuyama, *The End of History and the Last Man* (London, 1992).

2 Although postmodernism is one of those nebulous terms which conflates a kaleidoscope of intellectual trends across a range of disciplines, it does usefully categorise a growing body of work within critical theory which challenges the Enlightenment model of rationality by emphasising the discursive construction of the 'real' and the consequent disintegration of both the autonomous unified (centred) self and its grand narratives of emancipation. For useful introductions see Hal Foster (ed.), *Postmodern Culture* (London, 1985); E. Ann Kaplan, *Postmodernism and its Discontents. Theories, Practices* (London, 1988); Madan Sarup, *An Introductory Guide to Post-Structuralism and Postmodernism* (London, 1988); Steve Connor, *Postmodern Culture: An Introduction to Theories of the Contemporary* (London, 1989).

3 The best genealogies and summaries of this work are Lynn Hunt (ed.), *The New Cultural History* (Los Angeles, 1989); Geoff Eley, 'Is All The World A text? From Social History to the History of Society Two Decades Later', in T. MacDonald (ed.), *The Historical Turn in the Human Sciences* (Ann Arbor, 1992). For the suspicion towards the postmodern linguistic turn see the debate between Lawrence Stone, Catriona Kelly, Gabrielle M. Spiegel, and Patrick Joyce on 'History and Post-Modernism', *Past and Present*, 131 (1991), 217–18; *Past and Present*, 133 (1991), 204–9; *Past and Present*, 135 (1992), 189–208.

4 L. B. Namier, *The Structure of Politics at the Accession of George III* (London, 1929); Namier and J. Brooke (ed.), *The House of Commons, 1754–1790*, 3 vols. (London, 1964); M. J. Cowling, *1867: Disraeli, Gladstone and Revolution* (Cambridge, 1967); A. B. Cooke and J. R. Vincent, *The Governing Passion* (Brighton, 1974); N. Gash, *Aristocracy and People* (London, 1979); M. Bentley, *Politics Without Democracy, 1815–1914* (London, 1984). For a useful analysis of this tradition see R. Brent, 'Butterfield's Tories: "High Politics" and the writing of Modern British Political History', *Historical Journal*, 30, 4 (1987), 943–54. Here, and in what follows, it has been necessary to analyse often diverse historiographical traditions, whether tory, liberal, social democratic or marxist, as single coherent narratives.

5 D. C. Moore, *The Politics of Deference: A Study of the Mid Nineteenth-Century Political System* (Brighton, 1976); Cowling, *Disraeli, Gladstone and Revolution*.

6 Cooke and Vincent, *The Governing Passion*.

7 J. C. D. Clark, *English Society, 1688–1832: Ideology, Social Structure and Political Practice during the Ancien Regime* (Cambridge, 1985); Clark, *Revolution and Rebellion: State and Society in England in the Seventeenth and Eighteenth Centuries* (Cambridge, 1986); and 'Class Formation in England, 1750–1850', paper presented to Manchester Historical Association, January 1992.

8 Unfortunately responses to Clark's work, especially from the left, have often manifested themselves in the complacent form of doggedly repeating old maxims. An exception is Joanna Innes, 'Jonathan Clark, Social History and England's "Ancien Regime"', *Past and Present*, 115 (May 1987), 165–200.

9 There are (at least) two generations within this tradition, those whom Namier reacted against, and those who in turn reacted against Namier. For a representative sample see H. Jephson, *The Platform: Its Rise and Progress*, 2 vols. (London, 1892); M. Ostrogorski, *Democracy and the Organisation of Political Parties*, 2 vols. (London, 1902); C. Seymour, *Electoral Reform in England and Wales* (New Haven, 1915); G. S. Veitch, *The Genesis of Parliamentary Reform* (London, 1913); H. J. Hanham, *The Reformed Electoral System in Great Britain, 1832–1914* (London, 1968); J. A. Cannon, *Parliamentary Reform, 1640–1832* (Cambridge 1972); D. Fraser, *Urban Politics in Victorian England: The Structure of Politics in Victorian Cities*

(London, 1976); T. J. Nossiter, *Influence, Opinion and Political Idioms in Reformed England: Case Studies from the North-East* (Brighton, 1975); B. W. Hill, *British Parliamentary Parties, 1742–1832* (London, 1985).

10 A narrative which emerged from the work of such figures as A. S. A. Briggs, Henry Pelling, Jack Plumb, and Peter Clarke. Recent examples include John Brewer, *Party Ideology and Popular Politics at the Accession of George III* (Cambridge, 1976); Linda Colley, *In Defiance of Oligarchy: The Tory Party, 1714–1760* (Cambridge, 1982); Frank O'Gorman, *Voters, Patrons and Parties. The Unreformed Electoral System of Hanoverian England 1734–1832* (Oxford, 1989); Nicholas Rogers, *Whigs and Cities. Popular Politics in the Age of Walpole and Pitt* (Oxford, 1989); Eckhart Hellmuth (ed.)., *The Transformation of Political Culture: England and Germany in the Late Eighteenth Century* (Oxford, 1990).

11 E. P. Thompson, *The Making of the English Working Class*, (London, 1968 edn). Thompson elaborated his thesis elsewhere, see his, 'Eighteenth Century English Society: Class Struggle Without Class?' *Social History* 3 (1978), 133–65; 'Patrician Society and Plebian Culture', *Journal of Social History*, 7 (1974): and 'The Moral Economy of the English Crowd in the Eighteenth Century' *Past and Present*, 50, (1971), 76–131.

12 Useful summaries of these criticisms are to be found in Patrick Joyce (ed.), *The Historical Meanings of Work* (Cambridge, 1987); H. J. Kaye and K. McClelland (eds.), *E. P. Thompson: Critical Perspectives* (Cambridge, 1990).

13 William H. Sewell Jr., *Work and Revolution in France: The Language of Labour from the Old Regime to 1848* (Cambridge, 1980); Gareth Stedman Jones, *Languages of Class: Studies in English Working Class History 1832–1982* (Cambridge, 1983); W. M. Reddy, *The Rise of Market Culture: The Textile Trade and French Society 1750–1900* (Cambridge, 1984); Joan W. Scott, *Gender and the Politics of History* (London, 1988).

14 Robert Gray, 'The Deconstruction of the English Working Class', *Social History*, 11 (1986), 363–73; Joan W. Scott, 'On Language, Gender, and Working Class History', *International Labor and Working-Class History*, 31 (1987), 1–13; James Epstein, 'Rethinking the Categories of Working-Class History', *Labour/Le Travail*, 18, (1988); Patrick Joyce, *Visions of the People: Industrial England and the Question of Class, c. 1848–1914* (Cambridge, 1991). Others, however, have resisted change, see J. Foster, 'The Declassing of Language', *New Left Review*, 150, (1985), 29–45; N. Kirk, 'In Defence of Class: A Critique of Recent Revisionist Writing upon the Nineteenth Century English Working Class', *International Review of Social History*, 32, (1987) 2–47.

15 Joyce, *Visions of the People*; Scott, *Gender and the Politics of History*. Little work has yet been done on ethnic difference within this language although Nicola Richards' 'Stories of Belonging: National Identity in England and Scotland, 1788–1822', Ph.D. thesis (Manchester, forthcoming) promises to be an important contribution. See also Linda Colley, *Britons. Forging the Nation 1707–1837* (London, 1992).

16 Sally Alexander, 'Women, Class and Sexual Difference', *History Workshop Journal*, 17 (1984), 125–49; Terry Lovell (ed.), *British Feminist Thought: A Reader* (Oxford, 1990), 21ff.

17 Denise Riley, '*Am I That Name?' Feminism and the Category of Women in History* (Minneapolis, 1988); Scott, *Gender and the Politics of History*; and her 'The Evidence of Experience', *Critical Inquiry*, 17 (1991), 773–97.

18 Joan B. Landes, *Women and the Public Sphere in the Age of the French Revolution* (Ithaca, 1988). See also Jean Bethke Elshtain, *Public Man, Private Woman: Women in Social and Political Thought* (Princeton, 1981); Carole Pateman, *The Disorder of Women: Democracy, Feminism and Political Theory* (Cambridge, 1989); Catherine Hall, 'Private Persons versus Public Someones: Class, Gender and Politics in England, 1780–1850', in C. Steedman, C. Urwin and V. Walkerdine (eds.), *Language, Gender and Childhood* (London, 1985), pp. 10–33; Dorinda Outram, *The Body and the French Revolution: Sex, Class and Political Culture* (London, 1985); Harriet B. Applewhite and Darline G. Levy (eds.), *Women and Politics in the Age of the Democratic Revolution* (Ann Arbor, 1990).

19 Eley, 'Is All The World A Text?'; Joyce, 'History and Post-Modernism: Social Identity as Narrative in Nineteenth-Century England', *Democratic Subjects: Studies in the History of Identity in Nineteenth-Century England* (forthcoming).

20 Rogers, *Whigs and Cities*; O'Gorman, *Voters, Patrons and Parties*; Hellmuth (ed.), *The Transformation of Political Culture*; Joyce, *Visions of the People*; E. Biagini and A. Reid (eds.), *Currents of Radicalism: Popular Radicalism, Organised Labour and Party Politics in Britain, 1850–1914* (Cambridge, 1991); Jon Lawrence, 'Popular Radicalism and the Socialist Revival in Britain' *Journal of British Studies*, 31, 2 (1992), 163–86.

21 This idea owes much to the work of Jurgen Habermas, see his 'The Public Sphere: An Encyclopedia Article', *New German Critique* 1 (1974), 49–55; and *The Structural Transformation of the Public Sphere: An Inquiry into a Category of Bourgeois Society*, trans. T. Burger, (London, 1989). For some reflections on the utility of Habermas' model for modern British history see Eley, 'Rethinking the Political: Social History and Political Culture in Eighteenth- and Nineteenth-Century Britain', *Archiv Für Sozialgeschichte*, 21 (1981), 431–2; John Brewer, 'Public and Private: The Shifting of the Cultural Sphere in Eighteenth-Century England', paper presented to 'The Public Sphere in Eighteenth-Century Europe' conference, University of Exeter, May 1992.

22 The influence of much of this work has been Stedman Jones' 'Rethinking Chartism' and Ross McKibbin's, 'Class and Conventional Wisdom: the Conservative Party and the "Public" in Inter-War Britain' in his *Ideologies of Class: Social Relations in Britain, 1880–1950* (Oxford, 1990). See, for instance, albeit in a different key, Peter Mandler, *Aristocratic Government in the Age of Reform: Whigs and Liberals, 1830–1852* (Oxford, 1990).

23 A task begun by Joyce, *Visions of the People*.

24 Only Lewes has received any recent sort of historical attention, see John A. Phillips, *Electoral Behaviour in Unreformed England, 1761–1802* (Princeton, 1982); C. E. Brent, 'The Immediate Impact of the Second Reform Act on a Southern County Town: Voting Patterns at Lewes Borough in 1865 and 1868', *Southern History*, 2 (1980), 129–77. Otherwise we are still dependent on W. B. Mills, *Parliamentary History of the Borough of Lewes, 1795–1885* (London, 1908); H. F. Whitfield, *Plymouth and Devonport: In Times of War and Peace* (Plymouth, 1900); R. Newton, *Victorian Exeter, 1837–1914* (Leicester, 1968).

25 There has, however, been much debate about the scale of Oldham's industrialisation, see: J. Foster, *Class Struggle and the Industrial Revolution: Early Industrial Capitalism in Three English Towns* (London, 1974); D. S. Gadian, 'Class Consciousness in Oldham and Other North-West Industrial Towns 1830–50', *Historical Journal*, 21 (1978), 161–72; R. Sykes, 'Some Aspects of Working-Class Consciousness in Oldham 1830–42', *Historical Journal*, 23 (1980), 167–79. On East London's demography and economy see Gareth Stedman Jones, *Outcast London: A Study in the Relationship between Classes in Victorian London* (Oxford, 1971); Raphael Samuel, 'The Workshop of the World: Steam Power and Hand Technology in Mid-Victorian Britain', *History Workshop Journal*, 3 (1977); and 'Comers and Goers', in H. J. Dyos and M. Wolff (eds.), *The Victorian City: Images and Realities*, 1 (London, 1973), pp. 123–60.

I POWER LEGISLATED: THE STRUCTURE OF OFFICIAL POLITICS

1 Carole Pateman has argued that such exclusive definitions of property also entailed the notion of men's sexual ownership or property of women's bodies. Carole Pateman, *The Sexual Contract* (Cambridge, 1988). For general analyses of the deliberate exclusion of women in classical western liberal political theory see Elizabeth Fox Genovese, 'Property and Patriarchy in Classical Bourgeois Political Theory', *Radical History Review*, 1977, 36–59; Susan M. Okin, *Women in Western Political Thought* (Princeton, 1979); Jean Bethke Elshtain, *Public Man, Private Woman: Women in Social and Political Though* (Princeton, 1981); Anne Phillips, *Engendering Democracy* (Cambridge, 1991). For a specific historical treatment of this process in England see Hall, 'Private Persons versus Public Someones'.

2 To do so would require several books. See, for examples: Sidney and Beatrice Webb, *English Local Government from the Revolution to the Municipal Corporations Act: The Parish and the County* (London, 1963); Bryan Keith Lucas, *English Local Government Franchise* (Oxford, 1952); E. P. Hennock, *Fit and Proper Persons: Ideal and Reality in Nineteenth-Century Urban Government* (London, 1973); R. J. Olney, *Rural Society and County Government in Nineteenth-Century Lincolnshire* (Lincoln, 1979); Fraser, *Urban Politics in Victorian England*; Phillips, *Electoral Behaviour in Unreformed England*; John Garrard, *Leadership and Power in Victorian Industrial Towns, 1830–1880*

(Manchester, 1983); John Davis, *Reforming London: The London Govern-ment Problem, 1855–1900* (Oxford, 1988); O'Gorman, *Voters, Patrons and Parties*; John Prest, *Liberty and Locality: Parliament, Permissive Legislation and Ratepayers' Democracies in the Nineteenth Century* (Oxford, 1990).

3 With the notable exceptions of those listed above in n. 2.

4 Webbs, *English Local Government*, p. 5.

5 No historiographical work has analysed the official structure of vestry politics in any detail. The most useful accounts are Webbs, *English Local Government*; Keith Lucas, *English Local Government Franchise*; Fraser, *Urban Politics in Victorian England*; Garrard, *Leadership and Power in Victorian Towns*.

6 For a report of a vestry meeting of 2,000, 'a more numerous vestry meeting was scarcely ever held', see Butterworth MSS., August 1832.

7 *Manchester Guardian*, 3 November 1821, p. 3; *Morning Advertiser*, 28 March 1829, p. 3.

8 Keith Lucas, *English Local Government Franchise*, p. 13.

9 *Ibid.*, p. 165.

10 At a vestry poll in 1832 to elect a constable at Royton, under the Sturges Bourne regulations, women recorded votes for both candidates. See Butterworth MSS., 2 October 1832.

11 For the use of Sturges Bourne's system of plural voting in the permissive legislation of 1828–30, and in the procedure of the 1834 Poor Law Amendment Act to elect Guardians see Prest, *Liberty and Locality*, pp. 10–11, 15. Prest tends, however, to set up too great a dichotomy between nineteenth-century Benthamite rationalisation and the preceding stress on common law and permissive legislation. See David Lieberman, *The Province of Legislation Determined: Legal Theory in Eighteenth Century Britain* (Cambridge, 1990).

12 Keith Lucas, *English Local Government Franchise*, pp. 23–4.

13 *Ibid.*, pp. 25–6. Keith Lucas, Fraser, Davis, and Prest have all unfairly portrayed Toulmin Smith (1816–69) as a nostalgic Tory antiquarian, when, in fact, his campaign against centralisation was part of a long radical tradition which championed the rights of freeborn English-men to local self-government, as we shall see in chapter 5. Although his 'Anti-Centralization Union,' established in 1854, lasted for only 3 years, Toulmin Smith remained best known for his histories of constitutional law, and his support for Hungarian liberty in the late 1840s. In 1861 he defended the Kossuth against a charge of fraud by the Austrian government. See Keith Lucas, *English Local Government Franchise*, pp. 25–6; Fraser, *Urban Politics in Victorian England*, pp. 25–8; Davis, *Reforming London*, p. 10. See also *DNB*, LIII, pp. 94–5.

14 See Keith Lucas, *English Local Government Franchise*, pp. 120–1; Prest, *Liberty and Locality*, p. 11, esp. n. 16; chapter 3 below, p. 155.

15 For more detail on parochial reform campaigns of the 1820s, as well as those of the 1830s and 1850s, see chapter 5 below, pp. 200–3.

16 The secret ballot was not introduced at parliamentary level until 1872,

while women remained disenfranchised until 1918, although unmarried female householders were granted the municipal franchise in 1869.

17 The only time a vote was taken on the bill only 104 members passed through the lobby. See *Parliamentary Debates, 3rd Series* vii, pp. 879–91. Perhaps, as the Act was subsequently adopted in only 5 metropolitan parishes and 8 elsewhere, its radical implications were not lost on contemporaries.

18 Prest, *Liberty and Locality*, p. 11.

19 *Ibid.*, p. 11.

20 *Ibid.*, pp. 19–20.

21 V. Smith (ed.), *The Town Book of Lewes, 1702–1837*, I (Lewes, 1976), p. 103.

22 V. Smith (ed.), *The Town Book of Lewes, 1837–1901*, II (Lewes, 1976), p. 34 (my emphasis).

23 See T. W. Horsfield, *The History and Antiquities of Lewes*, II (Lewes, 1837), for a reprint of the Local Act (46th George 3rd).

24 *Sussex Weekly Advertiser*, 7 January 1845, p. 2.

25 Smith, *The Town Book of Lewes*, I, p. 300.

26 J. R. Somers Vine, *English Municipal Institutions: Their Growth and Development from 1835 to 1879* (London, 1879), p. 116.

27 The percentage of adult males is calculated by assuming that in the nineteenth century adult males accounted for 25.5 % of the population. See Phillips, *Electoral Behaviour in Unreformed England*, pp. 202–3.

28 Keith Lucas, *English Local Government Franchise*, p. 63.

29 Hartley Bateson, *A History of Oldham* (Oldham, 1949), pp. 125–8.

30 By 1866, 1,418 (61.2 %) of Oldham's 2,316 parliamentary voters were also municipal voters. The figures for Boston and Oldham's municipal electorates as a percentage of their populations were similar to those found by E. P. Hennock in Birmingham, Maidstone, Ipswich, and Leeds. See Hennock, *Fit and Proper Persons*, p. 12.

31 'Use of Small Tenements Act', *Parliamentary Papers, 1867*, (136) LVI, 449.

32 See Olney, *Rural Society and County Government*, pp. 5–13; B. D. Hayes, 'Politics in Norfolk, 1750–1832', Ph.D (Cambridge, 1958); Keith Lucas, *Local Government Franchise*, pp. 82–115.

33 Olney, *Rural Society and County Government*, pp. 98–104; Keith Lucas, *The Unreformed Local Government System* (London, 1980), pp. 48–50.

34 Keith Lucas, *English Local Government Franchise*, p. 84.

35 See Phillips, *Electoral Behaviour in Unreformed England*; O'Gorman, *Voters, Patrons and Parties*.

36 R. G. Thorne (ed.), *History of Parliament. The House of Commons, 1790–1820*, I (London, 1986), pp. 245–7. Phillips has even argued that the creation of freemen in this way was a highly effective means of mobilising political supporters. See Phillips, *Electoral Behaviour in Unreformed England*, p. 75.

37 L. B. Namier and J. Brooke (eds), *History of Parliament. The House of Commons, 1754–90*, I, (London, 1964), pp. 324–5. R. G. Thorne's con-

tention that Boston's electorate consisted of 'about 500' freemen voters between 1790 and 1820 presents a static picture of Boston's electorate which is difficult to square with the evidence. See Thorne (ed.), *The House of Commons, 1790–1820,* I, p. 245.

38 Phillips, *Electoral Behaviour in Unreformed England,* p. 88. Namier and Brooke slightly over-estimate the size of Lewes' electorate at approximately 250 people from the 4 contests between 1754 and 1790. Namier and Brooke, *The House of Commons, 1754–90,* I, pp. 393–5.

39 O'Gorman, *Voters, Patrons and Parties,* p. 59.

40 Namier and Brooke, *The House of Commons, 1754–90,* I, p. 249. Note that the figure for 1818 is the number of voters, not votes, polled. See *Trewmans Flying Post,* 2 July 1818, p. 4.

41 See Phillips, *Electoral Behaviour in Unreformed England,* pp. 190–3, 320–1; O'Gorman, *Voters, Patrons and Parties,* pp. 199–207.

42 It is, for instance, recognised that the distinction between categories like skilled craftsmen and semi/unskilled labourers rests on a materialist definition of 'skill' that denies the often flexible, culturally created, notions of skill. See Joyce (ed.), *The Historical Meanings of Work.*

43 See, for example, Cannon, *Parliamentary Reform, 1640–1832*; M. Brock, *The Great Reform Act* (London, 1973); Moore, *The Politics of Deference.*

44 Over 42 per cent of South Devon's electorate in 1835 and 1867 qualified as leaseholders, copyholders and tenants-at-will, officeholders, trustees, and mortgagees. See 'Returns of Counties, Cities and Boroughs,' *Parliamentary Papers,* 1866 (3626), LVII, 215.

45 Somers Vine, *English Municipal Institutions,* pp. 76–83.

46 Hall, 'Private Persons versus Public Someones.'

47 The figures for Tower Hamlets are infamously treacherous because of the size and mobility of its population. See Stedman Jones, *Outcast London*; Samuel, 'Comers and Goers'. For a more detailed analysis of the electorate of Tower Hamlets and other metropolitan boroughs see A. D. Taylor, 'Modes of Political Expression and Working Class Politics: The Manchester and London Examples, 1850–1880', Ph.D. (Manchester, 1992).

48 C. R. Dod, *Electoral Facts from 1832–52. Impartially Stated* (Brighton, 1972), p. 316.

49 Keith Lucas, *English Local Government Franchise,* p. 67.

50 'Number of £10 Compounded Householders in Boroughs', *Parliamentary Papers,* 1867 (305) LVI, 463.

51 'Borough Electors (Working Classes) Return', *Parliamentary Papers,* 1866 (17) LVIII, 47.

2 POWER IMAGINED: THE CULTURE OF OFFICIAL POLITICS

1 Lynn Hunt, *Politics, Culture and Class in the French Revolution* (Berkeley, 1984), p. 54.

2 There remains little work on the ceremonial calendar and symbolic repertoire of official political culture. For notable exceptions, see E.

Hammerton and D. Cannadine, 'Conflict and Consensus on a Cer-
emonial Occasion: The Diamond Jubilee in Cambridge 1897', *Historical Journal*, 24 (1981), 111–46; Cannadine, 'The Transformation of Civic Ritual in Modern Britain: The Colchester Oyster Feast', *Past and Present*, 94 (1982), 107–130; Cannadine, 'The Context, Performance and Meaning of Ritual: The British Monarchy and the "Invention of Tradition"', *c.* 1820–1977', in E. Hobsbawm and T. Ranger (eds.), *The Invention of Tradition* (Cambridge, 1983), pp. 101–64; L. Colley, 'The Apotheosis of George III: Loyalty, Royalty and the British Nation', *Past and Present*, 102 (1984), 93–129; William M. Kuhn, 'Ceremony and Politics: The British Monarchy 1871–1872', *Journal of British Studies*, 26 (1987), 133–62; F. O'Gorman, 'The Social Meaning of Elections: Campaign Rituals and Ceremonies in England during the Eighteenth and Nineteenth Centuries', *Past and Present*, 135 (1992), 79–115.

3 See for examples of this literature Emile Durkheim, *The Elementary Forms of Religious Life*, trans. J. W. Swain, (London, 1915); Victor Turner, *The Ritual Process: Structure and Anti-Structure* (London, 1969); Stephen Lukes, 'Political Ritual and Social Integration', in his *Essays in Social Theory* (London, 1977), pp. 63–73; R. Bocock, *Ritual in Industrial Society* (London, 1974); Sean Wilentz (ed.), *Rites of Power: Symbolism, Ritual and Politics Since the Middle Ages* (Philadelphia, 1985); David Cannadine and Simon Price (eds.), *Rituals of Royalty: Power and Ceremonial in Traditional Societies* (Cambridge, 1987); Tom Nairn, *The Enchanted Glass: Britain and its Monarchy* (London, 1988). For approaches more similar to my own see David I. Kertzer, *Ritual Politics and Power* (Yale, 1988); Mona Ozouf, *Festivals and Revolution: France 1789–1799* (Harvard, 1988).

4 P. Bailey, *Leisure and Class in Victorian England* (London, 1978); H. Cunningham, *Leisure in the Industrial Revolution* (London, 1980); E. and S. Yeo (eds.), *Popular Culture and Class Conflict* (Brighton, 1981); R. D. Storch, *Popular Culture and Custom in Nineteenth-Century England* (London, 1982); H. J. Dyos and J. Wolff (eds.), *The Victorian City: Images and Realities*, 2 vols (London, 1972); Fraser, *Urban Politics in Victorian England*, pp. 154–77; P. Waller, *Town, City and Nation, 1850–1914* (London, 1983); Peter Borsay, *The English Urban Renaissance: Culture and Society in the Provincial Town, 1660–1770* (Oxford, 1989); Mark Girouard, *Cities and People: A Social and Architectural History* (1989); and his *The English Town* (Yale, 1990).

5 The others were Bethnal Green Town Hall (1852), St George-in-the-East Vestry Hall (1860–2), Wapping Vestry Hall (1863), Hackney Town Hall (1864–6), Stoke Newington Vestry Hall (1866), Shoreditch Vestry Hall (1867–8), Poplar Public Offices (1869). See Colin Cunningham, *Victorian and Edwardian Town Halls* (London, 1981), pp. 252–99.

6 A. Briggs, *Victorian Cities* (London, 1968), p. 159.

7 Cunningham, *Victorian and Edwardian Town Halls*; C. Dellheim, *The Face of the Past: The Preservation of the Medieval Inheritance in Victorian England* (Cambridge, 1982).

8 Cunningham, *Victorian and Edwardian Town Halls*, p. 119.

9 See 'Contracts for Town Hall, 1842', OLSL.
10 *Manchester Gazette*, 1 March 1828, p. 3; Butterworth MSS., 20 February 1835; Bateson, *A History of Oldham*, pp. 114–17. For opposition to the proposal to build a new town hall in Leicester see Fraser, *Urban Politics in Victorian England*, pp. 167–9.
11 *The Oldham Chronical*, 2 September 1865, p. 3.
12 *The Western Times*, 26 October 1861, p. 6.
13 *The Lincolnshire Guardian News*, 11 October 1862, p. 4.
14 *The Western Times*, 26 October 1861, p. 6.
15 Cunningham, *Victorian and Edwardian Town Halls*, pp. 252–99.
16 Bateson, *A History of Oldham*, pp. 149–50.
17 In one of the few accounts we have of vestry politics Derek Fraser has written of the 'beer garden atmosphere' where 'rational argument was at a low premium'. Fraser, *Urban Politics in Victorian England*, pp. 26–7.
18 Smith (ed.), *The Town Book of Lewes 1702–1901*, 2 vols.
19 *The Manchester Observer*, 20 February 1819, p. 475.
20 Henry Jephson, *The Platform: Its Rise and Progress*, 1 (London, 1892), pp. 508–9.
21 *Flindell's Western Luminary*, 16 March 1813, p. 12.
22 See, for example, the Devon county meeting called to discuss the agricultural distress of 1822, when, although the reformers managed to pass a 'riding' amendment advocating parliamentary reform, the signatories of the petition were allowed to disassociate themselves from the amendment if they wished. See *The Alfred*, 5 February 1822, p. 2.
23 *The Manchester Guardian*, 3 November 1821, p. 3; *Morning Advertiser*, 28 March 1839, p. 3.
24 *The Sussex Weekly Advertiser*, 18 March 1811, p. 3.
25 Butterworth MSS., 10 May 1830.
26 *The Boston Gazette*, 20 September 1831, p. 2; *The Boston Herald*, 26 March 1839, p. 3.
27 *The Sussex Weekly Advertiser*, 21 November 1843, p. 2.
28 *The Morning Advertiser*, 20 December 1842, p. 3.
29 Butterworth MSS., 3 and 19 October 1832.
30 Jephson, *The Platform: Its Rise and Progress*, 1, p. 575.
31 *The Boston Gazette*, 5 May 1829, pp. 2–3.
32 *The Boston Gazette*, 5 January 1836, p. 2.
33 Kertzer, *Ritual Politics and Power*, p. 42.
34 *The Oldham Chronicle*, 18 November 1854, p. 3.
35 Bateson, *A History of Oldham*, p. 128.
36 Hunt, *Politics, Culture and Class in the French Revolution*, p. 54.
37 *The Boston Herald*, 30 May 1837, p. 3.
38 Bateson, *A History of Oldham*, pp. 163–4.
39 Colley, 'The Apotheosis of George III'. For conflicting chronologies see Cannadine, 'The British Monarchy and the "Invention of Tradition"', and Kuhn, 'Ceremony and Politics'.
40 *The Boston Guardian*, 18 October 1854, p. 2.
41 *The Boston Gazette*, 6 July 1830, p. 3.

42 Butterworth MSS., 15 July and 27 August 1830.
43 *The Sussex Weekly Advertiser*, 5 July 1830, p. 3.
44 Smith (ed.), *The Town Book of Lewes*, I, pp. 270–3.
45 For example, John Noble Boston's leading radical activist and occasional correspondent for *Drakard's Stamford News*, contested the *Boston Gazette's* report of a successful and popular royal proclamation in 1820: 'not *fifty* of the grown up people out of the 5,000 (saving the corporation) shouted – they *would* not shout. A man held up a paper as the procession was returning, on which was inscribed "Long Live Queen Caroline" which was heartily cheered.' *Drakard's Stamford News*, 28 February 1820, p. 3.
46 Butterworth MSS., 28 June 1838.
47 *Trewman's Flying Post*, 5 May 1814, p. 4.
48 *The Boston Gazette*, 28 June 1814, p. 3.
49 See N. Frye, *Anatomy of Criticism: Four Essays* (Princeton, 1957). For similar approaches to different historical subjects see Hayden White, *Metahistory: The Historical Imagination in Nineteenth-Century Europe* (Baltimore, 1973); Hunt, *Politics, Culture and Class in the French Revolution*, pp. 19–51; Thomas Lacqueur, 'The Queen Caroline Affair: Politics as Art in the Reign of George IV', *Journal of Modern History* 54 (1982), 439–66. The world of electoral ceremony is still largely uncharted, see Vernon, 'Drama at the Hustings. Conflict and Integration: A Study in Elections Rituals, 1780–1832', BA thesis (Manchester University, 1987); O'Gorman, 'The Social Meaning of Elections'.
50 *The Sussex Weekly Advertiser*, 5 October 1847, p. 5.
51 It was not unknown for potential candidates to refuse to stand if they thought the requisition was not large enough. See J. M. Cobbett's well publicised deliberations at Oldham in 1868. *The Oldham Standard*, 31 October 1868, p. 5.
52 'Election Posters: General Elections July and December, 1852', OLSL.
53 *Oldham Liberal Elector*, 7 November 1868, p. 4. For an excellent discussion of the importance of the local and the personal in selecting candidates before 1832 see O'Gorman, *Voters, Patrons and Parties*, pp. 126–8.
54 *The Boston Guardian*, 14 December 1830, p. 2; *The Sussex Weekly Advertiser*, 1 February 1813, p. 3.
55 *The Morning Advertiser*, 5 December 1832, p. 3.
56 Smith (ed.), *The Town Book of Lewes*, I, p. 294.
57 *The Sussex Weekly Advertiser*, 12 June 1826, p. 3.
58 There is some evidence that this type of highly organised procession was relatively new. See the reaction of Newark's Tories to the well-organised public entry of the reformer Serjeant Wilde. They held a rival procession with 'no laboured programme...no studied arrangement...no theatrical effect...in short, no artificial aid for excitement...all was in good old English stile [*sic*]'. Vernon, 'Drama at the Hustings', p. 15.
59 *Public Entry of John Fielden, Esq., M.P., and General Johnson, M.P., into Oldham* (Oldham, 1847), p. 1.
60 15,000 turned out for Lord John Russell's public entry to Plymouth during the 1832 South Devon election, just as 15–20,000 people turned

out for Gurney's public entry at the 1830 Norwich election. See *Devonport Chronicle*, 22 September 1832, p. 3; O'Gorman, 'The Social Meaning of Elections'.

61 Vernon, 'Drama at the Hustings', p. 21.
62 *The Boston Herald*, 18 July 1837, p. 3.
63 *The Sussex Agricultural Express*, 19 June 1852, p. 4.
64 *The Northern Star*, 5 June 1852, p. 6.
65 Letter from J. B. Cholwich to Sir T. D. Acland, dated 11 January 1817, EDRO.
66 For instance, at the 1830 Liverpool election the 'creation of the hustings... attracted as is wont a crowd of idlers who appeared to look on with deep interest, in joyous anticipation of the expected scenes the following week'. Vernon, 'Drama at the Hustings', p. 45.
67 Butterworth MSS., 12th December 1832. See also *East London Observer*, 8 July 1865, p. 2.
68 *The Northern Star*, 18 July 1846, p. 6.
69 *A Sketch of the Boston Election... 1830*, (Boston, 1830), pp. 21–22.
70 'Select Committee Appointed to Inquire into the Mode of Taking the Poll at Elections...' *Parliamentary Papers*, 1816–27 (394) iv.iii.
71 See chapter 3 below, pp. 123–4.
72 *The Sussex Weekly Advertiser*, 13 January 1812, p. 3.
73 Benjamin Grime, *Memory Sketches. Part 1 – Parliamentary Elections: Enfranchisement of the Borough in 1832, to General Election, 1852, both inclusive*, (Oldham, 1886), p. 245.
74 Vernon, 'Drama at the Hustings', p. 32.
75 Butterworth MSS., 20 July 1837.
76 *The Oldham Chronicle*, 21 November 1868, p. 7.
77 George Eliot, *Felix Holt, the Radical*, (London, 1887), p. 408.
78 *The Boston Gazette*, 3 May 1831, p. 1.
79 *The Sussex Weekly Advertiser*, 18 March 1816, p. 3.
80 See, 'Shaking Hands After the Battle', editorial *The Oldham Chronicle*, 4 April 1857, p. 2; *Records of the Election... Boston, 1852*, (Boston, 1852), p. 94.
81 *Records of the Election... Boston, 1852*, p. 81. There were no chairings in Oldham and Tower Hamlets, see chapter 6. pp. 230–1.
82 *The Boston Gazette*, 3 August 1830, p. 2 and 3 May 1831, p. 2. At the Nottingham election of 1820 no less than 30,000 people were reputed to have watched the chairing, while at Liverpool's election of 1806 over 10,000 people were estimated to have participated in the actual chairing procession alone. Vernon, 'Drama at the Hustings', p. 37.
83 *The Alfred*, 30 June 1818, p. 3.
84 *Trewman's Flying Post*, 11 June 1816, p. 3.
85 O'Gorman, 'The Social Meaning of Elections'. A similar destination is reached by Lacqueur, if by a more scenic route, see Lacqueur, 'The Queen Caroline Affair', pp. 465–6.
86 H. F. Whitfield, *Plymouth and Devonport: In Times of War and Peace* (Plymouth, 1900), p. 453.

87 Vernon, 'Drama at the Hustings', p. 66.
88 *Ibid.*, pp. 67–77. See also *The Lincoln, Rutland and Stamford Mercury*, 16 July 1852, p. 3 and 4 November 1853, p. 2.
89 *The Sussex Weekly Advertiser*, 19 June 1826, p. 3.
90 In spite of itself much of the body of work on corruption has affirmed the Whiggish impression that this legislation was liberating and enabled greater popular political expression. See Hanham, *Elections and Party Management*; Nossitor, *Influence, Opinion and Political Idioms in Reformed England*; Joyce, *Work, Society and Politics*; G. R. Searle, *Corruption in British Politics, 1895–1930* (Oxford, 1987). For the use of official force during elections see Donald Richter, 'The Role of Mob Riot in Victorian Elections, 1865–1885', *Victorian Studies*, 15, 1 (1971), 19–28; Richter *Riotous Victorians* (Ohio, 1981), pp. 1–19, 63–73; Mark Harrison, *Crowds in History; Mass Phenomena in English Town, 1790–1835* (Cambridge, 1988), pp. 202–32; Vernon, 'Drama at the Hustings', pp. 73–6; Ian Gilmour, *Riot, Rising and Revolution: Governance and Violence in Eighteenth Century England* (London, 1992).
91 'Number of Compounded Householders in Boroughs', *Parliamentary Papers*, 1867 (305) LVI, 463.
92 For a useful analysis of 'fair play' as a popular political attitude see Rohan McWilliam, 'The Tichborne Claimant and the Politics of "Fair Play"', in E. F. Biagini and A. J. Reid (eds.), *Currents of Radicalism: Popular Radicalism, Organised Labour and Party Politics in Britain* (Cambridge, 1991).
93 Whitfield, *Plymouth and Devonport*, p. 451.
94 *The Boston Herald*, 13 January 1835, p. 3.
95 Grime, *Memory Sketches*, pp. 283–5.
96 The England and Wales County Election Polls Act of 1853 (Vict. *c.* 15) further reduced polling at county elections from two days to a single day.
97 Bruce L. Kinzer, *The Ballot Question in Nineteenth-Century English Politics* (London, 1982).
98 *A Short History of the Corporation, Including a Descriptive Account of the Mace, Mayoral Robes, Chain and Badge*, OLSL.
99 Walter Bagehot, *The English Constitution* (London, 1963 edn).

3　THE MEDIUM AND THE MESSAGE: POWER, PRINT, AND THE
PUBLIC SPHERE

1 On the creation of 'the public' see J. A. W. Gunn, *Beyond Liberty and Property: The Process of self-Recognition in Eighteenth-Century Political Thought* (Montreal, 1983); Rocco L. Capraro, 'Typographical Politics: The Impact of Printing on the Political Life of Eighteenth-Century England' Ph.D. thesis (Washington, 1984); Catherine Hall, 'Private Persons Versus Public Someones', For more insightful French examples see, Keith Michael Baker, *Inventing the French Revolution: Essays on French Political Culture in the Eighteenth Century* (Cambridge, 1990); Joan B. Landes, *Women and the Public Sphere in the Age of the French Revolution*

(Ithaca, 1988);; Mona Ozouf, '"Public Opinion" at the End of the Old Regime', *Journal of Modern History*, 60 (1988), pp. 3–21. The original inspiration for much of this work was, of course, Jurgen Habermas, *The Structural Transformation of the Public Sphere* (Cambridge Mass., 1989).

2 Stefan Collini, Donald Winch, and John Burrow, *That Noble Science of Politics: A Study in Nineteenth-Century Intellectual History* (Cambridge, 1983), p. 189. For a fuller explanation of the transition from virtue as property to virtue as reason see chapter 8 below.

3 Genevieve Lloyd, *The Man of Reason: Male and Female in Western Philosophy* (London, 1984).

4 L. S. Stone, 'Literacy and Education in England, 1640–1900', *Past and Present*, 42, (1969); Michael Sanderson, 'Literacy and Social Mobility in the Industrial Revolution in England', *Past and Present*, 56 (1972), 75–104; Thomas W. Lacqueur, 'Debate: Literacy and Social Mobility in the Industrial Revolution in England', *Past and Present*, 64 (1974), 96–107; R. S. Schofield, 'Dimensions of Illiteracy, 1750–1850', *Explorations in Economic History*, 10, 4 (1973), 437–54. This account owes much to David Vincent's excellent, *Literacy and Popular Culture, England 1750–1914* (Cambridge, 1989), pp. 1–4, 22–41.

5 *Twelfth Annual Report of the Registrar General, 1853*. The figure for Tower Hamlets is an approximate one as it constitutes an average of the figures for the Unions of East London, Hackney, Shoreditch, Bethnal Green, Whitechapel, St George-in-the-East, Stepney and Poplar and consequently conceals wide discrepancies between these districts. For instance 50.8 per cent of women in Bethnal Green were illiterate, compared with 26.1 per cent in Hackney. The figure for Devon is taken from the 7th annual report of the Registrar General, 1845, which is an average of the figures between 1839 and 1844.

6 Vincent, *Literacy and Popular Culture*, pp. 17–18.

7 See Marshall McLuhan, *Understanding Media: The Extensions of Man* (New York, 1965); McLuhan and Q. Fiore, *The Medium is the Massage* (New York, 1967). For a recent attempt to rehabilitate McLuhan see Marjorie Ferguson, 'Marshall McLuhan Revisited: 1960s Zeitgeist or Pioneer Postmodernist', *Media, Culture and Society*, 13, 1 (1991), 71–96. See also Jean Baudrillard, *For a Critique of the Political Economy of the Sign* (St Louis, 1981), pp. 164–84; Walter J. Ong, *Orality and Literacy: The Technologizing of the Word* (London, 1982); D. I. LeMahieu, *A Culture for Democracy: Mass Communication and the Cultivated Mind in Britain between the Wars* (Oxford, 1988); Donald Lazere, 'Literacy and Mass Media: The Political Implications', in Cathy N. Davidson (ed.), *Reading in America: Literature and Social History* (Baltimore, 1989).

8 Victor Turner, *Dramas, Fields, and Metaphors*, (Ithaca, 1974).

9 Butterworth MSS., 12 December 1832 (my emphasis).

10 *East London Observer*, 3 November 1866, p. 2.

11 Fred Lawton, 'Skelmanthorpe's Flag of Freedom', *Hirst Buckley's Annual* (1926), 1–2.

12 Butterworth MSS., May 1832.
13 *The Oldham Standard*, 20 July 1859, p. 3.
14 Butterworth MSS., 12 December 1832 (my emphasis).
15 *The Manchester Guardian*, 14 July 1847, p. 7.
16 *The Boston Guardian*, 30 June 1830, p. 1; *The Alfred*, 5 December 1820, p. 3.
17 D. G. Wright, 'Politics and Opinion in Nineteenth-Century Bradford, 1832–1880' Ph.D. thesis (Leeds, 1966), pp. 228 and 337.
18 Both petitions protesting against the Act came from Coventry (with 5,000 signatures) and Spitalfields (with 1,800 signatures). See *Hansard*, 18, 20 March 1828, 1227.
19 *The Sussex Weekly Advertiser*, 3 August 1847, p. 5.
20 Butterworth MSS. 6 July 1835; *Plymouth Herald*, 18 February 1854, p. 6. See also Vernon, 'Drama at the Hustings', p. 61.
21 E. P. Thompson, 'Eighteenth-Century English Society: Class Struggle without Class?', *Social History*, 3, 2 (1978), 146.
22 *Public General Statutes*, 1827, George IV *c.* 36, 21 June 1827.
23 *Hansard*, 17, 1058.
24 For an example of the informal production of banners see, G. Linnaeus Banks, *The Manchester Man*, (Manchester, 1991 edn.), pp. 294–303.
25 *The Boston Gazette*, 12 June 1832, p. 3.
26 *The Shoreditch Observer*, 3 November 1860, p. 3.
27 'Robert Ballments Account... 1816', EDRO 1262m/13; 'Untitled Expenses for 181', EDRO 1262m/16; 'Memoranda of Bills Delivered... 1820', EDRO 1262m/19.
28 *Lincolnshire Guardian and News*, 3 November 1866, p. 2.
29 John Gorman, *Banner Bright* (London, 1973), pp. 49–65.
30 Huw Beynon and Terry Austin, 'The Iconography of the Durham Miners Gala', *Journal of Historical Sociology*, 2, 1 (1989), 68–9.
31 'Songs and Poems Envelope', Howell Papers, Bishopsgate Institute, (my emphasis).
32 James Epstein, 'Understanding the Cap of Liberty: Symbolic Practice and Social Conflict in Early Nineteenth-Century England', *Past and Present*, 122 (1989), 75–118.
33 *The Boston Herald*, 20 June 1837, p. 3.
34 *The Boston Herald*, 4 January 1848, p. 2.
35 Samuel Bamford, *Passages In The Life Of A Radical* (Oxford, 1984 edn), p. 145.
36 Mary Ryan, 'The American Parade: Representations of the Nineteenth-Century Social Order' in Hunt (ed.), *The New Cultural History*, p. 133.
37 Grime, *Memory Sketches*, p. 15.
38 June C. F. Barnes, 'Liberty or death', *Trans. of the Cumberland and Westmorland Antiquarian and Architectural Society*, 84 (1984), 205–14.
39 Marina Warner, *Monuments and Maidens: The Allegory of the Female Form* (London, 1985). See also the following debate in Eric Hobsbawm, 'Man

and Woman in Socialist Iconography', *History Workshop Journal*, 6 (1978), 121–38; M. Agulhon, 'On Political Allegory: A Reply to Eric Hobsbawm', *History Workshop Journal*, 8 (1979), 167–73; Sally Alexander, Anna Davin, and Eve Hostettler, 'On Political Allegory: A Reply to Eric Hobsbawm', *History Workshop Journal*, 8 (1979), 173–82.

40 Much remains to be done in this field see, Dave Russell, 'Popular Musical Culture and Popular Politics in the Yorkshire Textile Districts, 1880–1914', in John K. Walton and James Walvin (eds.), *Leisure in Britain, 1780–1939* (Manchester, 1983), pp. 99–116; Mark W. Booth, *The Experience of Songs* (New Haven, 1981); Roy Palmer, *The Sound of History: Songs and Social Comment* (Oxford, 1989). The work in progress of Phil Eva promises to be an important contribution; see his forthcoming thesis 'Popular Song and Social Identity', Manchester University.

41 Elizabeth L. Eisenstein, *The Printing Press as an Agent of Change* (Cambridge, 1980); Vincent, *Literacy and Popular Culture*. Here again historians of France are some way ahead, see F. Furet and J. Ozouf, *Reading and Writing: Literacy in France from Calvin to Jules Ferry* (Cambridge, 1982); Robert Darnton, 'What is the History of Books?' in Cathy N. Davidson (ed.), *Reading in America*; Roger Chartier, *The Cultural Uses of Print in Early Modern France* (Princeton, 1987); Chartier (ed.), *The Culture of Print: Power and the Uses of Print in Early Modern Europe* (Cambridge, 1989).

42 Thomas Carlyle, 'Stump Orator', *Latter Day Pamphlets* (London, 1858), pp. 158–90; O'Gorman, 'Social Meaning of Elections'.

43 *Woolmer's Exeter Gazette*, 17 January 1829, p. 2; *The Alfred*, 7 May 1831, p. 3.

44 T. Palmer Newbould, *Pages from a Life of Strife. Being Some Recollections of William Henry Chadwick, the Last of the Manchester Chartists* (London, 1911), p. 29 (my emphasis). All the following quotations are from this source.

45 M. Booth, *English Melodrama* (London, 1965); Peter Brooks, *The Melodramatic Imagination* (New Haven, 1976); Martha Vicinus, 'Helpless and Unbefriended: Nineteenth-Century Domestic Melodrama', *New Literary History*, 13, 1 (1981). For the general connection between theatre and oratory see, G. S. R. Kitson Clark, 'The Romantic Element, 1830 to 1850', in J. H. Plumb (ed.), *Studies in Social History: A Tribute to G. M. Trevelyan* (London, 1959) pp. 222–3.

46 *The Western Times*, 15 July 1837, p. 3.

47 *The Northern Star*, 4 September 1847, p. 5.

48 Not literally of course. Audiences liked to be flattered, not abused. For some this proved too much, as at the Tower Hamlets election of 1865, when one of the speakers 'retorted upon the crowd by insulting remarks as to their showing their unfitness for the franchise by their interruptions, and finally wound up by flourishing a thick stick and challenging them severally to fight'. *East London Observer*, 15 July 1865, p. 2.

49 *The Boston Herald*, 27 April 1847, p. 2.

50 D. A. Hamer, 'Gladstone: The Making of a Political Myth', *Victorian Studies*, 22, 1 (1978), 46.
51 *The Manchester Guardian*, 4 September 1852, p. 10.
52 For instance, George Holyoake remembered how as a parliamentary reporter he 'had opportunity of hearing nightly the speeches made in Parliament, I found that all the new ideas expressed there could easily be taken down in long hand, since they occurred seldom and were far between. A newspaper, not having space to report everything said, might entertain and much instruct its readers by giving merely the new ideas of the debates, or remarkable ways of presenting a familiar case.' G. J. Holyoake, *Sixty Years of an Agitator's Life*, II (London, 1892), p. 156.
53 Jan Vansina, *The Oral Tradition as History* (Wisconsin, 1985), p. 34.
54 Kenneth Burke, *A Rhetoric of Motives* (New York, 1969), p. 58.
55 Max Atkinson, *Our Master's Voices: The Language and Body-Language of Politics* (London, 1984), ch. 2.
56 Atkinson, *Our Master's Voices*, pp. 98–104.
57 *The Oldham Chronicle*, 15 July 1865, p. 2.
58 *East London Observer*, 12 September 1868, p. 6.
59 Grime, *Memory Sketches*, p. 248.
60 Smith, *The Town Book of Lewes* I, p. 262.
61 Grime, *Memory Sketches*, pp. 168–9.
62 Henry Mayhew, *The Morning Chronicle Survey of Labour and the Poor: The Metropolitan Districts*, (Horsham, 1981 edn.), esp. II, Letter XV, and V, Letter LV.
63 Mayhew, *The Morning Chronicle Survey of Labour and the Poor*, V, pp. 16–17.
64 Martha Vicinus, *The Industrial Muse* (London, 1974); J. S. Bratton, *Victorian Popular Ballads* (London, 1975); Brian Maidment, *The Poorhouse Fugitives: Self-Taught Poets and Poetry in Victorian Britain* (Manchester, 1987); Rohan McWilliam, 'The Tichborne Claimant and the People: Investigations into Popular Culture', Ph.D. thesis (Sussex, 1990); Joyce, *Visions of the People*.
65 McWilliam, 'The Tichborne Claimant and the People'; Joyce, *Visions of the People*.
66 While, as we shall see, there is much literature on the press, little has been written on other political uses of print, see Capraro, 'Typographical Politics'; Chartier (ed.), *The Culture of Print*, esp. Christian Jouhaud, 'Readability and Persuasion: Political Handbills'. On the relationship between print and image see M. Dorothy George, *English Political Caricature* (Oxford, 1954); Michael Duffy (ed.), *The English Satirical Print 1600–1832*, 7 vols. (Cambridge, 1986); Celina Fox, 'Graphic Journalism in England during the 1830s and 1840s', M. Phil. thesis (Oxford, 1974); Patricia Anderson, *The Printed Image and the Transformation of Popular Culture, 1790–1860* (Oxford, 1991).
67 O'Gorman, *Voters, Patrons and Parties*, p. 139.
68 Mayhew, *The Morning Chronicle Survey of Labour and the Poor*, II, p. 49.
69 Grime, *Memory Sketches*, pp. 145–6.

70 *The Morning Advertiser*, 11 August 1820, pp. 2–3.
71 *Reynold's Newspaper*, 27 June 1852, p. 14.
72 *The Morning Advertiser*, 15 March 1831, p. 3.
73 *The Sussex Weekly Advertiser*, 22 May 1826, p. 3 (my emphasis).
74 Butterworth MSS., 2 July 1835.
75 *East London Observer*, 16 May 1868, p. 6.
76 *A Correct Report of the Respectable Meeting of the Creditors of N. MacMullum, Esq., M.P....* (Boston, 1831), p. 2.
77 'Great Demonstration at Crompton, and Mr. Heald's Address to the Electors and Non-Electors of the Borough of Oldham, October 9 1852', Handbill in Election Posters: General Elections, July and December 1852, OLSL.
78 *A Sketch of the Boston Election... 1830*, p. 31.
79 Vincent, *Literacy and Popular Culture*, p. 238.
80 Nossiter, *Influence, Opinion, and Political Idioms in Reformed England*, p. 197.
81 The radical printers Tom Hynes (Plymouth), James Tucker (Exeter), John Knight (Oldham), Tom Jackson, John Noble, and Charles Barber (Boston) were, however, all fined or imprisoned for breaking these laws. Occasionally the local authorities went a step further and resolved to have a show of force, as at Exeter in 1819 when a 'number of London pamphlets, &c., considered to be of a seditious tendency, were on Friday last committed to the flames, in the market place of this city, by order of the Mayor'. See *The Alfred*, 14 September 1819, p. 3. The following year Tucker was convicted for publishing Hone's parodies, see *Republican*, 21 January 1820, pp. 47–51. For rival printers tipping off the authorities about unsigned bills see *The Boston Herald*, 27 August 1833, p. 4.
82 David Vincent, *Bread, Knowledge and Freedom: A Study in Nineteenth-Century Working Class Autobiography* (London, 1981).
83 Vincent, *Literacy and Popular Culture*, p. 235.
84 See P. Hollis, *The Pauper Press* (Oxford, 1970); Fox, 'Graphic Journalism in England during the 1830s and 1840s'; V. S. Berridge, 'Popular Journalism and Working-Class Attitudes, 1854–1886: A Study of Reynolds' Newspaper, Lloyd's Weekly Newspaper and the Weekly Times', Ph.D. thesis (London, 1976); R. Williams, 'The Press and Popular Culture: An Historical Perspective', in G. Boyce, J. Curran, and P. Wingate (eds.), *Newspaper History from the Seventeenth Century to the Present Day* (London, 1978); L. Brown, *Victorian News and Newspapers* (Oxford, 1985); Anderson, *The Printed Image and the Transformation of Popular Culture*.
85 Vincent, *Literacy and Popular Culture*, p. 235.
86 Vincent, *Literacy and Popular Culture*, p. 235.
87 Landes, *Women and the Public Sphere*, p. 61.
88 Brewer, *Party Ideology and Popular Politics*; Hollis, *The Pauper Press*.
89 *The Boston Gazette*, 29 March 1831, p. 3.
90 *The Boston Guardian*, 4 October 1854, p. 3.
91 Grime, *Memory Sketches*, p. 26.

92 Butterworth MSS., September 1836.
93 *The Oldham Chronicle*, 13 January 1853, p. 2.
94 Vincent, 'The Decline of the Oral Tradition in Popular Culture', in R. D. Storch (ed.), *Popular Culture and Custom in Nineteenth-Century England* (London, 1982), pp. 20–47.
95 *The Alfred*, 8 September 1818, p. 3.
96 Joyce, *Visions of the People*, p. 42.
97 Vincent, *The Formation of the British Liberal Party*, pp. 94–101.
98 *Mitchell's Newspaper Press Directory, 1851* (London, 1851).
99 Olivia Smith, *The Politics of Language, 1790–1819*, (Oxford, 1984).
100 *The Boston Herald*, 6 July 1841, p. 2.
101 *The Oldham Standard*, 9 March 1867, pp. 4–5.
102 Vincent, *Literacy and Popular Culture*, p. 183; Ong, *Orality and Literacy*, esp. ch. 4; Jack Goody, *The Domestication of the Savage Mind* (Cambridge, 1977).
103 See the articles by Giles Shaw on James and Edwin Butterworth in *Transactions of the Lancashire and Cheshire Antiquarian Society*, XXII (1904), pp. 61–72; *Ibid.*, XXVI (1908), pp. 124–32. Also Michael Winstanley 'News from Oldham', *Manchester Regional History Review*, 4, 1 (1990), pp. 3–10.
104 *A Record of the Boston Election...1847*, (Boston, 1847), p. 1.
105 *A Sketch of the Boston Election, 1830*, p. ix.
106 Vincent, *The Formation of the British Liberal Party*, p. 96.
107 Butterworth MSS., 12 December 1832. Butterworth had every right to be grateful for such treatment, see his comments on the vagaries of Oldham's weather and its effect on his reporting. Butterworth MSS., 31 January 1831 and 30 June 1835.
108 *The Devonport Chronicle*, 17 January 1829, p. 3.
109 *Flindell's Western Luminary*, 23 January 1837, p. 1; *The Manchester Guardian*, 4 December 1852, p. 1; *The Sussex Weekly Advertiser*, 12 January 1835, p. 2; *The East London Observer*, 21 November 1868, p. 5.
110 *The East London Observer*, 12 September 1868, p. 6.
111 *The East London Observer*, 12 September 1868, p. 6.
112 *Anecdotes of the Rt. Hon. W. E. Gladstone by an Oxford Man* (London, n.d.), p. 57. I am indebted to Tony Taylor for this reference. On Gladstone's oratory and his use of the press see H. G. C. Matthew, 'Rhetoric and Politics in Great Britain 1860–1950', in P. J. Waller (ed.), *Politics and Social Change: Essays Presented to A. F. Thompson* (London, 1987).
113 *The Alfred*, 27 April 1819, p. 2.
114 A technique pioneered by the Anti-Corn Law League see, Vincent, *Literacy and Popular Culture*, p. 239.
115 O'Gorman, 'Social Meaning of Elections'.
116 Keith Lucas, *English Local Government Franchise*, p. 24.
117 Keith Lucas, *English Local Government Franchise*, p. 124.
118 *The Boston Guardian*, 3 May 1854, p. 5. There were, of course, many other forms of 'corruption'. At Oldham the ballot papers were

supposedly delivered not to voters' homes but to the committee rooms of parties. Keith Lucas, *English Local Government Franchise*, p. 127.

119 *Parliamentary Papers*, 1876, no. 162, 'Minutes of Evidence', question 934.

120 Peter Clarke, *Lancashire and New Liberalism* (Cambridge, 1971), p. 251; Joyce, 'The Factory politics of Lancashire in the Later Nineteenth Century', *Historical Journal*, 18 (1975), 633–43.

121 See M. Ostrogorski, *Democracy and the Organisation of Political Parties*, 2 vols. (London, 1902)l; H. Hanham, *The Reformed Electoral System in Great Britain, 1832–1914* (London, 1968); Nossiter, *Influence, Opinion, and Political Idioms in Reformed England*; Kinzer, *The Ballot Question in Nineteenth-Century English Politics*.

4 A LANGUAGE OF PARTY?

1 For the eighteenth-century debate see L. B. Namier, *The Structure of Politics at the Accession of George III* (London, 1929); D. E. Ginter, *Whig Organisation in the General Election of 1790* (Berkeley, 1967); W. A. Speck, *Tory and Whig: The Struggle in the Constituencies, 1701–1715* (London, 1970); F. O'Gorman, *The Rise of Party in England: The Rockingham Whigs, 1760–1782* (London 1975); G. Holmes, *The Electorate and the National Will in the First Age of Party* (Kendall, 1976); O'Gorman, *The Emergence of the British Two Party System 1760–1832* (London, 1982); B. W. Hill, *British Parliamentary Parties, 1742–1832* (London, 1985); N. Rogers, *Whigs and Cities. Popular Politics in the Age of Walpole and Pitt* (Oxford, 1989); J. C. D. Clark, 'A General Theory of Party, Opposition and Government, 1688–1832', *Historical Journal*, 23 (1980), 295–325. For the nineteenth-century orthodoxy see, N. Gash, *Politics in the Age of Peel: A Study in the Technique of Parliamentary Representation, 1830–50* (London, 1953); Hanham, *Elections and Party Management in the Age of Gladstone and Disraeli*; Vincent, *The Formation of the British Liberal Party*; Nossiter, *Influence, Opinion and Political Idioms in Reformed England*; D. E. D. Beales, 'Parliamentary Politics and the "Independent" Member 1820–1860', in R. Robson (ed.), *Ideas and Institutions of Victorian Britain* (London, 1967) pp. 1–19; P. F. Clarke, 'Electoral Sociology of Modern Britain', *History*, 57 (1972), 31–55; Peter Fraser, 'Party Voting in the House of Commons, 1812–27', *English Historical Review*, 98 (1983), 763–84; Ian Newbould, 'The Emergence of a Two-Party System in England from 1830 to 1841: Roll Call and Consideration', *Parliaments, Estates and Representation*, 5 (1985), 25–32; Angus Hawkins, '"Parliamentary Government" and Victorian Political Parties, c. 1830–c. 1880', *English Historical Review*, (1989), 638–69; P. Gurowich, 'Party and Independence in the Early and Mid-Victorian House of Commons. Aspects of political theory and practice, 1832–1868, considered with special reference to the period, 1852–1868', Ph.D. thesis (Cambridge, 1986).

2 For a more complete re-assessment of the role of party in modern British

politics see papers from the 'Political Parties and Identities in Modern Britain, 1832–1964' Conference, Cambridge University, September 1991.

3 *The Stamford Mercury*, 9 July 1852, p. 3.

4 *The Stamford Mercury*, 4 June 1852, p. 2.

5 Those candidates were W. A. Maddocks (1802–1818), Major John Cartwright (1806), General Johnson (1820), John Wilks (1826–1835), Sir James Duke (1837–1849), David Wire (1847–1851), Hon. D. Pelham (1849) and, of course, Hankey himself.

6 *Notes and Queries*, 4th series, 2 and 3.

7 *The Morning Star*, 13 March 1857, p. 2.

8 For other contests over the use and meaning of colours see, K. J. Atton, 'Municipal and Parliamentary Politics in Ipswich, 1818–47', Ph.D thesis (London, 1981), p. 10; P. Searby, 'Weavers and Freemen in Coventry, 1820–61: Social and Political Traditionalism in an Early Victorian Town', Ph.D thesis (Warwick, 1972), p. 61.

9 See, for example, the ballads 'Ebrington's Victory; Or, The Laurel Wreath', EDRO, 1262M/16; 'The Mourning Oak' EDRO, 1148M/21 (i)/3.

10 R. J. Morris, 'Clubs, Societies and Associations', in F. M. L. Thompson (ed.), *The Cambridge Social History of Britain 1750–1950*, III (Cambridge, 1990), pp. 395–444; T. M. Parssinen, 'Association, Convention and Anti-Parliament in British Radical Politics, 1771–1848', *English Historical Review*, 87 (1973), 504–33.

11 *The Boston Herald*, 9 July 1833, p. 4, and 24 November 1835, p. 3.

12 *The Sussex Weekly Advertiser*, 30 May 1831, p. 3.

13 Oldham's radicals changed their formal organisational apparatus no less than six times between 1829 and 1838. See R. A. Sykes, 'Popular Politics and Trade Unionism in South East Lancashire, 1829–42', Ph.D. thesis (Manchester, 1982) II, pp. 412.

14 M. A. Baer, 'Politics of London, 1852–68: Parties, Voters and Representation', Ph.D. (Iowa, 1976); A. D. Taylor, 'Modes of Political Expression and Working Class Politics: The Manchester and London Examples, 1850–1880', Ph.D. thesis (Manchester, 1992).

15 *The Sussex Weekly Advertiser*, 10 October 1825, p. 3.

16 *The Boston Guardian*, 23 March 1857, p. 1.

17 '*United We Conquer*'. Boston Election. *1860*... (Boston, 1860), p. 11. As if this was not enough, Tuxford pleaded in his post-canvass address 'not to compel the Biographer of Herbert Ingram to record, as the climax of his political career, that with him expired the unity and energies of the old Blue cause for which he worked so earnestly and so well'. *Ibid.*, pp. 25–6.

18 *The Lincolnshire Guardian*, 3 November 1866, p. 2.

19 Grime, *Memory Sketches*, p. 105.

20 *The Oldham Ensign and Standard*, 31 July 1868, p. 3.

21 *The Sussex Weekly Advertiser*, 3 August 1847, p. 6.

22 *The Sussex Weekly Advertiser*, 23 June 1865, p. 3.

23 For accounts of this debate see J. A. W. Gunn, *Factions No More: Attitudes to Party in Government and Opposition in Eighteenth-Century England* (London, 1972); Brewer, *Party Ideology and Popular Politics*, pp. 55–76; Hawkins, '"Parliamentary Government" and Victorian Political Parties'.

24 *Records of the Election ... Boston, 1852*, pp. 26–7 and 84–5.

25 Grime, *Memory Sketches*, p. 44.

26 'England Expects Every Man To Do His Duty', by a 'Working Man' in 'Election Posters: General Elections July and December 1852', OLSL.

27 *The Alfred*, 16 June 1818, p. 3. Mark Kishlansky has traced many of these fears back into the sixteenth and seventeenth centuries. He argues that contested elections were perceived as so disruptive that they were avoided at all costs, preferring instead a method of 'selection'. Mark Kishlansky, *Parliamentary Selection: Social and Political Choice in Early Modern England* (Cambridge, 1986).

28 Jon Lawrence, 'Popular Politics and the Limitations of Party, Wolverhampton 1867–1900', in E. Biagini and A. Reid (eds.), *Currents of Radicalism: Popular Radicalism, Organised Labour and Party Politics in Britain, 1850–1914* (Cambridge, 1991), pp. 65–85.

29 *The Boston Guardian*, 2 May 1855, p. 2. For recent revisionist interpretations of Palmerstonianism see E. D. Steele, *Palmerston and Liberalism 1855–1865* (Cambridge, 1991); Taylor, 'Modes of Political Expression'.

30 *The Boston Herald*, 15 July 1834, p. 3. See also the creation of the 'Independent Reform Registration Society' at Boston in 1847, designed to nominate independent reforming candidates at municipal elections. *The Boston Herald*, 2 November 1847, p. 3.

31 Neil MacMaster, 'The Battle for Mousehold Heath 1857–1884. "Popular Politics" and the Victorian Public Park', *Past and Present*, 127 (1990), 144.

32 This is a glaring omission in the historiography. The exceptions are Beales, 'Parliamentary Politics and the "Independent Member"'; O'Gorman, *Voters, Patrons and Parties*, pp. 259–85; Gurowich, 'Party and Independence in the Early and Mid-Victorian House of Commons'.

33 Vernon, 'The languages of independence and the invention of party' (forthcoming); R. J. Olney, *Lincolnshire Politics*, pp. 49–55.

34 'To The Yeomanry Of Devon, 4 May 1816', EDRO.

35 *The Alfred*, 27 July 1818, p. 3.

36 'Mr. Heald's Address to the Joint Committee of the Late John Duncuft and John Duncuft and John Cobbett M.P., 28 July, 1852', in 'Election Posters: General Elections July and December 1852', OLSL.

37 Taylor, 'Modes of Political Expression and Working Class Politics'.

38 Bernard Deacon, *Liskeard and its People* (Redruth, 1989), p. 109.

39 See the discussion of W. A. Torrens in N. J. Gossman and J. O. Baylen (eds.), *Biographical Dictionary of Modern British Radicals*, II (London, 1979), pp. 500–5. My thanks to Tony Taylor for pointing out this connection to me and providing the reference.

40 'The Coalition RENEWED: but No Tricks upon Travellers', by 'Freeholder', EDRO, 1262M/19.

41 *The Sussex Weekly Advertiser*, 22 June 1818, p. 3.

42 *The Alfred*, 23 June 1816, p. 3.

43 *Supplement to the Western Times*, 18 July 1865, p. 1.

44 Vincent, *The Formation of the British Liberal Party*.

45 In the 25 years since the publication of Vincent's book, the only real addition to his thesis has been the fleshing out of the Conservative party's formation. See Joyce, 'Popular Toryism in Lancashire, 1860–1890', Ph.D. thesis (Oxford, 1975); Joyce, *Work, Society and Politics*, pp. 282–303.

46 Foster, *Class Struggle and the Industrial Revolution*, pp. 35–41.

47 G. Best, 'Popular Protestantism in Victorian Britain', in R. Robson (ed.), *Ideas and Institutions in Victorian Britain* (London, 1967); E. R. Norman, *Anti-Catholicism in Victorian England* (London, 1968); Joyce, 'Popular Toryism in Lancashire, 1860–1890'; Frank Neal, *Sectarian Violence: The Liverpool Experience 1819–1914: An Aspect of Anglo-Irish History* (Manchester, 1988); John Wolffe, *The Protestant Crusade in Great Britain 1829–60* (Oxford, 1991).

48 See Thorne, *The House of Commons, 1790–1820*, I, p. 396.

49 *The Sussex Express*, 30 May 1857, pp. 4–5.

50 Letter from John Carew to Sir Thomas Acland, dated 9 April 1831, EDRO, 1148M add/36/454.

51 *The Western Luminary*, 31 July 1837, p. 2.

52 *The Boston Guardian*, 23 June 1858, p. 3.

53 Ross McKibbin, 'Class and conventional wisdom'. See also 'Political Parties and Identities in Modern Britain 1832–1964' Conference, Cambridge University, September 1991.

54 Clark, 'A General Theory of Party, Opposition and Government, 1688–1832'; Fraser, 'Party Voting in the House of Commons, 1812–27'; Gurowich, 'Party and Independence in the Early and Mid-Victorian House of Commons'.

5 ORGANISATION AS SYMBOL

1 Ernest Jones, 'Pothouse Localities', in *Notes to the People*, II (London, 1967 edn), p. 623.

2 A task begun, as so often in political history, by historians of Chartism. See Eileen Yeo, 'Robert Owen and Radical Culture', in S. Pollard and J. Salt (eds.), *Robert Owen: Prophet of the Poor* (London, 1971), pp. 84–114; E. Yeo, 'Some Practices and Problems of Chartist Democracy', in J. Epstein and D. Thompson (eds.), *The Chartist Experience: Studies in Working Class Radicalism and Culture* (London, 1982), pp. 345–80; James Epstein, 'Some Organisational and Cultural Aspects of the Chartist Movement in Nottingham', in *ibid.*, pp. 221–68.

3 The term 'practical politics' is borrowed from Michael Savage, *The Dynamics of Working-Class Politics. The Labour Movement in Preston, 1880–1940* (Cambridge, 1987), although my emphasis is on the political not the social structure.

4 Fraser, *Urban Politics in Victorian England*.
5 Thorne, *The House of Commons, 1790–1820*, I, pp. 245–7 and 395–7. For the concept of selection see Kishlansky, *Parliamentary Selection*.
6 Thorne, *The House of Commons, 1790–1820*, I, pp. 95–9.
7 Joyce, *Work, Society and Politics*.
8 Morris, 'Clubs, societies and associations', pp. 396–406.
9 *The Boston Herald*, 5 April 1847, p. 3.
10 See the report in the *Sussex Express*, 19 October 1850, p. 4 and its refutation at a meeting of the Bundle of Sticks which resolved 'That the foregoing statement in the *Sussex Express*, that "candidates have been thrust upon the society without a proper consultation of their wishes " is at direct variance with the truth.' *The Sussex Weekly Advertiser*, 29 October 1850, p. 5.
11 *The Boston Gazette*, 9 June 1829, p. 2; *A Record of the Boston Election ... July 31, 1847* (Boston, 1847), p. 2.
12 *The Boston Guardian*, 23 May 1857, p. 1.
13 *The Boston Guardian*, 13 October 1860, p. 4; *The Poll Book for the Borough of Boston ... 1868* (Boston, 1868), pp. i–v; 'Report of Boston', in Howell Collection, 'Election Reports [no. 4060]', Bishopsgate Institute.
14 For a history of the debate about the concepts of the MP as representative and delegate see Henry Jephson, *The Platform, Its Rise and Progress*, II, pp. 133–47. Unfortunately I have not had the space to discuss radical uses of exclusive dealing which was, of course, part of the attempt to ensure the accountability of the electors by the non-electors. It was a means of reminding the enfranchised that their vote was a trust from the disenfranchised, and if they violated this trust by voting in the wrong way they would be held commercially accountable. Of course women, as the principal brokers of domestic expenditure, were afforded great power by the use of exclusive dealing. It empowered them, just as it empowered all the disenfranchised, to challenge exclusive official definitions of the public political sphere. Significantly, I have found evidence, or rather allegations, of exclusive dealing in all five constituencies, although it seems to have been used most extensively in Oldham.
15 Butterworth MSS., July and August 1832; Sykes, 'Popular Politics and Trade Unionism in South-East Lancashire, 1829–42', II pp. 388–9.
16 See *Cobbett's Manchester Lectures in Support of his Fourteen Reform Propositions* (London, 1832) and the account in Stewart A. Weaver, *John Fielden and the Politics of Popular Radicalism 1832–1847* (Oxford, 1987), pp. 53–60.
17 Weaver, *John Fielden and the Politics of Popular Radicalism*, pp. 64–5; Sykes, 'Some Aspects of Working-Class Consciousness in Oldham, 1830–1842' *Historical Journal*, 23 (1980), pp. 167–79.
18 *The Manchester Guardian*, 21 February 1846, p. 11, and 11 March 1846, p. 7.
19 Grime, *Memory Sketches*, pp. 41–51.
20 Weaver, *John Fielden and the Politics of Popular Radicalism*, p. 58.

21 *The Morning Advertiser*, 29 June 1832, p. 3; 15 August 1832, p. 2; 23 August 1832, p. 2; 11 October 1832, p. 2; *The Poor Man's Guardian*, 29 September 1832, p. 6.

22 Letters 898 and 902 Holyoake Papers, Co-Operative Union Library, Manchester; 'Report to the Electoral Committee' on the prospects of Edmond Beales' candidature at Tower Hamlets in 1868, in the Howell Collection, Bishopsgate Institute.

23 *The Morning Advertiser*, 15 August 1832, p. 2 and July 1847, p. 3.

24 *Mr. Cobbett at Royton*, in 'Election Posters: General Elections July and December 1852', OLSL.

25 *The Oldham Chronicle*, 4 February 1865, p. 8; *The Sussex Weekly Advertiser*, 30 January 1849, p. 5; *The Lincoln Gazette*, 24 July 1838, p. 3.

26 *The Alfred*, 2 July 1816, p. 3. Also *The Morning Advertiser*, 20 June 1818, p. 3; *The Sussex Weekly Advertiser*, 31 January 1831, p. 3.

27 Butterworth MSS., 13 April 1833. Also *The Boston Gazette*, 22 February 1831, p. 2; *The Sussex Weekly Advertiser*, 30 May 1848, p. 5.

28 *The Manchester Guardian*, 7 April 1852, p. 7. Also *The Boston Herald*, 24 July 1849, p. 2; *The Morning Advertiser*, 28 July 1847, p. 2.

29 See, for example, the vetting received by Lord John Russell from the Exeter Dissenters Committee at the 1835 election. Eventually they resolved to support Russell's candidature 'and called upon their Dissenting Brethren... to employ their utmost exertions to secure his return to Parliament'. *The Devonport Telegraph*, 2 May 1835, p. 3.

30 *The Sussex Weekly Advertiser*, 27 November 1826, p. 3.

31 On the fiction of democracy in Liberal and Conservative organisation see Vincent, *The Formation of the British Liberal Party*, pp. 118–31; Joyce, *Work, Society and Politics*, p. 269. For the National Liberal Federation see Robert Spence Watson, *The National Liberal Federation 1877–1906* (London, 1907).

32 As we shall see below, radical and reforming politics in Lewes and Devon were overwhelmingly concentrated on the parliamentary level. There were however a few minor ratepaying revolts at vestry level in Lewes, and a campaign (led by the veteran Exeter reformer J. Bowring) for the equalisation of the county rates in Devon during the 1860s.

33 *The Alfred*, 14 June 1821, p. 3.

34 *The Sussex Weekly Advertiser*, 10 October 1809, p. 3.

35 *The Sussex Weekly Advertiser*, 27 November 1809, p. 3.

36 Foster, *Class Struggle and the Industrial Revolution*, pp. 56–7; Sykes, 'Popular Politics and Trade Unionism in S.E. Lancashire', II pp. 476–80.

37 Bateson, *A History of Oldham*, pp. 98–9.

38 *The Manchester Guardian*, 17 November 1821, p. 3.

39 Weaver, *John Fielden and the Politics of Popular Radicalism*, pp. 168–206.

40 Butterworth MSS., 24 April 1839. For Taylor's protest against the appointment of special constables ('he was at a loss to conceive on what grounds they were deemed necessary') see Butterworth MSS., 1 May 1839.

41 Butterworth MSS., 2 January 1840.
42 *The Manchester Guardian*, 19 August 1843, p. 7.
43 *The Manchester Guardian*, 5 August 1848, p. 10.
44 Tower Hamlet's radicals had agitated on this issue with little success throughout the 1830s, opposing the New Police Act in 1830 and the New Police and Police Court Bill in 1839. As we shall see in chapter 6, the use of the police against the Chartists in 1842 and 1848, the prevention of radical meetings in Bishop's Bonner Fields in 1852, and the suppression of meetings at Primrose Hill in support of Garibaldi in 1864 and at Hyde Park in support of the Reform League in 1866, ensured that the issue remained at the centre of metropolitan political concerns.
45 At least half of the committee of Boston's Political Union during the early 1830s were Dissenters. The same was true of Birmingham's Political Union which also adopted the same practical political strategy, see Fraser, *Urban Politics in Victorian England*, pp. 43–4.
46 *The Boston Gazette*, 6 April 1830, p. 2 and January 1831, p. 2.
47 The radical controlled vestry had already refused to defray these expenses themselves, a resolution was passed blaming the violence 'on the palpable neglect of the magistrates', but as a compromise the expenses were deferred on to the county rate. See *The Boston Gazette*, 26 May 1831, p. 4.
48 *The Boston Herald*, 5 February 1833, p. 3.
49 *The Boston Herald*, 27 April 1839, p. 3. For the similar reaction of Leed's Anglicans see Fraser, *Urban Politics in Victorian England*, p. 34.
50 *The Boston Herald*, 15 July 1834, p. 3.
51 *The Boston Herald*, 1 December 1835, p. 3.
52 *The Boston Herald*, 29 September 1840, *p.* 3.
53 The link between these campaigns was evident in the title of Stepney's Anti-Church Rate and Parochial Reform Society established in 1846 to defeat 'any future attempt to saddle the parish with church rates; and the furtherance of parish reforms, and to watch over parochial expenditure'. *The Morning Advertiser*, 21 March 1846, p. 3.
54 See chapter 1 above, pp. 19–20.
55 Iorwerth Prothero, *Artisans and Politics in Early Nineteenth-Century London. John Gast and His Times* (London, 1981), pp. 300–27. Although Prothero has argued (p. 273) that during the 1820s the campaigns for parochial reform proved essential to the revival of the agitation for parliamentary reform.
56 *The Morning Advertiser*, 5 October 1844, p. 3; *The Morning Advertiser*; 12 January 1850, p. 3; *The East London Observer*, 21 November 1857, p. 4 and 15 May 1858, p. 4.
57 E. P. Hennock, 'Finance and Politics in Urban Local Government in England, 1835–1900', *Historical Journal*, 6, 2 (1963), 212–25; Taylor, 'Modes of Political Expression and Working Class Politics'. Both Iorwerth Prothero and John Garrard have, however, provided some warnings, from different ends of England, against such a position. See

Prothero, *Artisans and Politics in Early Nineteenth Century London*, pp. 273–4;
John Garrard, *Leadership and Power in Victorian Industrial Towns, 1830–80*
(Manchester, 1983), pp. 116–19.

58 *The East London Observer*, 15 May 1858, p. 4.

59 Others included the *Eastern Times and Tower Hamlets Gazette* (1859); *The
Shoreditch Advertiser* (1860); *Bethnal Green Times and East London Advertiser*
(1862); *Tower Hamlets Independent and East End Local Advertiser* (1866).

60 *The East London Observer*, 19 September 1857, p. 2.

61 For further discussion of Newton's appeal in 1852 see chapter 8 below,
pp. 266 and 311.

62 E. Yeo, 'Some Practices and Problems of Chartist democracy', p. 353.

63 *The Lincolnshire Guardian*, 27 September 1862, p. 3 and 1 November 1862,
p. 2; *The Western Times*, 9 March 1861, p. 7; *The Western Daily Mercury*,
1 January 1868, p. 3. The same pattern was repeated in Oldham where
the Ratepayers Reform Association was established in 1855 by radicals
and ex-Chartists like J. L. Quarmby, see *The Oldham Chronicle*, 29
September 1855, p. 3.

64 *The Northern Star*, 7 April 1838, p. 5; *The Boston Herald*, 5 March 1833,
p. 4.

65 Foster, *Class Struggle and the Industrial Revolution*, p. 61. Of course most
radical leaders had to make money out of politics just to survive. See
Paul A. Pickering, 'Chartism and the "Trade of Agitation" in Early
Victorian Britain', *History*, 76, (1991), 221–37.

66 *The Boston Herald*, 20 June 1837, p. 3.

67 *The Lincolnshire Guardian*, 27 October 1860, p. 2.

68 *The East London Observer*, 15 May 1858, p. 4.

69 Parssinen, 'Association, Convention and Anti-Parliament in British
Radical Politics', p. 532.

6 THE POLITICS OF CULTURE

1 Vincent, *The Formation of the Liberal Party*, p. 13.

2 Joyce, *Work, Society and Politics*, pp. 292–301.

3 For the concepts of selection and appropriation see respectively,
Raymond Williams, *The London Revolution* (London, 1965), pp. 67–76;
Pierre Bourdieu, *Distinction: A Social Critique of the Judgement of Taste*,
(Cambridge, Mass., 1984). Recent work has shown just how rich and
diverse the repertoire of popular political culture was, so much so that
this account can not attempt to be a definitive one. Much of the impetus
of this work has come from feminist studies, see especially E. Yeo,
'Robert Owen and Radical Culture'; Dorothy Thompson, 'Women
and nineteenth-century radical politics: a lost dimension', in Juliet
Mitchell and Ann Oakley (eds.), *The Rights and Wrongs of Woman*
(London, 1976), pp. 112–38; Barbara Taylor, *Eve and the New Jerusalem.
Socialism and Feminism in the Nineteenth Century* (London, 1983), esp. pp.
217–37; Scott, *Gender and the Politics of History*; Riley, '*Am I That Name?*';

see also the debate 'Politics and Culture in Women's History: A Symposium', *Feminist Studies*, 6 (1980), 26–63.

4 Eley, 'Rethinking the Political'; Epstein, 'Radical Dining, Toasting, and Symbolic Expression', pp. 273–4.

5 Riley, '*Am I That Name?*', p. 51.

6 There have been exceptions, see John Berger, 'The Nature of Mass Demonstrations', *New Society*, 23 May 1968, pp. 754–5; J. Mark Harrison, 'Symbolism, "Ritualism", and the Location of Crowds in early Nineteenth-Century English Towns', in D. Cosgrove and S. Daniels (eds.), *the Iconography of Landscape: Essays on Symbolic Representation, Design and Use of Past and Environments* (Cambridge, 1988); Susan G. Davies, *Parades and Power. Street-Theatre in Nineteenth-Century Philadelphia* (Berkeley, 1986), pp. 23–48.

7 Foster, *Class Struggle and the Industrial Revolution*, p. 39.

8 This contest was repeated elsewhere, see Thomas Cooper, *The Life of Thomas Cooper, Written by Himself* (London, 1872), p. 175.

9 Butterworth MSS., 17 April 1834.

10 There was, of course, a long tradition of carnivalesque in politics, see Peter Burke, *Popular Culture in Early Modern Europe*, (London, 1978), pp. 178–204. For its persistence see McWilliam, 'The Tichbourne Claimant and the People'.

11 Butterworth MSS., 22 and 29 May 1842. For Butterworth's description of the Kersal Moor meeting see 24 September 1838.

12 *The Oldham Standard*, 30 June 1866, p. 4. The Social Democratic Federation continued to stage such meetings at places like Blackstone Edge during the 1880s.

13 2 Kings, 18:4 and 2 Chronicles, 14:3. Oldham's Primitive Methodists also regularly staged 'camp-meetings' on Oldham Edge during the 1820s and 1830s, while Thomas Cooper thought Leicester's Chartist 'camp-meetings' very much like with Wesley's Cornish 'Gwennaps' – grand preaching places. Cooper, *Life of Thomas Cooper*, p. 174.

14 Malcolm Chase, *The People's Farm: English Radical Agrarianism, 1775–1840* (Oxford, 1988). Of course this fascination with reclaiming the land continued with the Commons, Open Spaces and Footpaths Preservation Society (1865), and then with the various mass trespasses of the 1930s. See W. G. Hoskins and Stamp Dudley, *The Common Lands of England and Wales*, (London, 1963); Howard Hill, *Freedom to Roam* (Ashbourne, 1981); Jan Marsh, *Back to the Land: The Pastoral Impulse in Victorian England from 1880–1914* (London, 1982); Marion Shoard, *This Land is Our Land: The Struggle for Britain's Countryside* (London, 1987); Tom Stephenson, *Forbidden Land: The Struggle for Access to Mountain and Moorland* (Manchester, 1989). For further analysis of the appeal of the land see chapter 8 below, pp. 315–16.

15 Roland Quinault, 'Outdoor Radicalism. Copenhagen Fields, 1795–1851', paper presented to the 'Metropolitan History Seminar' at the Institute of Historical Research, 18 January 1989.

16 See also Hugh Cunningham, 'The Metropolitan Fairs: A Case Study in the Social Control of Leisure', in A. P. Donajgrodzki (ed.), *Social Control in Nineteenth-Century Britain* (London, 1977), pp. 163–84.
17 *Reynold's Newspaper*, 4 July 1852, p. 4.
18 *The People's Paper*, 3 July 1852, p. 7 (my emphasis).
19 George Lansbury, *My Life* (London, 1928), p. 28.
20 Karl Marx and Friedrich Engels, *Collected Works* (London, 1980), XIV, p. 303. My thanks to Tony Taylor for this reference.
21 It was following this incident that Beales wrote his highly influential and much cited pamphlet on the history of the ancient constitutional rights of public assembly. Unfortunately no copies of this pamphlet appear to have survived, although it is referred to under Beales' entry in the *Dictionary of National Biography*, IV, p. 9.
22 Jephson, *The Rise of the Platform*, pp. 443–67; Donald Richter, 'The Struggle for Hyde Park in the 1860s', *Research Studies* 42, 4 (1974).
23 Ostrogorski, *Democracy and the Organisation of Political Parties*, II, pp. 395–6. During the 1880s both the SDF and the Socialist League continued to stage open-air meetings in the metropolis. See *Justice's* editorial in July 1885, arguing that the 'right of free speech practically depends upon the right to address their fellows in open spaces...' Brian Simon, *Education and the Labour Movement, 1870–1920* (London, 1965), p. 44. Of course this contest for the use of public spaces infamously climaxed at Trafalgar Square on Bloody Sunday (1887) and at the Battle of Boggart Hole Clough in Manchester (1896).
24 Not always however, see McMaster, 'The Battle for Mousehold Heath 1857–1884'.
25 See J. Money, 'Taverns, Coffee Houses and Clubs: Local Politics and Popular Articulacy in the Birmingham Area in the Age of the American Revolution', *Historical Journal*, 14 (1971), 15–47; Brian Harrison, 'Pubs', in Dyos and Wolff (eds.), *The Victorian City*, II, pp. 161–90; Peter Clark, *Sociability and Urbanity: Clubs and Societies in the Eighteenth-Century City* (Leicester, 1990).
26 Bateson, *A History of Oldham*, p. 98.
27 Brian Harrison, *Drink and the Victorians. The Temperance Question in England 1815–1872* (London, 1971), p. 61. See also Jacob Larwood and John Camden Hotten, *English Inn Signs* (New York, 1985 edn), pp. 48–9 and 292.
28 Thompson, *The Making of the English Working Class*, pp. 813–16; Trygve R. Tholfsen, *Working Class Radicalism in Mid-Victorian England* (London, 1976), pp. 61–72: Anna Clark, 'The Rhetoric of Chartist Domesticity: Gender, Language, and Class in the 1830s and 1840s', *Journal of British Studies*, 31, 1 (1992), 74–5.
29 Thompson, *The Making of the English Working Class*, p. 813.
30 *The Objects, Laws, &c. of the Crompton Political Union* (Oldham, 1832), p. 7.
31 Harrison, 'Pubs', p. 175.
32 Thompson, 'Women and Nineteenth-Century Radical Politics', p. 135.

33 *A Record of the Boston Election... 1847* (Boston, 1847), p. 16.
34 For more on Neesom see J. O. Bayley and N. J. Gossman, *Biographical Dictionary of Modern British Radicals*, II, pp. 367–9.
35 For the persistence of this metropolitan network see John Timbs, *Clubs and Club Life in London*, (London, 1872); Iain McCalman, *Radical Underworld: Prophets, Revolutionaries and Pornographers in London, 1795–1840* (London, 1988), pp. 113–16; Mary Thale, 'London Debating Societies in the 1790s', *Historical Journal*, 32, 1 (1989), 31–48; John Davis, 'Radical Clubs and London Politics, 1870–1900', in David Feldman and Gareth Stedman Jones (eds.), *Metropolis, London. Histories and Representations since 1800* (London, 1989), pp. 103–28; Taylor, 'Modes of Political Expression and Working Class Politics'.
36 Joyce, *Work Society and Politics*, p. 287.
37 Foster, *Class Struggle and the Industrial Revolution*, p. 218.
38 Ostrogorski, *Democracy and the Organisation of Political Parties*, I, pp. 250–86; Joyce, *Work, Society and Politics*, pp. 283–9; Martin Pugh, *The Tories and the People, 1880–1935* (Oxford, 1985); Jonathan Lawrence, 'Party Politics and the People: Continuity and Change in the Political History of Wolverhampton, 1815–1914', Ph.D. thesis (Cambridge, 1990), pp. 53–75.
39 It is interesting to speculate on the role of women in this move, for plebeian dissenting congregations like these had long afforded women one of their few public platforms. See Deborah Valenze, 'Cottage Religion and the Politics of Survival', in Jane Rendall (ed.), *Equal or Different. Women's Politics 1800–1914* (Oxford, 1987), pp. 31–56.
40 Butterworth MSS., 4 January 1832.
41 Butterworth MSS., 14 March 1835.
42 *The East London Observer*, 18 August 1860, p. 2 (my emphasis).
43 Although this licensing system was created by the Seditious Meetings Act of 1819, it continued to be strictly enforced, as James Dawson of Lees would testify. In 1841 he was fined £20 for presiding at a Chartist meeting in an unlicensed room, he was later imprisoned for not paying the fine. Butterworth MSS., 26 October 1841.
44 Gordan Howard-Smith, 'The Oldham Branch of the Owenite Socialist Movement, 1838–46', Diploma in Political, Economic, and Social Studies, (Nottingham, 1979).
45 *New Moral World*, 12, pp. 296 and 334; Taylor, *Eve and the New Jerusalem*, pp. 324–7.
46 *The Northern Star*, 13 March 1844, p. 6 (my emphasis).
47 *The Manchester Guardian*, 24 June 1848, p. 8.
48 *The Northern Star*, 16 January 1841, p. 2.
49 Boston's Chartists were frequently refused use of the town hall so they relied on the use of rooms above shops, and other locations owned by those sympathetic to the cause. During the early 1830s Caister and Wedd's Granary was known as 'Blue Town Hall' because of its regular use for radical meetings, see *The Boston Gazette*, 10 August 1830, p. 1.

50 Sykes, 'Popular Politics and Trade Unionism in South-East Lancashire, 1829–42', II, pp. 625–31.
51 Winstanley, 'News from Oldham', p. 4.
52 *Drakard's Stamford News*, 18 October 1822, p. 3.
53 Butterworth MSS., 25 March 1834.
54 Butterworth MSS., 20 December 1832.
55 Butterworth MSS., 5 November 1833.
56 *The Northern Star*, 22 August 1840, p. 1.
57 *The Northern Star*, 23 November 1839, p. 7.
58 Grime, *Memory Sketches*, p. 186.
59 *The East London Observer*, 13 June 1868, p. 2.
60 *The East London Observer*, 21 November 1868, p. 5.
61 *The Devonport Telegraph*, 30 May 1835, p. 4.
62 Butterworth MSS., 12 April 1841; *The Morning Advertiser*, 8 February 1839, p. 3, and 28 January 1842, p. 3.
63 Holyoake Papers, Letter 761, Co-Operative Union Library, Manchester. My thanks to Tony Taylor for this reference.
64 *The East London Observer*, 29 February 1868, p. 5.
65 Ostrogorski, *Democracy and the Organisation of Political Parties*, II, p. 383.
66 Taylor, *Eve and the New Jerusalem*, p. 229.
67 *The Poll Book…Boston* (Boston, 1826), p. 10.
68 *Cobbett's Political Register*, 22 December 1832, p. 723.
69 *The Sussex Weekly Advertiser*, 21 January 1833, p. 3.
70 *Cobbett's Political Register*, 22 December 1832, p. 722.
71 *The Boston Herald*, 13 January 1835, p. 2.
72 O'Gorman, *Voters, Patrons and Parties*, esp. ch. 3.
73 *The Poll Book…Boston, 1847*, p. 10. Also *The Sussex Weekly Advertiser*, 1 April 1818, p. 3.
74 Bamford, *Passages in the Life of a Radical*, p. 131.
75 Vincent, *Bread, Knowledge and Freedom*, pp. 174–7.
76 For earlier political uses and meanings of these forms see David Cressy, *Bonfires and Bells: National Memory and the Protestant Calendar in Elizabethan and Stuart England* (London, 1989); Rogers, *Whigs and Cities*, pp. 348–386; Kathleen Wilson, 'The Rejection of Deference: Urban Political Culture in England, 1715–1785', Ph.D. (Yale University, 1985); Brewer, *Party Ideology and Popular Politics at the Accession of George III*, ch. 9; Alan Booth, 'Popular Loyalism and Public Violence in the North-West of England, 1790–1800', *Social History*, 8 (1983), 295–313; R. D. Storch, '"Please to Remember the Fifth of November": Conflict, Solidarity and Public Order in Southern England, 1815–1900', in Storch (ed.), *Popular Culture and Custom in Nineteenth-Century England* (London, 1982); D. G. Paz, 'Bonfire Night in Mid-Victorian Northants: The Politics of Popular Revel' *Historical Research*, 63 (1990), 316–28.
77 Storch, 'Please to Remember the Fifth of November', pp. 75–82.
78 Butterworth MSS., 5 November 1830.
79 *The Boston Gazette*, 8 November 1832, p. 3.

80 Butterworth MSS., 8 November 1838, (my emphasis).
81 Storch, 'Please to Remember the Fifth of November', p. 79.
82 Butterworth MSS., 9 March 1838.
83 Thompson, 'Women in Nineteenth-Century Radical Politics', p. 137; John Boshtedt, 'The Myth of the Feminine Food Riot: Women as Proto-Citizens in English Community Politics, 1790–1810', in Applewhite and Levy (eds.), *Women and Politics in the Age of Democratic Politics*, (Ann Arbor, 1990), pp. 21–60.
84 Jephson, *The Platform*, p. 245.
85 Jephson, *The Platform*, p. 249.
86 Thompson, *The Chartists*, p. 129.
87 Thompson, 'Chartism as a Historical Subject', *Bulletin of Society for the Study of Labour History*, 20 (1970), p. 12. John Stevenson has also argued that the period 1848–70 represented 'the transition to order'. John Stevenson, *Popular Disturbances in England 1700–1870* (London, 1979), p. 275. This process seems to have been less marked in southern England which was after all effectively by-passed by Chartism, see J. W. Morris, 'A Disappearing Crowd? Collective Action in Late Nineteenth-Century Croydon', *Southern History*, 11 (1990), 90–113.
88 Butterworth MSS, 27 November 1841.
89 *The East London Observer*, 20 October 1866, p. 4; 3 November 1866, p. 2; 3 October 1868, p. 5. There were however a few signs of unease within the Reform League's local and national leadership about these forms of cultural politics. See Harrison, 'Pubs', p. 176; *The Shoreditch Observer*, 3 November 1866, p. 3.
90 *The East London Observer*, 3 October 1868, p. 5.
91 *Boston Election…1868* (Boston, 1868), p. vii.
92 *The Lincolnshire Guardian*, 10 November 1858, p. 3.
93 *The Manchester Guardian*, 4 September 1847, p. 8.
94 Storch, 'Please to Remember the Fifth of November', p. 82.
95 *The Lewes Times*, 12 November 1858, p. 4.
96 J. E. Ethrington, 'Lewes Bonfire Riots of 1847', *Sussex History*, 1, 6 (1978), 2–16.
97 For the role of counter-attractive events in the reform of popular culture see Hugh Cunningham, *Leisure in the Industrial Revolution c.1780–c.1880* (London, 1980), pp. 40–1, 98–100, 179–80; Peter Bailey, *Leisure and Class in Victorian England. Rational Recreation and the Contest for Control, 1830–1885* (London, 1978), chs. 2 and 4; Harrison, *Drink and the Victorians*, pp. 22, 184, 225; Robert Poole, 'Oldham Wakes', in John K. Walton and James Walvin (eds.), *Leisure in Britain, 1780–1939* (Manchester, 1983), pp. 71–98.
98 Butterworth MSS., 2 September, 5 November 1834 and 21 April 1835.
99 Butterworth MSS., 1 April 1839.
100 Butterworth MSS., 12 April 1841.
101 *The Manchester Guardian*, 2 September 1843, p. 7.
102 *The Boston Herald*, 13 May 1834, p. 2. This was so successful they

repeated it the following year, *The Boston Herald*, 7 April 1835, p. 3. For the political uses of the theatre in Oldham see Butterworth MSS., 7 March and 5 December 1840.

103 Yeo, 'Robert Owen and Radical Culture', pp. 99–103; Epstein, 'Radical Dining and Symbolic Expression'.

104 M. I. Thomis and J. Grimmett, *Women in Protest 1800–1850* (London, 1983); Rendall (ed.), *Equal or Different*; Applewhite and Levy (eds.), *Women and Politics in the Age of Democratic Politics*.

105 *The Sussex Weekly Advertiser*, 22 July 1833, p. 3.

106 *The Sussex Weekly Advertiser*, 12 August 1833, p. 3.

107 *The Lewes Times*, 20 July 1866, p. 7.

108 *The Boston Herald*, 4 July 1837, p. 3.

109 *The Lincolnshire Guardian*, 18 August 1858, p. 3.

110 *Boston Election. The Poll Book... 1868*, p. vi.

111 Butterworth MSS., 10 August 1837 (my emphasis).

112 Butterworth MSS., 17 August 1837.

113 Butterworth MSS., 5 January 1838.

114 Taylor, *Eve and the New Jerusalem*, p. 217.

115 Howard-Smith, 'The Oldham Branch of the Owenite Socialist Movement, 1838–46', p. 41.

116 Taylor, *Eve and the New Jerusalem*, p. 230.

117 Butterworth MSS., 4 January 1839 (my emphasis).

118 *The Manchester Guardian*, 1 September 1852, p. 8.

119 Grime, *Memory Sketches*, pp. 218–19.

120 *The Free Trader*, 16 October 1852, p. 2.

121 Grime, *Memory Sketches*, p. 218.

122 *The Manchester Guardian*, 19 February 1853, p. 10, and 24 September 1853, p. 9.

123 Joyce, *Work, Society and Politics*, p. 283.

124 'Toryism in Oldham: Club Histories', newspaper cuttings from *The Oldham Standard* (1909), p. 14.

125 Pugh, *The Tories and the People, 1880–1935*, ch. 3.

126 *The Western Luminary*, 23 January 1837, pp. 1–2.

127 *The Charter*, 16 February 1840, p. 14.

128 *The Northern Star*, 17 October 1840, p. 1.

129 Eley, 'Rethinking the Political'; Epstein, 'Radical Dining, Toasting, and Symbolic Expression', pp. 273–4.

130 Ostrogorski, *Democracy and the Organisation of Political Parties*, II, pp. 475ff; Linda E. Walker, 'The Women's Movement in England in the Late Nineteenth and Early Twentieth Centuries' Ph.D. thesis (Manchester, 1984); Walker, 'Party Political Women: A Comparative Study of Liberal Women and the Primrose League, 1890–1914', in Rendall (ed.), *Equal or Different. Women's Politics 1800–1914* (Oxford, 1987), pp. 165–191.

131 Robert Michels, *Political Parties. A Sociological Study of the Oligarchic Tendencies of Modern Democracy* (London, 1962 edn.).

132 James Vernon, 'The Languages of Independence and the Mid-Victorian Invention of Party' (forthcoming).

7   THE IDOL AND THE ICON: LEADERS AND THEIR POPULAR
CONSTITUENCIES

1 Thomas Carlyle, *Heroes and Hero-Worship* (London, 1888 edn.), pp. 186–7.
2 See James Epstein, *The Lion of Freedom: Feargus O'Connor and the Chartist Movement, 1832–1842* (London, 1982); John Belchem, '*Orator Hunt*': *Henry Hunt and English Working-Class Radicalism* (Oxford, 1985); Stuart A. Weaver, *John Fielden and the Politics of Popular Radicalism* (London, 1988); Patrick Joyce, 'Paradoxes of Party: The Re-Invention of Party in Victorian Politics', paper delivered at the 'Political Parties and Identities in Modern Britain, 1832–1964' conference, Cambridge, September 1991; Peter Clarke, *A Question of Leadership: Gladstone to Thatcher* (London, 1991).
3 On 'The Cult of Veneration Among the Masses' see Michels, *Political Parties*, pp. 93–8. On political leaders in the world of entertainment see Michael Diamond, 'Political Heroes of the Victorian Music Hall', *History Today*, (January 1990), 33–9; Phillip Waller, 'Laughter at the Palace of Varieties', *Times Higher Educational Supplement*, 8 June 1990, pp. 13 and 18. For the infusion of politics in football see Lawrence, 'Party Politics and the People', ch. 3.
4 A phrase taken from Lynn Hunt, *Politics, Culture and Class in the French Revolution*, ch. 6.
5 Peter Karsten, *Patriot-Heroes in England and America. Political Symbolism and Changing Values Over Three Centuries* (Wisconsin, 1978); Stephen Wilson (ed.), *Saints and their Cults. Studies in Religious Sociology, Folklore, and History* (Cambridge, 1983); John M. Thielman, 'Political Canonization and Political Symbolism in Medieval England', *Journal of British Studies*, 29, 3 (1990), 241–266.
6 Significantly these gifts often reflected the leader's popular image. Thus Wilkes was fittingly given food, drink, and tobacco, while Gladstone 'the woodman' was forever presented with silver axes. Brewer, *Party Ideology and Popular Politics*, pp. 176–7; Hamer, 'Gladstone: The Making of a Political Myth', pp. 37–8.
7 'Ebrington and Independence', EDRO, 1262m/16.
8 Brewer, *Party Ideology and Popular Politics*, pp. 163–200.
9 Thompson, *The Chartists*, p. 52; Vincent, *Literacy and Popular Culture*, pp. 243–253.
10 During the 1890s when Jack London visited the room of an old socialist the only decoration was a portrait of Garibaldi. See Taylor, 'Modes of Political Expression in Working Class Politics'.
11 *The Northern Star*, 9 January 1841, p. 8.
12 *The Beehive*, 25 January 1868, p. 1.

13 Brewer, *Party Ideology and Popular Politics*, pp. 163–4; A. W. Yarrington, 'The Commemoration of the Hero 1800–1864. Monuments to the British Victors of the Napoleonic Wars' Ph.D. thesis (Cambridge, 1980), pp. 40–1; Gerald Jordan and Nicholas Rogers, 'Admirals as Heroes: Patriotism and Liberty in Hanoverian England', *Journal of British Studies*, 28 (1989), 211–22.

14 Brewer, *Party Ideology and Popular Politics*, p. 185. See also Pickering, 'Chartism and the "Trade of Agitation" in Early Victorian Britain'.

15 *The Sussex Weekly Advertiser*, 12 December 1825, p. 3. See also Christopher Brunel and Peter M. Jackson, 'Notes on Tokens as a Source of Information on the History of the Labour and Radical Movement', *Society for the Study of Labour History*, 15 (1967), 26–40.

16 J. Larwood and J. C. Hotten, *English Inn Signs. A Revised and Modernized Version of the History of Signboards*, (London, 1985 edn), pp. 48–9; Leslie Dunkling and Gordon Wright, *A Dictionary of Pub Names* (London, 1987).

17 Larwood and Hotten, *English Inn Signs*, p. 37.

18 Thompson, 'Women and Nineteenth-Century Radical Politics', p. 122.

19 Ernest H. Kantorowicz, *The King's Two Bodies: A Study in Medieval Political Theology* (Princeton, 1957); M. Axton, *The Queen's Two Bodies: Drama and the Elizabethan Succession* (London, 1977); S. Hanley, *The Lit de Justice of the Kings of France* (Princeton, 1983); M. Bloch, 'The Ritual of the Royal Bath in Madagascar: The Dissolution of Death, Birth and Fertility into Authority', and M. Gilbert, 'The Person of the King: Ritual and Power in a Ghanaian State' in D. Cannadine and S. Price (eds.), *Rituals of Royalty: Power and Ceremonial in Traditional Societies*, (Cambridge, 1987).

20 Jordan and Rogers, 'Admirals as Heroes', p. 221; Hamer, 'Gladstone: The Making of a Political Myth', p. 37; Derek Beales, 'Garibaldi in England: The Politics of Italian Enthusiasm', paper presented to 'Popular Radicalism and Party Politics in Britain 1848–1914', Churchill College, Cambridge, April 1989.

21 C. I. Hamilton, 'Naval Hagiography and the Victorian Hero', *Historical Journal*, 23, 2 (1980), 381–98; J. S. A. Adamson, 'Eminent Victorians: S. R. Gardiner and the Liberal as Hero', *Historical Journal*, 33, 3 (1990), 641–57. Also on proliferation of Gladstone biographies see Hamer, 'Gladstone: The Making of a Political Myth', pp. 29–35.

22 Thompson, *The Making of the English Working Class*, p. 682; Epstein, *The Lion of Freedom*, pp. 90–4; Belchem, '*Orator Hunt*', pp. 3–12; Joyce, *Visions of the People*, 45–52.

23 'An Englishman', *County Election. 8 May, 1816, Plymouth*. WDRO, 74/273.

24 *The Sussex Weekly Advertiser*, 13 May 1811, p. 3.

25 *The East London Observer*, 7 November 1868, p. 6 (my emphasis).

26 Letter no. 5, E. Beales to Howell, dated 30 October 1868, in Howell Collection (Letters), Bishopsgate Institute. See also 'Edmond Beales, President of the Reform League', in Howell's unpublished biography

vol. c, d. p. 43; *Reform Songs to be sung at the Agricultural Hall by the Reform Minstrels on the day of the Great National Demonstration. Also a Memoir of Edmond Beales, Esq., M.A., President of the League* (London, 1867).

27 William Cobbett still awaits his Epstein or Belchem. Several have grappled with this most contradictory of men, but none entirely successfully. See G. D. H. Cole, *The Life of William Cobbett* (London, 1925); J. W. Osborne, *William Cobbett: His Thought and his Times* (New Brunswick, 1966); J. Sambrook, *William Cobbett* (London, 1973); Daniel Green, *Great Cobbett: The Noblest Agitator* (Oxford, 1985).

28 Butterworth MSS., 5 January 1832.

29 *The Oldham Standard*, 14 July 1860, p. 4.

30 Butterworth MSS., 4 December 1834 (my emphasis).

31 *Oldham Election – Mr. Cobbett at Hollinwood* in 'Election Posters: General Elections July and December 1852', OLSL.

32 'Toryism in Oldham', p. 4.

33 Thompson, *The Chartists*, pp. 98–9.

34 *The Morning Advertiser*, 11 October 1832, p. 2.

35 Beales, *England and Italy 1859–60* (London, 1961); Taylor, 'Modes of Political Expression and Working Class Politics'.

36 Bateson, *A History of Oldham*, p. 181; Winston Churchill, *My Early Life: A Roving Commission* (London, 1941), pp. 368–74.

37 Thompson, *The Making of the English Working Class*, pp. 682–3.

38 *Reynolds Newspaper*, 4 April 1852, p. 9.

39 *Reynolds Newspaper*, 16 May 1852, p. 12. For a profile of Newton see Bellamy and Saville (eds.), *Dictionary of Labour Biography*, II, pp. 270–6.

40 *Election Address by W. J. Fox to the Electors of the Borough of Oldham, 1 July 1847*, in 'Election Posters: General Elections July and December 1852', OLSL.

41 *The Manchester Guardian*, 18 April 1846, p. 10.

42 *The Manchester Guardian*, 10 July 1852, p. 5.

43 *The Times*, 31 July 1847, p. 3 (my emphasis).

44 *The East London Observer*, 14 November 1868, p. 2.

45 *The Lincolnshire Guardian*, 27 April 1859, p. 4.

46 *The Lincolnshire Guardian*, 27 April 1859, p. 4.

47 Weaver, *John Fielden and the Politics of Popular Radicalism*, p. 26.

48 *The Oldham Chronicle*, 5 September 1857, p. 3.

49 *The Oldham Chronicle*, 9 September 1857, p. 3.

50 O'Gorman, *Voters, Patrons and Parties*, pp. 122–4.

51 *The Oldham Chronicle*, 26 April 1868, p. 7.

52 *Oldham Liberal Elector*, no. 7, November 1868, p. 4.

53 Thomas Mottershead, 'Report to the Electoral Committee of Mr. Beales at Tower Hamlets', in Howell Collection, Bishopsgate Institute.

54 Butterworth MSS, 12 December 1832.

55 Weaver, *John Fielden and the Politics of Popular Radicalism*.

56 Hamer, 'Gladstone: The Making of a Political Myth', p. 46.

57 Hamer, 'Gladstone: The Making of a Political Myth'. p. 37–8.

58 *The Oldham Ensign and Standard*, 18 September 1868, p. 2 (my emphasis).

59 *The Oldham Chronicle*, 7 November 1868, p. 3.

60 *Oldham Liberal Elector*, 3 October 1868, p. 3.

61 *The Oldham Ensign and Standard*, 29 July 1868, p. 3.

62 *The Oldham Standard*, 14 July 1860, p. 4.

63 *The Rising Sun*, 2 October 1852, p. 3.

64 *The Manchester Guardian*, 18 April 1846, p. 10.

65 Richard Garnett, *The Life of W. J. Fox: Public Teacher and Social Reformer 1786–1864* (London, 1910), p. 294.

66 At the funeral of Oldham's veteran radical leader John Knight in 1838, the cortège alone consisted of 2,500 people, and 'the streets through which they passed were crowded by thousands of spectators'. See Butterworth MSS., 9 September 1838. Few could compete with the 40 thousand present at William Aitken's funeral in neighbouring Ashton during 1864. See Joyce, *Visions of the People*, p. 37.

67 Grime, *Memory Sketches*, p. 203.

68 Grime, *Memory Sketches*, pp. 113–4.

69 Grime, *Memory Sketches*, p. 112.

70 *Boston Election … 127th November, 1868* (Boston, 1868), p. v.

71 Foster, *Class Struggle and the Industrial Revolution*, pp. 134–5.

72 Grime, *Memory Sketches*, p. 110.

73 Grime, *Memory Sketches*, p. 110.

74 Gemini, '*No go*' – *The Sublime Watchword of the Mongrel Politicians of Oldham* in 'Election Posters and Scraps, 1849–1852', OLSL.

75 *The Manchester Guardian*, 4 December 1852, p. 9.

76 Grime, *Memory Sketches*, p. 73.

77 Grime, *Memory Sketches*, p. 57.

78 *Hymn to be Sung in the Working Man's Hall on Monday Evening, the 27th Septr., 1852, In Respect to the Memory of The Late JAMES HOLLADAY ESQR., Who died in this Hall, on Monday evening, the 20th Inst.* in 'Ballads, Broadsides and Songs', p. 74, OLSL.

79 *Lines on the Death of James Holladay, Esq., Addressed to the Electors and Non-Electors of the Borough of Oldham*, in 'Election Posters: General Elections, July and December 1852', OLSL.

80 *The Oldham Chronicle*, 10 June 1865, p. 6.

81 Thompson, *The Making of the English Working Class*, p. 683; Epstein, *The Lion of Freedom*, pp. 90–3.

82 Sykes, 'Popular Politics and Trade Unionism in South East Lancashire, 1829–1842', II, pp. 394–6; D. Vincent, *Bread, Knowledge, and Freedom. A Study of Nineteenth-Century Working Class Autobiography* (London, 1981), pp. 174–7.

83 Yeo, 'Some Practices and Problems of Chartist Democracy', pp. 355–60.

84 This profile of Knott was compiled from reports in the local press, the Butterworth MSS., and the obituary in *The Oldham Chronicle*, 20 August 1892, p. 3.

85 Foster, *Class Struggle and the Industrial Revolution*, ch. 6.

86 This profile of Browne was compiled from reports in the local press, the *Lewes Town Book*, and the obituary in the *East Sussex News*, 26 January 1877, p. 3.

87 This profile of Noble was compiled from reports in the local press and poll books, and the obituary in the *Stamford Mercury*, 17 August 1866, p. 6.

88 *Dictionary of National Bibliography*, XLI, p. 81.

8   THE NATION AND ITS PEOPLE: THE DISCOURSE OF POPULAR
    CONSTITUTIONALISM

1 Roland Barthes, 'Introduction to the Structural Analysis of Narratives', in his *Image, Music, Text*, trans. S. Heath (New York, 1977), p. 79.

2 Northrop Frye, *The Anatomy of Criticism* (Princeton, 1957); Fredric Jameson, *The Political Unconscious: Narrative as a Socially Symbolic Act* (New York, 1981); Hayden White, *The Content of the Form: Narrative Discourse and Historical Representation* (Baltimore, 1989).

3 White, *The Content of the Form*, p. 157.

4 Christopher Hill, 'The Norman Yoke' in his *Puritanism and Revolution* (London, 1955), pp. 50–122; H. T. Dickinson, 'The Eighteenth-Century Debate on the Glorious Revolution', *History*, 61 (1976), 28–45; Dickinson, *Liberty and Property: Political Ideology in Eighteenth-Century Britain* (London, 1977); Anne Pallister, *Magna Carta. The Heritage of Liberty* (Oxford, 1977); J. G. A. Pocock (ed.), *Three British Revolutions* (Princeton, 1982); Pocock, *The Ancient Constitution and the Feudal Law: A Study of English Historical Thought in the Seventeenth Century. A Re-issue with a Retrospect* (Cambridge, 1987 edn); R. J. Smith, *The Gothic Bequest; Medieval Institutions In British Political Thought, 1688–1863* (Cambridge, 1987); Kathleen Wilson, 'Inventing Revolution: 1688 and Eighteenth-Century Popular Politics', *Journal of British Studies*, 28 (October, 1989), 349–86.

5 For similar uses of this idea of a master narrative see Sewell, *Work And Revolution in France*; Sean Wilentz, *Chants Democratic: New York City and the Rise of the American Working Class, 1788–1850* (New York, 1984); Epstein, 'Understanding the Cap of Liberty', p. 117; Epstein 'The Constitutional Idiom: Radical Reasoning, Rhetoric and Action in Early Nineteenth-Century England', *Journal of Social History*, 23, 3 (Spring 1990), 568.

6 Thompson, *The Making of the English Working Class*, p. 88. It should be noted that this account received widespread support from historians on all sides of the political spectrum. See Foster, *Class Struggle and the Industrial Revolution*, pp. 34–43; John Cannon, *Parliamentary Reform 1640–1832* (Cambridge, 1973), ch. 6; Brewer, 'Theater and Counter-Theater in Georgian Politics: The Mock Elections at Garrat', *Radical History Review*, 22 (1979–80), 7–40.

7 McCalman, *Radical Underworld*; McCalman, 'New Jerusalems: Proph-

ecy, Judaism and Radical Restorationism in London, 1786–1832',
paper presented to Modern History Seminar, Manchester University,
1992; Prothero, 'Religion and Radicalism', paper presented to Modern
History Seminar, Manchester University, February 1987; Gregory
Claeys, *Citizens and Saints, Politics and Anti-Politics in Early British Socialism*
(Cambridge, 1989). Recent work has also concentrated on the varieties
of Whiggism and Liberalism, see J. G. A. Pocock, 'The Varieties of
Whiggism from Exclusion to Reform: A History of Ideology and
Discourse' in his *Virtue, Commerce and History: Essays on Political Thought
and History, Chiefly in the Eighteenth Century* (Cambridge, 1985), pp.
215–311; Stefan Collini, Donald Winch, and John Burrow, *That Noble
Science of Politics: A Study in Nineteenth-Century Intellectual History*
(Cambridge, 1983); Biancamaria Fontana, *Rethinking the Politics of
Commercial Society: The Edinburgh Review, 1802–1832* (Cambridge, 1985);
Peter Mandler, *Aristocratic Government in the Age of Reform: Whigs and
Liberals, 1830–1852* (Oxford, 1990); Richard Bellamy (ed.), *Victorian
Liberalism: Nineteenth-Century Political Thought and Practice* (London,
1990).

8 John Belchem, 'Henry Hunt and the Evolution of the Mass Platform',
English Historical Review, 93 (1978), 739–48; Belchem, 'Republicanism,
Constitutionalism and the Radical Platform', *Social History*, 6, 1 (1981),
1–32; Belchem, '1848: Feargus O'Connor and the Collapse of the Mass
Platform', in Epstein and Thompson (eds.), *The Chartist Experience*, pp.
269–310. Epstein, 'Radical Dining and Symbolic Expression'; Epstein,
'Understanding the Cap of Liberty'; Epstein 'The Constitutional
Idiom'.

9 Stedman Jones, 'Rethinking Chartism'; Biagini and Reid (eds), *Currents
of Radicalism*; Joyce, *Visions of the People*; Jon Lawrence, 'Popular
Radicalism and the Socialist Revival in Britain', *Journal of British Studies*,
31, 2 (1992), 163–86.

10 Stedman Jones, *Languages of Class*; Foster, 'The Declassing of Lan-
guage'; Gray, 'The Deconstruction of the English Working Class';
J. W. Scott, 'On Language, Gender, and Working Class History';
N. Kirk, 'In Defence of Class'; Joyce, *Visions of the People*.

11 Belchem, '*Orator Hunt*', p. 5.

12 Epstein, 'The Constitutional Idiom', p. 568; Epstein, 'Understanding
the Cap of Liberty', p. 117. It is an approach taken from Jameson, *The
Political Unconscious*, pp. 83–4.

13 A fact recognised by Joyce himself, see his 'Postmodernism and the Fall
of Class: Social Identity as Narrative in Nineteenth-Century England',
paper presented to Pacific Coast Conference on British Studies,
University of San Diego, March 1992.

14 'Prospectus of East London Democratic Association' 1837, quoted in
D. Thompson, *The Early Chartists* (London, 1971), p. 56.

15 In some radical circles there was a great deal of admiration for both the
American and French constitutions, especially the former. Henry

Pelling, *America and the British Left from Bright to Bevan* (London, 1956); C. Bonwick, *English Radicals and the American Revolution* (London, 1977); Dickinson, *Liberty and Property*; Claeys, *Citizens and Saints*.

16 *Western Luminary*, 23 January 1837, p. 2.

17 Wilson, 'Inventing Revolution', p. 384.

18 Wilentz, *Chants Democratic*. On English Francophobia and Russophobia see Gerald Newman, 'Anti-French propaganda and British Liberal Nationalism in the Early Nineteenth Century: Suggestions towards a General Interpretation', *Victorian Studies*, 18 (1975), 385–418; Stella Cottrell, 'The Devil on Two Sticks: Francophobia in 1803', in Raphael Samuel (ed.), *Patriotism, The Making and Unmaking of British National Identity. Vol. I: History and Politics*, pp. 259–74; J. H. Gleason, *The Genesis of Russophobia in Great Britain* (Cambridge, Mass., 1950). On anti-Catholicism more generally see G. Best, 'Popular Protestantism in Victorian Britain', in R. Robson (ed.), *Ideas and Institutions of Victorian Britain*; E. R. Norman, *Anti-Catholicism in Victorian England* (London, 1968).

19 For the genealogy of this belief see W. Haller, *Foxe's Book of Martyrs and the Elect Nation* (London, 1963); Peter Furtado, 'National Pride in Seventeenth-Century England', in Samuel (ed.), *Patriotism*, I, pp. 44–56; John Wolffe, *The Protestant Crusade in Great Britain, 1820–1860* (Oxford, 1991).

20 *The Sussex Agricultural Express*, 30 May 1857, p. 5.

21 *The Devon Weekly Times*, 24 July 1868, p. 5.

22 *Woolmer's Exeter and Plymouth Gazette*, 7 August 1858, p. 7.

23 Foster, *Class Struggle and the Industrial Revolution*, pp. 217–20; Joyce, *Work, Society and Politics*; Sykes, 'Popular Politics and Trade Unionism', II, pp. 455–65; Frank Neal, 'The Manchester Origins of the English Orange Order', *Manchester Regional History Review*, 4, 2 (1990/1).

24 Quoted in Jonathan Fulcher, 'Contests Over Constitutionalism: The Faltering of Reform in England, 1819–1820', paper given at Postgraduate Seminar in Modern British History, University of Cambridge, Sidney Sussex College, November 1990. The following paragraphs owe much to Fulcher's stimulating paper.

25 Fulcher, 'Contests over Constitutionalism'.

26 Fulcher, 'Contests over Constitutionalism'.

27 Fulcher, 'Contests over Constitutionalism'.

28 *The Morning Advertiser*, 18 September 1832, p. 3.

29 *The Boston Herald*, 24 July 1849, p. 2.

30 *The Western Times*, 24 June 1843, p. 3.

31 See n. 7 above.

32 See n. 4 above.

33 Pocock of course never denied the import, just the primacy, of the Lockean tradition, despite the accusations of Kramnick in his *Republicanism and Bourgeois Radicalism. Political Ideology in Late Eighteenth-Century England and America* (New York, 1990). See Pocock, 'Between

Gog and Magog; The Republican Thesis and the *Ideologia Americana*', *Journal of the History of Ideas*, (1987), 325–45.

34 Epstein, 'The Constitutional Idiom', pp. 558–63; Claeys, *Machinery, Money and the Millennium*.

35 Mandler, *Aristocratic Government in the Age of Reform*.

36 Colley, 'Radical Patriotism in Eighteenth-Century England', in Samuel (ed.), *Patriotism*, 1 pp. 169–87.

37 McCalman, *Radical Underworld*; Joel H. Weiner, *Radicalism and Freethought in Nineteenth-Century Britain: The Life of Richard Carlile* (Westport, 1983).

38 Taylor, 'Modes of Political Expression and Working Class Politics'. Also Edward Royle, *Radical Politics 1790–1900; Religion and Unbelief* (London, 1971); and his *Radicals, Secularists and Republicans 1866–1914* (Manchester, 1980).

39 *The Northern Star*, 23 January 1841, p. 2.

40 Prothero, 'Religion and Radicalism'; McCalman, 'New Jerusalems'; Historians such as Prothero and McCalman seem to be working towards the conclusion that Paine's politics was just one source of belief within the radical underworld; it did not always claim primacy over other progressive causes such as Judaism, vegetarianism, or homoeopathy, to name but a few. See also Logie Barrow, *Independent Spirits: Spiritualism and English Plebeians* (London, 1986).

41 *Drakard's Stamford News*, 1 November 1822, p. 2.

42 Hugh Cunningham, 'The Language of Patriotism', in Samuel (ed.), *Patriotism*, I, pp. 57–89.

43 This part of Knight's career is excluded from Foster's account. For these activities see Thompson, *The Making of the English Working Class*, pp. 676–8. See also William Fitton's obituary of Knight which was at great pains to stress Knight's attachment to constitutionalism, *The Northern Star*, 22 September 1838, p. 7.

44 Butterworth MSS., 13 October 1831. For Knight's repetition of this homespun, biblical motto in 1819 and 1838 see Appendix 4 and *The Northern Star*, 10 March 1838, p. 7.

45 *The Northern Star*, 14 July 1838, p. 6.

46 Istvan Hont and Michael Ignatieff (eds.), *Wealth and Virtue: The Shaping of Political Economy in the Scottish Enlightenment* (Cambridge, 1983); Noel Thompson, *The People's Science: The Popular Political Economy of Exploitation and Crisis, 1816–1834* (Cambridge, 1984); Thompson, *The Market and its Critics: Socialism and Political Economy in Nineteenth-Century Britain* (London, 1988); Claeys, *Machinery, Money and the Millennium: From Moral Economy to Socialism, 1815–1860* (Cambridge, 1987).

47 Foster, *Class Struggle and the Industrial Revolution*, p. 140.

48 Thompson, *The People's Science*, pp. 221–2. Kirk, 'In Defence of Class'.

49 Belchem, 'Radical Language and Ideology in Early Nineteenth-Century England: The Challenge to the Platform', *Albion*, 20, 2 (1988), 250.

50 *The Morning Advertiser*, 18 April 1842, p. 7.
51 *Mr. Heald's Address to the Joint Committees of Duncuft and Cobbett, 28 July 1852*, in 'Election Posters: General Elections July and December 1852', OLSL.
52 Wally Seccombe, 'Patriarchy Stabilized: The Construction of the Male Breadwinner Wage Norm in Nineteenth-Century Britain', *Social History*, 11 (1986), 53–76.
53 *Reynold's Newspaper*, 25 April 1852, p. 6.
54 F. E. Gillespie, *Labor and Politics in England, 1850–1867* (Durham, N. Carolina, 1927), p. 132.
55 *Reynold's Newspaper*, 2 April 1854, p. 3.
56 Butterworth MSS., 9 March 1840.
57 *Reynold's Newspaper*, 27 June 1852, p. 12.
58 *The Northern Star*, 26 June 1852, p. 6.
59 John Rule, 'The Property of Skill in the Period of Manufacture', in Joyce (ed.), *The Historical Meanings of Work* (Cambridge, 1988), pp. 99–118; Sally Alexander, 'Women, Class and Sexual Differences in the 1830s and 1840s: Some Reflections on the Writing of a Feminist History', *History Workshop Journal*, 17 (1984), 132–5.
60 See n. 59 above and Seccombe, 'Partriarchy Stabilized'.
61 Anna Clark, 'The Rhetoric of Chartist Domesticity: Gender, Language, and Class in the 1830s and 1840s', *Journal of British Studies*, 31, 1 (1992), 69.
62 *The Morning Advertiser*, 6 October 1826, p. 2.
63 Leonore Davidoff and Catherine Hall, *Family Fortunes. Men and Women of the English Middle Class, 1780–1850* (London, 1987), pp. 108–13; Hall, 'Private Persons versus Public Someones', Clark, 'The Rhetoric of Chartist Domesticity'.
64 Pocock, 'The Varieties of Whiggism from Exclusion to Reform', p. 485; Stefan Collini, 'The Idea of "Character" in Victorian Political Thought', *Transactions of the Royal Historical Society*, 5th series, 35 (1985), pp. 29–50.
65 *The Western Luminary*, 23 January 1837, p. 2.
66 The following paragraph owes much to Malcolm Chase's, *The People's Farm: English Radical Agrarianism 1775–1840* (Oxford, 1988).
67 Staves, *Married Women's Separate Property in England, 1680–1833* (Harvard, 1990).
68 *Reynold's Newspaper*, 25 April 1852, p. 6 and 9 May 1852, p. 13.
69 Howell Papers 333.3 57 (20), Bishopsgate Institute.
70 *The East London Observer*, 14 January 1860, p. 2.
71 *The East London Observer*, 31 October 1868, p. 7.
72 *Reynold's Newspaper*, 9 November 1856, p. 6.
73 For the recent re-interpretation of utopian politics generally see, E. P. Thompson, *William Morris: Romantic to Revolutionary* (London, 1976 edn.); Stedman Jones, 'Utopian Socialism Reconsidered', in R. Samuel (ed.), *People's History and Socialist Theory* (London, 1981), pp. 138–41;

Taylor, *Eve and the New Jerusalem*, pp. xiii–xviii; Peter Alexander and Roger Gill (eds.), *Utopias* (London, 1984).

74 *The Manchester Observer*, 2 October 1819, p. 731.
75 Quoted in G. S. R. Kitson Clark, 'The Romantic Element, 1830 to 1850', in J. H. Plumb (ed.), *Studies in Social History: A Tribute to G. M. Trevelyan* (London, 1955), p. 222.
76 *The Western Times*, 3 February 1849, p. 6.
77 W. H. G. Armytage, *Heaven's Below: Utopian Experiments in England, 1560–1960* (London, 1961); Armytage, *Yesterdays Tomorrows: A Historical Survey of Future Societies* (London, 1968); J. F. C. Harrison, *The Second Coming: Popular Millenarianism, 1780–1850* (London, 1979); J. C. Davis, *Utopia and the Ideal Society : A Study of English Utopian Writing 1516–1700* (Cambridge, 1981).
78 *The Northern Star*, 4 September 1847, p. 5.
79 *The Northern Star*, 11 August 1838, p. 5.
80 *The Manchester Gazette*, 23 January 1819, p. 411.
81 *The Morning Advertiser*, 27 September 1841, p. 3.
82 *The Morning Advertiser*, 8 May 1848, p. 2.
83 Dorothy Thompson, *Queen Victoria: Gender and Power* (London, 1990), p. 92.
84 *The Northern Star*, 16 October 1847, p. 1,
85 Taylor, 'Modes of Political Expression'.
86 *The East London Observer*, 12 March 1859, p. 3.
87 Steele, *Palmerston and Liberalism 1855–1865*; Taylor, 'Modes of Political Expression and Working-Class Politics'.
88 *The East London Observer*, 18 August 1860, p. 2.
89 *The East London Observer*, 23 June 1860, p. 3.
90 'Memoir of Edmond Beales, Esq., M.A. President of the League. (Extracted from the *Commonwealth*.)' in the Howell Papers 40 (2), Bishopsgate Institute. For details of Beales' pamphlet on the rights of public assembly see chapter 6 above, n. 21.
91 *The East London Observer*, 3 January 1866, p. 2.
92 Bellamy (ed.), *Liberalism*, p. 8.
93 Joyce, *Visions of the People*, pp. 48–54.
94 'A word to the New Electors, especially the Working Men from the President of the Reform League', p. 4, Howell Papers, Election Envelope, Bishopsgate Institute.
95 'A word to the New Electors, especially the Working Men from the President of the Reform League', p. 2.
96 *The Royal Devonport Telegraph*, 10 January 1835, p. 2.
97 *The Manchester Gazette*, 1 March 1828, p. 3.
98 *Reynold's Newspaper*, 16 May 1852, p. 12.
99 *The Metropolitan Working Men's Conservative Association*, Howell Papers, Political Parties Envelope, Bishopsgate Institute.
100 *The Northern Star*, 1 April 1848, p. 6.
101 *The Oldham Ensign and Standard*, 29 July 1868, p. 3.

102 *The Oldham Standard*, 26 July 1867, p. 3.
103 *Oldham Standard*, 26 July 1867, p. 8.
104 Tower Hamlets was reputed to boast approximately 7,000 Jewish *voters* by 1868, see *The East London Observer*, 15 August 1868, p. 3. According to Foster about 7 per cent or 8,000 of Oldham's population in 1861 were Irish, see his *Class Struggle and the Industrial Revolution*, p. 244.
105 Taylor, 'Modes of Political Expression and Working-Class Politics'.
106 *The Morning Advertiser*, 5 February 1848, p. 3.
107 Clark, 'The Rhetoric of Chartist Domesticity'.
108 See, for example, *The Northern Star*, 8 July 1848, p. 1.
109 Riley, *Am I That Name?* p. 67.
110 *The East London Observer*, 12 September 1868, p. 5 and 31 October 1868, p. 7.
111 J. L. Reisser, 'The Married Women's Property Bills of Great Britain, 1857–1882', Ph.D. thesis (California, Irvine, 1989).
112 Epstein, 'Constitutional Idiom', p. 567.
113 Thomas Lacqueur, 'The Queen Caroline Affair: Politics as Art in the Reign of George IV', *Journal of Modern History*, 54 (1982), 417–66; Clark, 'Queen Caroline and the Sexual Politics of Popular Culture in London, 1820', *Representations*, 31 (1990), 47–68; Clark, 'The Rhetoric of Chartist Domesticity', 67–9; Joyce, 'Postmodernism and the Fall of Class'.
114 Booth, *English Melodrama*; Brooks, *The Melodramatic Imagination*; Vicinus, '"Helpless and Unbefriended"'.
115 Epstein, 'Understanding the Cap of Liberty'; Pickering, 'Class Without Words'.
116 Joyce, *Visions of the People*, pp. 329–42.

CONCLUSION

1 See for example Clark, *English Society, 1688–1832*; J. Obelkivich, L. Roper, and R. Samuel (eds.), *Disciplines of Faith: Studies in Religion, Politics and Patriarchy* (London, 1987).
2 A project already begun by a number of scholars, see the forthcoming James Vernon (ed.), *Re-reading the Constitution: new narratives in the history of English Politics*.
3 R. Rosaldo, 'Celebrating Thompson's Heroes: Social Analysis in History and Anthropology', in Kaye and McClelland (eds.), *E. P. Thompson: Critical Perspectives*.

Select Bibliography

LOCAL HISTORIES, PAST AND PRESENT

Aspects of Nineteenth-Century Boston and District, History of Boston Series, No. 8 (Boston, 1972).

Bagley, G. S. *Boston. Its Story and People* (Boston, 1986).

Bateson, H. *A History of Oldham* (Oldham, 1949).

Butterworth, E. *Historical Sketches of Oldham* (Oldham, 1856).

Butterworth, J. *An Historical and Descriptive Account of the Town and Parochial Chapelry of Oldham* (Oldham, 1826).

Gill, C. *Plymouth. A New History 1603 to the Present Day*, 2 vols. (London, 1979).

Horsfield, T. W. *The History and Antiquities of Lewes*, 2 vols. (Lewes, 1837).

Mills, D. R. (ed.). *Twentieth-Century Lincolnshire* (Lincoln, 1989).

Mills, W. B. *The Parliamentary History of the Borough of Lewes, 1795–1885* (Lewes, 1908).

Newton, R. *Victorian Exeter, 1837–1914* (Leicester, 1968).

Porter, H. *Boston: Some of the Happenings in its History, 1800–1868*, 3 vols. (Lincoln, 1941–3).

Smith, V. (ed.). *The Town Book of Lewes 1702–1901*, 2 vols. (Lewes, 1973–6).

Thompson, P. *The History and Antiquities of Boston and the Villages of Skirbeck, Fishtoft, Freiston, Butterwick, Leverton, Leake, and Wrangle; Comprising the Hundreds of Skirbeck, in the County of Lincoln. Including also a History of the East, West, and Wildmore Fens, and Copious Notices of the Holland of Hauteiuntre Fen; a History of the River Watham; the Biography of Celebrated Persons, Natives of, or Connected with, the Neighbourhood; Sketches of the Geology, Natural History, Botany, and Agriculture of the District; A Very Extensive Collection of Archaisms and Provincial Words, Local Dialect, Phrases, Proverbs, Omens and Superstitions, etc.* (Boston, 1856).

Whitfield, H. F. *Plymouth and Devonport: In Times of War and Peace* (Plymouth, 1900).

BIOGRAPHIES AND AUTOBIOGRAPHIES

Anecdotes of the Rt. Hon. W. E. Gladstone by an Oxford Man (London, n.d.).

Acland, Anne. *Sir Thomas Dyke Acland: Memoirs and Letters* (Privately Printed, 1902).

Bamford, Samuel. *Early Days* (London, 1849).
 Passages in the Life of a Radical (Oxford, 1984 edn).
Cooper, Thomas. *The Life of Thomas Cooper, Written by Himself* (London, 1872).
Garnett, R. *The Life of W. J. Fox: Public Teacher and Social Reformer 1786–1864* (London, 1910).
Grime, Benjamin. *Memory Sketches. Part One – Parliamentary Elections: Enfranchisement of the Borough in 1832, to General Election, 1852, Both Inclusive* (Oldham, 1887).
Holyoake, G. J. *Sixty Years of an Agitator's Life*, 2 vols. (London, 1893).
Lansbury, George. *My Life* (London, 1931).
Middleton, James. *Election Recollections* (Oldham, 1925).
Newbould, T. Palmer. *Pages from a Life of Strife. Being Some Recollections of William Henry Chadwick, the Last of the Manchester Chartists* (London, 1911).

MANUSCRIPT SOURCES AND ESTATE PAPERS

Butterworth Manuscript Diaries, OLSL.
Parliamentary Election Newspapers, 1852, OLSL.
Ballads, Broadsides, and Songs, OLSL.
Election Posters and Scraps, 1849–52, OLSL.
Election Posters: General Elections July and December 1852, OLSL.
Howell Papers, Bishopsgate Institute, London.
Holyoake Papers, Co-operative Union Library, Manchester.
Boston Borough Records, Town Hall, Boston.
Acland MSS, EDRO.
Fortescue MSS, EDRO.
Palk MSS, EDRO.
Bastard MSS. WDRO.
Shiffner MSS., ESRO.
Moberly MSS. ESRO.

NEWSPAPERS

Cobbett's Political Register.
The Poor Man's Guardian.
The Working Man's Friend.
The Charter.
The Northern Star.
Notes to the People.
The People's Paper.
The Reasoner.
Reynold's Newspaper.
The Beehive.
The Parochial Chronicle.

The Parochial Expositer; or Anti-Church Rate Payers Gazette.
East London News.
The Shoreditch Observer.
Bethnal Green Times and East London Advertiser.
Eastern Times and Tower Hamlets Gazette.
Tower Hamlets Independent and East End Local Advertiser.
The Times.
The Morning Advertiser.
Cowdrey's Manchester Gazette and Weekly Advertiser.
The Manchester Times.
The Manchester Observer.
The Manchester Political Register.
The Manchester Guardian.
Oldham Free Press.
The Oldham Reformer, and General Advertiser.
The Oldham Advertiser.
The Oldham Ensign and Standard.
The Oldham Express.
The Oldham Times.
The Oldham Standard.
The Oldham Chronicle.
Noble's Boston Advertiser, Railway Guide, and Monthly Register.
The Champion of the East.
Drakard's Stamford News, and General Advertiser for the Counties of Lincoln,
*   Rutland, Northampton, Huntingdon, Leicester, Nottingham, and Other Parts*
*   Adjacent.*
The Boston Gazette and Lincolnshire Commercial Advertiser.
Lincolnshire, Boston, and Spalding Free Press and Eastern Counties Advertiser.
The Lincoln, Rutland and Stamford Mercury.
The Boston, Lincoln, Louth and Spalding Herald.
The Boston Guardian and Lincolnshire Advertiser.
Trewman's Flying Post, or Plymouth and Cornish Advertiser.
Flindell's Western Luminary: The Family Newspaper of the Nobility and Gentry,
*   Farmers and Traders of the Counties of Devon, Cornwall, Dorset and Somerset.*
The Alfred; West of England Journal, and General Advertiser.
Besley's Devonshire Chronicle and Exeter News.
Woolmer's Exeter and Plymouth Gazette.
The Devonport Independent, and Plymouth and Stonehouse Gazette.
The Devon Weekly Times.
The Western Express.
The Voice of the People and Magna Charta Review.
The Daily Eastern Mercury.
The Western Morning News.
The Exeter Journal and West of England Advertiser.
The West of England Conservative and General Advertiser.
Exeter Weekly Times and West of England General Advertiser.

Plymouth and Devonport Weekly Journal and General Advertiser for Devon, Cornwall,
   Somerset, and Dorset.
Plymouth, Devonport and Stonehouse Herald.
The Royal Devonport Telegraph, and Plymouth Chronicle.
The Sussex Weekly Advertiser: or Lewes Journal.
The Sussex Agricultural Express, Surrey Standard, Weald of Kent Mail, and County
   Advertiser.
The Lewes Times and County General Advertiser.

POLL BOOKS AND PAMPHLETS

A Correct State of the Poll (Boston, 1812).
History of the Boston Election (Boston, 1818).
The Addresses, Squibs, and Other Publications (Boston, 1820).
A Correct and Alphabetical State of the Poll (Boston, 1820).
The Poll Book (Alphabetically Arranged) Together with the Addresses (Boston,
   1826).
A Sketch of the Boston Election (Boston, 1830).
Boston Election Sketches (Boston, 1831).
A Correct Report of the Respectable Meeting of the Creditors of N. MacMullum
   (Boston, 1831).
The Poll of the Burgesses (Boston, 1837).
A Correct List of the Poll (Alphabetically Arranged) (Boston, 1837).
A Record of the Boston Election (Boston, 1841).
A Correct List of the Poll (Boston, 1843).
A Record of the Boston Election (Boston, 1847).
The Poll Book (Boston, 1847).
The Poll Book (Boston, 1849).
Records of the Election, for the Borough of Boston, 1852 (Boston, 1852).
The Poll Book (Boston, 1852).
Boston Election. The Poll Book (Boston, 1859).
'United We Conquer'. Boston Election 1860 (Boston, 1860).
Statement of Circumstances Connected with the Candidature of Samuel C. Ridley for the
   Representation of Boston (Boston, 1860).
Boston Election, 1865 (Boston, 1865).
Boston Election. The Poll Book (Boston, 1865).
Boston Election. The Poll Book (Boston, 1868).
A List of the Voters (Manchester 1832).
Oldham Election. The Poll Book (Oldham, 1835).
The Remembrancer, Shewing how the Electors of the Borough of Oldham Voted at the
   General Election which took Place, July 30th 1847 (Oldham, 1847).
The Second Remembrancer, Shewing how the Electors of the Borough of Oldham Voted
   at the General Election which took Place, July 8th 1852 (Oldham, 1852).
The Third Remembrancer, Shewing how the Electors of the Borough of Oldham Voted
   at the Election which took Place, Dec. 2nd, 1852 (Oldham, 1852).
Election, 1857. The Oldham Poll Book (Oldham, 1857).

Election, 1859. The Oldham Poll Book (Oldham, 1859).
Election, 1865. The Oldham Poll Book (Oldham, 1865).
Election, 1868. Oldham Borough Poll Book (Oldham, 1868).
Borough of Lewes – to Wit. A Poll (Lewes, 1812).
Borough of Lewes – to Wit. A Poll (Lewes, 1816).
A Poll Taken by Mr. Wm. Smart and Mr. Thos. Whiteman (Lewes, 1818).
Lewes Election, 1826. A Poll (Lewes, 1826).
Borough of Lewes. A Poll (Lewes, 1830).
A Poll Taken by Mr. George Bailey (Lewes, 1835).
A Poll Taken by Mr. Plumer Verrall (Lewes, 1837).
A Poll Taken by Mr. Nehemiah Wimble (Lewes, 1841).
A Poll Taken by Mr. Benjamin Flint and Mr. John Hilton (Lewes, 1847).
A Poll Taken by Mr. Richard Lambe and Mr. Charles Parsons (Lewes, 1859).
A Poll Taken by Mr. Henry S. Gorringe (Lewes, 1865).
A Poll Taken by Mr. James Broad (Lewes, 1868).
The Objects, Laws, &c., of the Crompton Political Union (Oldham, 1832).
Public Entry of John Fielden, Esq., M.P. and General Johnson, M.P. into Oldham (Oldham, 1847).
'Toryism in Oldham: Club Histories', *Oldham Standard*, 1909.

SECONDARY SOURCES: BOOKS

Abelove, H. et al. (eds.), *Visions of History* (New York, 1983).
Alexander, P. and Gill, R. (eds.). *Utopias* (London, 1984).
Anderson, P. *The Printed Image and the Transformation of Popular Culture* (Oxford, 1991).
Applewhite, H. B. and Levy, D. G. (eds.). *Women and Politics in the Age of Democratic Revolution* (Ann Arbor, 1990).
Atkinson, M. *Our Master's Voices: The Language and Body Language of Politics* (London, 1984).
Bagehot, W. *The English Constitution* (London, 1963 edn.).
Bailey, P. *Leisure and Class in Victorian England. Rational Recreation and the Contest for Control* (London, 1978).
Music Hall: The Business of Pleasure (Milton Keynes, 1986).
Baker, K. M. *Inventing the French Revolution: Essays on French Political Culture in the Eighteenth Century* (Cambridge, 1990).
Barrow, L. *Independent Spirits: Spiritualism and English Plebeians* (London, 1986).
Barrows, F. D. and Mock, D. B. (eds.). *A Dictionary of Obituaries of Modern British Radicals* (London, 1989).
Belchem, J. *'Orator' Hunt: Henry Hunt and English Working-Class Radicalism* (Oxford, 1985).
Bellamy, J. M. and Saville, J. (eds.). *Dictionary of Labour Biography*, 8 vols. (London, 1972–87).
Bellamy, R. (ed.). *Victorian Liberalism: Nineteenth-Century Political Thought and Practice* (London, 1990).

Best, G. *Mid-Victorian Britain* (Glasgow, 1979).
Biagini, E. and Reid, A. (eds.). *Currents of Radicalism: Popular Radicalism, Organised Labour and Party Politics in Britain, 1850–1914* (Cambridge, 1991).
Bonwick, C. *English Radicals and the American Revolution* (London, 1977).
Booth, M. *English Melodrama* (London, 1965).
Booth, M. W. *The Experience of Songs* (New Haven, 1981).
Borsay, P. *The English Urban Renaissance: Culture and Society in the Provincial Town, 1660–1770* (Oxford, 1989).
Boshtedt, J. *Riot and Community Politics in England and Wales, 1790–1810* (Cambridge, Mass., 1983).
Bourdieu, P. *Distinction. A Social Critique of the Judgement of Taste* (London, 1984).
Bratton, J. *Victorian Popular Ballads* (London, 1975).
Bratton, J. (ed.). *The Victorian Music Hall: Performance and Style* (Milton Keynes, 1987).
Brock, M. *The Great Reform Act* (London, 1972).
Brooks, P. *The Melodramatic Imagination* (New Haven, 1976).
Burke, K. *A Rhetoric of Motives* (New York, 1969).
Burke, P. *Popular Culture in Early Modern Europe* (London, 1978).
Burke, P. and Porter, R. (eds.). *The Social History of Language*, 2 vols. (Cambridge, 1988–1990).
Bushaway, B. *By Rite: Custom, Ceremony and Community in England 1700–1850* (London, 1982).
Calhoun, C. *The Question of Class Struggle: Social Foundations of Popular Radicalism during the Industrial Revolution* (Chicago, 1982).
Cannadine, D. and Price, S. (eds.). *Rituals of Royalty: Power and Ceremonial in Traditional Societies* (Cambridge, 1987).
Cannon, J. A. *Parliamentary Reform, 1640–1832* (Cambridge, 1972).
Carlyle, T. *Heroes and Hero-Worship* (London, 1888).
Chartier, R. *The Cultural Uses of Print in Early Modern France* (Princeton, 1987).
Chartier, R. (ed.). *The Culture of Print: Power and the Uses of Print in Early Modern Europe* (Cambridge, 1989).
Chase, M. *The People's Farm: English Radical Agrarianism, 1775–1840* (Oxford, 1988).
Claeys, G. *Machinery, Money and the Millennium: From Moral Economy to Socialism, 1815–1860* (Cambridge, 1987).
  Citizens and Saints: Politics and Anti-Politics in Early British Socialism (Cambridge, 1989).
Clark, J. C. D. *English Society, 1688–1832: Ideology, Social Structure and Political Practice during the Ancien Regime* (Cambridge, 1985).
  Revolution and Rebellion: State and Society in England in the Seventeenth and Eighteenth Centuries (Cambridge, 1986).
Clark, P. *Sociability and Urbanity: Clubs and Societies in the Eighteenth-Century City* (Leicester, 1990).

Clarke, P. F. *Lancashire and the New Liberalism* (Cambridge, 1971).

A Question of Leadership: Gladstone to Thatcher (London, 1991).

Cobbett, W. *The Parliamentary History of England*, 36 vols. (London, 1806–1820).

Colley, L. *In Defiance of Oligarchy: The Tory Party, 1714–1760* (Cambridge, 1982).

Collini, S., Winch, D. and Burrow, J. *That Noble Science of Politics: A Study in Nineteenth-Century Intellectual History* (Cambridge, 1983).

Colls, R. *The Colliers Rant: Song and Culture in the Industrial Village* (London, 1977).

The Pitmen of the Northern Coalfield: Work, Culture and Protest, 1790–1850 (Manchester, 1987).

Colls, R. and Dodd, P. (eds.). *Englishness: Essays in Politics and Culture* (London, 1986).

Cosgrove, D. and Daniels, S. (eds.). *The Iconography of Landscape: Essays on Symbolic Representation, Design and Use of Past and Environments* (Cambridge, 1988).

Cressy, D. *Bonfires and Bells: National Memory and the Protestant Calendar in Elizabethan and Stuart England* (London, 1989).

Cunningham, H. *Leisure in the Industrial Revolution* (London, 1980).

Davidoff, L. and Hall, C. *Family Fortunes: Men and Women of the English Middle Class, 1780–1850* (London, 1987).

Davies, Susan G. *Parades and Power: Street-Theatre in Nineteenth-Century Philadelphia* (Berkeley, 1986).

Davis, J. *Reforming London: The London Government Problem, 1855–1900* (Oxford, 1988).

Davis, J. C. *Utopia and the Ideal Society: A Study of English Utopian Writing 1516–1700* (Cambridge, 1981).

Dellheim, C. *The Face of the Past: The Preservation of the Medieval Inheritance in Victorian England* (Cambridge, 1982).

Denning, M. *Mechanic Accents: Dime Novels and Working Class Culture in America* (New York, 1987).

Dickinson, H. T. *Liberty and Property: Political Ideology in Eighteenth Century Britain* (London, 1977).

Dod, C. R. *Electoral Facts from 1832–52. Impartially Stated* (Brighton, 1972).

Dozier, R. B. *For King, Constitution and Country: The English Loyalists and the French Revolution* (Kentucky, 1983).

Durkheim, E. *The Elementary Forms of Religious Life* (London, 1915).

Dyos, H. J. and Wolff, M. (eds.). *The Victorian City: Images and Realities*, 2 vols. (London, 1973).

Eisenstein, E. L. *The Printing Press as an Agent of Change* (Cambridge, 1990).

Elshtain, J. B. *Public Man, Private Woman: Women in Social and Political Thought* (Princeton, 1981).

Emsley, C. *British Society and the French Wars 1793–1815* (London, 1979).

Epstein, J. *The Lion of Freedom. Feargus O'Connor and the Chartist Movement, 1832–1842* (London, 1982).

Epstein, J. and Thompson, D. (eds.). *The Chartist Experience: Studies in Working-Class Radicalism and Culture* (London, 1982).

Feldman, D. and Stedman Jones, G. (eds.). *Metropolis, London: Histories and Representations since 1800* (London, 1989).

Fontana, B. *Rethinking the Politics of Commercial Society: The Edinburgh Review, 1802–1832* (Cambridge, 1985).

Foster, J. *Class Struggle and the Industrial Revolution: Early Industrial Capitalism in Three English Towns* (London, 1974).

Foster, H. (ed.). *Postmodern Culture* (London, 1985).

Fraser, D. *Urban Politics in Victorian England: The Structure of Politics in Victorian Cities* (London, 1976).

Frye, N. *The Anatomy of Criticism* (Princeton, 1957).
    The Secular Scripture (Cambridge, Mass., 1976).

Fukuyama, F. *The End of History and the Last Man* (London, 1992).

Furet, F. and Ozouf, J. *Reading and Writing: Literacy in France from Calvin to Jules Ferry* (Cambridge, 1982).

Gammage, R. G. *History of the Chartist Movement* (London, 1894 edn.).

Garrard, J. *Leadership and Power in Victorian Industrial Towns, 1830–80* (Manchester, 1983).

Gash, N. *Politics in the Age of Peel: A Study in the Technique of Parliamentary Representation, 1830–1850* (London, 1953).

Geertz, C. *The Interpretation of Cultures* (New York, 1973).
    Local Knowledge: Further Essays in Interpretive Anthropology (New York, 1983).

Gellner, E. *Culture, Identity and Politics* (Cambridge, 1987).

Gillespie, F. E. *Labor and Politics in England, 1850–1867* (Durham, N. Carolina, 1927).

Gilmour, I. *Riot, Rising and Revolution: Governance and Violence in Eighteenth-Century England* (London, 1992).

Ginter, D. E. *Whig Organisation in the General Election of 1790* (Berkeley, 1967).

Girouard, M. *Cities and People: A Social and Architectural History* (London, 1989).
    The English Town (Yale, 1990).

J. H. Gleason, *The Genesis of Russophobia in Great Britain* (Cambridge, Mass., 1950).

Glen, R. *Urban Workers in the Early Industrial Revolution* (London, 1983).

Golby, J. M. and Purdue, A. W. *The Civilization of the Crowd: Popular Culture in England 1750–1900* (London, 1984).

Goody, J. *The Domestication of the Savage Mind* (Cambridge, 1977).

Gorman, J. *Banner Bright* (London, 1973).

Gossman, N. J. and Baylen, J. O. (eds.). *Dictionary of Modern British Radicals*, 2 vols. (London, 1979).

Gray, R. *The Aristocracy of Labour in Nineteenth Century Britain c. 1850–1900* (London, 1981).

Gunn, J. A. W. *Factions No More: Attitudes to Party in Government and Opposition in Eighteenth Century England* (London, 1972).

Beyond Liberty and Property: The Process of Self-Recognition in Eighteenth-Century Political Thought (Montreal, 1983).

Habermas, J. *The Structural Transformation of the Public Sphere: An Inquiry into a Category of Bourgeois Society* (London, 1989).

Hanham, H. J. *Elections and Party Management: Politics in the Time of Gladstone and Disraeli* (London, 1959).

The Reformed Electoral System in Great Britain, 1932–1914 (London, 1968).

Harrison, B. *Drink and the Victorians. The Temperance Question in England 1815–1872* (London, 1971).

Harrison, J. F. C. *The Second Coming: Popular Millenarianism, 1780–1850* (London, 1979).

Harrison, M. *Crowds in History: Mass Phenomena in English Towns, 1790–1835* (Cambridge, 1988).

Harrison, R. *Before the Socialists: Studies in Labour and Politics, 1861–1881* (London, 1981).

Hellmuth, E. (ed.). *The Transformation of Political Culture: England and Germany in the Late Eighteenth Century* (Oxford, 1990).

Hennock, E. P. *Fit and Proper Persons: Ideal and Reality in Nineteenth Century Urban Government* (London, 1973).

Hill, B. W. *English Parliamentary Parties, 1742–1832* (London, 1985).

Hill, C. *Puritanism and Revolution* (London, 1955).

Hobsbawm, E. and Ranger, T. (eds.). *The Invention of Tradition* (Cambridge, 1983).

Hollis, P. *The Pauper Press* (Oxford, 1970).

Hont, I. and Ignatieff, M. (eds.). *Wealth and Virtue: The Shaping of Political Economy in the Scottish Enlightenment* (Cambridge, 1983).

Hunt, L. *Politics, Culture and Class in the French Revolution* (Berkeley, 1984).

(ed.). *The New Cultural History* (Los Angeles, 1989).

Ionescu, G. and Gellner, E. (eds.). *Populism, its Meaning and Characteristics* (London, 1969).

Jameson, F. *The Political Unconscious: Narrative as a Socially Symbolic Act* (New York, 1981).

Jephson, H. *The Platform: Its Rise and Progress*, (London, 1892).

Johnson, R. (ed.). *Making Histories: Studies in History, Writing and Politics* (London, 1982).

Jones, G. Stedman. *Outcast London: A Study in the Relationship between Classes in Victorian Society* (Oxford, 1971).

Languages of Class: Studies in English Working-Class History 1832–1982 (Cambridge, 1983).

Joyce, P. *Work, Society and Politics. The Culture of the Factory in Later Victorian England* (London, 1982 edn.).

Visions of the People: Industrial England and the Question of Class, c. 1848–1914 (Cambridge, 1991).

Joyce, P. (ed.). *The Historical Meanings of Work* (Cambridge, 1988).

Kantorowicz, E. *The King's Two Bodies: A Study in Medieval Political Theory* (Princeton, 1957).

Kaplan, E. A. *Postmodernism and its Discontents. Theories, Practices* (London, 1988).

Karsten, P. *Patriot-Heroes in England and America. Political Symbolism and Changing Values Over Three Centuries* (Wisconsin, 1978).

Kaye, H. J. and McClelland, K. (eds.). *E. P. Thompson: Critical Perspectives* (Cambridge, 1990).

Kertzer, D. I. *Ritual Politics and Power* (Yale, 1988).

Kidd, A. J. and Roberts, K. W. (eds.). *City, Class and Culture: Studies of Social Policy and Cultural Production in Victorian Manchester* (Manchester, 1985).

Kinzer, B. L. *The Ballot Question in Nineteenth Century English Politics* (London, 1982).

Kirk, N. *The Growth of Working Class Reformism in Mid-Victorian England* (London, 1985).

Kishlansky, M. *Parliamentary Selection: Social and Political Choice in Early Modern England* (Cambridge, 1986).

Kramnick, I. *Republicanism and Bourgeois Radicalism. Political Ideology in Eighteenth-Century England and America* (New York, 1990).

Landes, J. B. *Women and the Public Sphere in the Age of the French Revolution* (Ithaca, 1988).

Larwood, J. and Hotten, J. C. *English Inn Signs. A Revised and Modernised Version of the History of Signboards* (London, 1985 edn.).

LeMahieu, D. I. *A Culture for Democracy; Mass Communication and the Cultivated Mind in Britain between the Wars* (Oxford, 1988).

Lewis, G. C. Sir. *Remarks on the Use and Abuse of Political Terms* (Oxford, 1877).

Lieberman, D. *The Province of Legislation Determined: Legal Theory in Eighteenth-Century Britain* (Cambridge, 1990).

Lloyd, G. *The Man of Reason: Male and Female in Western Philosophy* (London, 1984).

Lucas, B. Keith *English Local Government Franchise* (Oxford, 1952).

Lukes, S. *Essays in Social Theory* (London, 1977).

Lyotard, J. F. *The Postmodern Condition: A Report on Knowledge* (Minneapolis, 1979).

McCalman, I. *Radical Underworld: Prophets, Revolutionaries and Pornographers in London, 1795–1840* (Cambridge, 1988).

McKibbin, R. *Ideologies of Class: Social Relations in Britain, 1880–1950* (Oxford, 1990).

McLuhan, M. and Fiore, Q. *The Medium is the Massage* (New York, 1967).

Maidment, B. *The Poorhouse Fugitives: Self-Taught Poets and Poetry in Victorian Britain* (Manchester, 1987).

Malcolmson, R. W. *Popular Recreations in English Society, 1700–1850* (Cambridge, 1973).

Mandler, P. *Aristocratic Government in the Age of Reform: Whigs and Liberals, 1830–1850* (Oxford, 1990).

Mayhew, H. *The Morning Chronicle Survey of Labour and the Poor*, 6 vols. (Horsham, 1981).

Medick, H. and Sabean, D. W. (eds.). *Interests and Emotion: Essays on the Study of Family and Kinship* (Cambridge, 1984).

Michels, R. *Political Parties. A Sociological Study of the Oligarchic Tendencies of Modern Democracy* (London, 1962 edn).

Money, J. *Experience and Identity: Birmingham and the West Midlands 1760–1800* (Manchester, 1977).

Moore, D. C. *The Politics of Deference: A Study of the Mid-Nineteenth Century Political System* (Brighton, 1976).

Morris, R. (ed.). *Class, Power and Social Structure in British Nineteenth Century Towns* (Leicester, 1986).

Nairn, T. *The Enchanted Glass: Britain and its Monarchy* (London, 1988).

Namier, L. B. *The Structure of Politics at the Accession of George III* (London, 1929).

Namier, L. B. and Brooke, J. (eds.). *The House of Commons, 1754–1790*, 3 vols. (London, 1964).

Newman, G. *The Rise of English Nationalism: A Cultural History, 1740–1830* (London, 1988).

Nossiter, T. J. *Influence, Opinion and Political Idioms in Reformed England: Case Studies from the North-East* (Brighton, 1975).

O'Gorman, F. *The Rise of Party in England: The Rockingham Whigs, 1760–1782* (London, 1975).

The Emergence of the British Two Party System, 1760–1832 (London, 1982).

Voters, Patrons and Parties. The Unreformed Electoral System of Hanoverian England 1734–1832 (Oxford, 1989).

Obelkivich, J., Roper, L. and Samuel, R. (eds.). *Disciplines of Faith: Studies in Religion, Politics and Patriarchy* (London, 1987).

Okin, S. M. *Women in Western Political Thought* (Princeton, 1979).

Olney, R. J. *Lincolnshire Politics, 1832–1885* (Oxford, 1973).

Rural Society and County Government in Nineteenth Century Lincolnshire (Lincoln, 1979).

Ong, W. J. *Orality and Literacy: The Technologizing of the Word* (London, 1982).

Ostrogorski, M. *Democracy and the Organisation of Political Parties*, 2 vols. (London, 1902).

Outram, D. *The Body and the French Revolution: Sex, Class and Political Culture* (London, 1985).

Ozouf, M. *Festivals and Revolution: France 1789–1799* (Harvard, 1988).

Pallister, A. *Magna Carta. The Heritage of Liberty* (Oxford, 1977).

Palmer, R. *Sound of History: Songs and Social Comment* (Oxford, 1988).

Parry, J. P. *Democracy and Religion: Gladstone and the Liberal Party, 1867–75* (Cambridge, 1986).

Pateman, C. *The Sexual Contract* (Cambridge, 1988).

The Disorder of Women: Democracy, Feminism and Political Thought (Cambridge, 1989).

Pelling, H. *America and the British Left from Bright to Bevan* (London, 1956).

Phillips, A. *Engendering Democracy* (Cambridge, 1991).

Phillips, J. A. *Electoral Behaviour in Unreformed England, 1761–1802* (Princeton, 1982).

Phillipson, U. *Political Slang, 1750–1850* (London, 1941).

Pocock, J. G. A. *Virtue, Commerce and History: Essays on Political Thought and History, Chiefly in the Eighteenth Century* (Cambridge, 1985).

The Ancient Constitution and the Feudal Law: A Study of English Historical Thought in the Seventeenth Century. A Re-issue with a Retrospect (Cambridge, 1987).

Pocock, J. G. A. (ed.). *Three British Revolutions* (Princeton, 1982).

Poster, M. *Foucault, Marxism and History. Mode of Production Versus Mode of Information* (Cambridge, 1984).

Prest, J. *Liberty and Locality: Parliament, Permissive Legislation and Ratepayers' Democracies in the Nineteenth Century* (Oxford, 1990).

Prothero, I. *Artisans and Politics in Early Nineteenth-Century London: John Gast and His Times* (London, 1981).

Pugh, M. *The Tories and the People, 1880–1935* (Oxford, 1985).

Rabinow, P. (ed.). *The Foucault Reader* (London, 1984).

Ranciere, J. *The Nights of Labour* (New York, 1989).

Reddy, W. M. *The Rise of Market Culture. The Textile Trade and French Society, 1750–1990* (Cambridge, 1984).

Rendall, J. (ed.). *Equal or Different. Women's Politics 1800–1914* (Oxford, 1987).

Richter, D. *Riotous Victorians* (Ohio, 1981).

Riley, D. *'Am I That Name?' Feminism and the Category of 'Women' in History* (London, 1988).

Rogers, N. *Whigs and Cities. Popular Politics in the Age of Walpole and Pitt* (Oxford, 1989).

Royle, E. *Radical Politics 1790–1900: Religion and Unbelief* (London, 1971).

Radicals, Secularists, and Republicans, 1866–1914 (Manchester, 1980).

Rule, J. *The Labouring Classes in Early Industrial England* (London, 1986).

Samuel, R. (ed.). *People's History and Socialist Theory* (London, 1981).

Patriotism. The Making and Unmaking of British National Identity, 3 vols. (London, 1989).

Savage, M. *The Dynamics of Working Class Politics. The Labour Movement in Preston, 1880–1940* (Cambridge, 1987).

Saville, J. *1848: The British State and the Chartist Movement* (Cambridge, 1987).

Scott, J. W. *Gender and the Politics of History* (New York, 1988).

Searle, G. R. *Corruption in British Politics, 1895–1930* (Oxford, 1987).

Seymour, C. *Electoral Reform in England and Wales* (New Haven, 1915).

Sewell, jun. W. H. *Work and Revolution in France: The Language of Labour from the Old Regime to 1848* (Cambridge, 1980).

Simon, B. *Education and the Labour Movement, 1870–1920* (London, 1965).

Smith, F. B. *The Making of the Second Reform Bill* (Cambridge, 1966).

Smith, O. *The Politics of Language, 1791–1819* (Oxford, 1981).

Smith, R. J. *The Gothic Bequest: Medieval Institutions in British Thought* (Cambridge, 1987).

Snell, K. *Annals of the Labouring Poor* (Cambridge, 1985).

Staves, S. *Married Women's Separate Property in England, 1680–1833* (Harvard, 1990).

Steele, E. D. *Palmerston and Liberalism 1855–1865* (Cambridge, 1991).

Stevenson, J. *Popular Disturbances in England 1700–1870* (London, 1979).

Stevenson, J. and Quinault, R. (eds.). *Popular Protest and Public Order: Six Studies in British History, 1790–1820* (London, 1974).

Storch, R. D. *Popular Culture and Custom in Nineteenth Century England* (London, 1982).

Taylor, B. *Eve and the New Jerusalem. Socialism and Feminism in the Nineteenth Century* (London, 1983).

Tholfsen, T. R. *Working Class Radicalism in Mid-Victorian England* (London, 1976).

Thomis, M. I. and Holt, P. *Threats of Revolution in Britain* (London, 1977).

Thompson, D. *The Chartists: Popular Politics in the Industrial Revolution* (London, 1984).

Queen Victoria: Gender and Power (London, 1990).

Thompson, E. P. *The Making of the English Working Class* (London, 1968 edn).

William Morris: Romantic to Revolutionary (London, 1976 edn).

Thompson, N. *The People's Science: The Popular Political Economy of Exploitation and Crisis, 1816–1834* (Cambridge, 1984).

The Market and its Critics: Socialism and Political Economy in Nineteenth-Century Britain (London, 1988).

Thorne, R. G. (ed.). *History of Parliament. The House of Commons, 1790–1820*, 2 vols. (London, 1986).

Timbs, J. *Clubs and Club Life in London* (London, 1872).

Trevelyan, G. M. *The Two-Party System in English Constitutional History* (Oxford, 1926).

Turner, V. *The Ritual Process: Structure and Anti-Structure* (London, 1967).

Dramas, Fields, and Metaphors (Ithaca, 1974).

Vansina, J. *The Oral Tradition as History* (Wisconsin, 1985).

Veitch, G. S. *The Genesis of Parliamentary Reform* (London, 1913).

Vicinus, M. *The Industrial Muse* (London, 1974).

Vincent, D. *Bread, Knowledge and Freedom: A Study of Nineteenth-Century Working Class Autobiography* (London, 1981).

Literacy and Popular Culture, England 1750–1914 (Cambridge, 1989).

Vincent, J. *Poll Books: How Victorians Voted* (Cambridge, 1967).

The Formation of the British Liberal Party 1857–1868 (London, 1972 edn.).

Vincent, J. and Stenton, M. *McCalman's Parliamentary Poll Book 1832–1914* (Brighton, 1971).

Vine, J. R. Somers. *English Municipal Institutions: Their Growth and Development from 1835 to 1879* (London, 1879).

Waller, P. *Town, City and Nation, 1850–1914* (London, 1983).

Walton, J. K. and Walvin, J. (eds.). *Leisure in Britain, 1780–1939* (Manchester, 1983).

Warner, M. *Monuments and Maidens: The Allegory of the Female Form* (London, 1985).

Weaver, S. A. *John Fielden and the Politics of Popular Radicalism* (London, 1987).

Webb, S. and B. *English Local Government from the Revolution to the Municipal Corporations Act: The Parish and the County* (London, 1963).

The Manor and the Borough, Part One (London, 1908).

Weiner, J. H. *Radicalism and Freethought in Nineteenth Century Britain: The Life of Richard Carlile* (Westport, 1983).

Wells, R. *Insurrection: The British Experience, 1795–1803* (Gloucester, 1983).

White, H. *Metahistory: The Historical Imagination in Nineteenth-Century Europe* (Baltimore, 1973).

The Content of the Form: Narrative Discourse and Historical Representation (Baltimore, 1987).

Wilentz, S. *Chants Democratic: New York City and the Rise of the American Working Class* (New York, 1984).

Wilentz, S. (ed.). *Rites of Power: Symbolism, Ritual and Politics Since the Middle Ages* (Philadelphia, 1985).

Williams, G. A. *Artisans and Sans-Culottes: Popular Movements in France and Britain during the French Revolution* (London, 1968).

Williams, R. *The Long Revolution* (London, 1965).

Wilson, S. (ed.). *Saints and their Cults. Studies in Religious Sociology, Folklore and History* (Cambridge, 1983).

Wolffe, J. *The Protestant Crusade in Great Britain 1829–1860* (Oxford, 1991).

Wright, D. G. *Popular Radicalism: The Working Class Experience 1780–1880* (London, 1988).

Yeo, E. and S. (eds.). *Popular Culture and Class Conflict* (Brighton, 1981).

SECONDARY SOURCES: ARTICLES

Adamson, J. S. A. 'Eminent Victorians: S. R. Gardiner and the Liberal as Hero', *Historical Journal*, 33, 3 (1990), 641–57.

Alexander, S. 'Women, Class and Sexual Differences in the 1830s and 1860s: Some Reflections on the Writing of Feminist History', *History Workshop Journal*, 17 (1984), 125–49.

Bailey, P. '"Will the Real Bill Banks Please Stand Up?" Role Analysis of Victorian Working-Class Respectability', *Journal of Social History*, 12 (1979), 336–53.

'Ally Sloper's Half Holiday: Comic Art in the 1880s' *History Workshop Journal*, 16 (1983), 4–31.

Barker, P. 'The Domestication of Politics: Women and American Political Society, 1780–1920', *American Historical Review*, 89 (1984), 620–47.

Baxter, J. L. and Donelly, F. K. 'The Revolutionary Underground in the West Riding: myth or reality', *Past and Present*, 64 (1974), 124–36.

Beales, D. E. D. 'Parliamentary Politics and the "Independent Member" 1820–1860', in R. Robson (ed.), *Ideas and Institutions in Victorian Britain* (London, 1967), pp. 1–19.

Behlmer, G. 'Theory and Anti-Theory in Nineteenth-Century British Social History', *Journal of British Studies*, 26, 1 (1987), 123–32.

Belchem, J. 'Henry Hunt and the Evolution of the Mass Platform', *English Historical Review*, 93 (1978), 739–73.
'Republicanism, Popular Constitutionalism and the Radical Platform in the Early Nineteenth-Century England', *Social History*, 6 (1981), 1–35.
'Radical Language and Ideology in Early Nineteenth-Century England: The Challenge of the Platform', *Albion*, 20 (1988), 247–59.
Berger, John. 'The Nature of Mass Demonstrations', *New Society*, 23 May 1968, pp. 754–55.
Best, G. 'Popular Protestantism in Victorian Britain', in R. Robson (ed.), *Ideas and Institutions in Victorian Britain* (London, 1967).
Booth, A. 'Popular Loyalism and Public Violence in the North-West of England, 1790–1800', *Social History*, 8 (1983), 295–313.
Brent, C. E. 'The Immediate Impact of the Second Reform Act on a Southern County Town: Voting Patterns at Lewes Borough in 1865 and 1868' *Southern History*, 2 (1980), 129–77.
Brent, R. 'Butterfield's Tories: "High Politics" and the Writing of Modern British History', *Historical Journal*, 30, 4 (1987), 943–54.
Brewer, J. 'Theater and Counter-Theater in Georgian Politics: The Mock Elections at Garrat', *Radical History Review*, 22 (1979–80), 7–40.
'The Number 45: A Wilkite Political Symbol', in Stephen Baxter (ed.), *Englands Rise to Greatness: England from the Restoration to the American War* (Berkeley, 1980), pp. 349–80.
'Commercialisation in Politics', in N. McKendrick (ed.), *The Birth of a Consumer Society* (London, 1982), 197–262.
Briggs, A. 'The Language of "Class" in Early Nineteenth-Century England', in Briggs and J. Saville (eds.), *Essays in Labour History* (London, 1960).
'The Language of "Mass" and "Masses" in Nineteenth-Century Britain', in D. E. Martin and D. Rubenstein (eds.), *Ideology and the Labour Movement: Essays Presented to John Saville* (London, 1979).
Brunel, C. and Jackson, P. M. 'Notes on Tokens as a Source of Information on the History of the Labour and Radical Movements', *Society for the Study of Labour History*, 15 (1967), 26–40.
Cannadine, D. 'The Transformation of Civic Ritual in Modern Britain: The Colchester Oyster Feast', *Past and Present*, 94 (1982), 107–30.
'The Past and Present in the English Industrial Revolution', *Past and Present*, 103 (1984), 131–72.
'The Context, Performance and Meaning of Ritual: The British Monarchy and the "Invention of Tradition", c. 1820–1977', in E. Hobsbawm and T. Ranger (eds.), *The Invention of Tradition* (Cambridge, 1983), pp. 101–64.
Cannadine, D. and Hammerton, E. 'Conflict and Consensus on a Ceremonial Occasion: The Diamond Jubilee in Cambridge in 1897', *Historical Journal*, 24 (1981), 111–46.
Chase, M. 'From Millennium to Anniversary: The Concept of Jubilee in Late Eighteenth- and Nineteenth-Century England', *Past and Present*, 129 (1990), pp. 132–47.

Claeys, G. 'The Triumph of Class Conscious Reform in British Radicalism, 1790–1860', *Historical Journal*, 26, 4 (1983), 969–85.

Clark, A. 'Queen Caroline and the Sexual Politics of Popular Culture in London, 1820', *Representations*, 31 (1990), 47–68.

'The Rhetoric of Chartist Domesticity: Gender, Language and Class in the 1830s and 1840s', *Journal of British Studies*, 31, 1 (1992), 62–88.

Clark, G. S. R. Kitson. 'The Romantic Element, 1830 to 1850', in J. H. Plumb (ed.), *Studies in Social History: A Tribute to G. M. Trevelyan* (London, 1955).

Clark, J. C. D. 'A General Theory of Party, Opposition and Government, 1688–1832', *Historical Journal*, 23, 2 (1980), 295–325.

Clarke, P. F. 'Electoral Sociology of Modern Britain', *History*, 57 (1972), 31–55.

Colley, L. 'The Apotheosis of George III: Loyalty, Royalty and the British Nation', *Past and Present*, 102 (1984), 94–129.

'Whose Nation? Class and National Consciousness in Britain, 1750–1830', *Past and Present*, 113 (1986), 97–117.

'The Politics of Eighteenth-Century British History', *Journal of British Studies*, 25, 4 (1986), 359–79.

Collini, S. 'The Idea of "Character" in Victorian Political Thought', *Transactions of the Royal Historical Society*, 5th Series, 35 (1985), 29–55.

Cunningham, H. 'The Metropolitan Fairs: A Case Study in the Social Control of Leisure', in A. Donajgrodzki (ed.), *Social Control in Nineteenth-Century Britain* (London, 1977), pp. 163–84.

'The Language of Patriotism, 1750–1914', *History Workshop*, 12 (1981), 8–33.

Diamond, H. 'Political Heroes of the Victorian Music Hall', *History Today*, (1990), 33–9.

Dinwiddy, J. 'Sir Francis Burdett and Burdettite Radicalism', *History*, 65 (1980), 17–31.

Drescher, S. 'Cart Whipp and Billy Roller: Or Anti-Slavery and Reform Symbolism in Industrialising Britain', *Journal of Social History*, 15, 1 (1981), 3–24.

Dunbabin, J. P. D. 'British Local Government Reform: The Nineteenth Century and After', *English Historical Review*, 92 (1977), 777–805.

Eley, G. 'Rethinking the Political: Social History and Political Culture in Eighteenth- and Nineteenth-Century Britain' *Archiv für Sozialgeschichte*, 21 (1981), 427–57.

'Is All The World a Text? From Social History to the History of Society Two Decades Later', in T. MacDonald (ed.), *The Historical Turn in the Human Sciences* (Ann Arbor, 1992).

Emsley, C. 'Repression, "Terror" and the Role of the Law in England during the Decade of the French Revolution', *English Historical Review*, 100 (1985), 801–25.

'An Aspect of Pitt's "Terror": Prosecutions for Sedition during the 1790s', *Social History*, 6 (1981), 155–84.

Epstein, J. 'Rethinking the Categories of Working Class History', *Labour/Le Travail*, 18, (1988).

'Radical Dining, Toasting and Symbolic Expression in Early Nineteenth-Century Lancashire: Rituals of Solidarity', *Albion*, 20, 2 (1988), 271–91.

'Understanding the Cap of Liberty: Symbolic Practice and Social Conflict in Early Nineteenth-Century England', *Past and Present*, 122, (1989), 75–118.

'The Constitutional Idiom: Radical Reasoning, Rhetoric and Action in Early Nineteenth-Century England', *Journal of Social History*, 23, 3 (Spring, 1990), 553–74.

'"Bred as a Mechanic": Plebeian Intellectuals and Popular Politics in Early Nineteenth-Century England', in Leon Fink et al. (eds.), *Intellectuals and Social Action* (forthcoming Cornell, 1993).

Feldman, D. 'There was an Englishman, an Irish Man and a Jew... Immigrants and Minorities in Britain', *Historical Journal*, 26, 1 (1983), 185–99.

Ferguson, M. 'Marshall McLuhan Revisited: 1960s Zeitgeist Victim or Pioneer Postmodernist?', *Media, Culture and Society*, 13, 1 (1991), 71–90.

Foster, J. 'The Declassing of Language', *New Left Review*, 150, (1985), 29–45.

Gadian, D. S. 'Class Consciousness in Oldham and other North-West Industrial Towns 1830–1850', *Historical Journal*, 21, 1 (1978), 161–72.

Genovese, E. Fox. 'Property and Patriarchy in Classical Bourgeois Theory', *Radical History Review*, (1977), 36–59.

Gray, R. 'The Deconstruction of the English Working Class', *Social History*, 11 (1986), 363–73.

Gunn, J. A. W. 'Influence, Parties, and the Constitution: Changing Attitudes, 1783–1832', *Historical Journal*, 17, 2 (1974), 301–28.

Habermas, J. 'The Public Sphere: An Encyclopedia Article', *New German Critique*, 1 (1974), pp. 43–55.

Hall, C. 'Private Persons versus Public Someones: Class, Gender and Politics in England, 1780–1850', in C. Steedman, C. Urwin, and V. Walkerdine (eds.), *Language, Gender and Childhood* (London, 1985), pp. 10–33.

Hamer, D. A. 'Gladstone: The Making of a Political Myth', *Victorian Studies*, 22, 1 (1978), 29–50.

Hamilton, C. I. 'Naval Hagiography and the Victorian Hero', *Historical Journal*, 23, 2 (1980), 381–98.

Hawkins, A. '"Parliamentary Government" and Victorian Political Parties, c. 1830–c. 1880', *English Historical Review*, (1989), 638–69.

Hennock, E. P. 'Finance and Politics in Urban Local Government in England, 1835–1900', *Historical Journal*, 6, 2 (1963), 212–25.

Hill, C. 'God and the English Revolution', *History Workshop Journal*, 17 (1984), 19–31.

Howkins, A. and Dyck, I. C. '"The Time's Alteration": Popular Ballads,

Rural Radicalism and William Cobbett', *History Workshop*, 23 (1987), 20–38.

Innes, J. 'Jonathan Clark, Social History and England's "Ancien Regime"', *Past and Present*, 115 (1987), 165–200.

Jordan, G. and Rogers, N. 'Admirals as Heroes: Patriotism and Liberty in Hanoverian England', *Journal of British Studies*, 28 (1989), 201–24.

Joyce, P. 'Work', in F. M. L. Thompson (ed.), *The Cambridge Social History of Great Britain 1750–1950*, II (Cambridge, 1990).

Kent, C. 'Presence and Absence: History, Theory and the Working Class', *Victorian Studies*, 29, 3 (1986), 437–62.

Kirk, N. 'In Defence of Class: A Critique of Recent Revisionist Writing upon the Nineteenth-Century English Working Class', *International Review of Social History*, 32 (1987), 2–47.

Kuhn, W. M. 'Ceremony and Politics: The British Monarchy, 1971–2', *Journal of British Studies*, 26, 2 (1987), 133–62.

Lacqueur, T. W. 'Debate: Literacy and Social Mobility in the Industrial Revolution in England', *Past and Present*, 64 (1974), 96–107.

'The Queen Caroline Affair: Politics as Art in the Reign of George IV', *Journal of Modern History*, 54, (1982), 417–66.

Lawrence, J. 'Popular Radicalism and the Socialist Revival in Britain', *Journal of British Studies*, 31, 2 (1992), 163–86.

Matthew, H. G. C. 'Rhetoric and Politics in Great Britain, 1860–1950', in P. J. Waller (ed.), *Politics and Social Change in Modern Britain, Essays Presented to A. F. Thompson* (Brighton, 1987), pp. 34–58.

McKibbin, R. 'Why was there no Marxism in Great Britain?', *English Historical Review*, 99 (1984), 297–331.

McMaster, N. 'The Battle for Mousehold Heath 1857–1884. "Popular Politics" and the Victorian Public Park', *Past and Present*, 127, (1990), 117–54.

Money, J. 'Taverns, Coffee Houses and Clubs: Local Politics and Popular Articulacy in the Birmingham Area in the Age of the American Revolution', *Historical Journal*, 14 (1971), 15–47.

Morris, R. J. 'Clubs, Societies, and Associations', in F. M. L. Thompson (ed.), *Cambridge Social History of Britain 1750–1950*, III (Cambridge, 1990).

Neal, F. 'The Birkenhead Garibaldi Riots of 1862', *Transactions of the Historic Society of Lancashire and Cheshire*, 131 (1982), 87–111.

Nicholls, D. 'The English Middle Class and the Ideological Significance of Radicalism, 1760–1888', *Journal of British Studies*, 24, 4 (1985), 415–33.

Ozouf, M. '"Public Opinion" at the End of the Old Regime', *Journal of Modern History*, 60 (1988), 3–21.

Parssinen, T. M. 'Association, Convention and Anti-Parliament in British Radical Politics, 1771–1848', *English Historical Review*, 88 (1973), 504–33.

Paz, D. G. 'Bonfire Night in Mid-Victorian Northants: The Politics of Popular Revel', *Historical Research*, 63 (1990), 316–28.

Pickering, P. 'Class Without Words: Symbolic Communication in the Chartist Movement', *Past and Present*, 112 (1986), 144–62.

'Chartism and the "Trade of Agitation" in Early Victorian Britain', *History*, 76 (1991), 221–37.

Poole, R. 'Oldham Wakes', in J. K. Walton and J. Walvin (eds.), *Leisure in Britain 1780–1939* (Manchester, 1983), pp. 71–98.

Prothero, I. 'William Benbow and the Concept of the "General Strike"', *Past and Present*, 63 (1974), 132–71.

Ranciere, J. 'The Myth of the Artisan: Critical Reflections on a Category of Social History', *International Labour and Working-Class History*, 24, (1983), 1–16.

Richter, D. 'The Role of Mob Riot in Victorian Elections, 1865–1885', *Victorian Studies*, 15, 1 (1971), 19–28.

Rubinstein, W. D. 'The End of "Old Corruption" in Britain 1780–1860', *Past and Present*, 101 (1984), 55–86.

'British Radicalism and the "Dark Side" of Populism', in Rubinstein, *Elites and the Wealthy in Modern British History* (Brighton, 1988).

Russell, D. 'Popular Musical Culture and Popular Politics in the Yorkshire Textile Districts, 1880–1914', in J. K. Walton and J. Walvin (eds.), *Leisure in Britain 1780–1939* (Manchester, 1983), 99–116.

Sanderson, M. 'Literacy and Social Mobility in the Industrial Revolution in England', *Past and Present*, 56 (1972), 75–104.

Schofield, R. S. 'Dimensions of Illiteracy, 1750–1850', *Explorations in Economic History*, 10, 4 (1973), 437–54.

Schottler, P. 'Historians and Discourse Analysis', *History Workshop Journal*, 27 (1989), 37–64.

Seccombe, W. 'Patriarchy Stabilized: The Construction of the Male Breadwinner Wage Norm in Nineteenth-Century Britain', *Social History*, 11 (1986), 53–76.

Seed, J. 'Unitarianism, Political Economy, and the Antinomies of Liberal Culture in Manchester, 1830–50', *Social History*, 7, 1 (1982), 1–25.

Smail, J. 'New Languages for Labour and Capital: The Transformation of Discourse in the Early Years of the Industrial Revolution', *Social History*, 12, 1 (1987).

Stone, L. S. 'Literacy and Education in England, 1640–1900', *Past and Present*, 42, (1969).

Sykes, R. A. 'Some Aspects of Working-Class Consciousness in Oldham, 1830–1842', *Historical Journal*, 23, 1 (1980), 167–79.

Thompson, D. 'Women and Nineteenth-Century Radical Politics: a Lost Dimension', in J. Mitchell and A. Oakely (eds.), *The Rights and Wrongs of Women* (London, 1976).

'The Language of Class', *Bulletin of the Society for the Study of Labour History*, 52, (1987), 54–7.

Thompson, E. P. 'The Moral Economy of the English Crowd in the Eighteenth Century', *Past and Present*, 50 (1971), 76–136.

'Patrician Society and Plebeian Culture', *Journal of Social History*, 7 (1974), 383–405.
'Eighteenth-Century English Society: Class Struggle Without Class?', *Social History*, 3 (1978), 133–65.
Vicinus, M. 'Helpless and Unbefriended: Nineteenth-Century Domestic Melodrama', *New Literary History*, 13, 1 (1981).
Vincent, D. 'Reading in the Working-Class Home', in J. K. Walton and J. Walvin (eds.), *Leisure in Britain 1780–1939* (Manchester, 1983), pp. 207–26.
Waller, P. J. 'Democracy and Dialect, Speech and Class', in P. J. Waller (ed.), *Politics and Social Change in Modern Britain, Essays Presented to A. F. Thompson* (Brighton, 1987), pp. 1–33.
Wilson, K. 'Empire, Trade, and Popular Politics in Mid-Hanoverian England: The Case of Admiral Vernon', *Past and Present*, 121 (1988) 74–109.
'Inventing Revolution: 1688 and Eighteenth-Century Popular Politics', *Journal of British Studies*, 28 (1989), 349–86.
Winstanley, M. 'News from Oldham', *Manchester Regional History Review*, 4, 1 (1990), 3–10.
Yeo, E. 'Robert Owen and Radical Culture', in S. Pollard and J. Salts (eds.), *Robert Owen Prophet of the Poor* (London, 1971).
'Christianity in Chartist Struggle 1838–1842', *Past and Present*, 91 (1981), pp. 109–39.

UNPUBLISHED THESES

Andrews, J. H. 'Political Issues in the County of Kent, 1820–1846', M.Phil. thesis (London, 1967).
Atton, A. J. 'Municipal and Parliamentary Politics in Ipswich, 1818–1847', Ph.D. thesis (London, 1981).
Baer, M. A. 'Politics of London, 1852–1868: Parties, Voters and Representation', Ph.D. thesis (Iowa, 1976).
Berridge, V. 'Popular Journalism and Working Class Attitudes 1854–1886: A Study of *Reynolds' Newspaper*, *Lloyd's Weekly Newspaper* and the *Weekly Times*' Ph.D. thesis (London, 1976).
Bickerstaffe, D. 'Politics and Party Organisation in Oldham, 1832–1914', MA thesis (Durham, 1965).
Capraro, R. L. 'Typographical Politics: The Impact of Printing on the Political Life of Eighteenth-Century England', Ph.D. thesis (Washington, 1984).
Deacon, G. C. 'Popular Song and Social History. A Study of the Miners of the North-East', Ph.D. thesis (Essex, 1987).
Fox, C. 'Graphic Journalism in England During the 1830s and 1840s', D.Phil. thesis (Oxford, 1974).
Gadian, D. S. 'A Comparative Survey of Popular Movements in North-West Industrial Towns 1830–1850', Ph.D. thesis (Lancaster, 1976).

Gurowich, P. 'Party and Independence in the Early and Mid-Victorian House of Commons. Aspects of Political Theory and Practice, 1832–1868, Considered with Special Reference to the Period, 1852–1868', Ph.D. thesis (Cambridge, 1986).

Hayes, B. D. 'Politics in Norfolk, 1750–1832', Ph.D. thesis (Cambridge, 1958).

Jaggard, E. K. G. 'Patrons, Principles and Parties: Cornwall Politics 1760–1910', Ph.D. thesis (Washington, 1980).

Lawrence, J. 'Party Politics and the People: Continuity and Change in the Political History of Wolverhampton, 1815–1914', Ph.D. thesis (Cambridge, 1990).

McWilliam, R. 'The Tichborne Claimant and the People: Investigations into Popular Culture, 1867–1886', D.Phil. thesis (Sussex, 1990).

Reisser, J. L. 'The Married Women's Property Bills of Great Britain, 1857–1882' Ph.D. thesis (California, Irvine, 1989).

Searby, P. 'Weavers and Freemen in Coventry, 1820–1861: Social and Political Traditionalism in an Early Victorian Town', Ph.D. thesis (Warwick, 1972).

Smith, G. Howard. 'The Oldham Branch of the Owenite Socialist Movement, 1838–46', Diploma in Political, Economic and Social Studies (Nottingham, 1979).

Smith, J. 'Politics and Ideology in Early Nineteenth-Century Bradford: Conflict and Compromise, 1825–1852', M.Phil. thesis (York, 1983).

Sykes, R. A. 'Popular Politics and Trade Unionism in South-East Lancashire, 1829–42', Ph.D. thesis (Manchester, 1982).

Taylor, A. D. 'Modes of Political Expression and Working-Class Politics: The Manchester and London Examples, 1850–1880', Ph.D. thesis (Manchester, 1992).

Trainor, R. H. 'Authority and Social Structure in an Industrialised Area: A Study of Three Black Country Towns, 1840–90', D.Phil. thesis (Oxford, 1983).

Walker, L. E. 'The Women's Movement in England in the Late Nineteenth and Early Twentieth Centuries', Ph.D. thesis (Manchester, 1984).

Wilson, Kathleen. 'The Rejection of Deference: Urban Political Culture in England, 1715–1785', Ph.D. thesis (Yale, 1985).
'Political Radicalism in the North East of England 1830–60: Issues in Historical Sociology', Ph.D. thesis (Durham, 1988).

Wright, D. G. 'Politics and Opinion in Nineteenth-Century Bradford, 1832–80', Ph.D. thesis (Bradford, 1968).

Yarrington, A. W. 'The Commemoration of the Hero 1800–1864. Monuments to the British Victors of the Napoleonic Wars', Ph.D. thesis (Cambridge, 1980).

UNPUBLISHED PAPERS

Beales, D. 'Garibaldi in England. The Politics of Italian Enthusiasm', paper presented to the 'Popular Radicalism and Party Politics in Britain 1848–1914' conference, Churchill College, Cambridge, April 1989.

Brewer, J. 'Public and Private: The Shifting of the Cultural Sphere in Eighteenth-Century England', paper presented to 'The Public Sphere in Eighteenth-Century Europe' conference, University of Exeter, May 1992.

Chartier, R. 'The Uses of Literacy. "Popular" Readers in Early Modern France', paper presented to the 'Popular Culture in Question' conference, Essex University, April 1991.

Clark, J. C. D. 'Class Formation in England, 1750–1850', paper presented to Manchester Historical Association, January 1992.

Epstein, J. 'In Liberty's Defense: T. J. Wooler and the Law', in his *Repertoires of Resistance* (forthcoming).

Fulcher, J. 'Contests Over Constitutionalism: The Faltering of Reform in England, 1819–1820', paper presented to Postgraduate Seminar in Modern British History, University of Cambridge, Sidney Sussex College, 12 November 1990.

Joyce, P. 'History and Postmodernism: Social Identity as Narrative in Nineteenth-Century England' in his *Democratic Subjects: Studies in the History of Identity in Nineteenth-Century England* (forthcoming).

McCalman, I. 'New Jerusalems, Prophecy, Judaism and Radical Restorationism in London, 1786–1832', paper presented to the Modern History Seminar, Manchester University, May 1992.

Prothero, I. 'Religion and Radicalism', paper presented to the Modern History Seminar, Manchester University, February 1987.

Quinault, R. 'Outdoor Radicalism. Copenhagen Fields, 1795–1851', unpublished paper presented to the 'Metropolitan History Seminar' at the Institute of Historical Research, January 1989.

Index

Printed in the United Kingdom by
Lightning Source UK Ltd., Milton Keynes
141508UK00001B/10/P